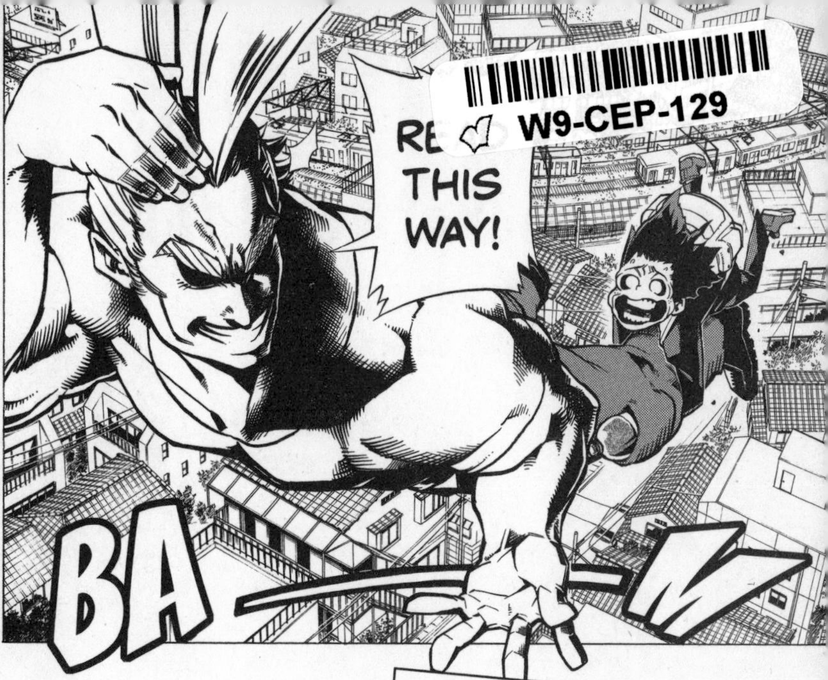
RE
THIS
WAY!
BA—M

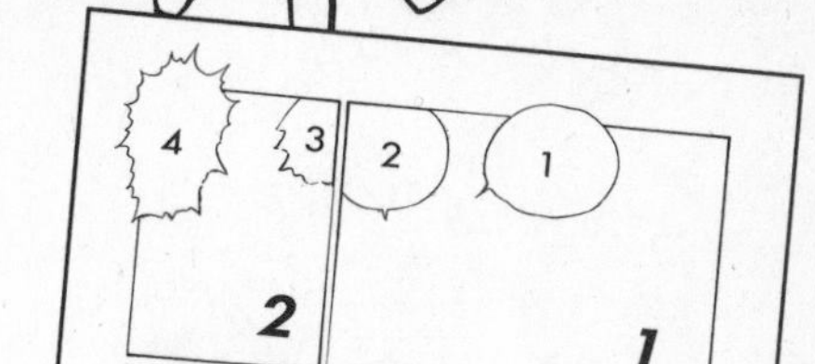

MY HERO ACADEMIA

reads from right to left, starting in the upper-right corner. Japanese is read from right to left, meaning that action, sound effects and word-balloon order are completely reversed from English order.

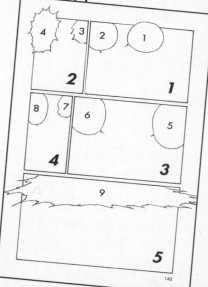

HORIKOSHI'S ASSISTANTS

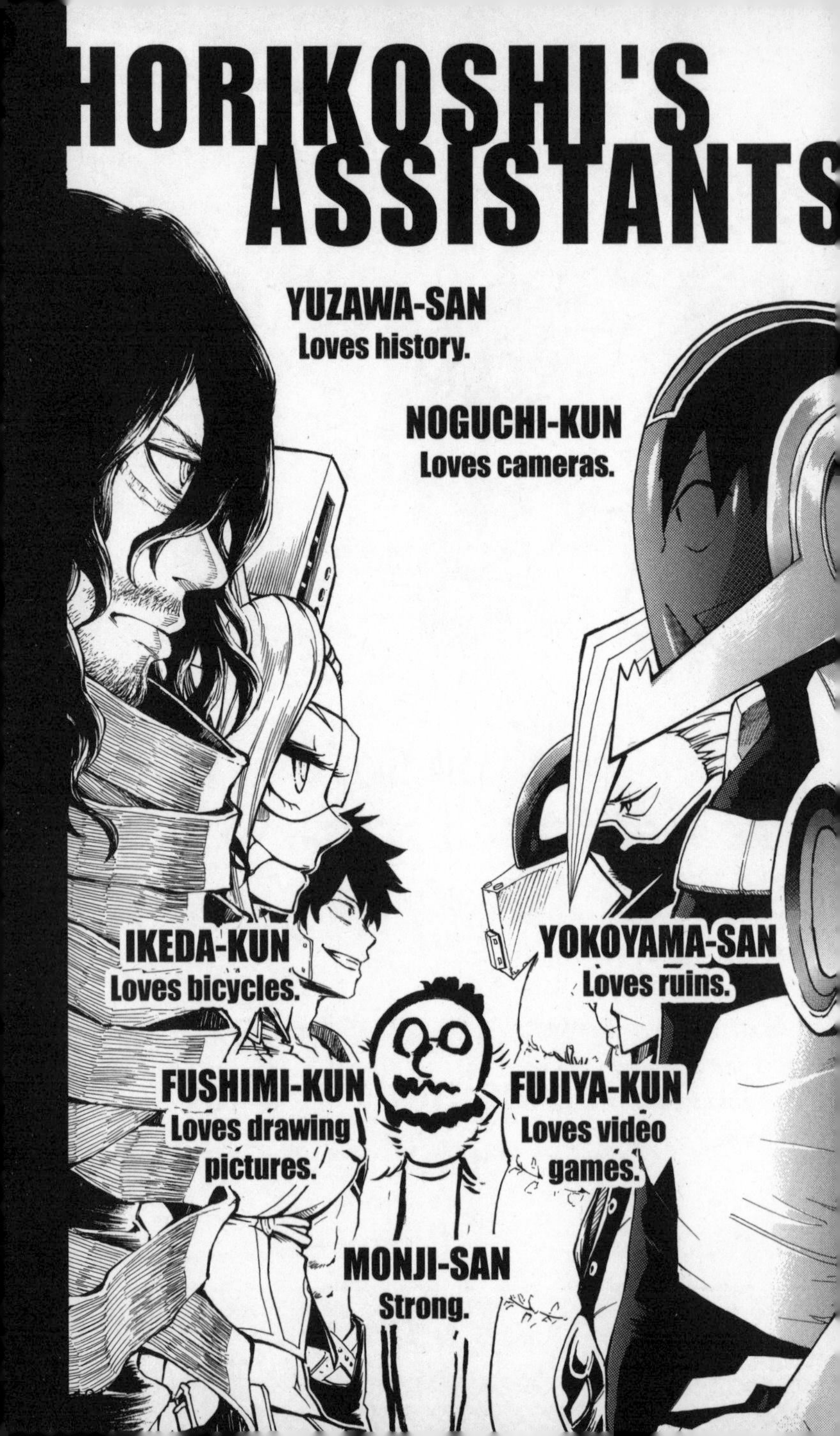
YUZAWA-SAN
Loves history.
NOGUCHI-KUN
Loves cameras.
YOKOYAMA-SAN
Loves ruins.
IKEDA-KUN
Loves bicycles.
FUJIYA-KUN
Loves video games.
FUSHIMI-KUN
Loves drawing pictures.
MONJI-SAN
Strong.

This is volume 12!! Things are getting out of hand!

KOHEI HORIKOSHI

12

SHONEN JUMP Manga Edition

STORY & ART **KOHEI HORIKOSHI**

TRANSLATION & ENGLISH ADAPTATION **Caleb Cook**
TOUCH-UP ART & LETTERING **John Hunt**
DESIGNER **Julian [JR] Robinson**
SHONEN JUMP SERIES EDITOR **John Bae**
GRAPHIC NOVEL EDITOR **Mike Montesa**

BOKU NO HERO ACADEMIA © 2014 by Kohei Horikoshi
All rights reserved.
First published in Japan in 2014 by SHUEISHA Inc., Tokyo.
English translation rights arranged by SHUEISHA Inc.

Printed in the U.S.A.

Published by VIZ Media, LLC
P.O. Box 77010
San Francisco, CA 94107

10 9 8 7 6 5 4 3
First printing, April 2018
Third printing, December 2018

MY HERO ACADEMIA

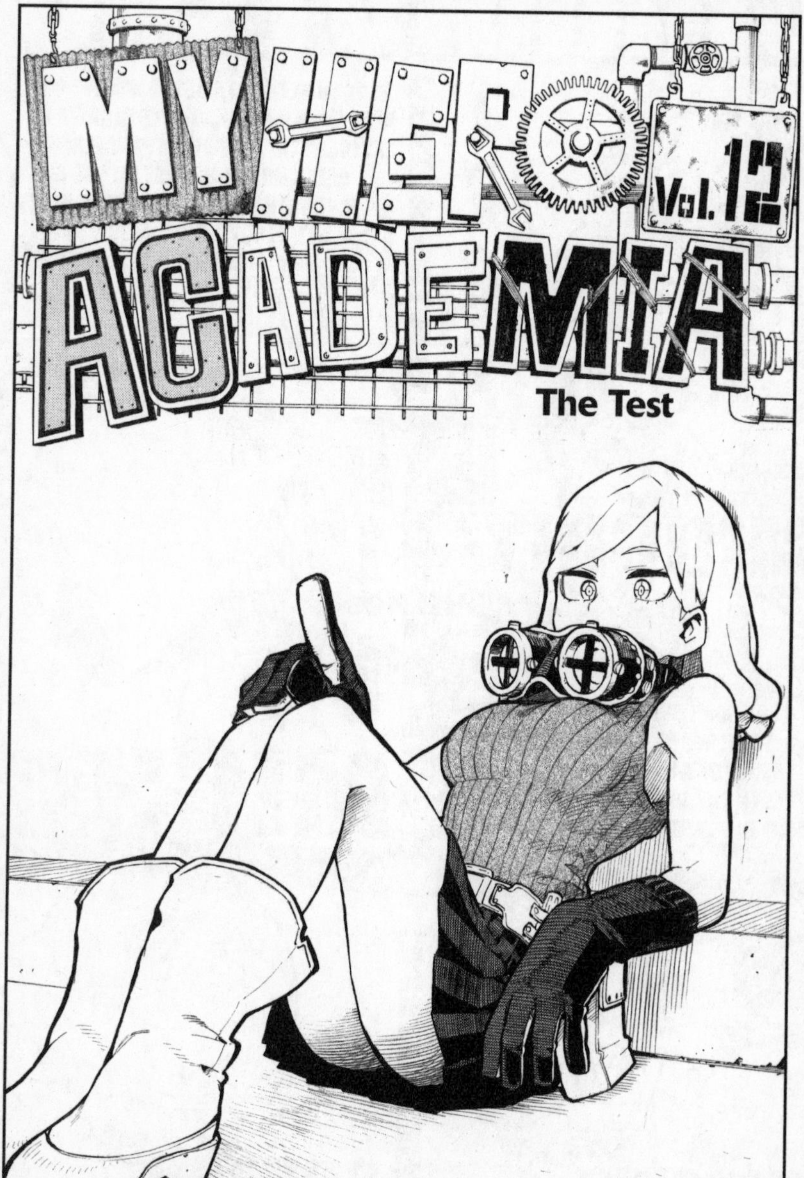
MY HERO ACADEMIA
Vol. 12
The Test

KOHEI HORIKOSHI

SHONEN JUMP MANGA

CHARACTERS

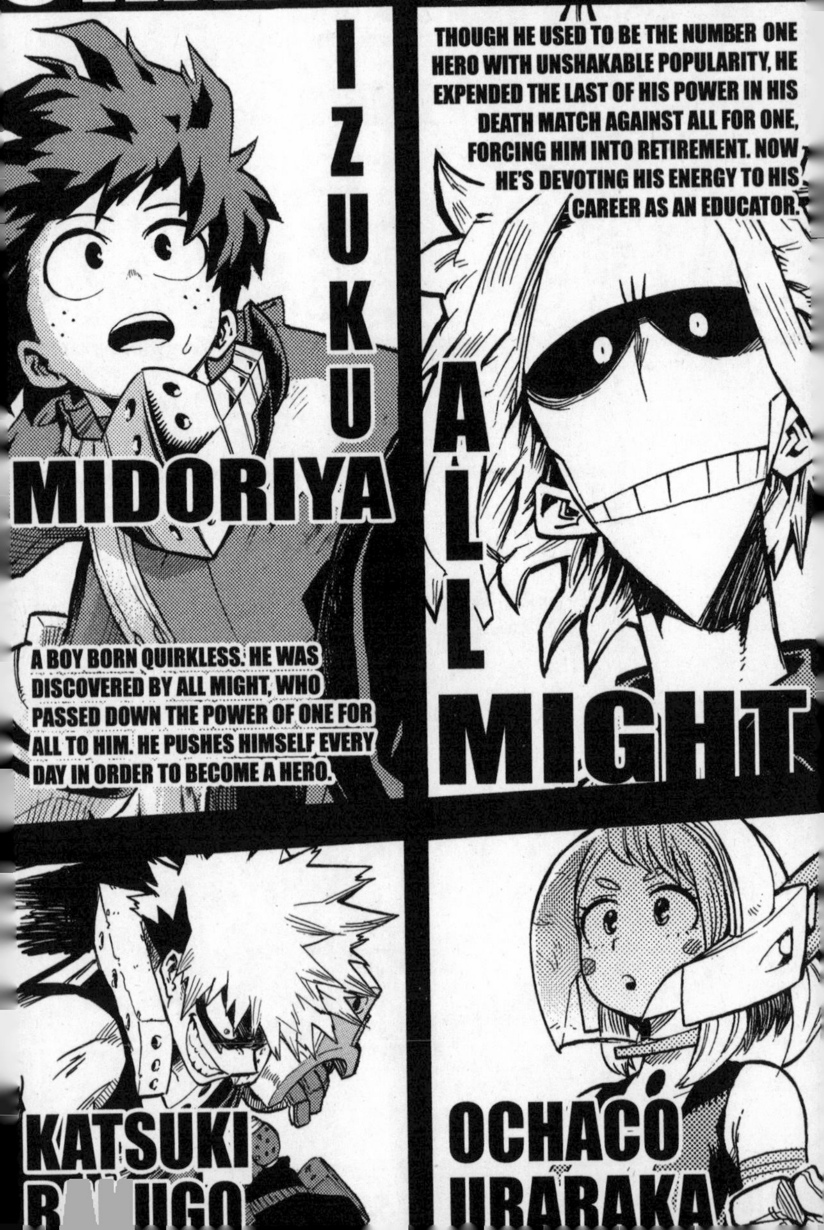

THOUGH HE USED TO BE THE NUMBER ONE HERO WITH UNSHAKABLE POPULARITY, HE EXPENDED THE LAST OF HIS POWER IN HIS DEATH MATCH AGAINST ALL FOR ONE, FORCING HIM INTO RETIREMENT. NOW HE'S DEVOTING HIS ENERGY TO HIS CAREER AS AN EDUCATOR.
ALL MIGHT
IZUKU MIDORIYA
A BOY BORN QUIRKLESS. HE WAS DISCOVERED BY ALL MIGHT, WHO PASSED DOWN THE POWER OF ONE FOR ALL TO HIM. HE PUSHES HIMSELF EVERY DAY IN ORDER TO BECOME A HERO.
OCHACO URARAKA
KATSUKI

STORY

One day, people began manifesting special abilities that came to be known as "Quirks," and before long, the world was full of superpowered humans. But with the advent of these exceptional individuals came an increase in crime, and governments alone were unable to deal with the situation. At the same time, others emerged to oppose the spread of evil! As if straight from the comic books, these heroes keep the peace and are even officially authorized to fight crime. Our story begins when a certain Quirkless boy and lifelong hero fan meets the world's number one hero, starting him on his path to becoming the greatest hero ever!

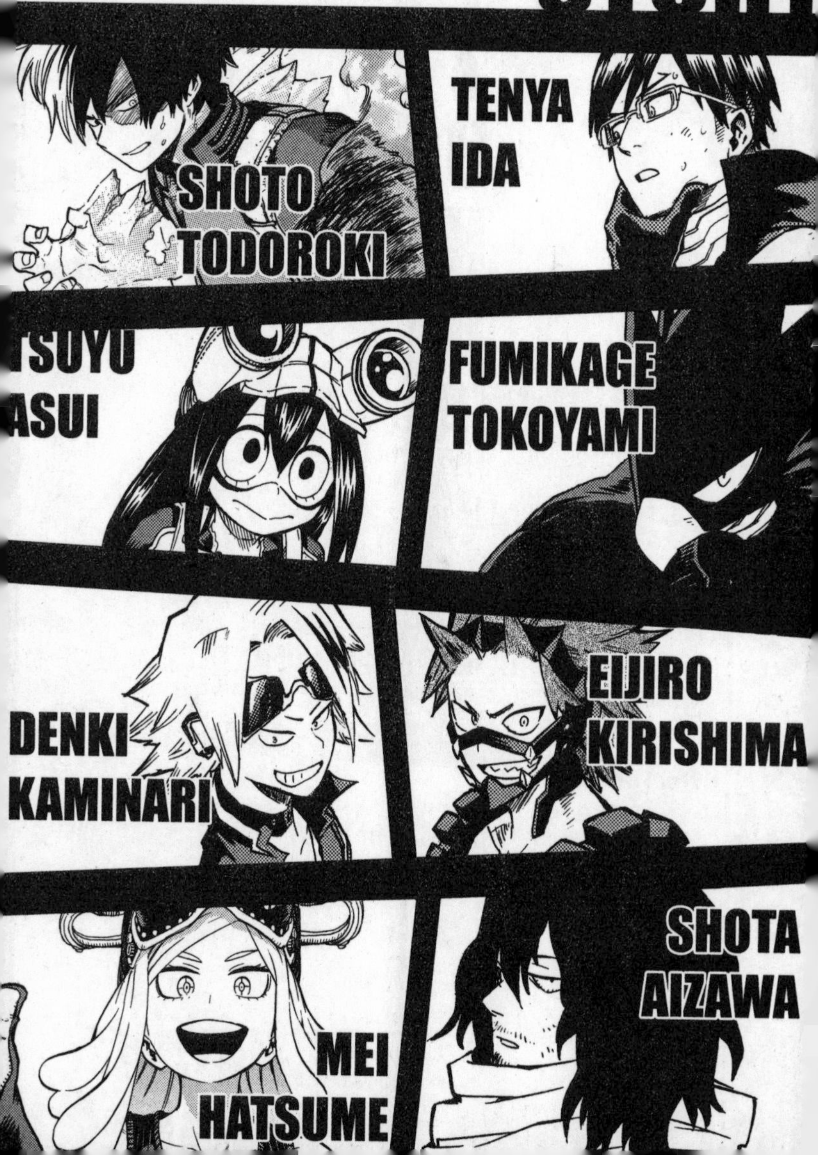
TENYA IDA
SHOTO TODOROKI
FUMIKAGE TOKOYAMI
TSUYU ASUI
EIJIRO KIRISHIMA
DENKI KAMINARI
SHOTA AIZAWA
MEI HATSUME

Vol.12

MY HERO ACADEMIA

CONTENTS

The Test

NOOO NOOO

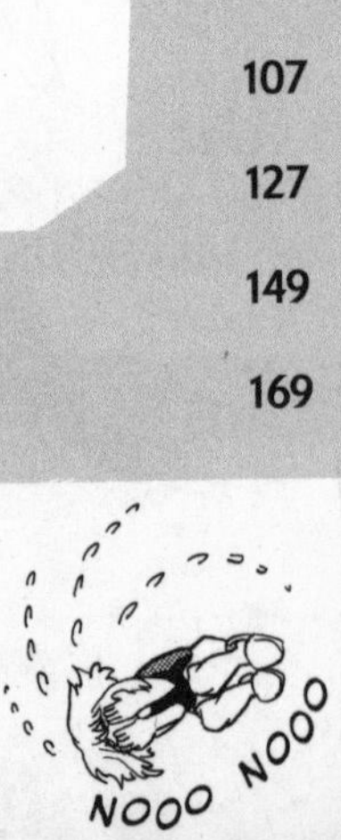

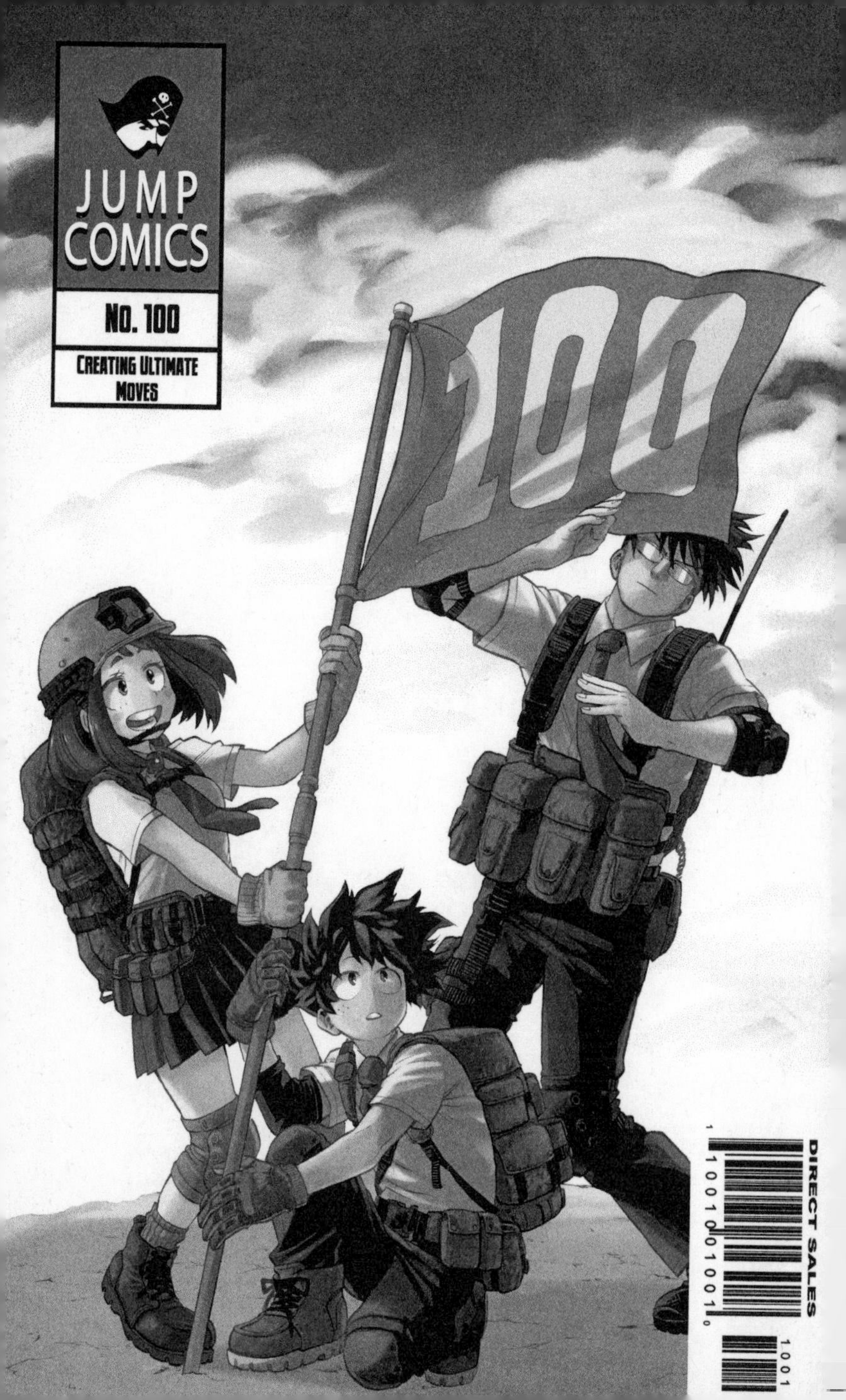
JUMP
COMICS
No. 100
Creating Ultimate
Moves
100
DIRECT SALES

MY HERO ACADEMIA

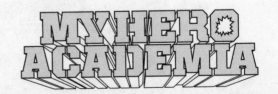

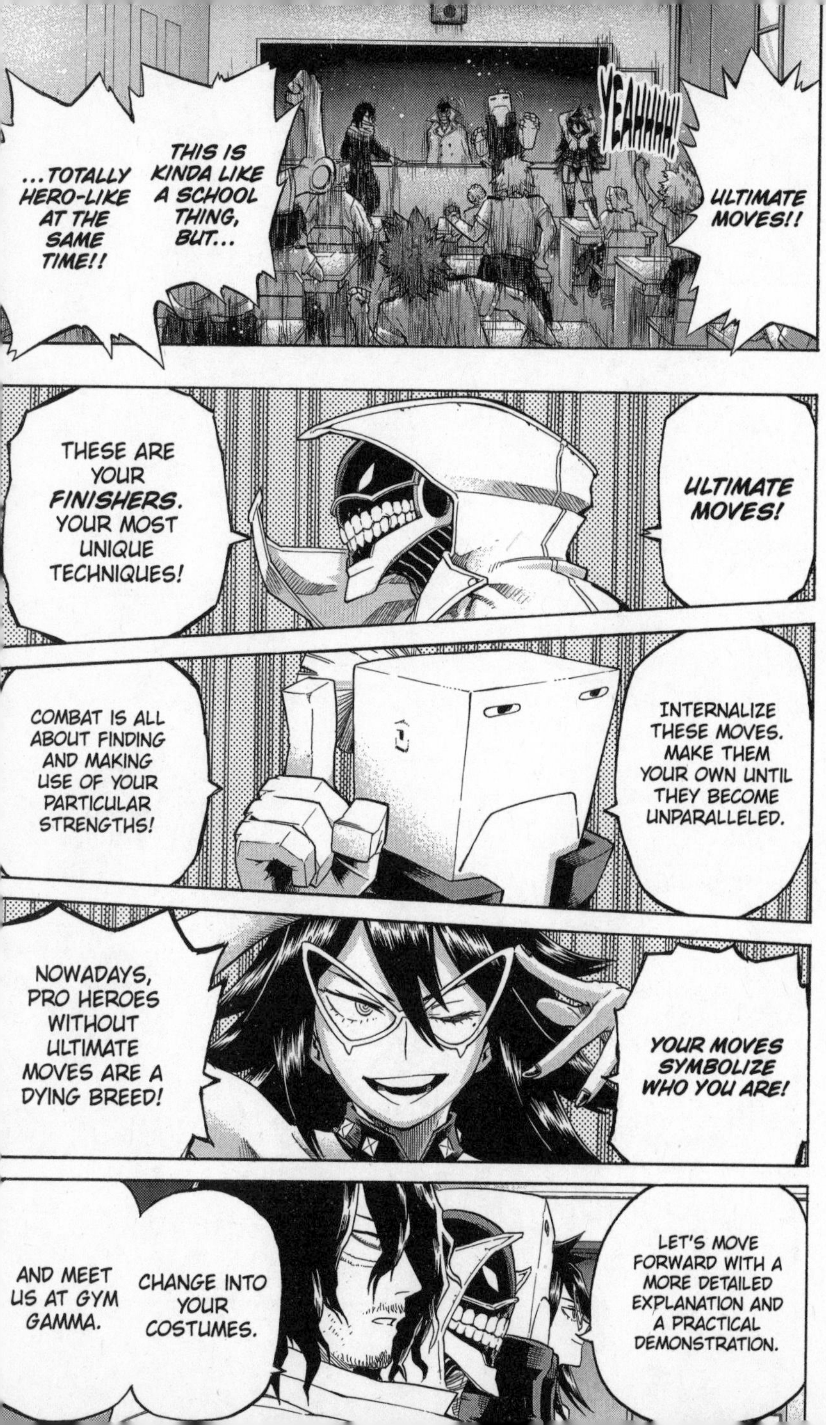
ULTIMATE MOVES!!
YEAHHHH!
THIS IS KINDA LIKE A SCHOOL THING, BUT...
...TOTALLY HERO-LIKE AT THE SAME TIME!!
ULTIMATE MOVES!
THESE ARE YOUR FINISHERS. YOUR MOST UNIQUE TECHNIQUES!
INTERNALIZE THESE MOVES. MAKE THEM YOUR OWN UNTIL THEY BECOME UNPARALLELED.
COMBAT IS ALL ABOUT FINDING AND MAKING USE OF YOUR PARTICULAR STRENGTHS!
YOUR MOVES SYMBOLIZE WHO YOU ARE!
NOWADAYS, PRO HEROES WITHOUT ULTIMATE MOVES ARE A DYING BREED!
LET'S MOVE FORWARD WITH A MORE DETAILED EXPLANATION AND A PRACTICAL DEMONSTRATION.
CHANGE INTO YOUR COSTUMES.
AND MEET US AT GYM GAMMA.

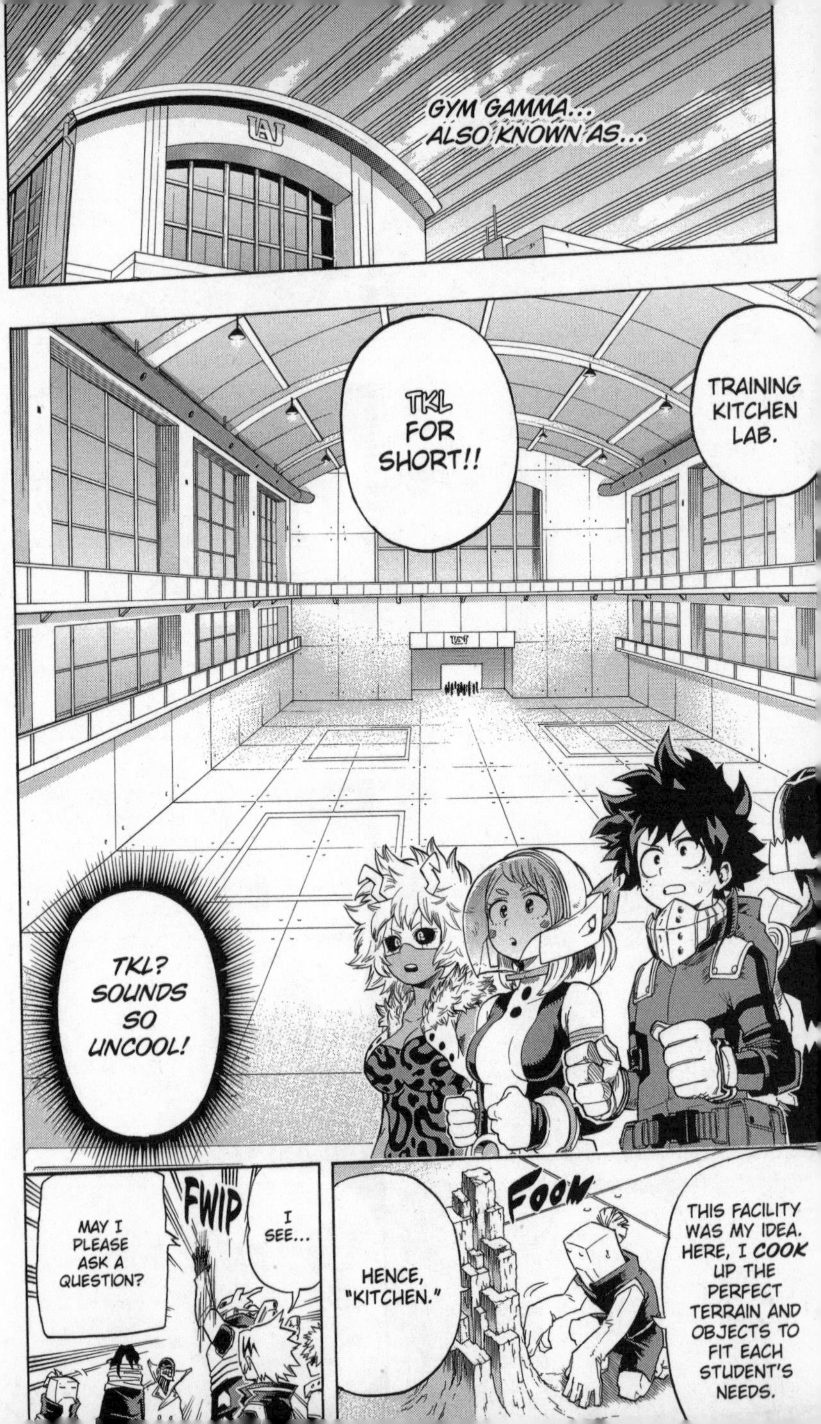
GYM GAMMA... ALSO KNOWN AS...
TRAINING KITCHEN LAB.
TKL FOR SHORT!!
TKL? SOUNDS SO UNCOOL!
THIS FACILITY WAS MY IDEA. HERE, I **COOK** UP THE PERFECT TERRAIN AND OBJECTS TO FIT EACH STUDENT'S NEEDS.
FOOM
HENCE, "KITCHEN."
I SEE...
FWIP
MAY I PLEASE ASK A QUESTION?

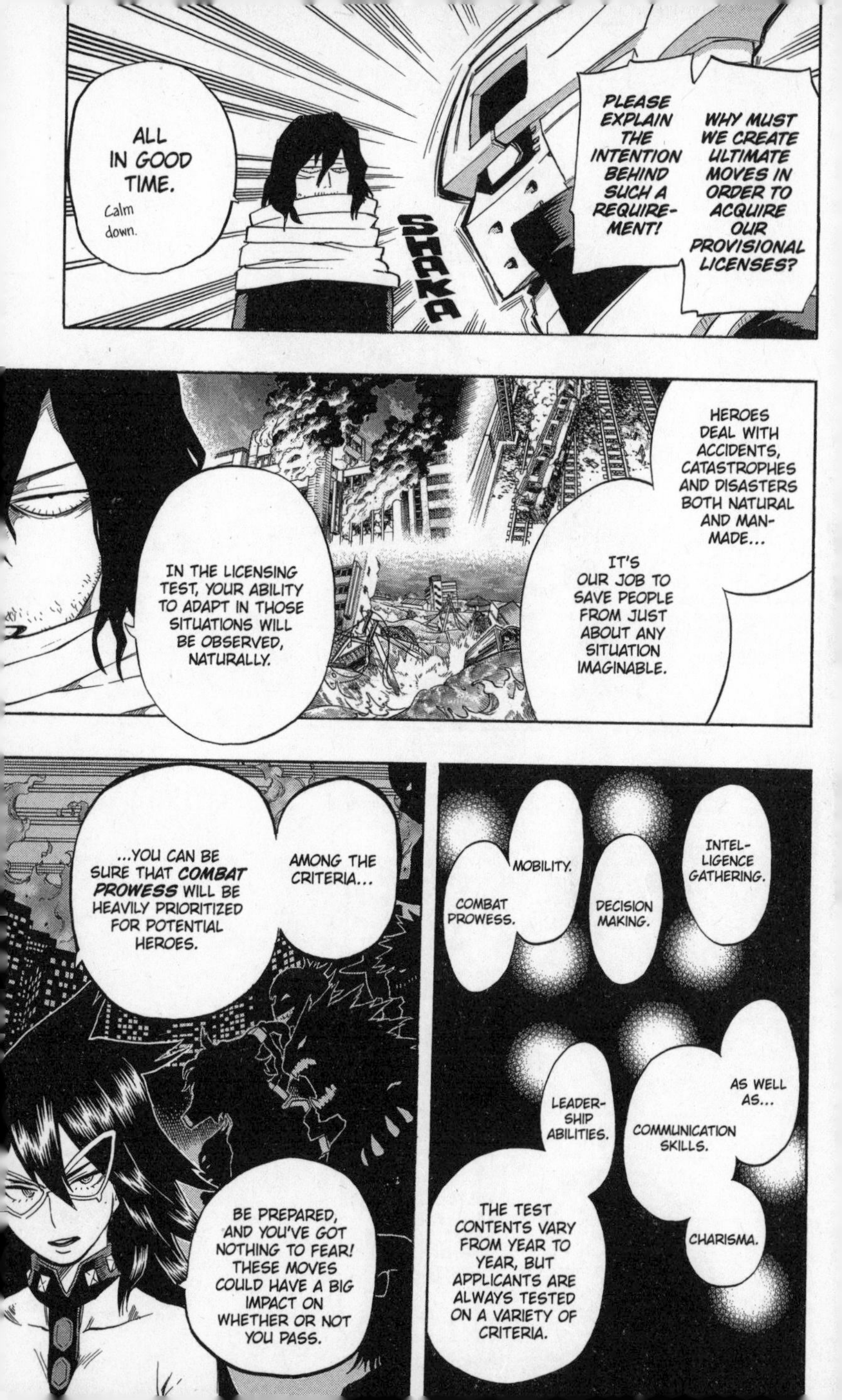
WHY MUST WE CREATE ULTIMATE MOVES IN ORDER TO ACQUIRE OUR PROVISIONAL LICENSES?
PLEASE EXPLAIN THE INTENTION BEHIND SUCH A REQUIRE-MENT!
SHAKA
ALL IN GOOD TIME.
Calm down.
HEROES DEAL WITH ACCIDENTS, CATASTROPHES AND DISASTERS BOTH NATURAL AND MAN-MADE...
IT'S OUR JOB TO SAVE PEOPLE FROM JUST ABOUT ANY SITUATION IMAGINABLE.
IN THE LICENSING TEST, YOUR ABILITY TO ADAPT IN THOSE SITUATIONS WILL BE OBSERVED, NATURALLY.
THE TEST CONTENTS VARY FROM YEAR TO YEAR, BUT APPLICANTS ARE ALWAYS TESTED ON A VARIETY OF CRITERIA.
INTEL-LIGENCE GATHERING.
DECISION MAKING.
MOBILITY.
COMBAT PROWESS.
AS WELL AS...
COMMUNICATION SKILLS.
LEADER-SHIP ABILITIES.
CHARISMA.
AMONG THE CRITERIA...
...YOU CAN BE SURE THAT *COMBAT PROWESS* WILL BE HEAVILY PRIORITIZED FOR POTENTIAL HEROES.
BE PREPARED, AND YOU'VE GOT NOTHING TO FEAR! THESE MOVES COULD HAVE A BIG IMPACT ON WHETHER OR NOT YOU PASS.

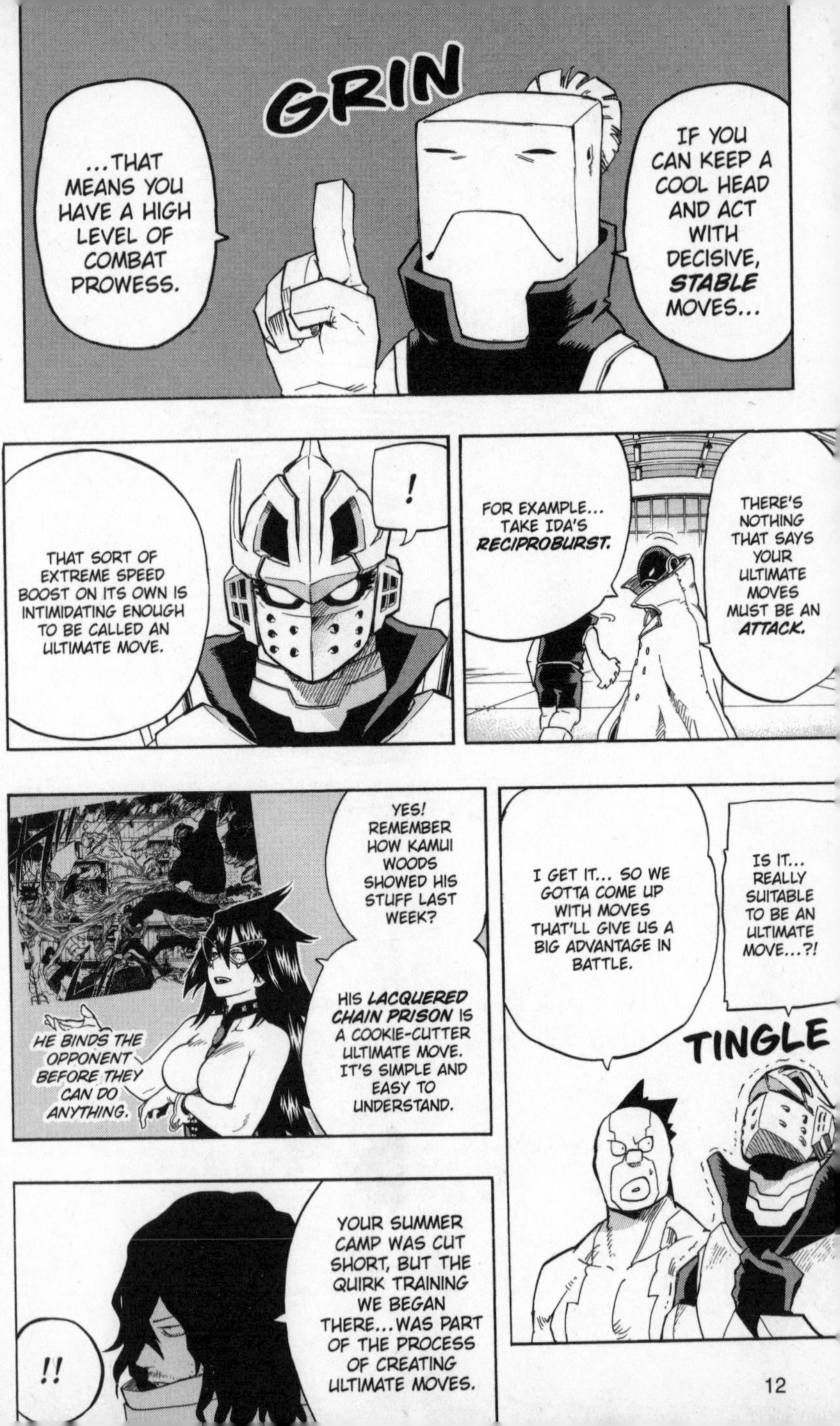

IF YOU CAN KEEP A COOL HEAD AND ACT WITH DECISIVE, ***STABLE*** MOVES...
GRIN
...THAT MEANS YOU HAVE A HIGH LEVEL OF COMBAT PROWESS.
THERE'S NOTHING THAT SAYS YOUR ULTIMATE MOVES MUST BE AN ***ATTACK.***
FOR EXAMPLE... TAKE IDA'S ***RECIPROBURST.***
!
THAT SORT OF EXTREME SPEED BOOST ON ITS OWN IS INTIMIDATING ENOUGH TO BE CALLED AN ULTIMATE MOVE.
IS IT... REALLY SUITABLE TO BE AN ULTIMATE MOVE...?!
I GET IT... SO WE GOTTA COME UP WITH MOVES THAT'LL GIVE US A BIG ADVANTAGE IN BATTLE.
TINGLE
YES! REMEMBER HOW KAMUI WOODS SHOWED HIS STUFF LAST WEEK?
HIS ***LACQUERED CHAIN PRISON*** IS A COOKIE-CUTTER ULTIMATE MOVE. IT'S SIMPLE AND EASY TO UNDERSTAND.
HE BINDS THE OPPONENT BEFORE THEY CAN DO ANYTHING.
YOUR SUMMER CAMP WAS CUT SHORT, BUT THE QUIRK TRAINING WE BEGAN THERE...WAS PART OF THE PROCESS OF CREATING ULTIMATE MOVES.
!!

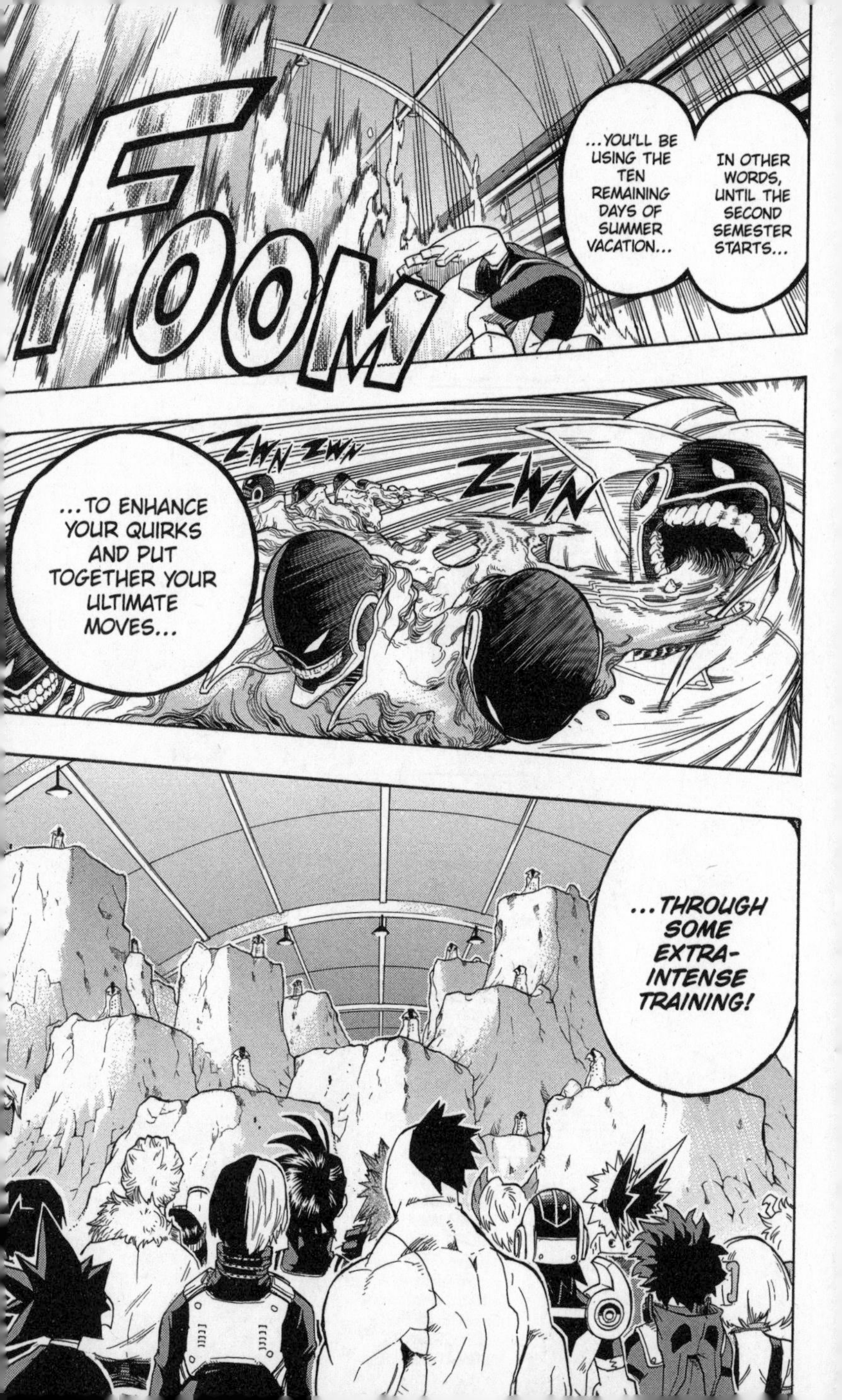
IN OTHER WORDS, UNTIL THE SECOND SEMESTER STARTS...
...YOU'LL BE USING THE TEN REMAINING DAYS OF SUMMER VACATION...
FOOM
ZWN
ZWN ZWN
...TO ENHANCE YOUR QUIRKS AND PUT TOGETHER YOUR ULTIMATE MOVES...
...THROUGH SOME EXTRA-INTENSE TRAINING!

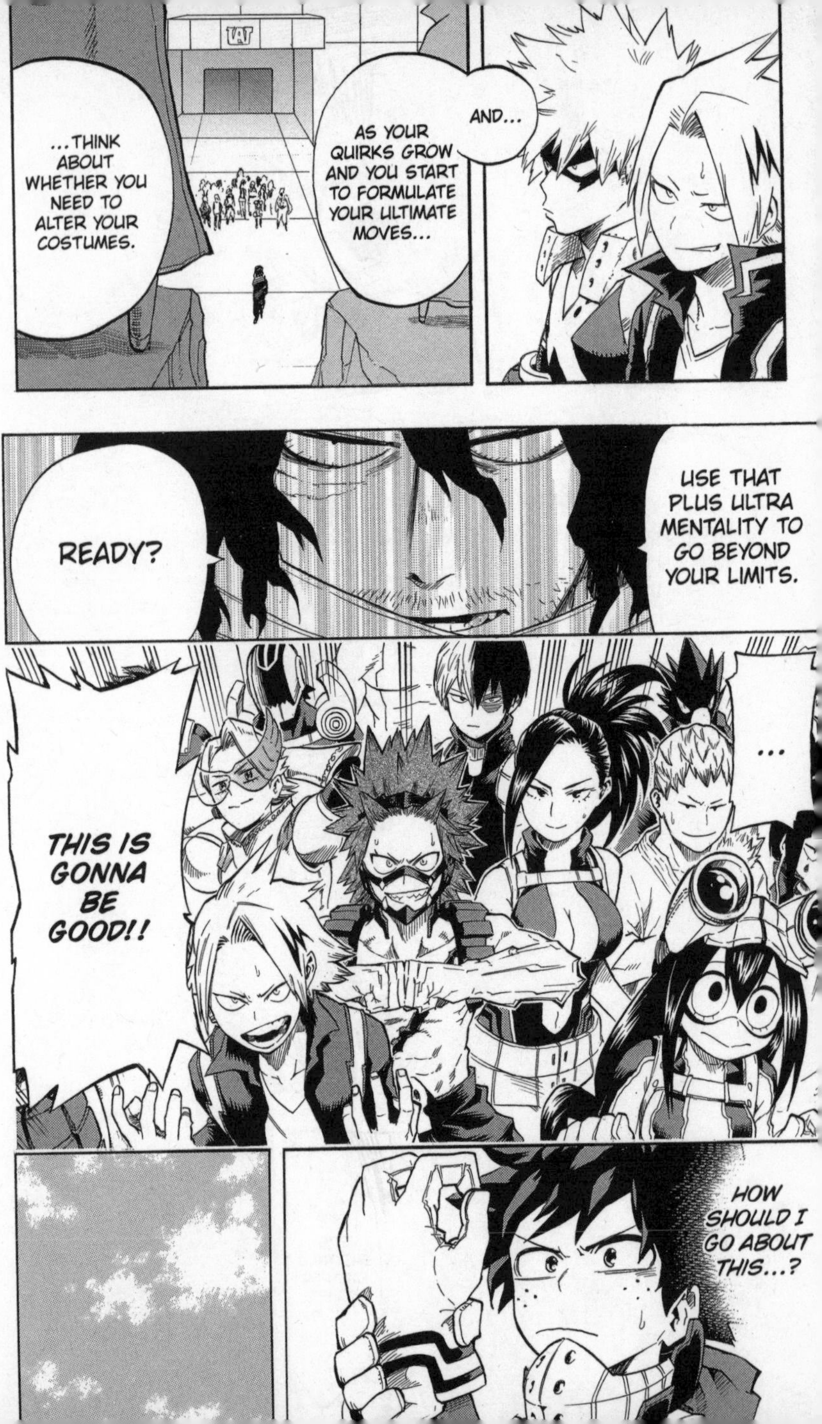
AND...
AS YOUR QUIRKS GROW AND YOU START TO FORMULATE YOUR ULTIMATE MOVES...
...THINK ABOUT WHETHER YOU NEED TO ALTER YOUR COSTUMES.
USE THAT PLUS ULTRA MENTALITY TO GO BEYOND YOUR LIMITS.
READY?
...
THIS IS GONNA BE GOOD!!
HOW SHOULD I GO ABOUT THIS...?

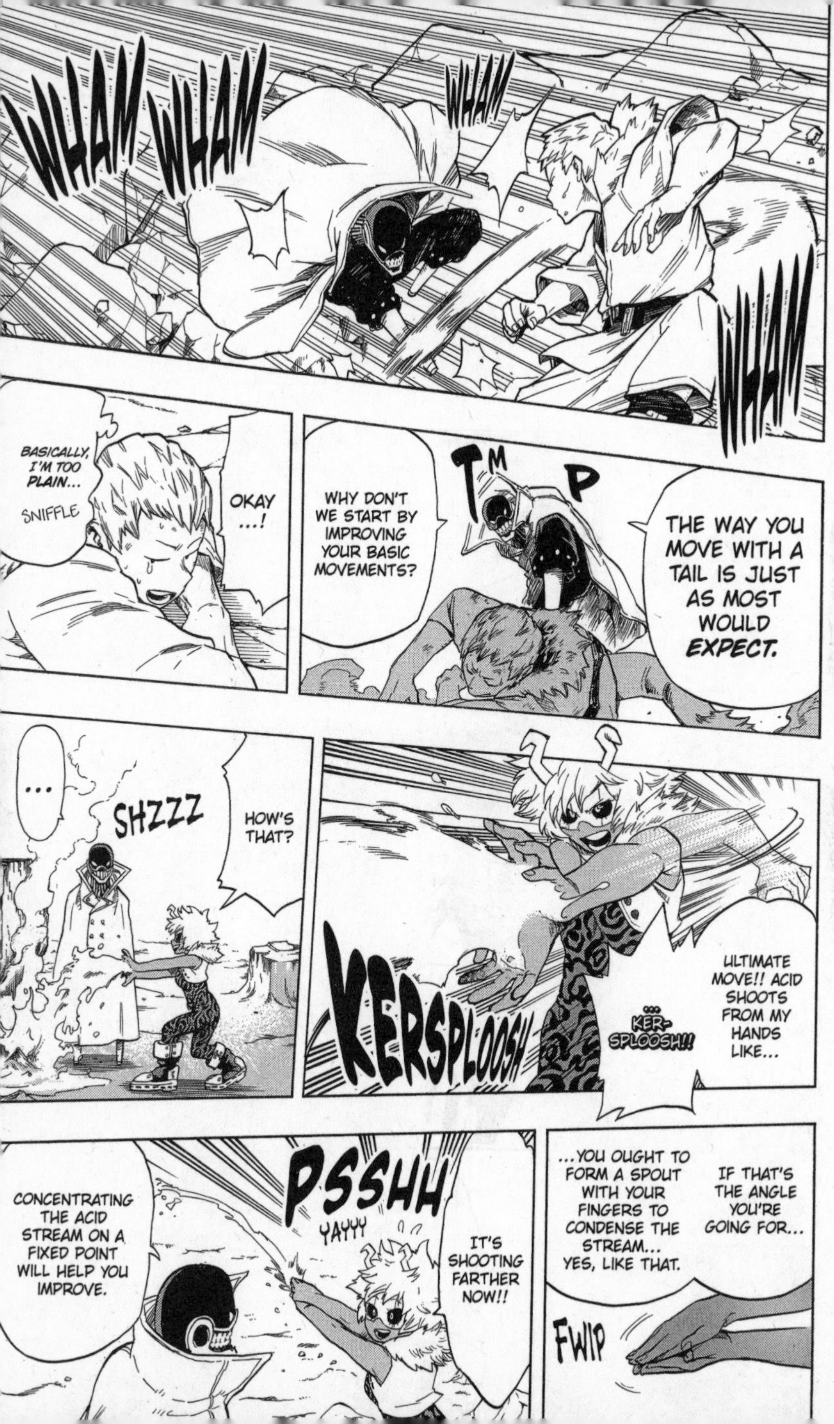
WHAM
WHAM
WHAM WHAM
T M P
THE WAY YOU MOVE WITH A TAIL IS JUST AS MOST WOULD EXPECT.
WHY DON'T WE START BY IMPROVING YOUR BASIC MOVEMENTS?
OKAY ...!
BASICALLY, I'M TOO PLAIN...
SNIFFLE
ULTIMATE MOVE!! ACID SHOOTS FROM MY HANDS LIKE...
...KER-SPLOOSH!!
KERSPLOOSH
HOW'S THAT?
SHZZZ
...
IF THAT'S THE ANGLE YOU'RE GOING FOR...
...YOU OUGHT TO FORM A SPOUT WITH YOUR FINGERS TO CONDENSE THE STREAM... YES, LIKE THAT.
FWIP
IT'S SHOOTING FARTHER NOW!!
PSSHH
YAYYY
CONCENTRATING THE ACID STREAM ON A FIXED POINT WILL HELP YOU IMPROVE.

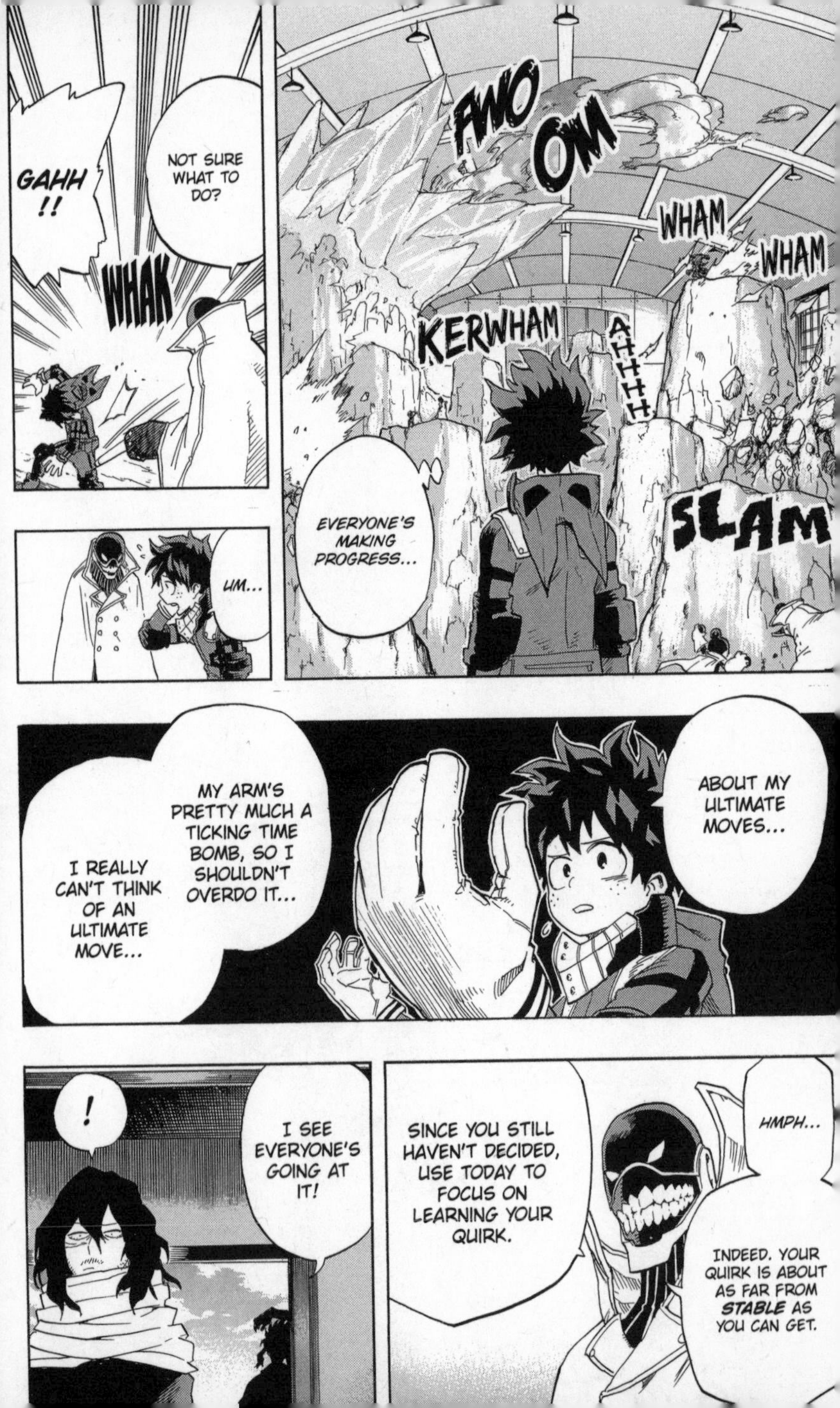
WHAM
WHAM
FWOOM
KERWHAM
AHHHHH
SLAM
EVERYONE'S MAKING PROGRESS...
NOT SURE WHAT TO DO?
GAHH !!
WHAK
UM...
ABOUT MY ULTIMATE MOVES...
MY ARM'S PRETTY MUCH A TICKING TIME BOMB, SO I SHOULDN'T OVERDO IT...
I REALLY CAN'T THINK OF AN ULTIMATE MOVE...
HMPH...
SINCE YOU STILL HAVEN'T DECIDED, USE TODAY TO FOCUS ON LEARNING YOUR QUIRK.
INDEED. YOUR QUIRK IS ABOUT AS FAR FROM STABLE AS YOU CAN GET.
I SEE EVERYONE'S GOING AT IT!
!

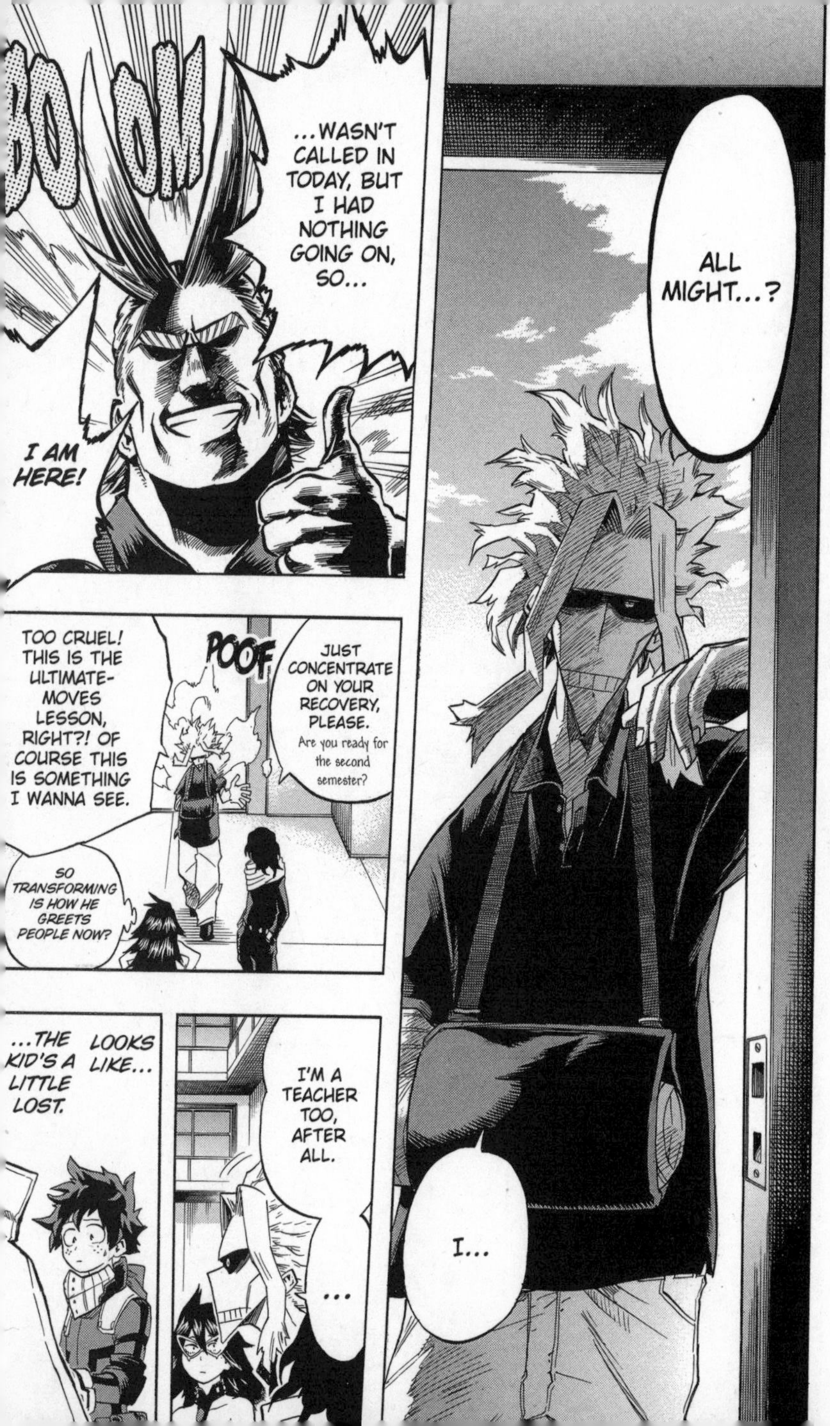
ALL MIGHT...?
I...
...WASN'T CALLED IN TODAY, BUT I HAD NOTHING GOING ON, SO...
BOOM
I AM HERE!
JUST CONCENTRATE ON YOUR RECOVERY, PLEASE.
Are you ready for the second semester?
POOF
TOO CRUEL! THIS IS THE ULTIMATE-MOVES LESSON, RIGHT?! OF COURSE THIS IS SOMETHING I WANNA SEE.
SO TRANSFORMING IS HOW HE GREETS PEOPLE NOW?
I'M A TEACHER TOO, AFTER ALL.
...
LOOKS LIKE...
...THE KID'S A LITTLE LOST.

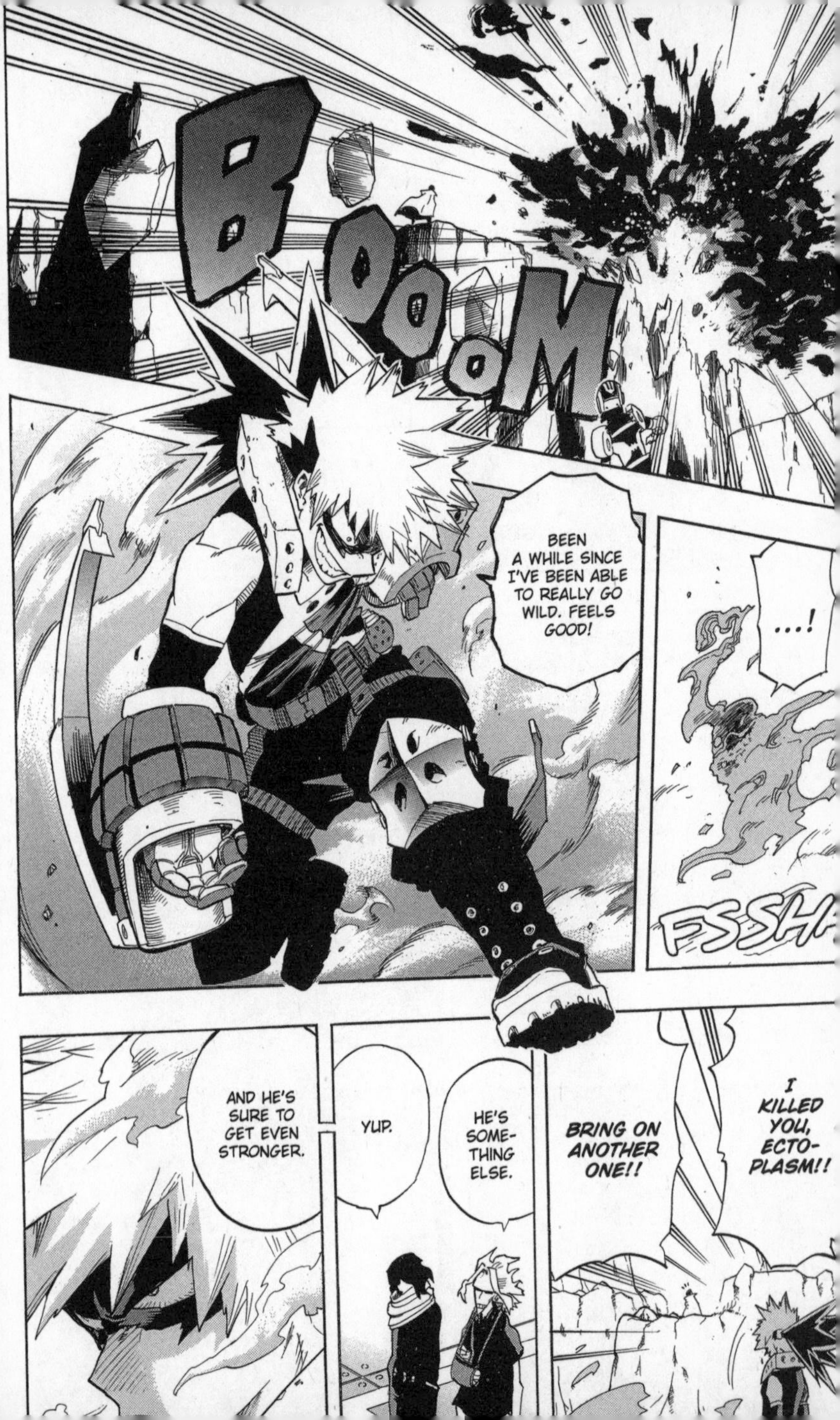
BOOOM
...!
FSSH
BEEN A WHILE SINCE I'VE BEEN ABLE TO REALLY GO WILD. FEELS GOOD!
I KILLED YOU, ECTO-PLASM!!
BRING ON ANOTHER ONE!!
HE'S SOME-THING ELSE.
YUP.
AND HE'S SURE TO GET EVEN STRONGER.

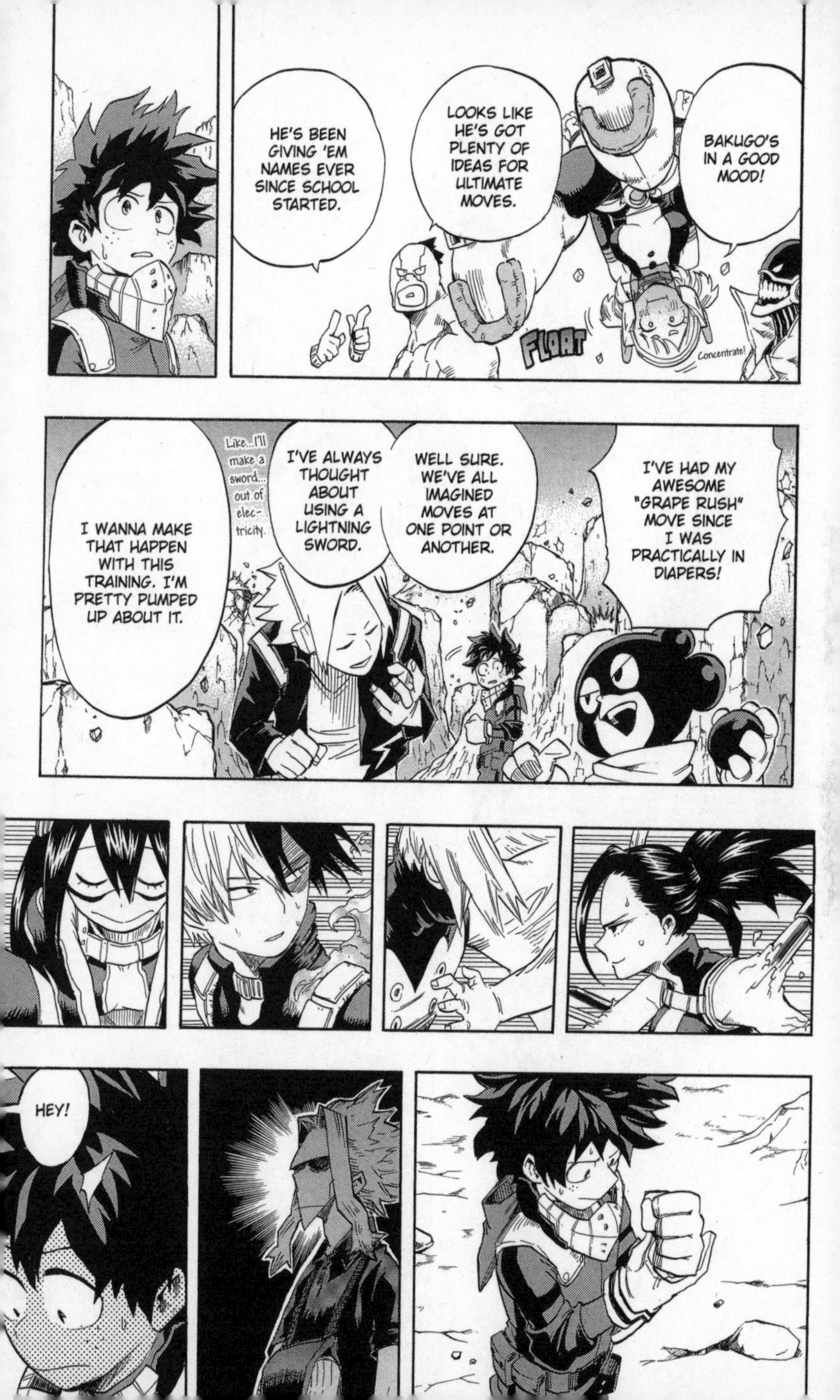
BAKUGO'S IN A GOOD MOOD!
Concentrate!
FLOAT
LOOKS LIKE HE'S GOT PLENTY OF IDEAS FOR ULTIMATE MOVES.
HE'S BEEN GIVING 'EM NAMES EVER SINCE SCHOOL STARTED.
I'VE HAD MY AWESOME "GRAPE RUSH" MOVE SINCE I WAS PRACTICALLY IN DIAPERS!
WELL SURE. WE'VE ALL IMAGINED MOVES AT ONE POINT OR ANOTHER.
I'VE ALWAYS THOUGHT ABOUT USING A LIGHTNING SWORD.
Like...I'll make a sword... out of elec-tricity.
I WANNA MAKE THAT HAPPEN WITH THIS TRAINING. I'M PRETTY PUMPED UP ABOUT IT.
HEY!

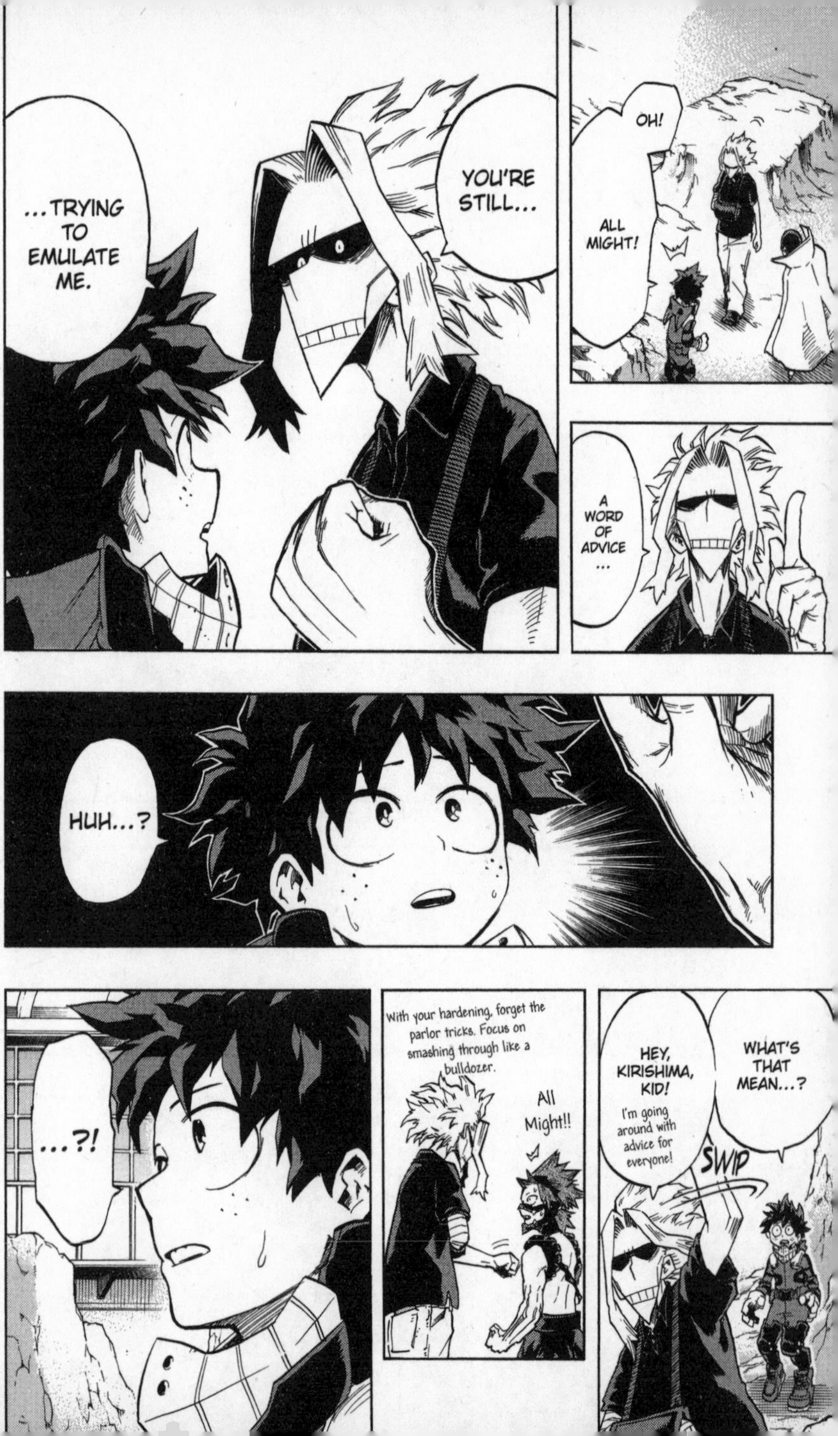
OH!
ALL MIGHT!
A WORD OF ADVICE...
YOU'RE STILL...
...TRYING TO EMULATE ME.
HUH...?
WHAT'S THAT MEAN...?
HEY, KIRISHIMA, KID!
I'm going around with advice for everyone!
SWIP
With your hardening, forget the parlor tricks. Focus on smashing through like a bulldozer.
All Might!!
...?!

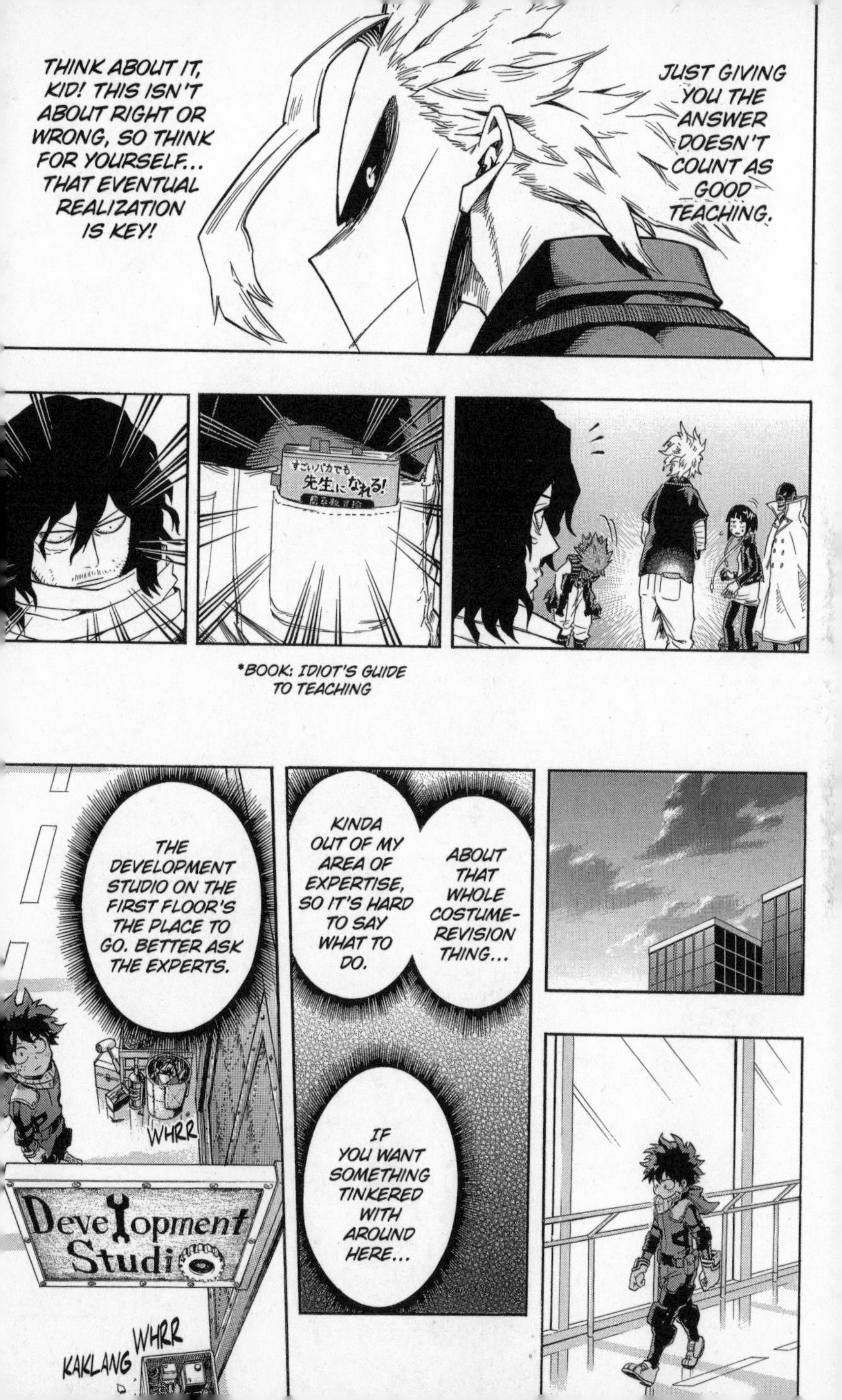
JUST GIVING YOU THE ANSWER DOESN'T COUNT AS GOOD TEACHING.
THINK ABOUT IT, KID! THIS ISN'T ABOUT RIGHT OR WRONG, SO THINK FOR YOURSELF... THAT EVENTUAL REALIZATION IS KEY!
すごいバカでも先生になれる!
*BOOK: IDIOT'S GUIDE TO TEACHING
ABOUT THAT WHOLE COSTUME-REVISION THING...
KINDA OUT OF MY AREA OF EXPERTISE, SO IT'S HARD TO SAY WHAT TO DO.
IF YOU WANT SOMETHING TINKERED WITH AROUND HERE...
THE DEVELOPMENT STUDIO ON THE FIRST FLOOR'S THE PLACE TO GO. BETTER ASK THE EXPERTS.
WHRR
Development Studio
WHRR
KAKLANG

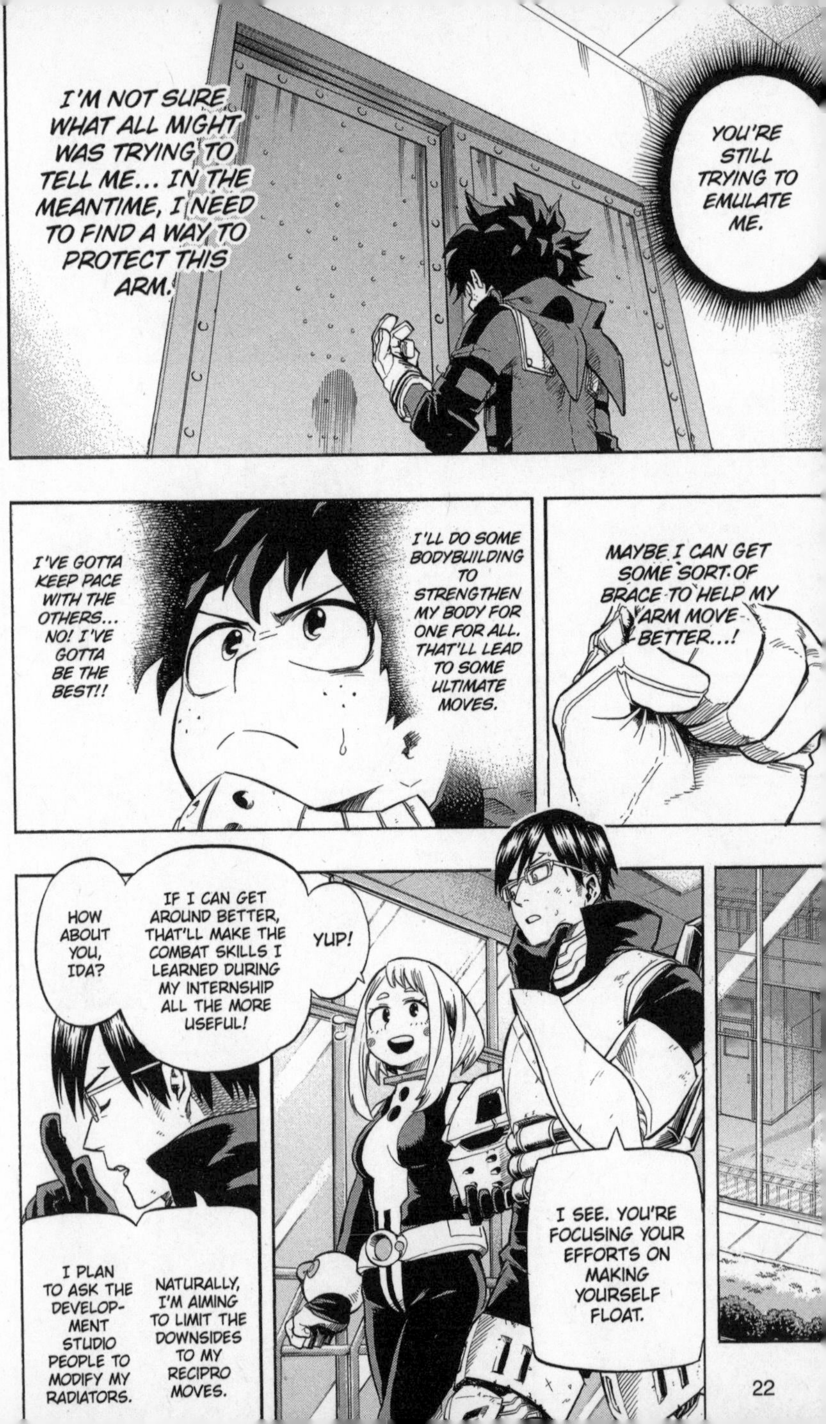
YOU'RE STILL TRYING TO EMULATE ME.
I'M NOT SURE WHAT ALL MIGHT WAS TRYING TO TELL ME... IN THE MEANTIME, I NEED TO FIND A WAY TO PROTECT THIS ARM.
MAYBE I CAN GET SOME SORT OF BRACE TO HELP MY ARM MOVE BETTER...!
I'LL DO SOME BODYBUILDING TO STRENGTHEN MY BODY FOR ONE FOR ALL. THAT'LL LEAD TO SOME ULTIMATE MOVES.
I'VE GOTTA KEEP PACE WITH THE OTHERS... NO! I'VE GOTTA BE THE BEST!!
YUP!
IF I CAN GET AROUND BETTER, THAT'LL MAKE THE COMBAT SKILLS I LEARNED DURING MY INTERNSHIP ALL THE MORE USEFUL!
HOW ABOUT YOU, IDA?
I SEE. YOU'RE FOCUSING YOUR EFFORTS ON MAKING YOURSELF FLOAT.
NATURALLY, I'M AIMING TO LIMIT THE DOWNSIDES TO MY RECIPRO MOVES.
I PLAN TO ASK THE DEVELOPMENT STUDIO PEOPLE TO MODIFY MY RADIATORS.

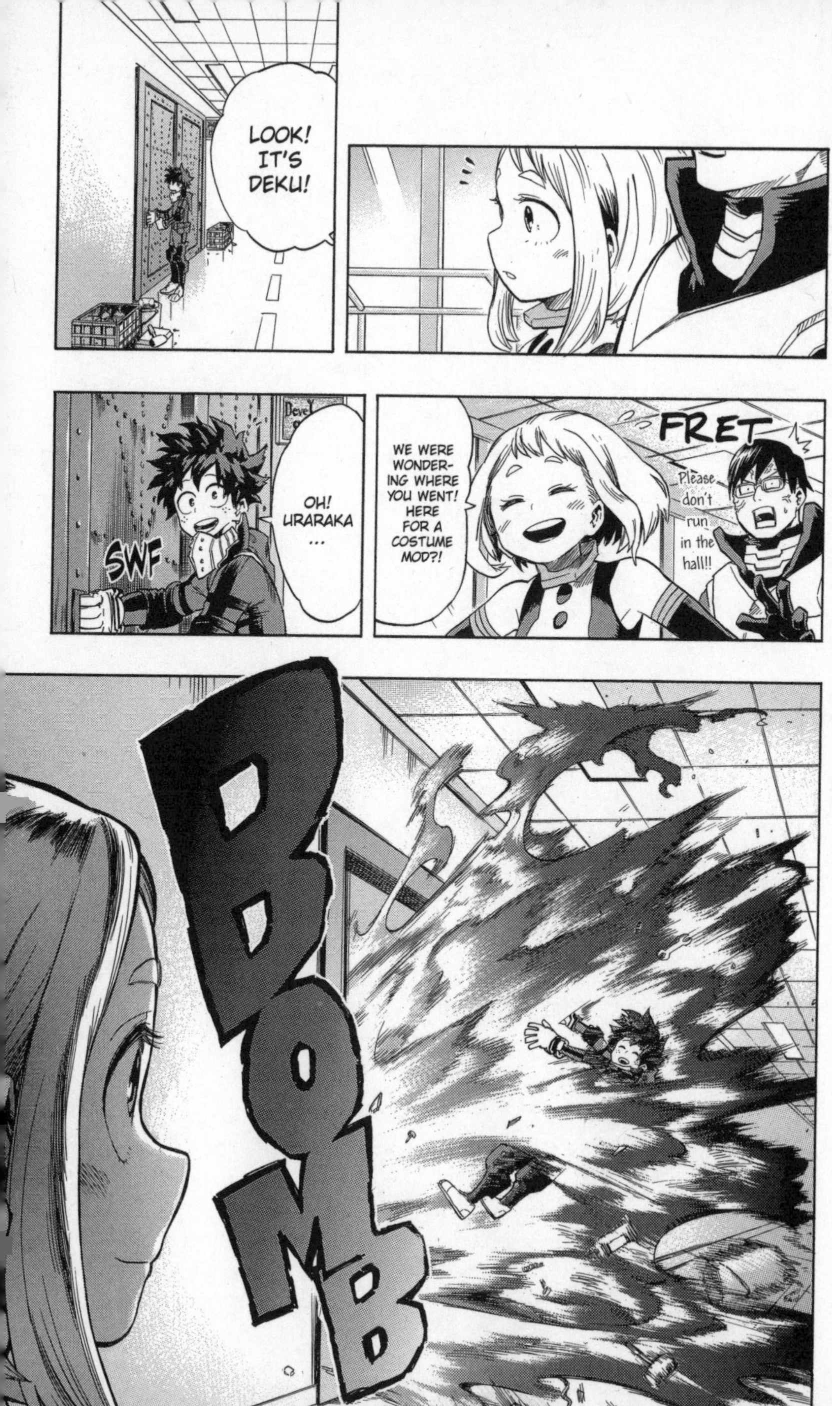
LOOK! IT'S DEKU!
FRET
WE WERE WONDERING WHERE YOU WENT! HERE FOR A COSTUME MOD?!
Please don't run in the hall!!
OH! URARAKA ...
SWF
BOMB

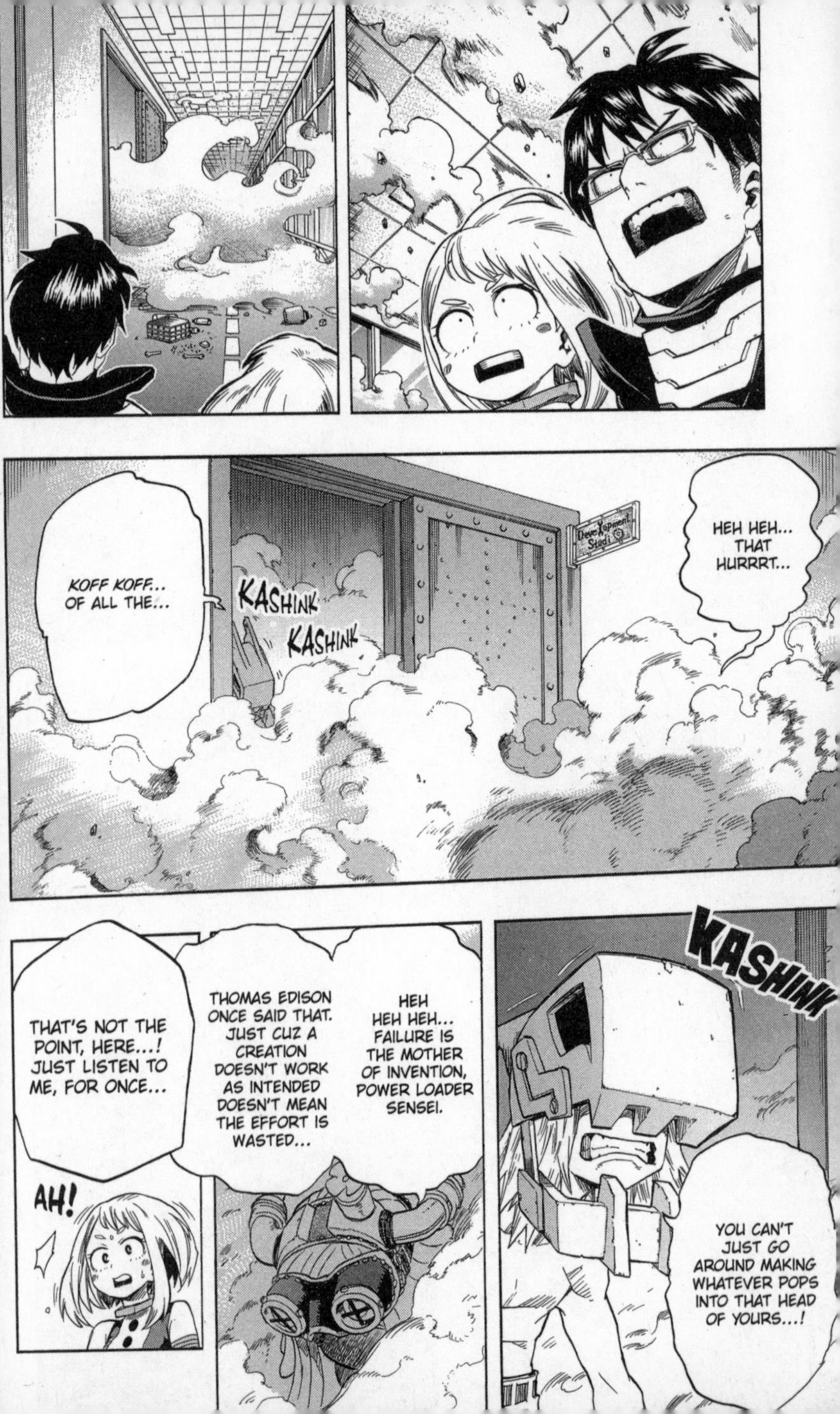
HEH HEH... THAT HURRRT...
KASHINK
KASHINK
KOFF KOFF... OF ALL THE...
KASHINK
YOU CAN'T JUST GO AROUND MAKING WHATEVER POPS INTO THAT HEAD OF YOURS...!
HEH HEH HEH... FAILURE IS THE MOTHER OF INVENTION, POWER LOADER SENSEI.
THOMAS EDISON ONCE SAID THAT. JUST CUZ A CREATION DOESN'T WORK AS INTENDED DOESN'T MEAN THE EFFORT IS WASTED...
THAT'S NOT THE POINT, HERE...! JUST LISTEN TO ME, FOR ONCE...
AH!

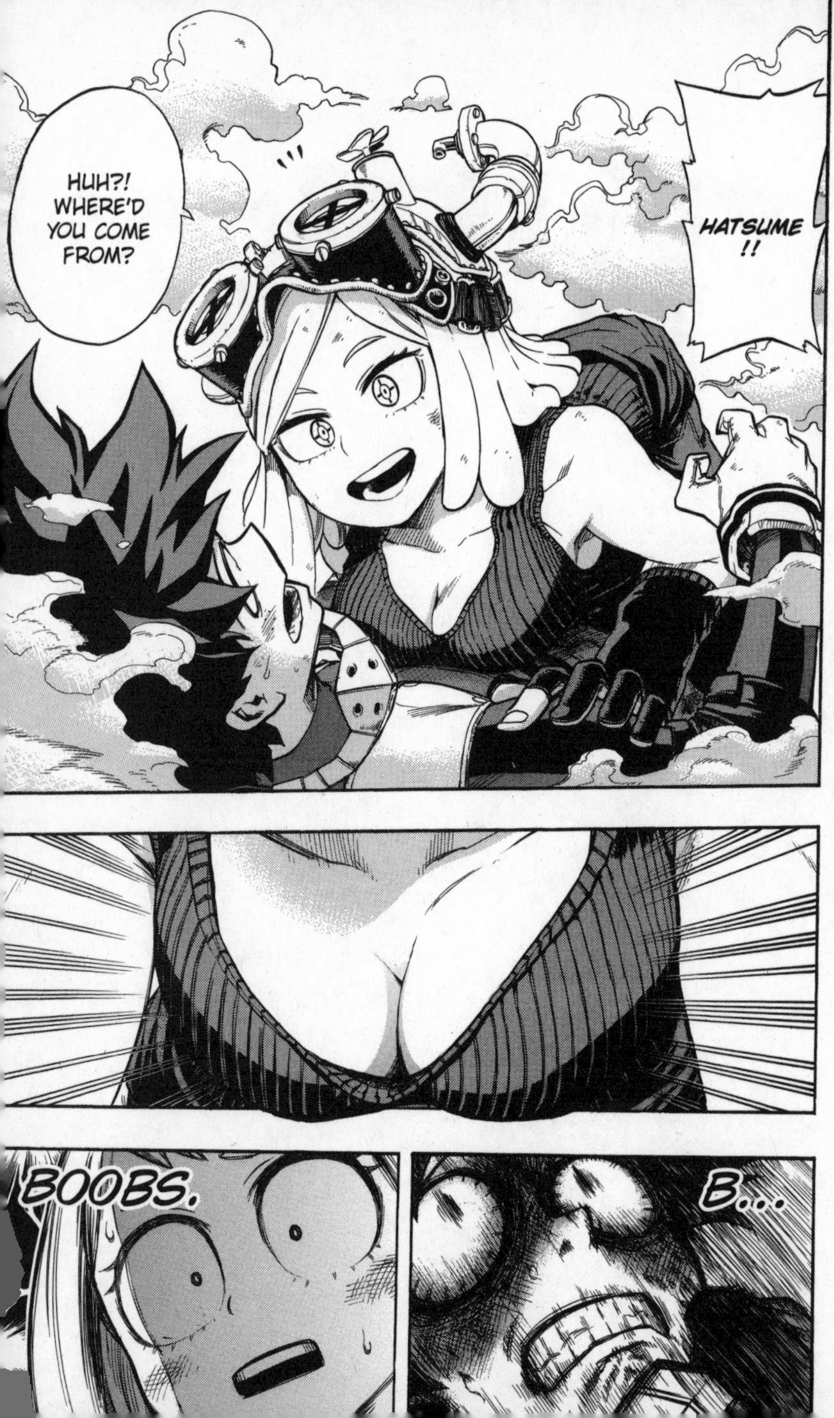
HATSUME !!
HUH?! WHERE'D YOU COME FROM?
B...
BOOBS.

THE·100

Thanks to you readers, we made it to three-digit chapters! Amazing!

Deku sure has earned himself a bunch of scars. Sometimes I don't draw them all in, but even back when the series first got serialized, I was ready to carve him up like that. He's accrued those scars way faster than I thought, though.

We've been through a lot already, but the week of chapter 100 was a particularly emotional one for me. Pretty crazy that a milestone chapter like that ended with boobs. I'm sure I was just tired.

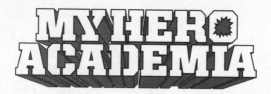

MY HERO ACADEMIA

No. 101 - The Girl Called Mei Hatsume

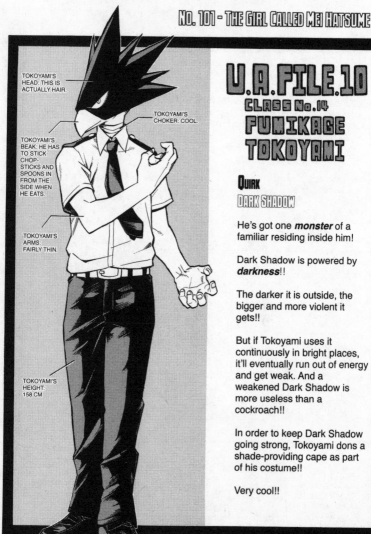

TOKOYAMI'S HEAD: THIS IS ACTUALLY HAIR.
TOKOYAMI'S CHOKER: COOL.
TOKOYAMI'S BEAK: HE HAS TO STICK CHOP-STICKS AND SPOONS IN FROM THE SIDE WHEN HE EATS.
TOKOYAMI'S ARMS: FAIRLY THIN.
TOKOYAMI'S HEIGHT: 158 CM

U.A. FILE.10

CLASS No.14

FUMIKAGE TOKOYAMI

Quirk

Dark Shadow

He's got one ***monster*** of a familiar residing inside him!

Dark Shadow is powered by ***darkness***!!

The darker it is outside, the bigger and more violent it gets!!

But if Tokoyami uses it continuously in bright places, it'll eventually run out of energy and get weak. And a weakened Dark Shadow is more useless than a cockroach!!

In order to keep Dark Shadow going strong, Tokoyami dons a shade-providing cape as part of his costume!!

Very cool!!

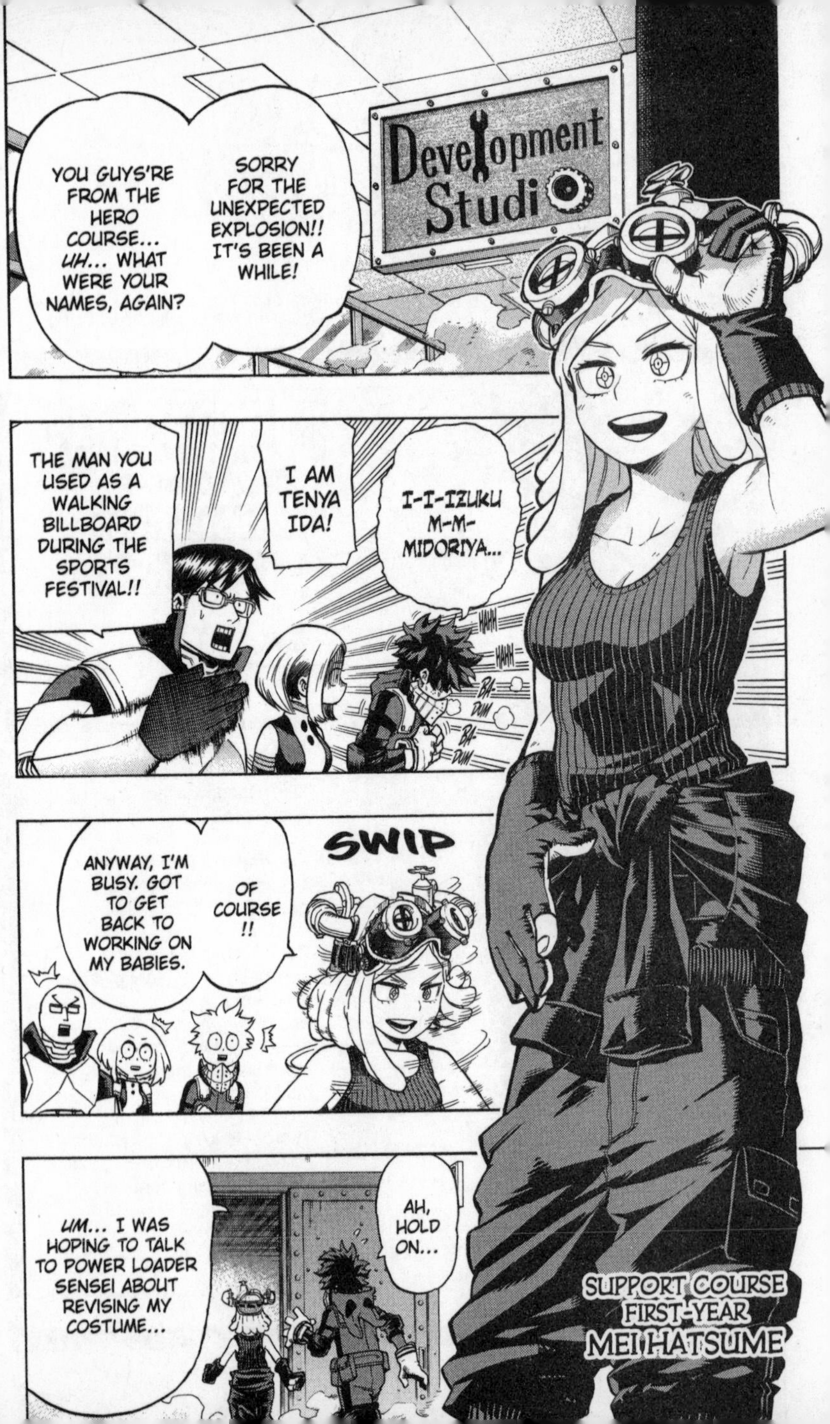

Development Studio
SORRY FOR THE UNEXPECTED EXPLOSION!! IT'S BEEN A WHILE!
YOU GUYS'RE FROM THE HERO COURSE... *UH*... WHAT WERE YOUR NAMES, AGAIN?
I-I-IZUKU M-M-MIDORIYA...
HAHH
HAHH
BA-DUM
BA-DUM
I AM TENYA IDA!
THE MAN YOU USED AS A WALKING BILLBOARD DURING THE SPORTS FESTIVAL!!
SWIP
OF COURSE !!
ANYWAY, I'M BUSY. GOT TO GET BACK TO WORKING ON MY BABIES.
AH, HOLD ON...
UM... I WAS HOPING TO TALK TO POWER LOADER SENSEI ABOUT REVISING MY COSTUME...
SUPPORT COURSE FIRST-YEAR MEI HATSUME

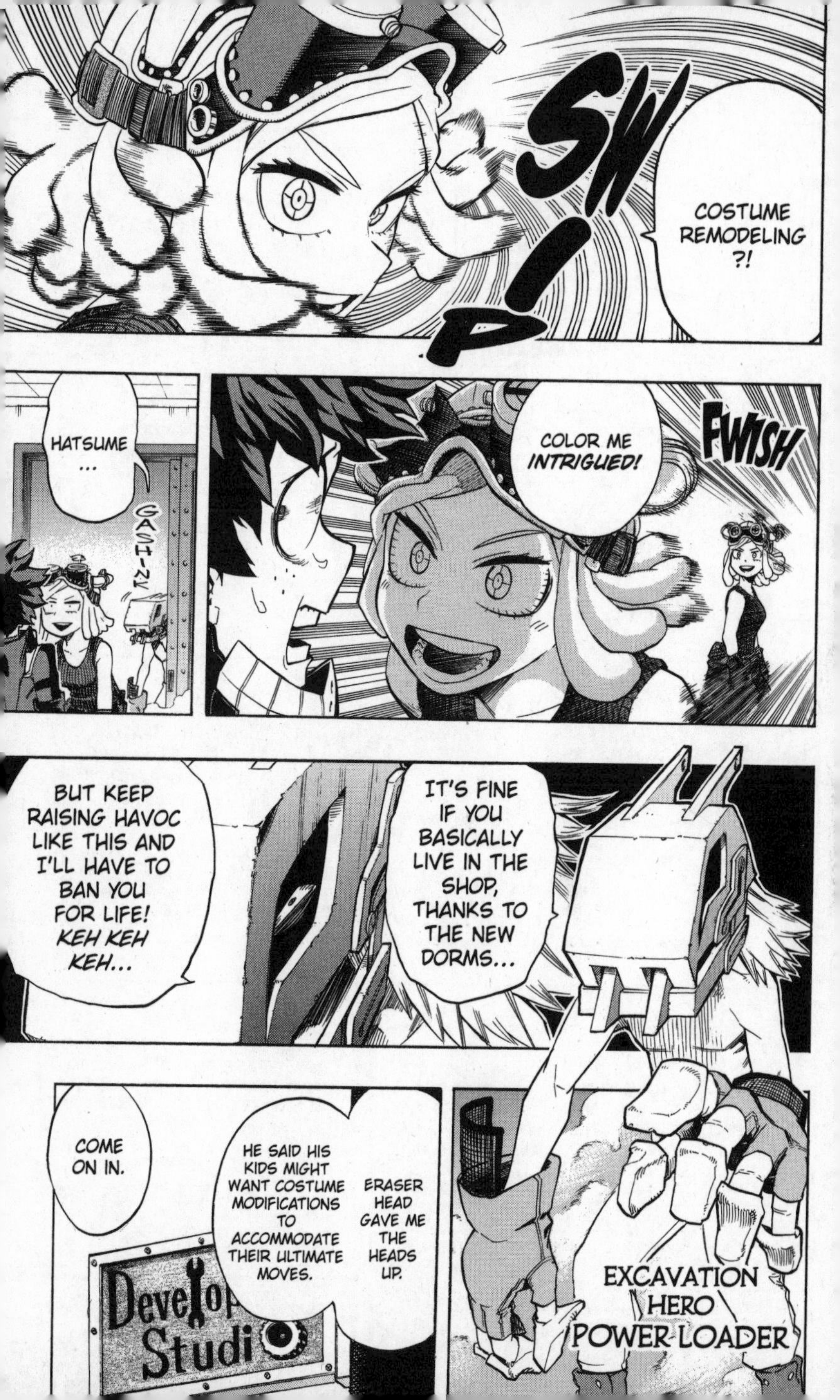
COSTUME REMODELING ?!
SWIP
FWISH
COLOR ME *INTRIGUED!*
HATSUME ...
GASHINK
IT'S FINE IF YOU BASICALLY LIVE IN THE SHOP, THANKS TO THE NEW DORMS...
BUT KEEP RAISING HAVOC LIKE THIS AND I'LL HAVE TO BAN YOU FOR LIFE! *KEH KEH KEH...*
EXCAVATION HERO POWER LOADER
ERASER HEAD GAVE ME THE HEADS UP.
HE SAID HIS KIDS MIGHT WANT COSTUME MODIFICATIONS TO ACCOMMODATE THEIR ULTIMATE MOVES.
COME ON IN.
Develop
Studi

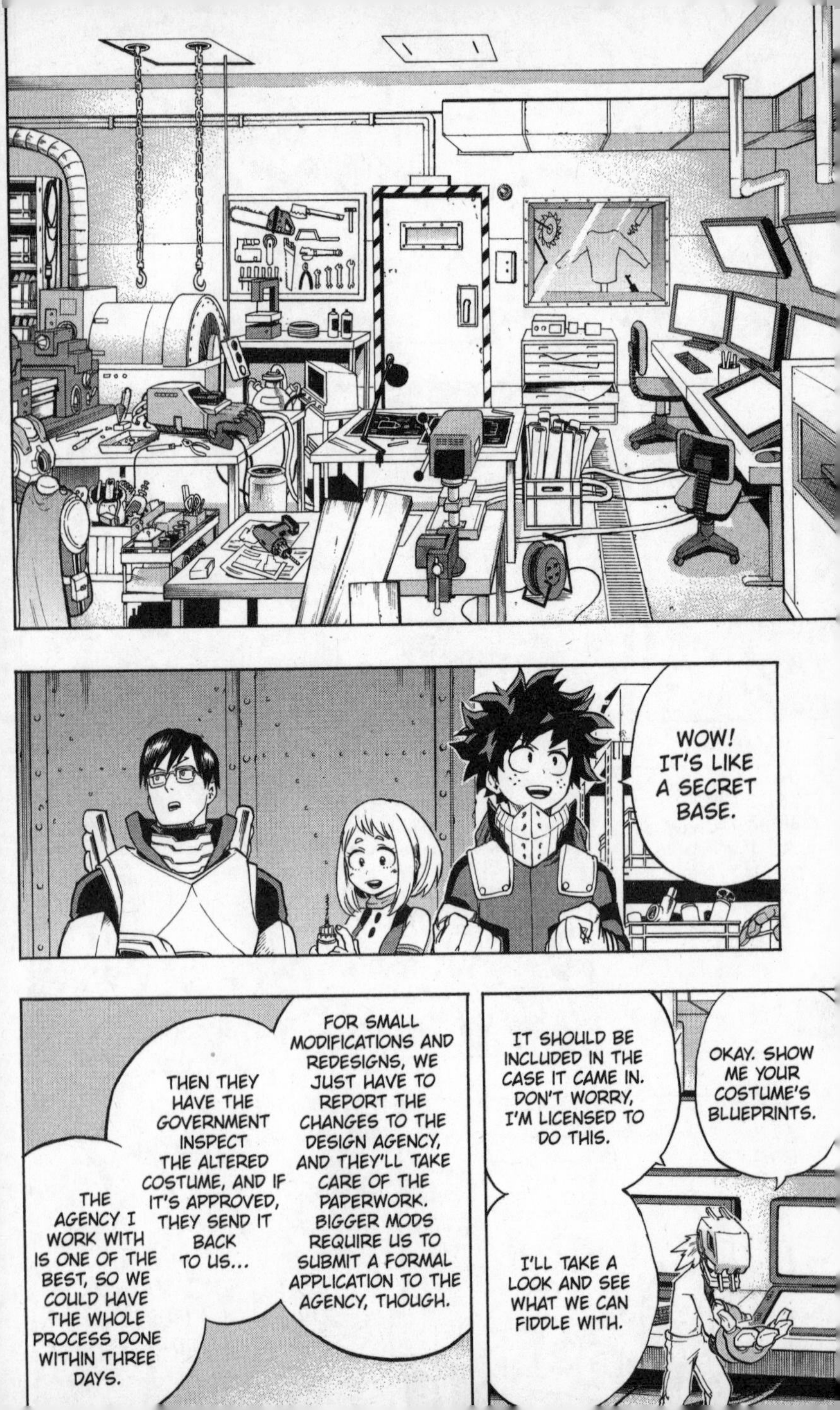
WOW! IT'S LIKE A SECRET BASE.
OKAY. SHOW ME YOUR COSTUME'S BLUEPRINTS.
IT SHOULD BE INCLUDED IN THE CASE IT CAME IN. DON'T WORRY, I'M LICENSED TO DO THIS.
I'LL TAKE A LOOK AND SEE WHAT WE CAN FIDDLE WITH.
FOR SMALL MODIFICATIONS AND REDESIGNS, WE JUST HAVE TO REPORT THE CHANGES TO THE DESIGN AGENCY, AND THEY'LL TAKE CARE OF THE PAPERWORK. BIGGER MODS REQUIRE US TO SUBMIT A FORMAL APPLICATION TO THE AGENCY, THOUGH.
THEN THEY HAVE THE GOVERNMENT INSPECT THE ALTERED COSTUME, AND IF IT'S APPROVED, THEY SEND IT BACK TO US...
THE AGENCY I WORK WITH IS ONE OF THE BEST, SO WE COULD HAVE THE WHOLE PROCESS DONE WITHIN THREE DAYS.

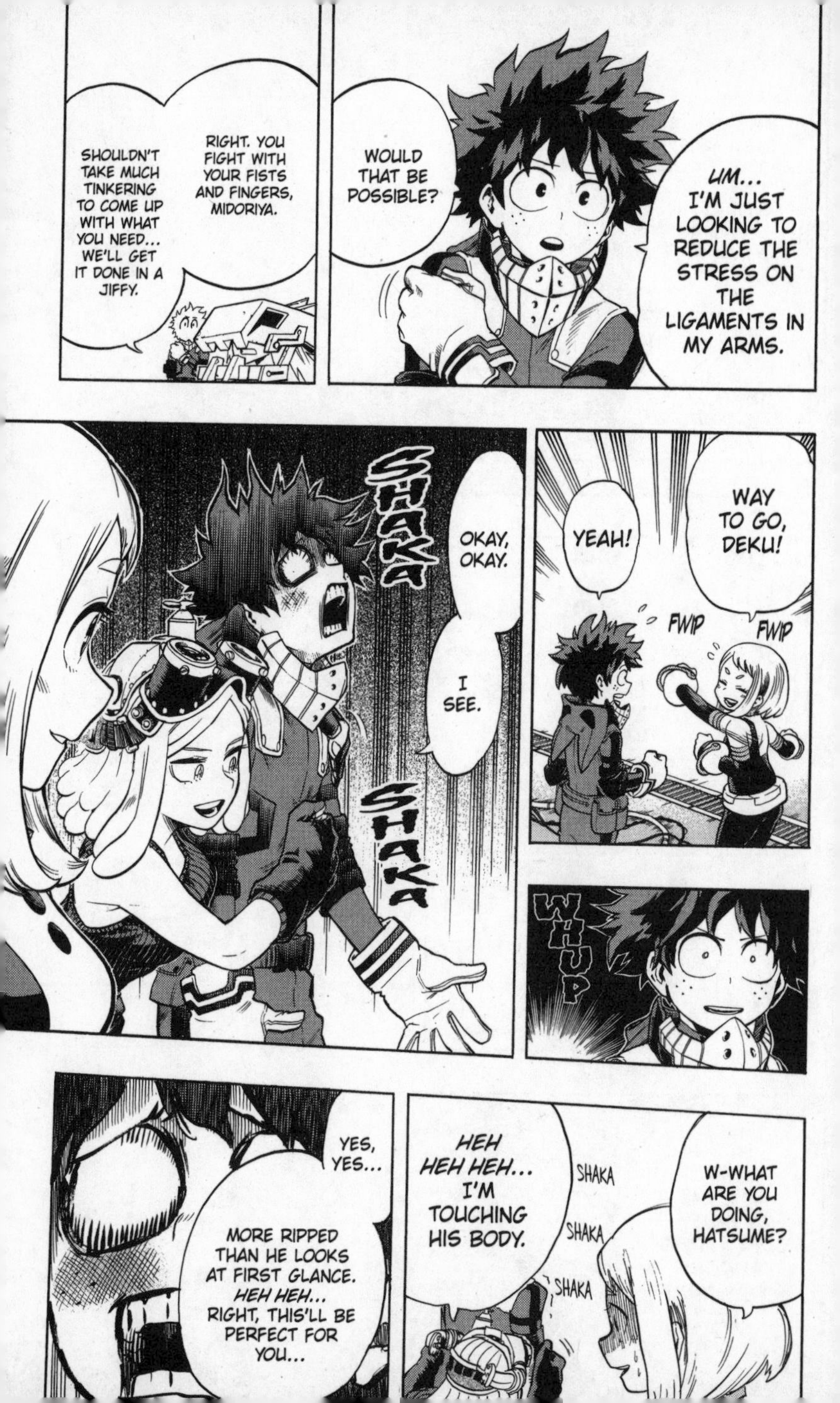

UM... I'M JUST LOOKING TO REDUCE THE STRESS ON THE LIGAMENTS IN MY ARMS.
WOULD THAT BE POSSIBLE?
RIGHT. YOU FIGHT WITH YOUR FISTS AND FINGERS, MIDORIYA.
SHOULDN'T TAKE MUCH TINKERING TO COME UP WITH WHAT YOU NEED... WE'LL GET IT DONE IN A JIFFY.
WAY TO GO, DEKU!
YEAH!
FWIP
FWIP
WHUP
SHAKA
OKAY, OKAY.
I SEE.
SHAKA
W-WHAT ARE YOU DOING, HATSUME?
SHAKA
SHAKA
SHAKA
HEH HEH HEH... I'M TOUCHING HIS BODY.
YES, YES...
MORE RIPPED THAN HE LOOKS AT FIRST GLANCE. HEH HEH... RIGHT, THIS'LL BE PERFECT FOR YOU...

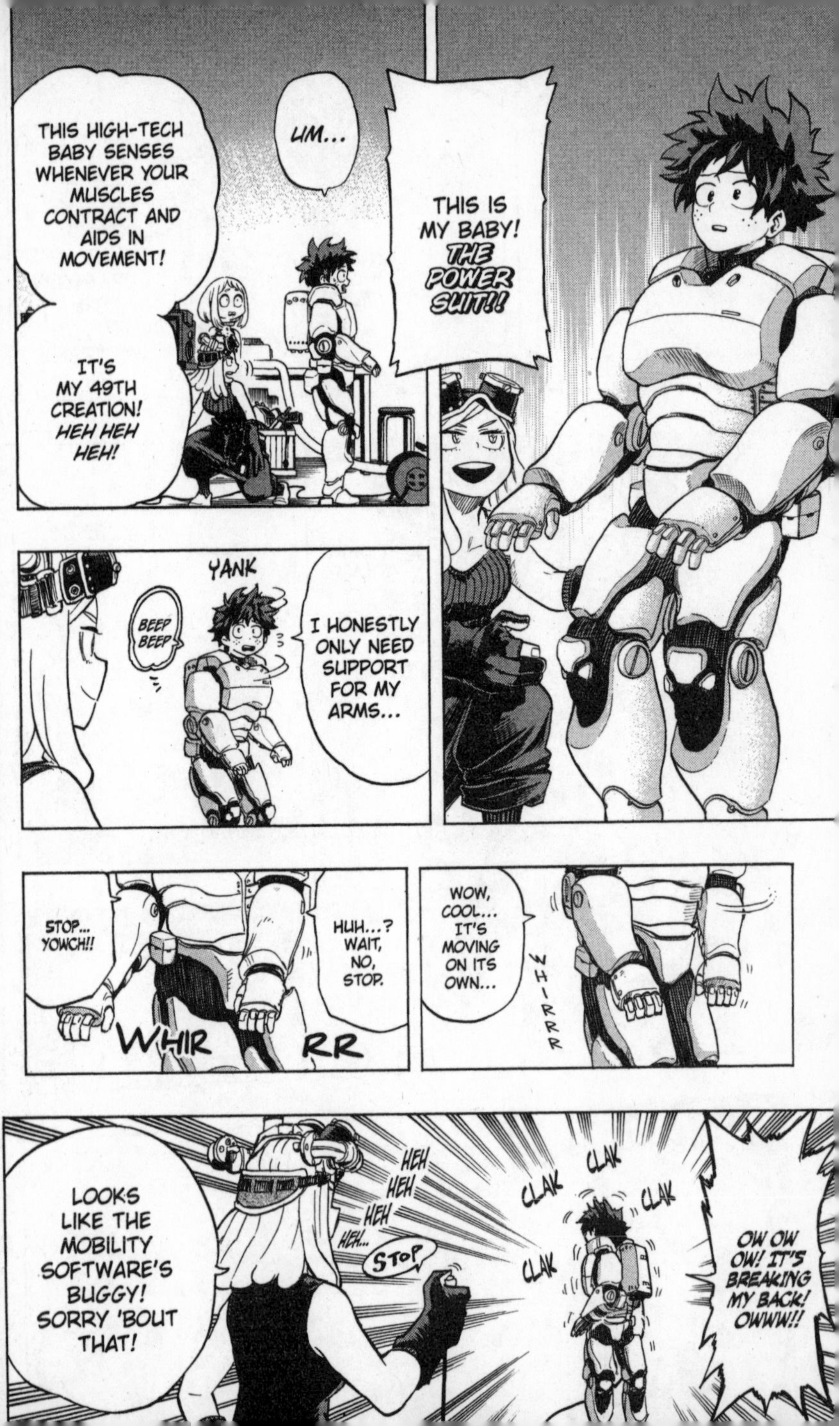

THIS IS MY BABY! THE POWER SUIT!!
UM...
THIS HIGH-TECH BABY SENSES WHENEVER YOUR MUSCLES CONTRACT AND AIDS IN MOVEMENT!
IT'S MY 49TH CREATION! HEH HEH HEH!
YANK
I HONESTLY ONLY NEED SUPPORT FOR MY ARMS...
BEEP BEEP
WOW, COOL... IT'S MOVING ON ITS OWN...
WHIRRR
HUH...? WAIT, NO, STOP.
STOP... YOWCH!!
WHIRRR
OW OW OW! IT'S BREAKING MY BACK! OWWW!!
CLAK
CLAK
CLAK
CLAK
STOP
HEH HEH HEH HEH...
LOOKS LIKE THE MOBILITY SOFTWARE'S BUGGY! SORRY 'BOUT THAT!

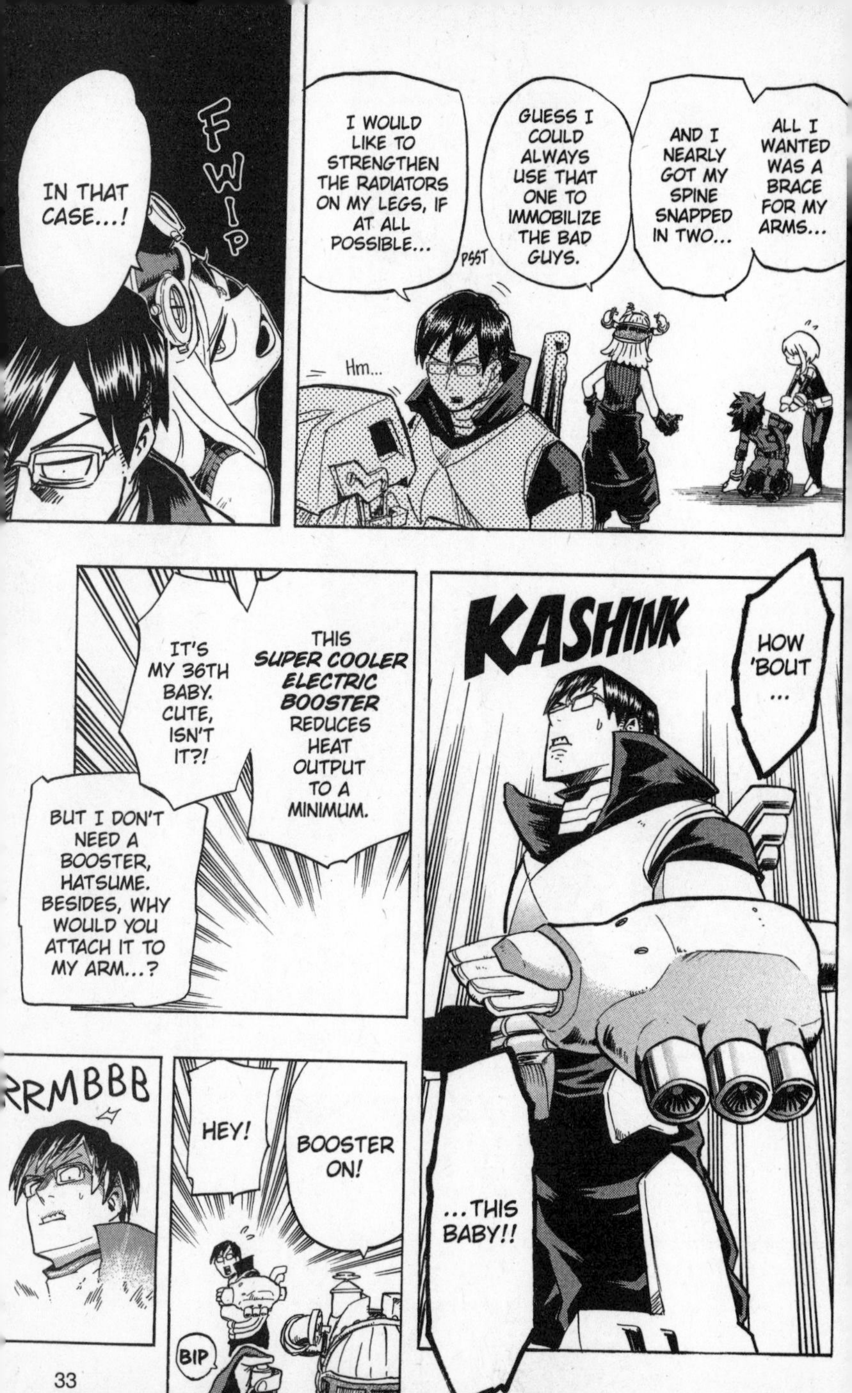
ALL I WANTED WAS A BRACE FOR MY ARMS...
AND I NEARLY GOT MY SPINE SNAPPED IN TWO...
GUESS I COULD ALWAYS USE THAT ONE TO IMMOBILIZE THE BAD GUYS.
PSST
I WOULD LIKE TO STRENGTHEN THE RADIATORS ON MY LEGS, IF AT ALL POSSIBLE...
Hm...
FWIP
IN THAT CASE...!
KASHINK
HOW 'BOUT...
...THIS BABY!!
THIS **SUPER COOLER ELECTRIC BOOSTER** REDUCES HEAT OUTPUT TO A MINIMUM.
IT'S MY 36TH BABY. CUTE, ISN'T IT?!
BUT I DON'T NEED A BOOSTER, HATSUME. BESIDES, WHY WOULD YOU ATTACH IT TO MY ARM...?
BOOSTER ON!
HEY!
BIP
RRMBBB

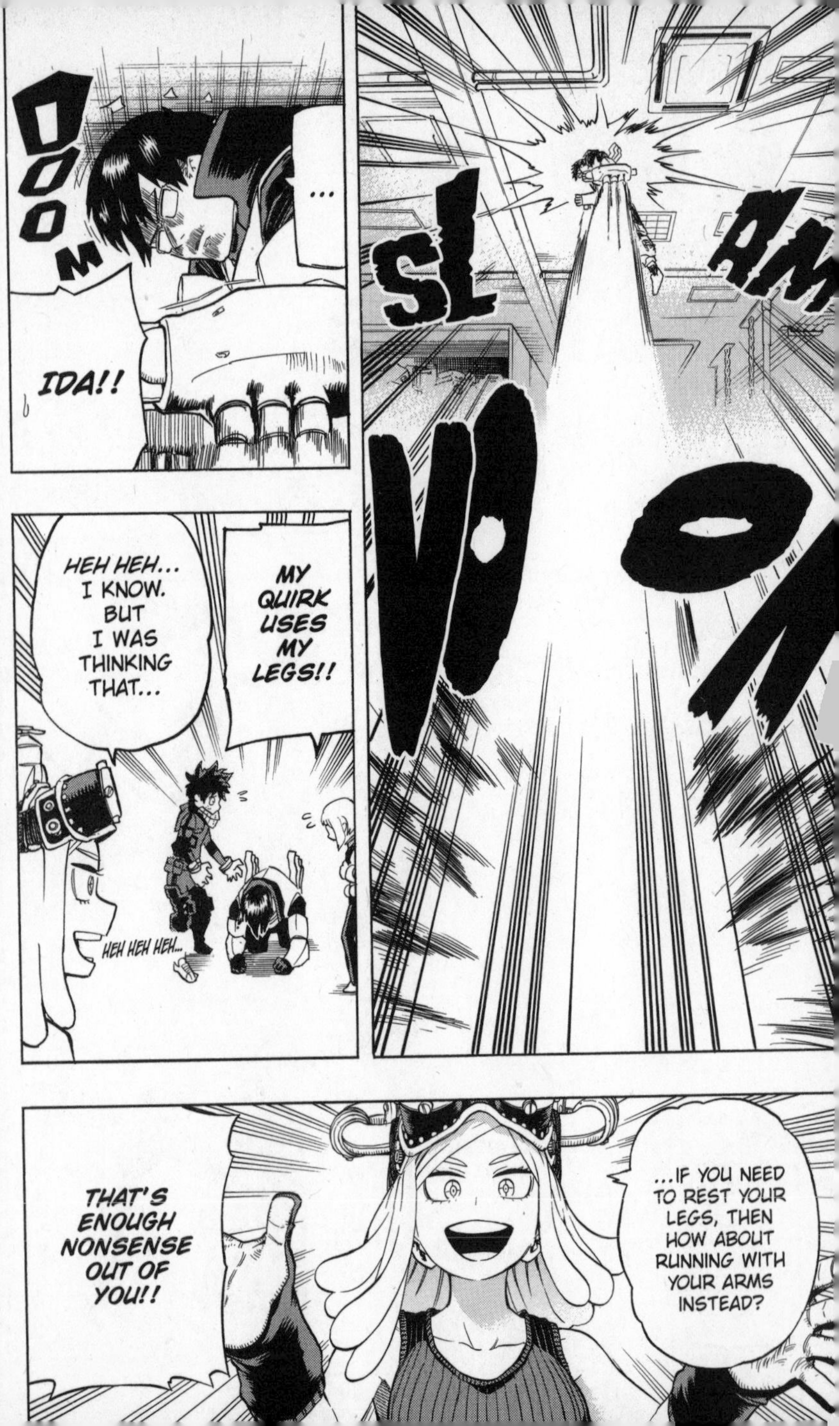
SLAM
VOOM
DOOOM
...
IDA!!
MY QUIRK USES MY LEGS!!
HEH HEH... I KNOW. BUT I WAS THINKING THAT...
HEH HEH HEH...
...IF YOU NEED TO REST YOUR LEGS, THEN HOW ABOUT RUNNING WITH YOUR ARMS INSTEAD?
THAT'S ENOUGH NONSENSE OUT OF YOU!!

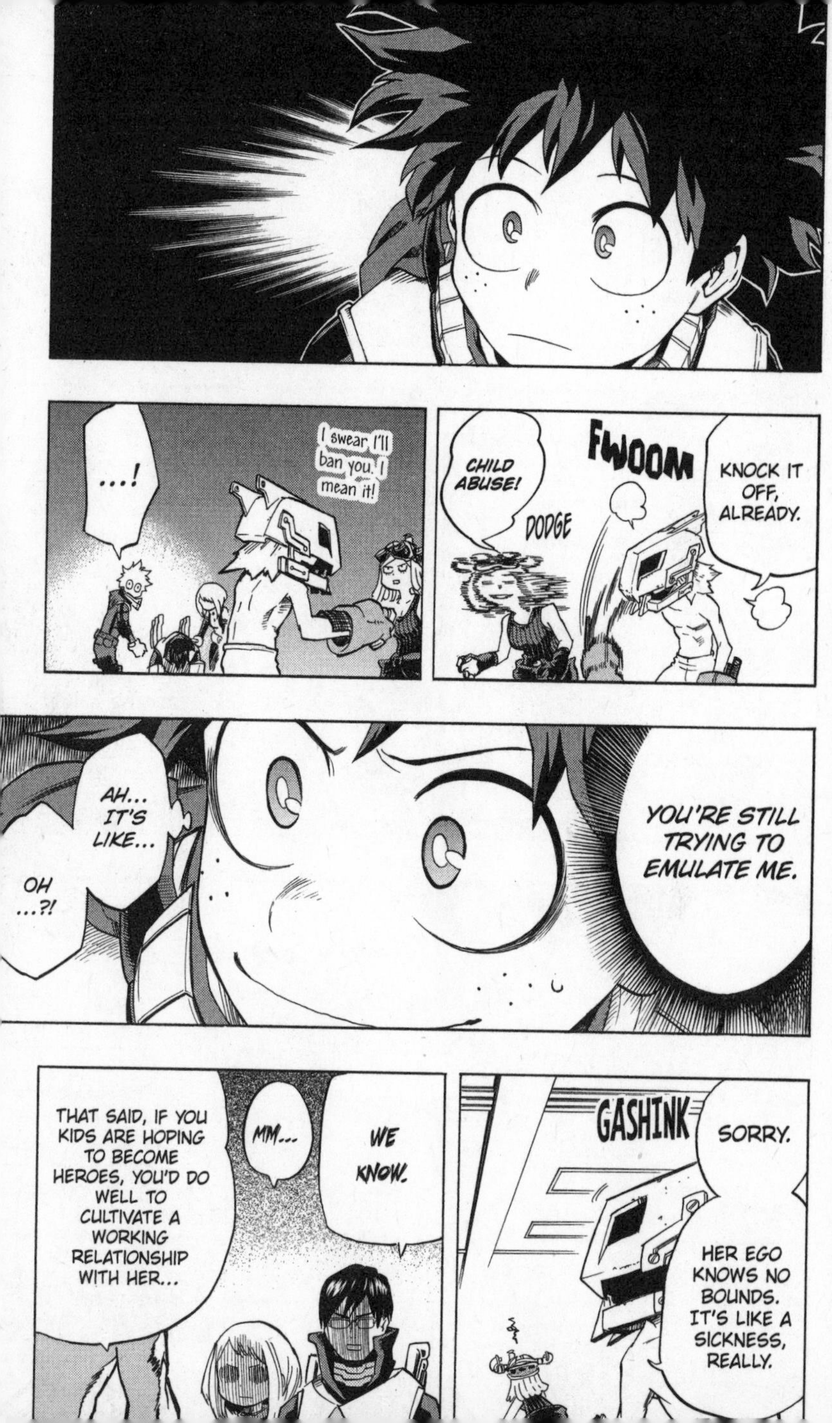
KNOCK IT OFF, ALREADY.
FWOOM
CHILD ABUSE!
DODGE
I swear I'll ban you. I mean it!
...!
YOU'RE STILL TRYING TO EMULATE ME.
AH... IT'S LIKE...
OH ...?!
SORRY.
GASHINK
HER EGO KNOWS NO BOUNDS. IT'S LIKE A SICKNESS, REALLY.
WE KNOW.
MM...
THAT SAID, IF YOU KIDS ARE HOPING TO BECOME HEROES, YOU'D DO WELL TO CULTIVATE A WORKING RELATIONSHIP WITH HER...

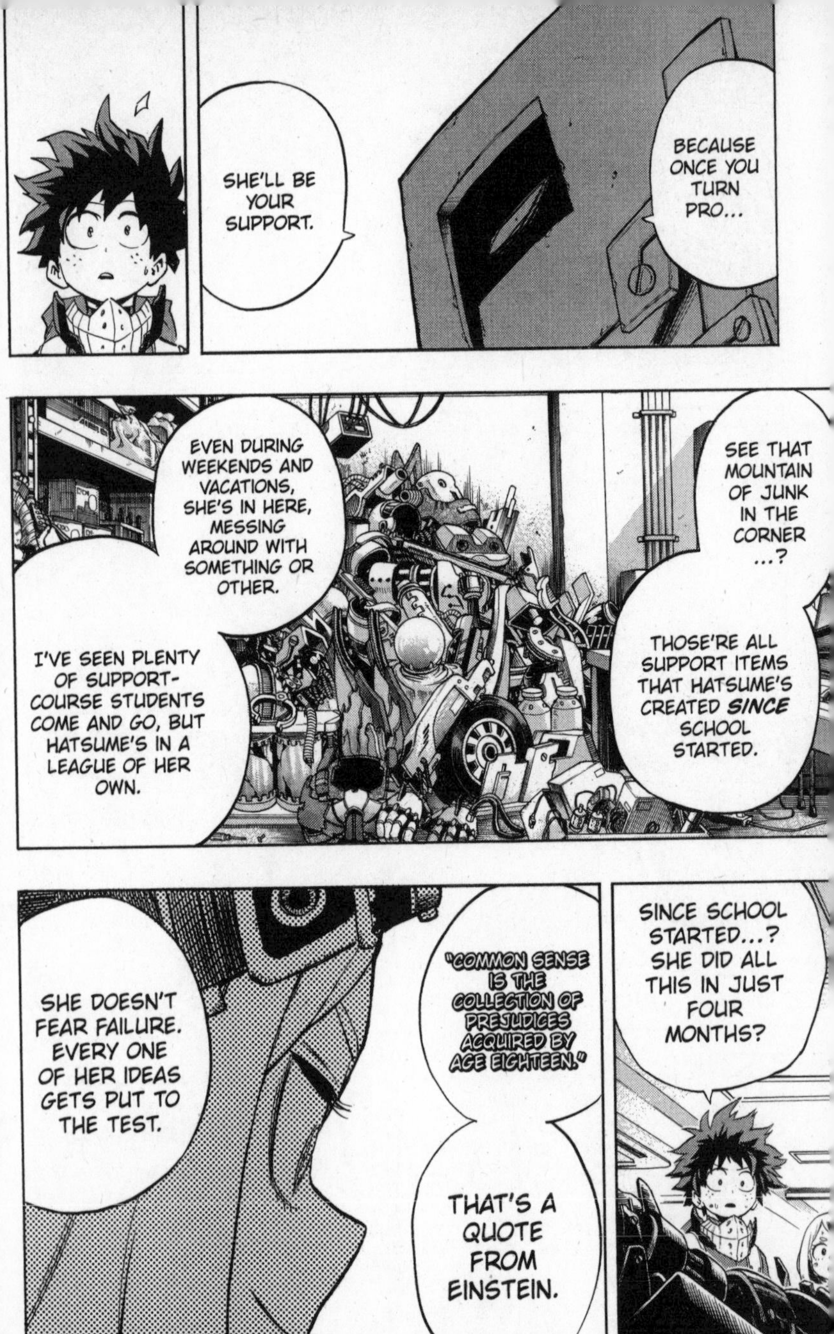
BECAUSE ONCE YOU TURN PRO...
SHE'LL BE YOUR SUPPORT.
SEE THAT MOUNTAIN OF JUNK IN THE CORNER ...?
THOSE'RE ALL SUPPORT ITEMS THAT HATSUME'S CREATED *SINCE* SCHOOL STARTED.
EVEN DURING WEEKENDS AND VACATIONS, SHE'S IN HERE, MESSING AROUND WITH SOMETHING OR OTHER.
I'VE SEEN PLENTY OF SUPPORT-COURSE STUDENTS COME AND GO, BUT HATSUME'S IN A LEAGUE OF HER OWN.
SINCE SCHOOL STARTED...? SHE DID ALL THIS IN JUST FOUR MONTHS?
"COMMON SENSE IS THE COLLECTION OF PREJUDICES ACQUIRED BY AGE EIGHTEEN."
THAT'S A QUOTE FROM EINSTEIN.
SHE DOESN'T FEAR FAILURE. EVERY ONE OF HER IDEAS GETS PUT TO THE TEST.

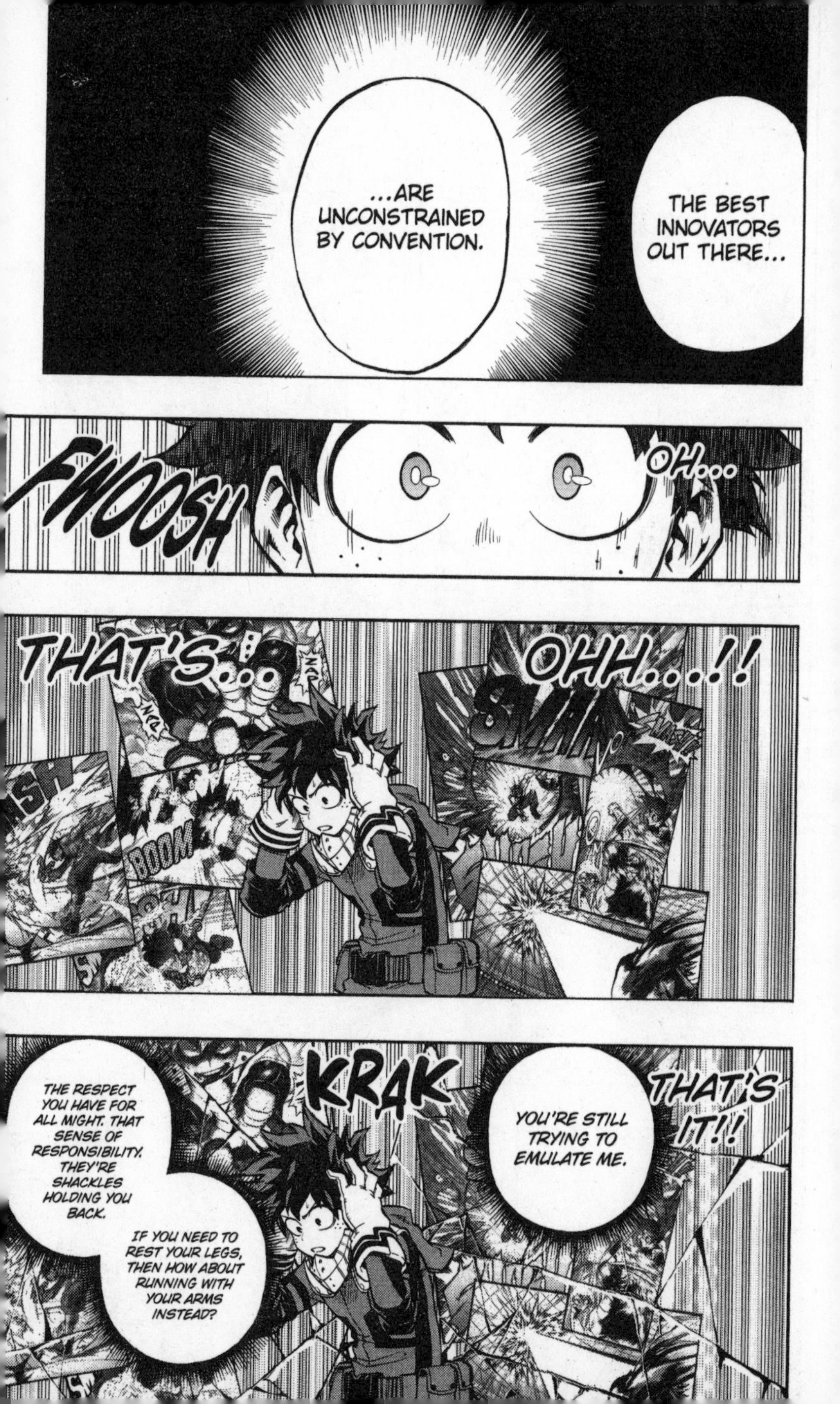
THE BEST INNOVATORS OUT THERE...
...ARE UNCONSTRAINED BY CONVENTION.
OH...
FWOOSH
OHH...!!
THAT'S...
BOOM
THAT'S IT!!
YOU'RE STILL TRYING TO EMULATE ME.
KRAK
THE RESPECT YOU HAVE FOR ALL MIGHT. THAT SENSE OF RESPONSIBILITY. THEY'RE SHACKLES HOLDING YOU BACK.
IF YOU NEED TO REST YOUR LEGS, THEN HOW ABOUT RUNNING WITH YOUR ARMS INSTEAD?

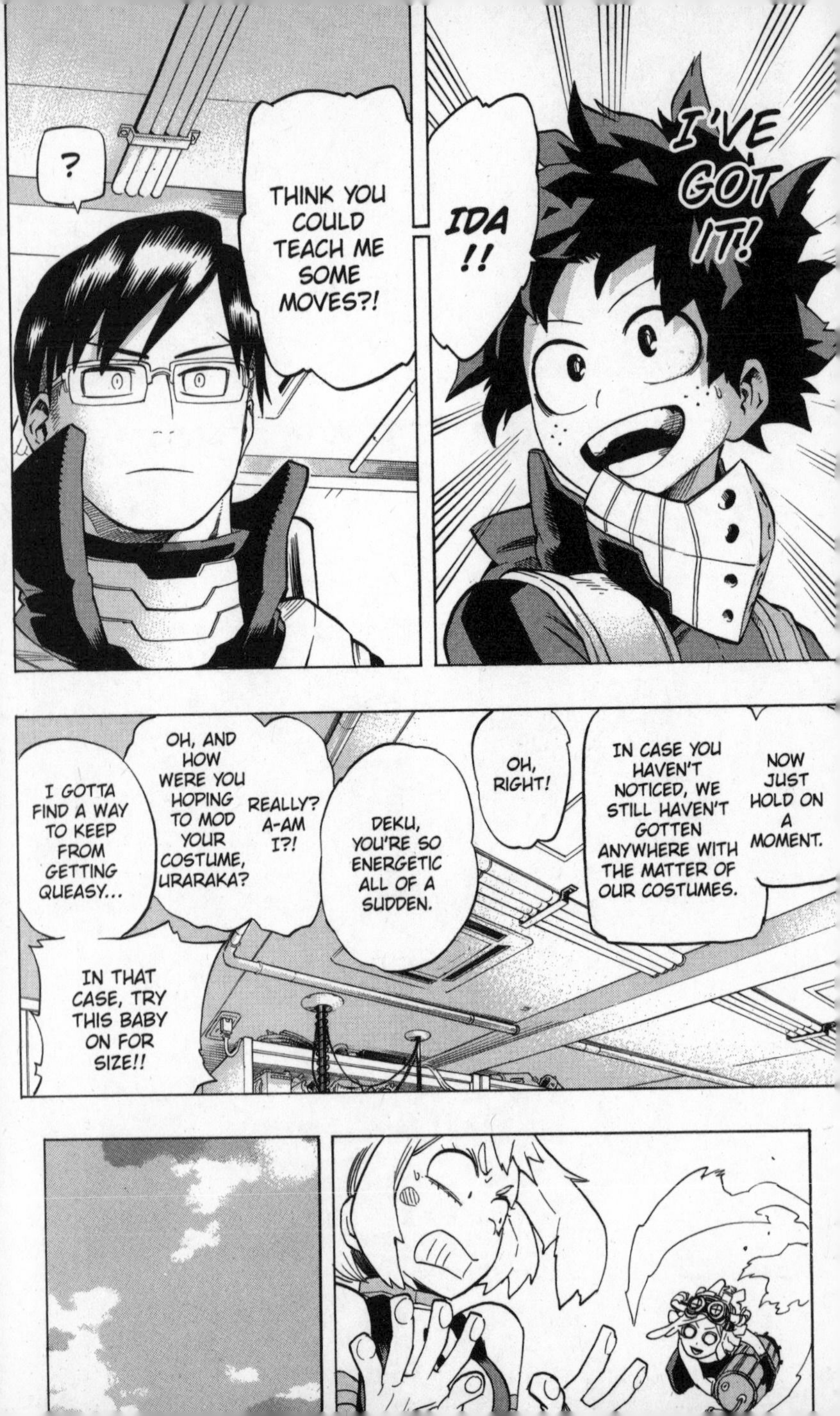
I'VE GOT IT!
IDA!!
THINK YOU COULD TEACH ME SOME MOVES?!
?
NOW JUST HOLD ON A MOMENT.
IN CASE YOU HAVEN'T NOTICED, WE STILL HAVEN'T GOTTEN ANYWHERE WITH THE MATTER OF OUR COSTUMES.
OH, RIGHT!
DEKU, YOU'RE SO ENERGETIC ALL OF A SUDDEN.
REALLY? A-AM I?!
OH, AND HOW WERE YOU HOPING TO MOD YOUR COSTUME, URARAKA?
I GOTTA FIND A WAY TO KEEP FROM GETTING QUEASY...
IN THAT CASE, TRY THIS BABY ON FOR SIZE!!

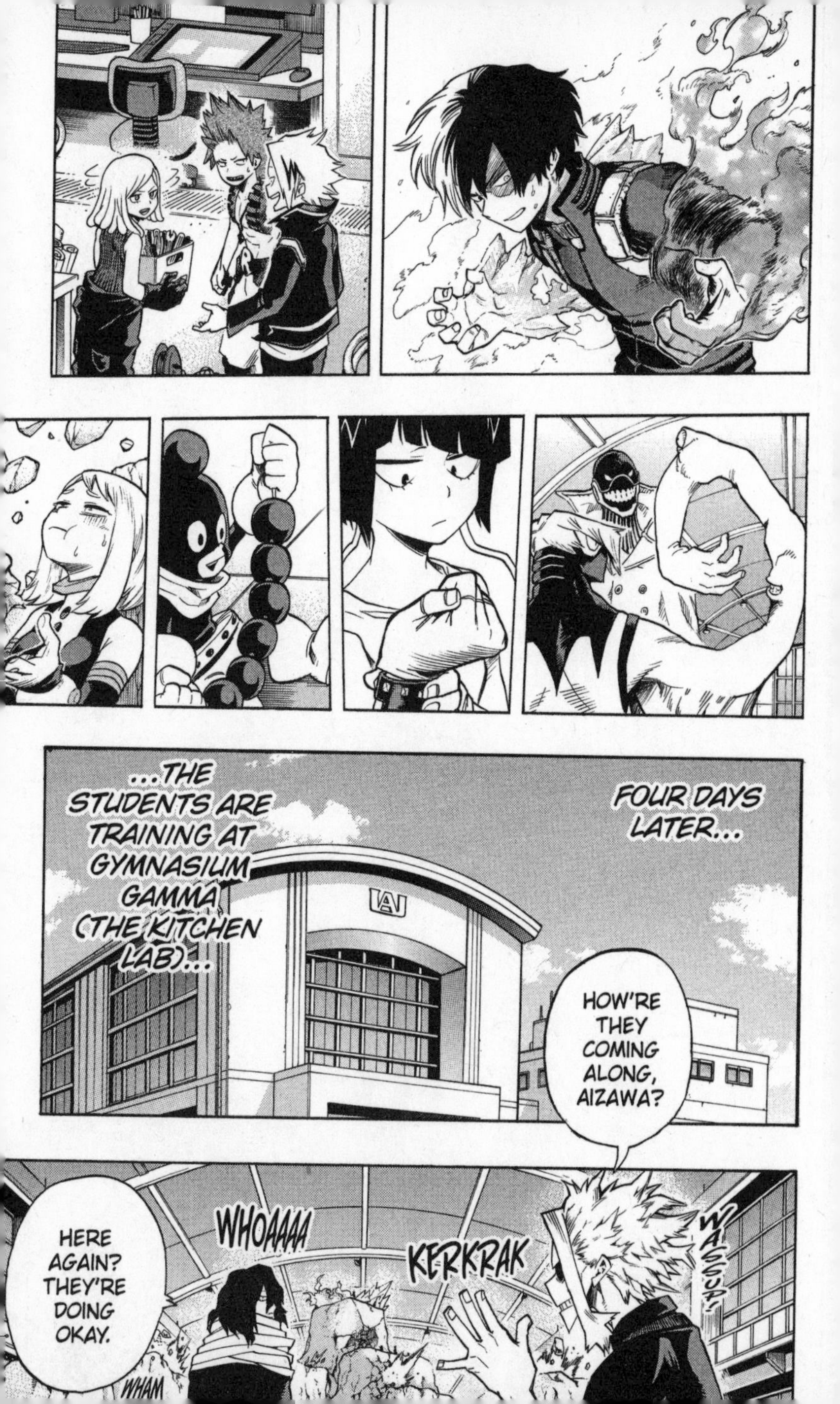
FOUR DAYS LATER...
...THE STUDENTS ARE TRAINING AT GYMNASIUM GAMMA (THE KITCHEN LAB)...
HOW'RE THEY COMING ALONG, AIZAWA?
WASSUP!
KERKRAK
WHOAAAA
HERE AGAIN? THEY'RE DOING OKAY.
WHAM

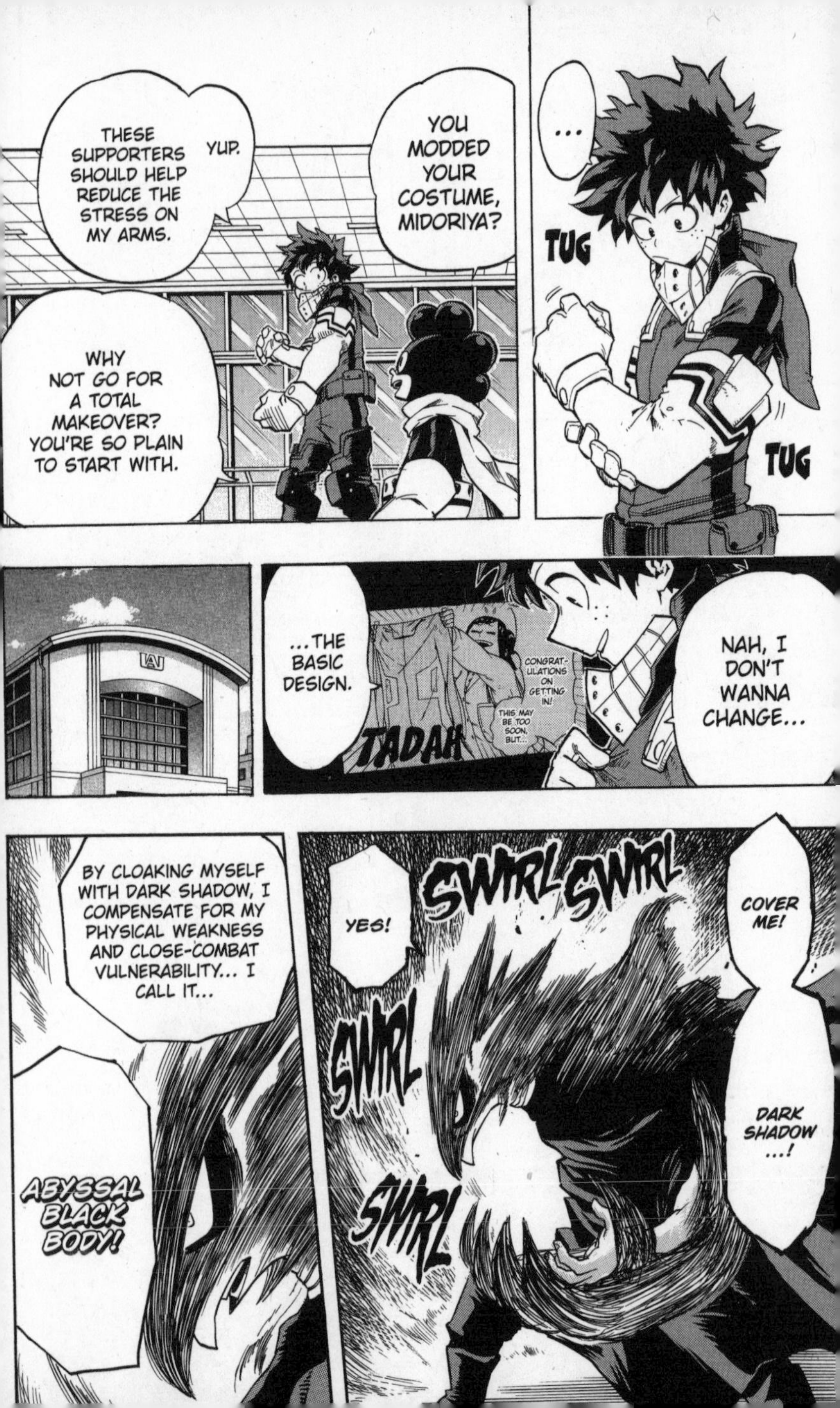
...
TUG
TUG
YOU MODDED YOUR COSTUME, MIDORIYA?
YUP.
THESE SUPPORTERS SHOULD HELP REDUCE THE STRESS ON MY ARMS.
WHY NOT GO FOR A TOTAL MAKEOVER? YOU'RE SO PLAIN TO START WITH.
NAH, I DON'T WANNA CHANGE...
...THE BASIC DESIGN.
CONGRAT-ULATIONS ON GETTING IN!
THIS MAY BE TOO SOON, BUT...
TADAH
COVER ME!
SWIRL SWIRL
YES!
SWIRL
DARK SHADOW ...!
SWIRL
BY CLOAKING MYSELF WITH DARK SHADOW, I COMPENSATE FOR MY PHYSICAL WEAKNESS AND CLOSE-COMBAT VULNERABILITY... I CALL IT...
ABYSSAL BLACK BODY!

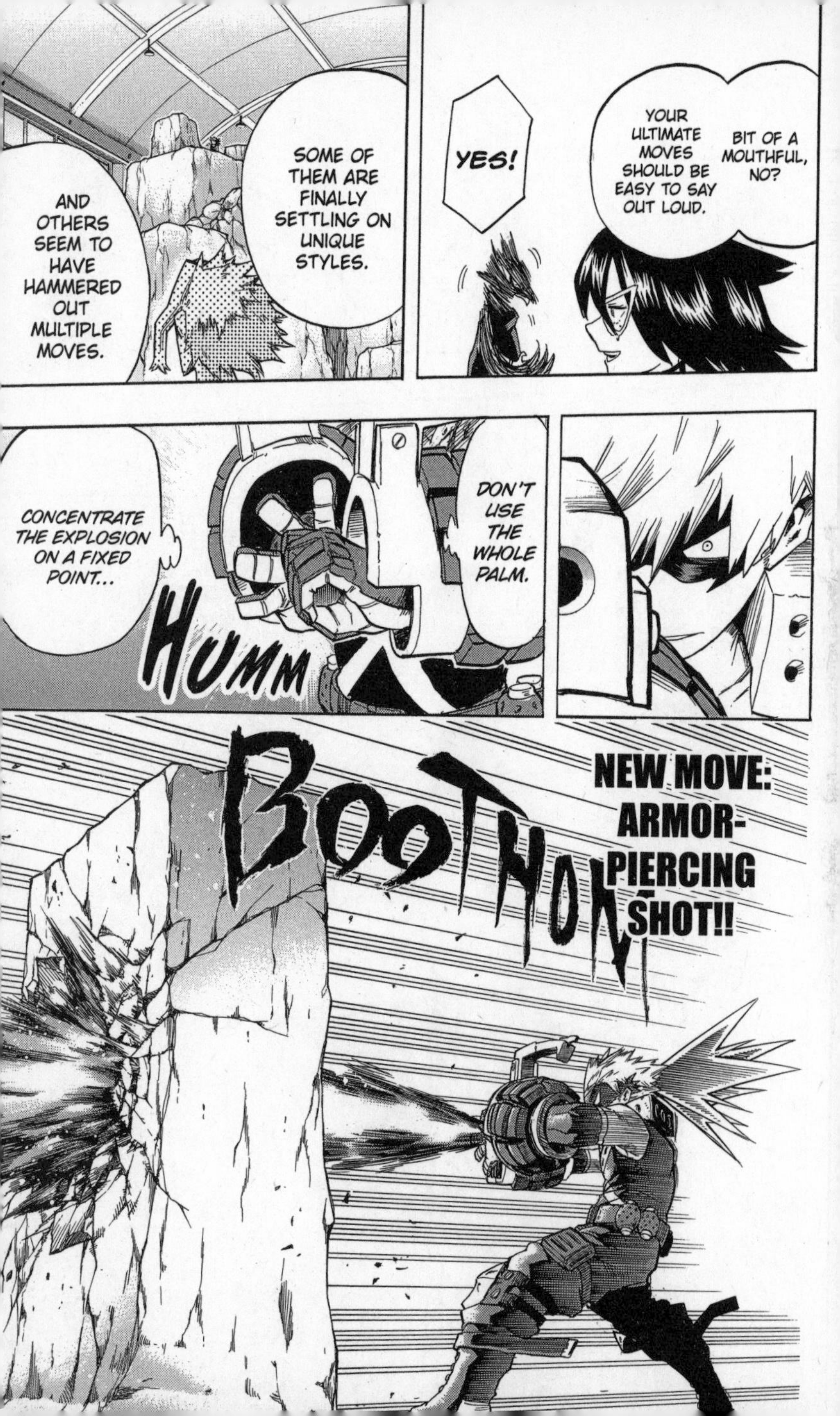

BIT OF A MOUTHFUL, NO?
YOUR ULTIMATE MOVES SHOULD BE EASY TO SAY OUT LOUD.
YES!
SOME OF THEM ARE FINALLY SETTLING ON UNIQUE STYLES.
AND OTHERS SEEM TO HAVE HAMMERED OUT MULTIPLE MOVES.
DON'T USE THE WHOLE PALM.
CONCENTRATE THE EXPLOSION ON A FIXED POINT...
HUMM
NEW MOVE: ARMOR-PIERCING SHOT!!
BOOTHOM

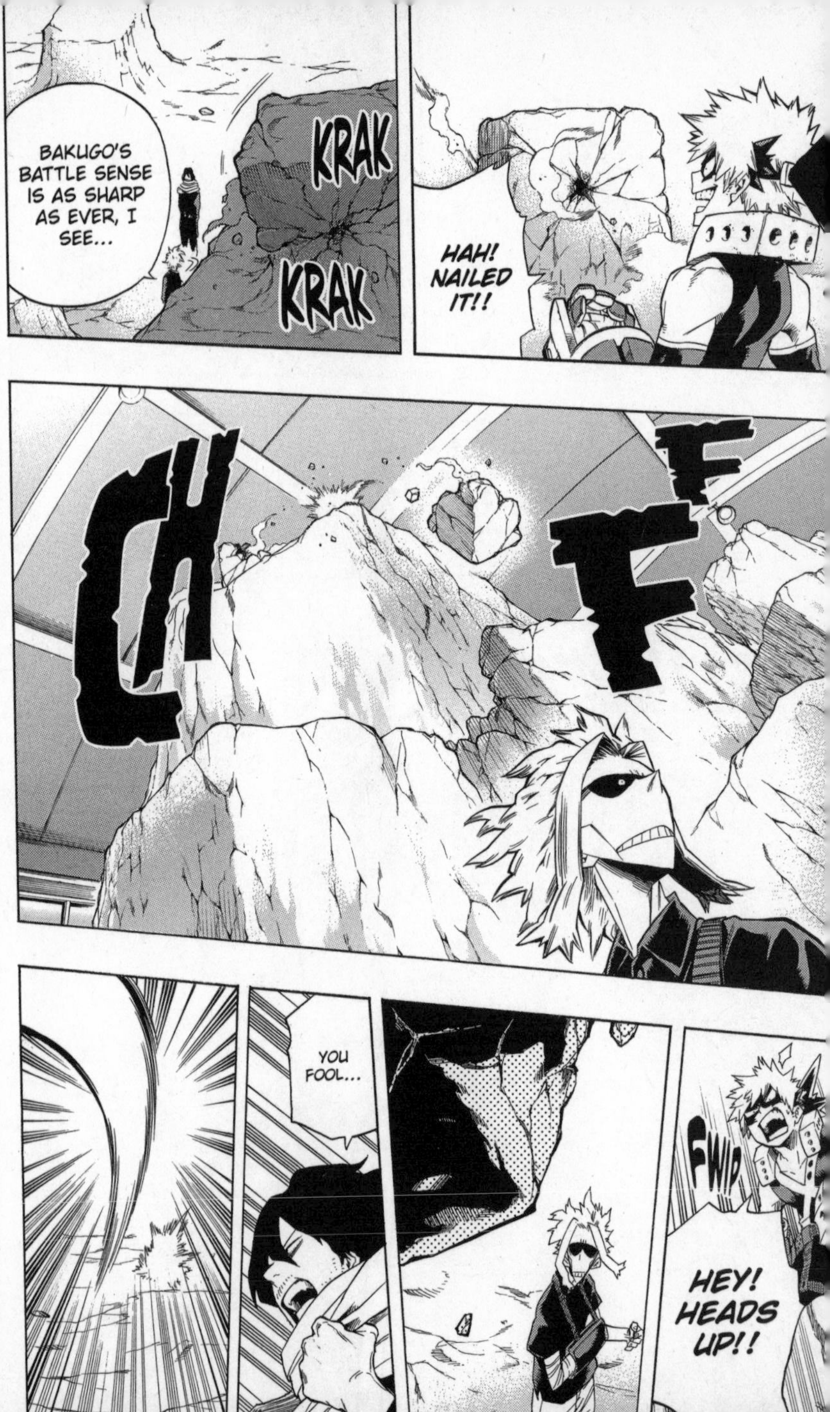
HAH! NAILED IT!!
KRAK
KRAK
BAKUGO'S BATTLE SENSE IS AS SHARP AS EVER, I SEE...
CHFF
FWIP
HEY! HEADS UP!!
YOU FOOL...

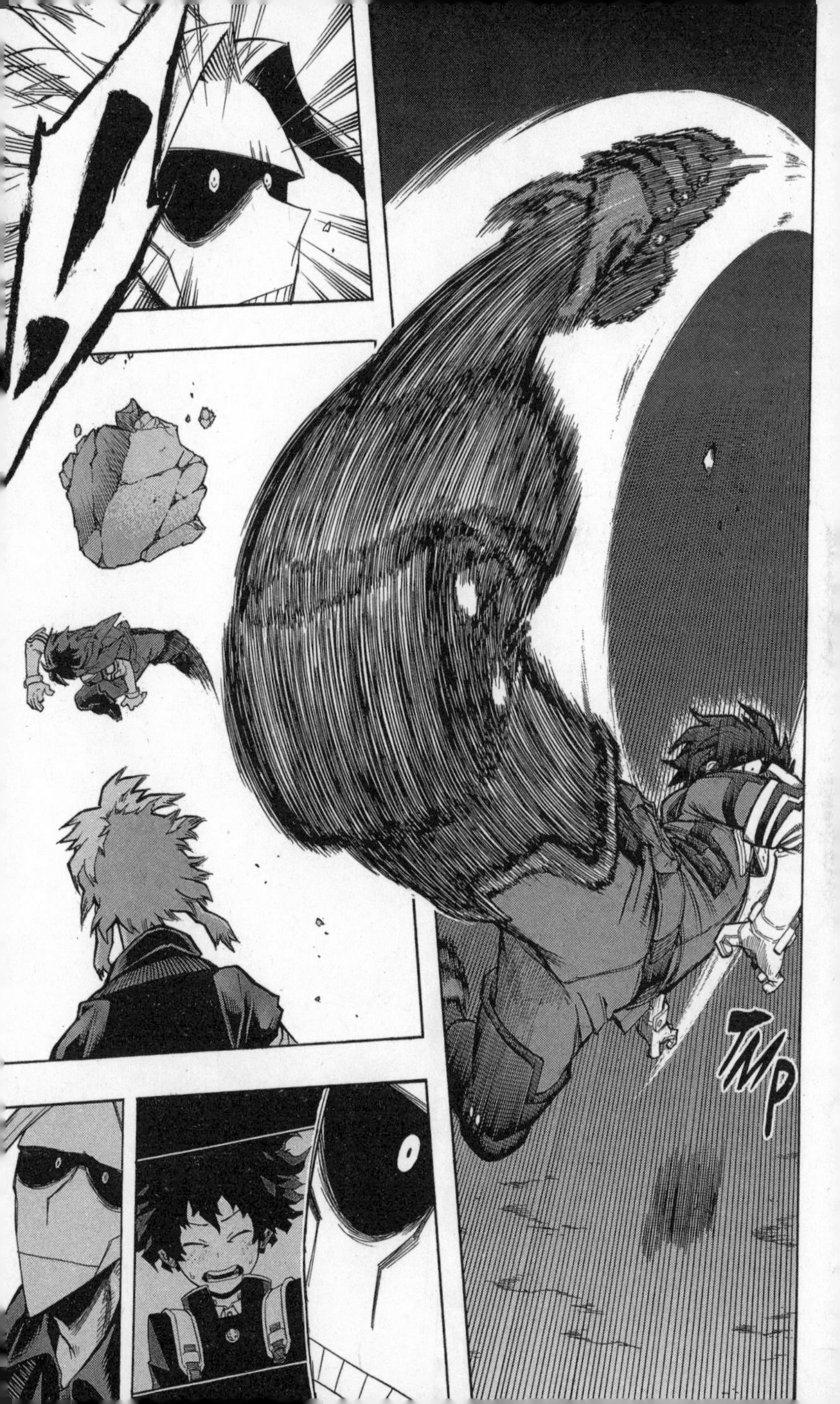
TMP

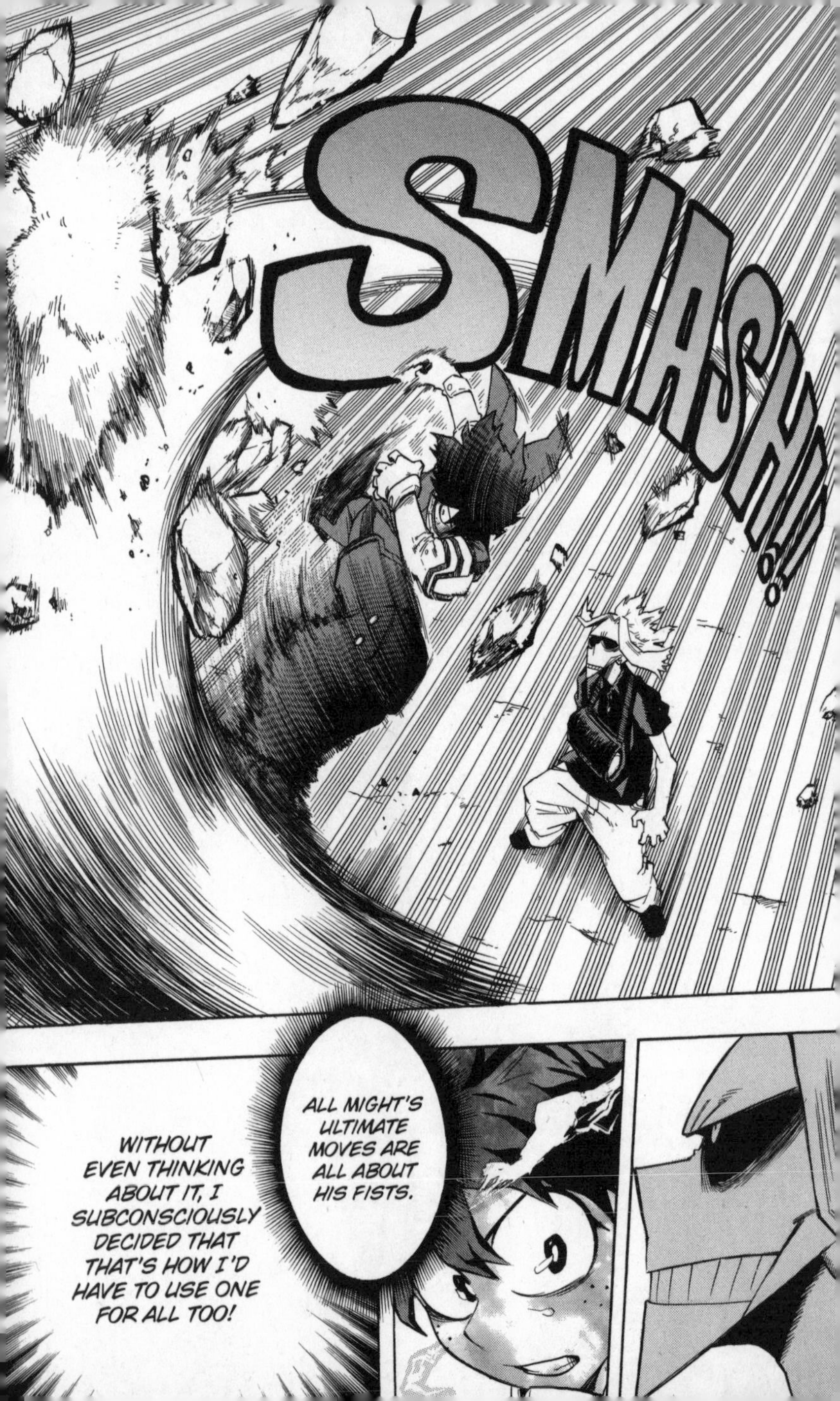
SMASH!!
ALL MIGHT'S ULTIMATE MOVES ARE ALL ABOUT HIS FISTS.
WITHOUT EVEN THINKING ABOUT IT, I SUBCONSCIOUSLY DECIDED THAT THAT'S HOW I'D HAVE TO USE ONE FOR ALL TOO!

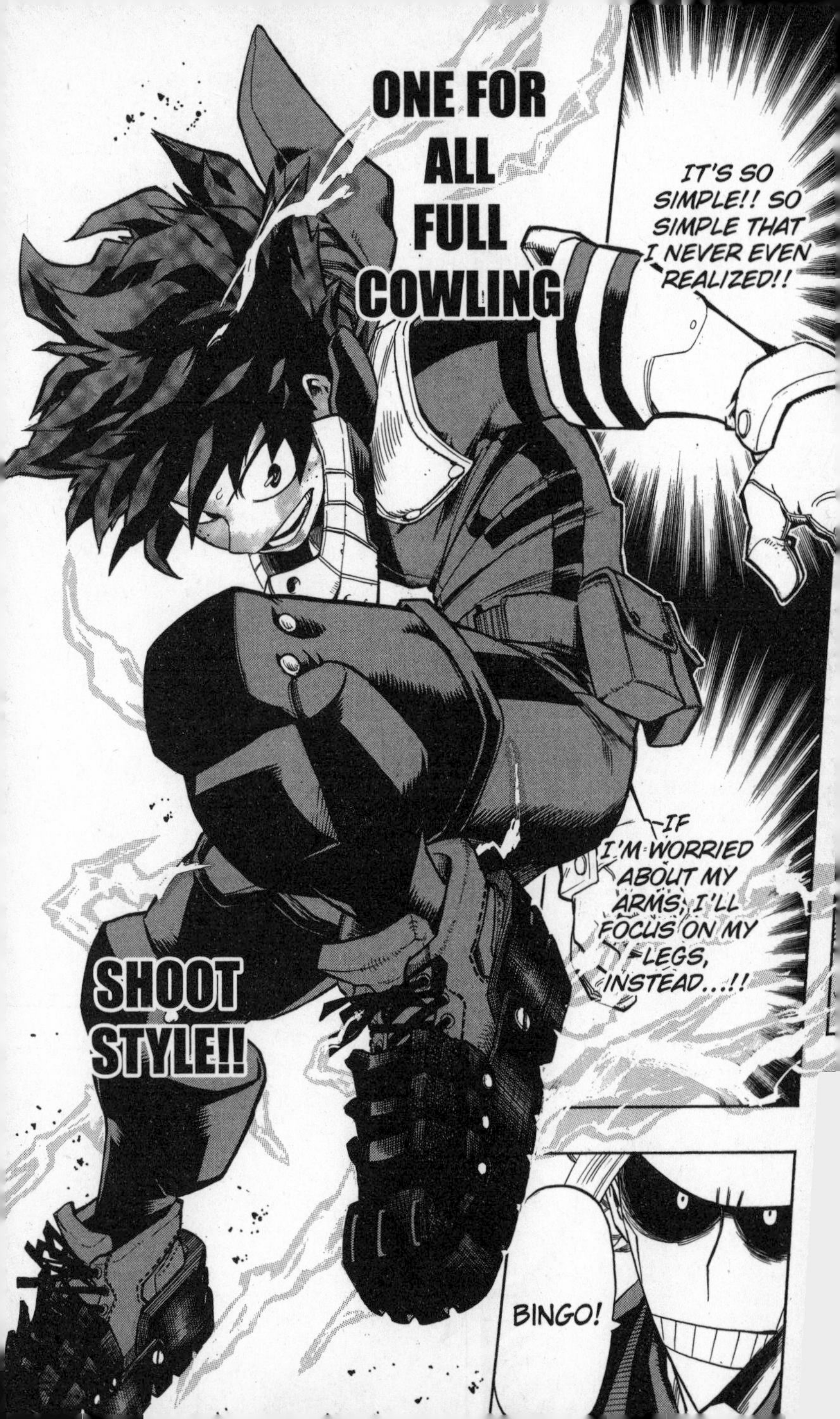
IT'S SO SIMPLE!! SO SIMPLE THAT I NEVER EVEN REALIZED!!
IF I'M WORRIED ABOUT MY ARMS, I'LL FOCUS ON MY LEGS, INSTEAD...!!
ONE FOR ALL FULL COWLING
SHOOT STYLE!!
BINGO!

HERO

POWER LOADER [40] [HIGARI MAIJIMA]

STREET CLOTHES

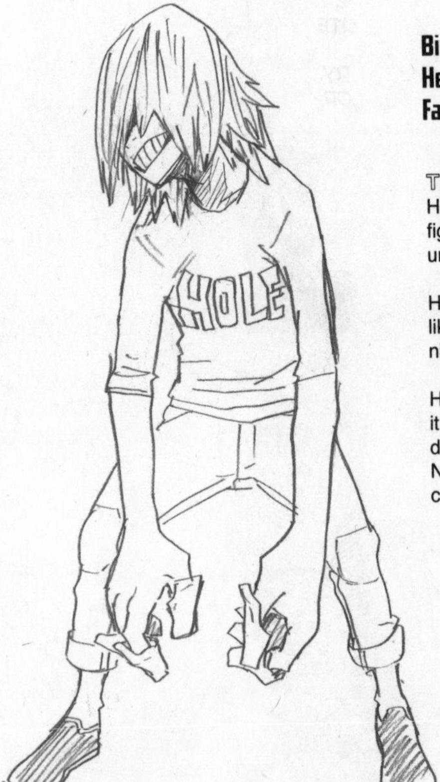

Birthday: 9/17
Height: 155 cm
Favorite Thing: Cars

THE SUPPLEMENT

His Quirk is Iron Claws. He fights by digging his way underground, like a mole.

His costume is actually more like armor. Drawing it is a nightmare.

He's also a genius when it comes to support item development, but he's got a Napoleon complex when it comes to his short stature.

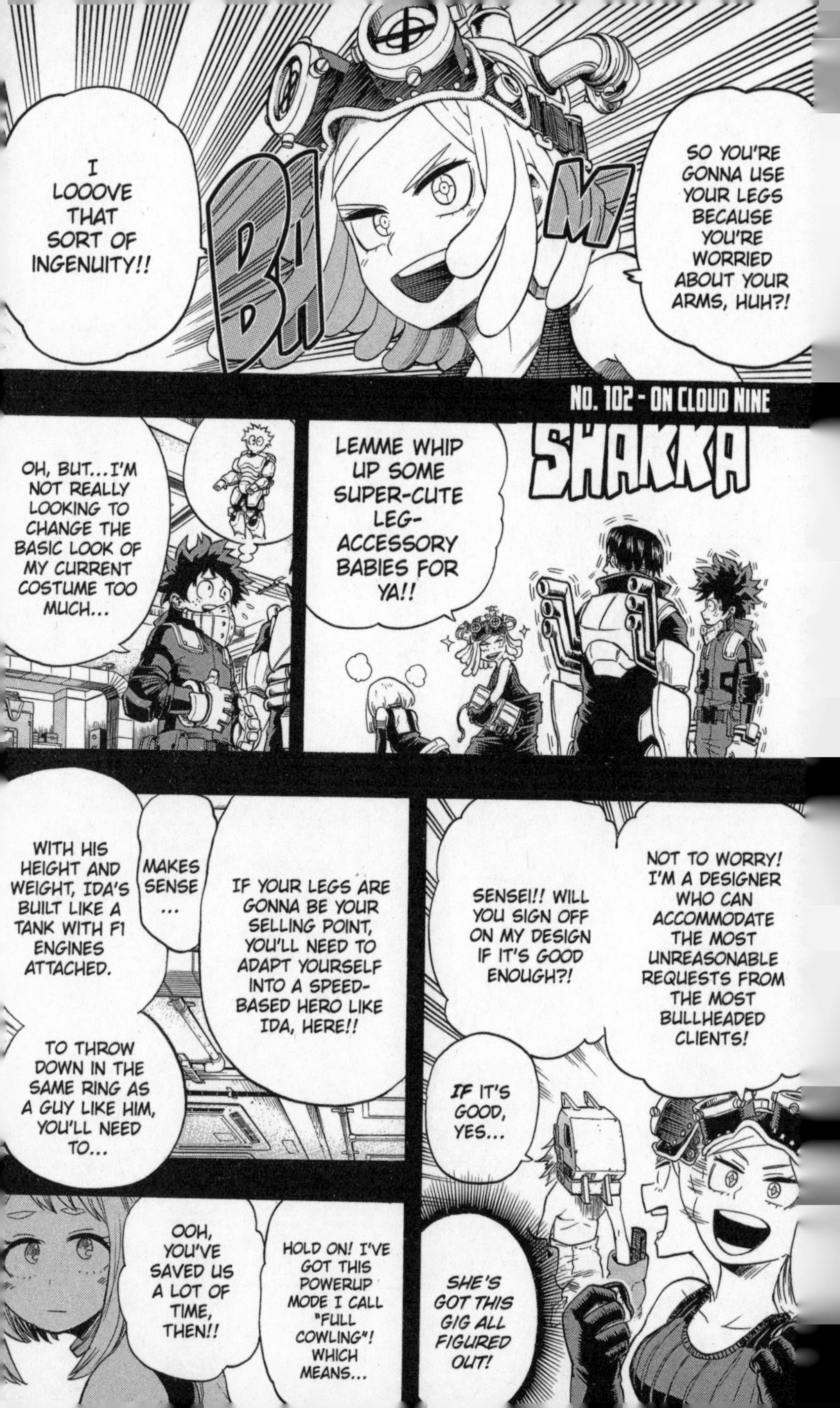
SO YOU'RE GONNA USE YOUR LEGS BECAUSE YOU'RE WORRIED ABOUT YOUR ARMS, HUH?!
BAM
I LOOOVE THAT SORT OF INGENUITY!!
NO. 102 - ON CLOUD NINE
SHAKKA
LEMME WHIP UP SOME SUPER-CUTE LEG-ACCESSORY BABIES FOR YA!!
OH, BUT...I'M NOT REALLY LOOKING TO CHANGE THE BASIC LOOK OF MY CURRENT COSTUME TOO MUCH...
NOT TO WORRY! I'M A DESIGNER WHO CAN ACCOMMODATE THE MOST UNREASONABLE REQUESTS FROM THE MOST BULLHEADED CLIENTS!
SENSEI!! WILL YOU SIGN OFF ON MY DESIGN IF IT'S GOOD ENOUGH?!
IF IT'S GOOD, YES...
SHE'S GOT THIS GIG ALL FIGURED OUT!
IF YOUR LEGS ARE GONNA BE YOUR SELLING POINT, YOU'LL NEED TO ADAPT YOURSELF INTO A SPEED-BASED HERO LIKE IDA, HERE!!
MAKES SENSE...
WITH HIS HEIGHT AND WEIGHT, IDA'S BUILT LIKE A TANK WITH F1 ENGINES ATTACHED.
TO THROW DOWN IN THE SAME RING AS A GUY LIKE HIM, YOU'LL NEED TO...
HOLD ON! I'VE GOT THIS POWERUP MODE I CALL "FULL COWLING"! WHICH MEANS...
OOH, YOU'VE SAVED US A LOT OF TIME, THEN!!

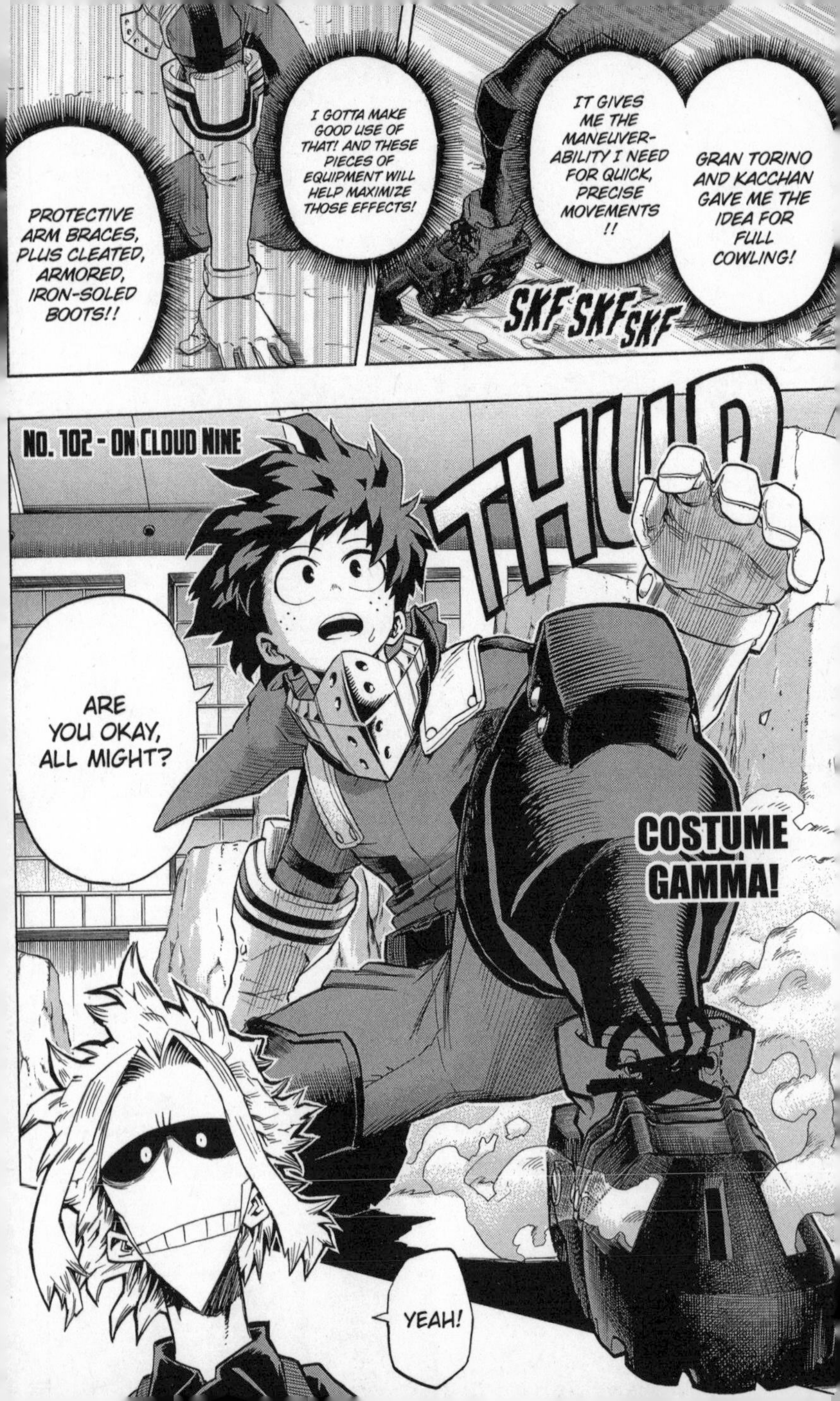
GRAN TORINO AND KACCHAN GAVE ME THE IDEA FOR FULL COWLING!
IT GIVES ME THE MANEUVER-ABILITY I NEED FOR QUICK, PRECISE MOVEMENTS !!
I GOTTA MAKE GOOD USE OF THAT! AND THESE PIECES OF EQUIPMENT WILL HELP MAXIMIZE THOSE EFFECTS!
PROTECTIVE ARM BRACES, PLUS CLEATED, ARMORED, IRON-SOLED BOOTS!!
SKF SKF SKF
THUD
No. 102 - On Cloud Nine
COSTUME GAMMA!
ARE YOU OKAY, ALL MIGHT?
YEAH!

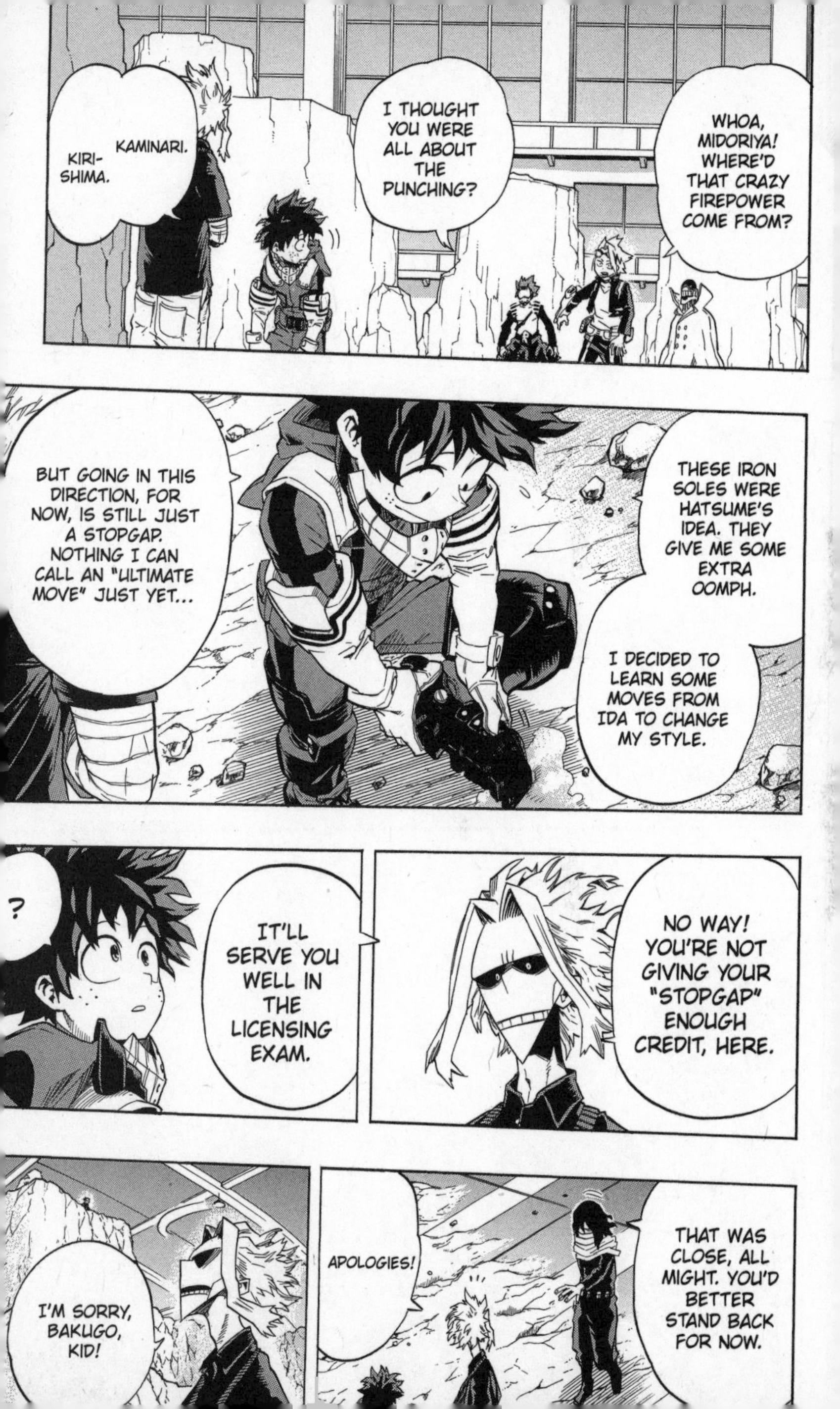
WHOA, MIDORIYA! WHERE'D THAT CRAZY FIREPOWER COME FROM?
I THOUGHT YOU WERE ALL ABOUT THE PUNCHING?
KAMINARI.
KIRI-SHIMA.
THESE IRON SOLES WERE HATSUME'S IDEA. THEY GIVE ME SOME EXTRA OOMPH.
I DECIDED TO LEARN SOME MOVES FROM IDA TO CHANGE MY STYLE.
BUT GOING IN THIS DIRECTION, FOR NOW, IS STILL JUST A STOPGAP. NOTHING I CAN CALL AN "ULTIMATE MOVE" JUST YET...
NO WAY! YOU'RE NOT GIVING YOUR "STOPGAP" ENOUGH CREDIT, HERE.
IT'LL SERVE YOU WELL IN THE LICENSING EXAM.
?
THAT WAS CLOSE, ALL MIGHT. YOU'D BETTER STAND BACK FOR NOW.
APOLOGIES!
I'M SORRY, BAKUGO, KID!

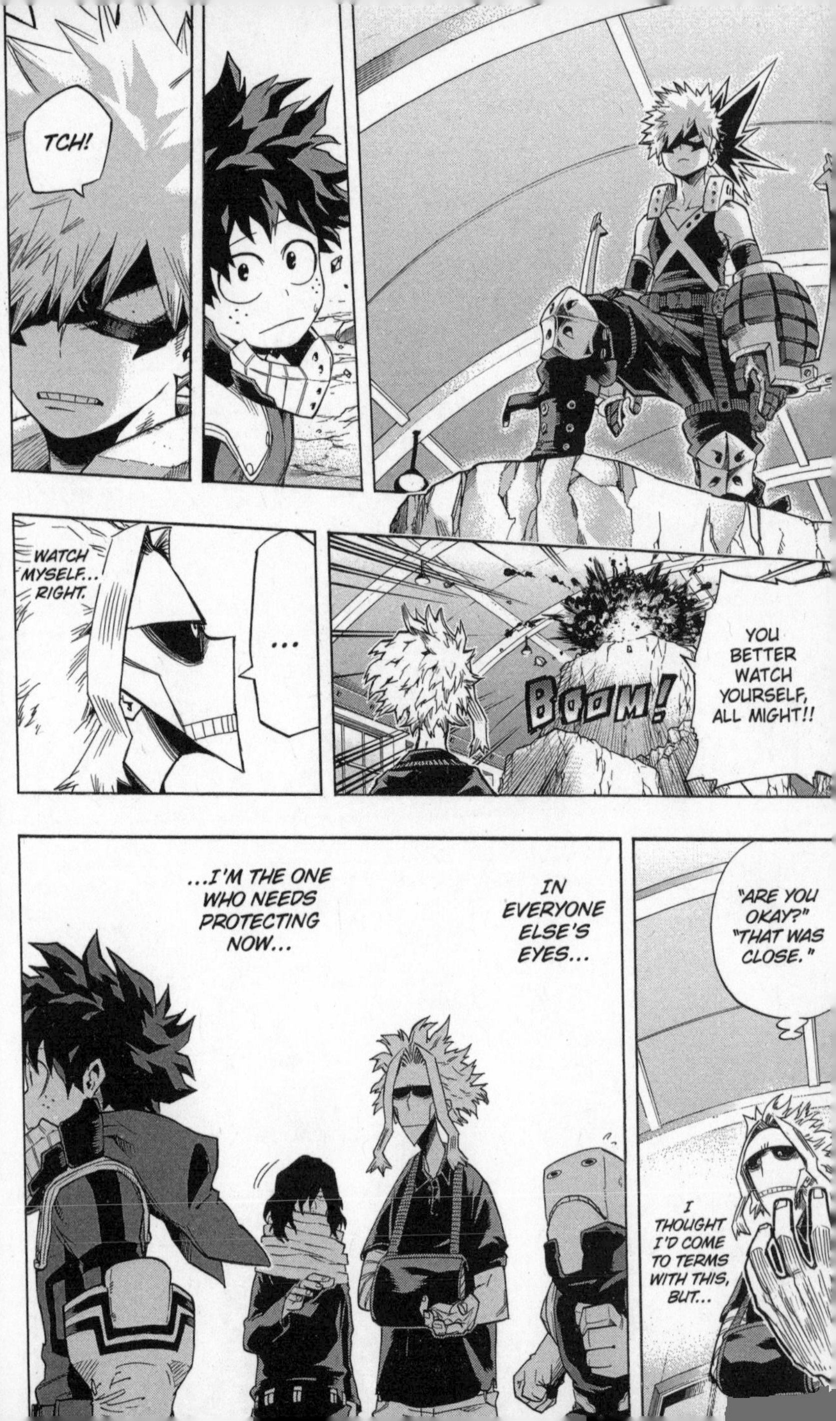
TCH!
YOU BETTER WATCH YOURSELF, ALL MIGHT!!
BOOM!
WATCH MYSELF... RIGHT.
...
"ARE YOU OKAY?" "THAT WAS CLOSE."
I THOUGHT I'D COME TO TERMS WITH THIS, BUT...
IN EVERYONE ELSE'S EYES...
...I'M THE ONE WHO NEEDS PROTECTING NOW...

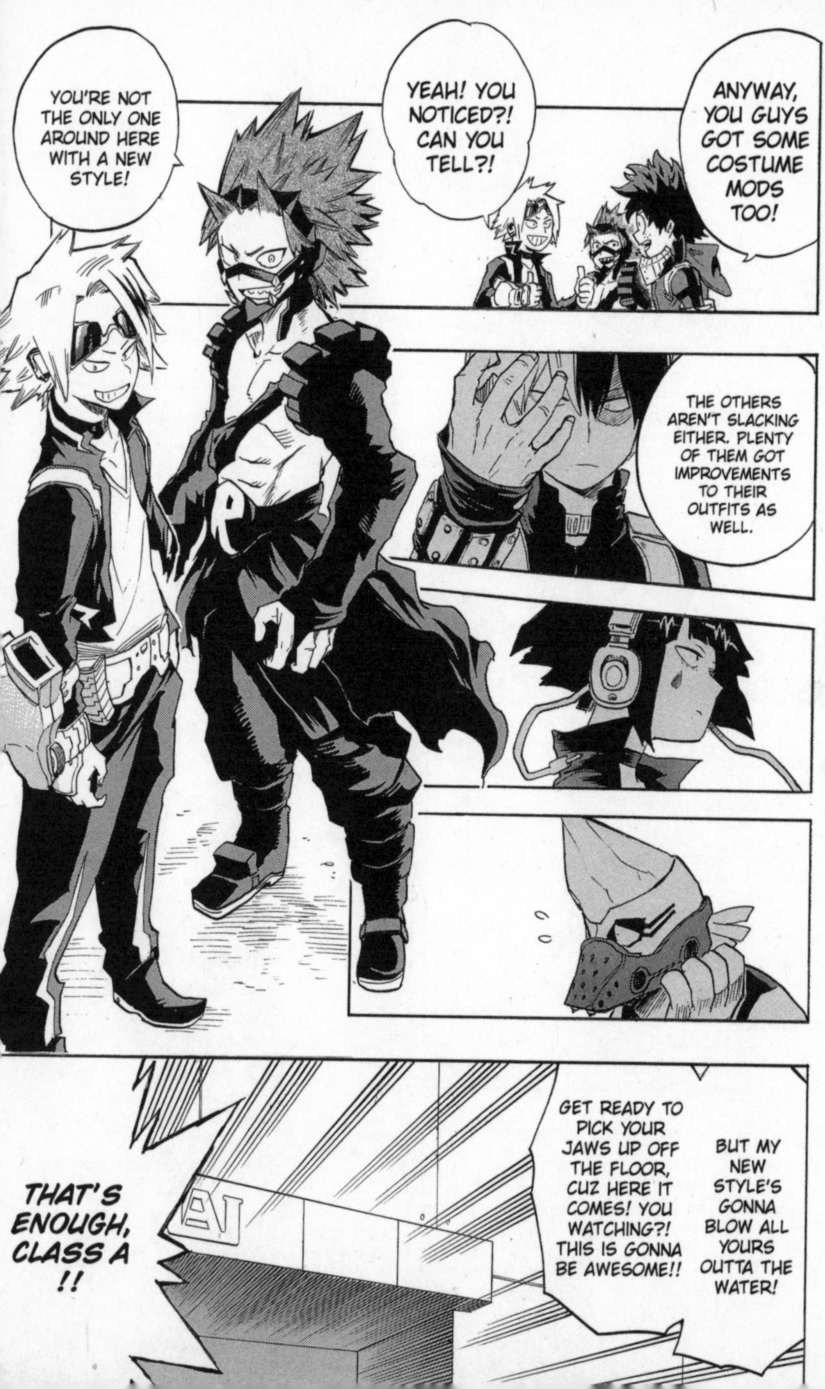

ANYWAY, YOU GUYS GOT SOME COSTUME MODS TOO!
YEAH! YOU NOTICED?! CAN YOU TELL?!
YOU'RE NOT THE ONLY ONE AROUND HERE WITH A NEW STYLE!
THE OTHERS AREN'T SLACKING EITHER. PLENTY OF THEM GOT IMPROVEMENTS TO THEIR OUTFITS AS WELL.
BUT MY NEW STYLE'S GONNA BLOW ALL YOURS OUTTA THE WATER!
GET READY TO PICK YOUR JAWS UP OFF THE FLOOR, CUZ HERE IT COMES! YOU WATCHING?! THIS IS GONNA BE AWESOME!!
THAT'S ENOUGH, CLASS A!!

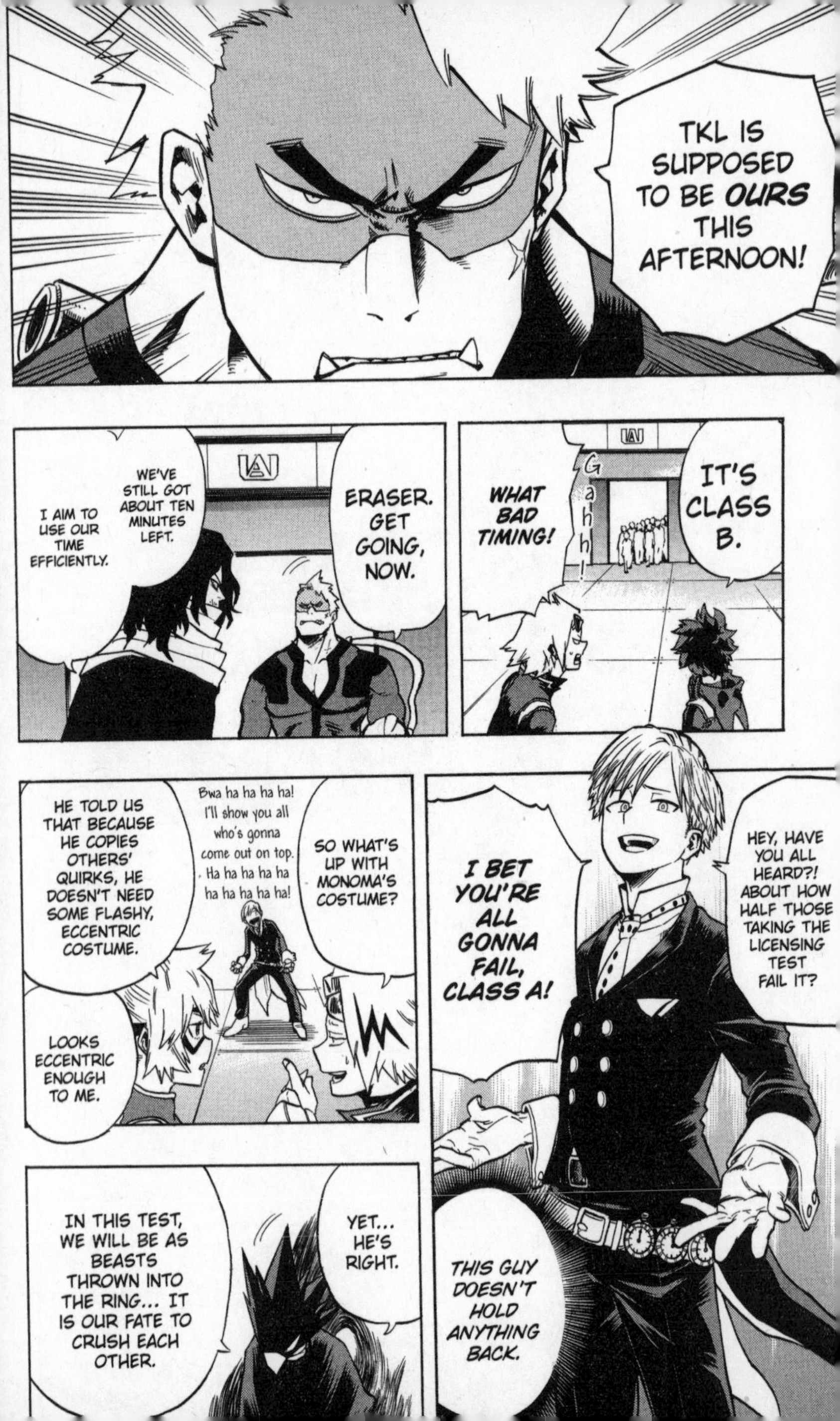
TKL IS SUPPOSED TO BE OURS THIS AFTERNOON!
IT'S CLASS B.
WHAT BAD TIMING!
Gahh!
ERASER. GET GOING, NOW.
WE'VE STILL GOT ABOUT TEN MINUTES LEFT.
I AIM TO USE OUR TIME EFFICIENTLY.
HEY, HAVE YOU ALL HEARD?! ABOUT HOW HALF THOSE TAKING THE LICENSING TEST FAIL IT?
I BET YOU'RE ALL GONNA FAIL, CLASS A!
THIS GUY DOESN'T HOLD ANYTHING BACK.
SO WHAT'S UP WITH MONOMA'S COSTUME?
Bwa ha ha ha ha! I'll show you all who's gonna come out on top. Ha ha ha ha ha ha ha ha ha ha!
HE TOLD US THAT BECAUSE HE COPIES OTHERS' QUIRKS, HE DOESN'T NEED SOME FLASHY, ECCENTRIC COSTUME.
LOOKS ECCENTRIC ENOUGH TO ME.
YET... HE'S RIGHT.
IN THIS TEST, WE WILL BE AS BEASTS THROWN INTO THE RING... IT IS OUR FATE TO CRUSH EACH OTHER.

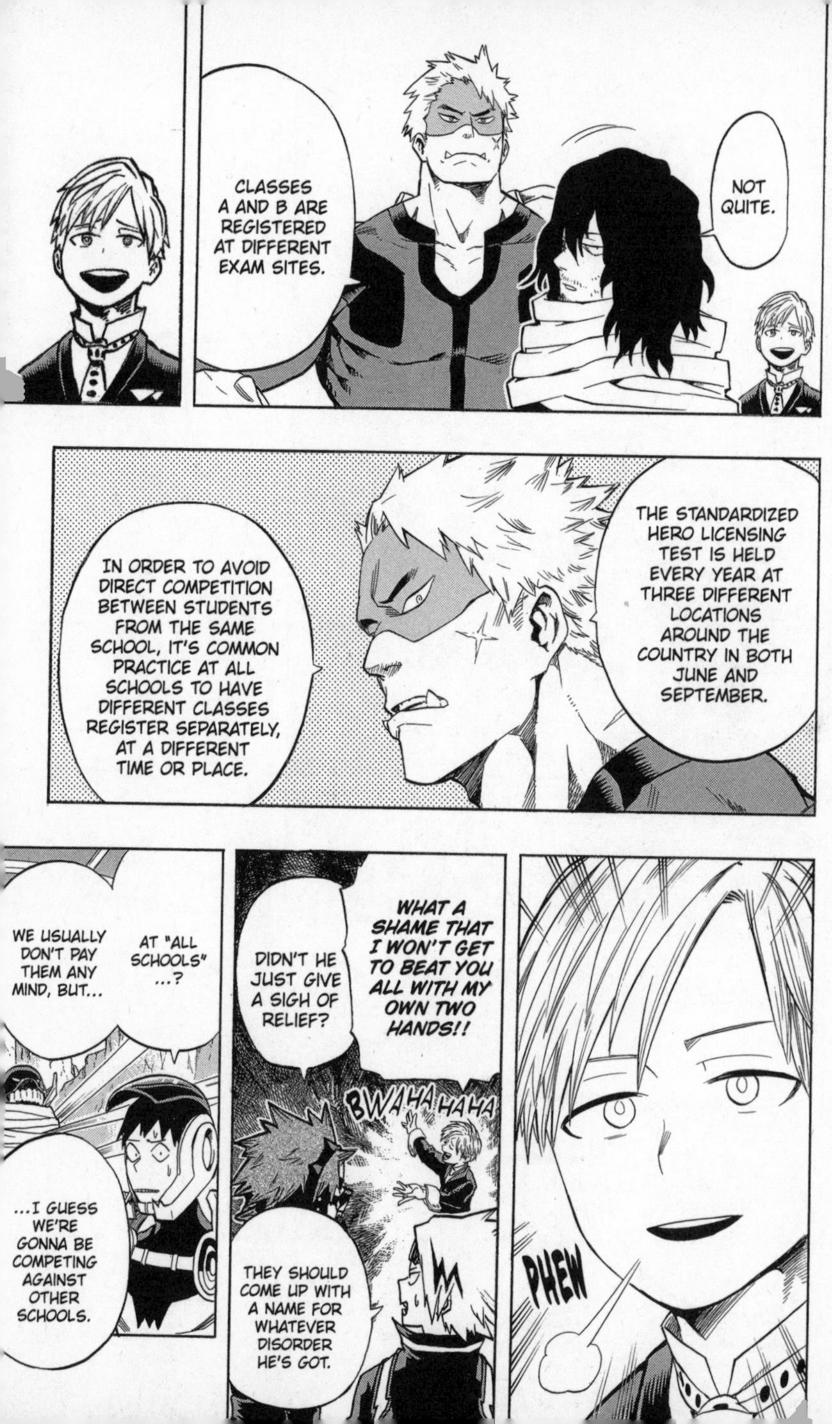
NOT QUITE.
CLASSES A AND B ARE REGISTERED AT DIFFERENT EXAM SITES.
THE STANDARDIZED HERO LICENSING TEST IS HELD EVERY YEAR AT THREE DIFFERENT LOCATIONS AROUND THE COUNTRY IN BOTH JUNE AND SEPTEMBER.
IN ORDER TO AVOID DIRECT COMPETITION BETWEEN STUDENTS FROM THE SAME SCHOOL, IT'S COMMON PRACTICE AT ALL SCHOOLS TO HAVE DIFFERENT CLASSES REGISTER SEPARATELY, AT A DIFFERENT TIME OR PLACE.
PHEW
WHAT A SHAME THAT I WON'T GET TO BEAT YOU ALL WITH MY OWN TWO HANDS!!
BWAHAHAHA
DIDN'T HE JUST GIVE A SIGH OF RELIEF?
THEY SHOULD COME UP WITH A NAME FOR WHATEVER DISORDER HE'S GOT.
AT "ALL SCHOOLS" ...?
WE USUALLY DON'T PAY THEM ANY MIND, BUT...
...I GUESS WE'RE GONNA BE COMPETING AGAINST OTHER SCHOOLS.

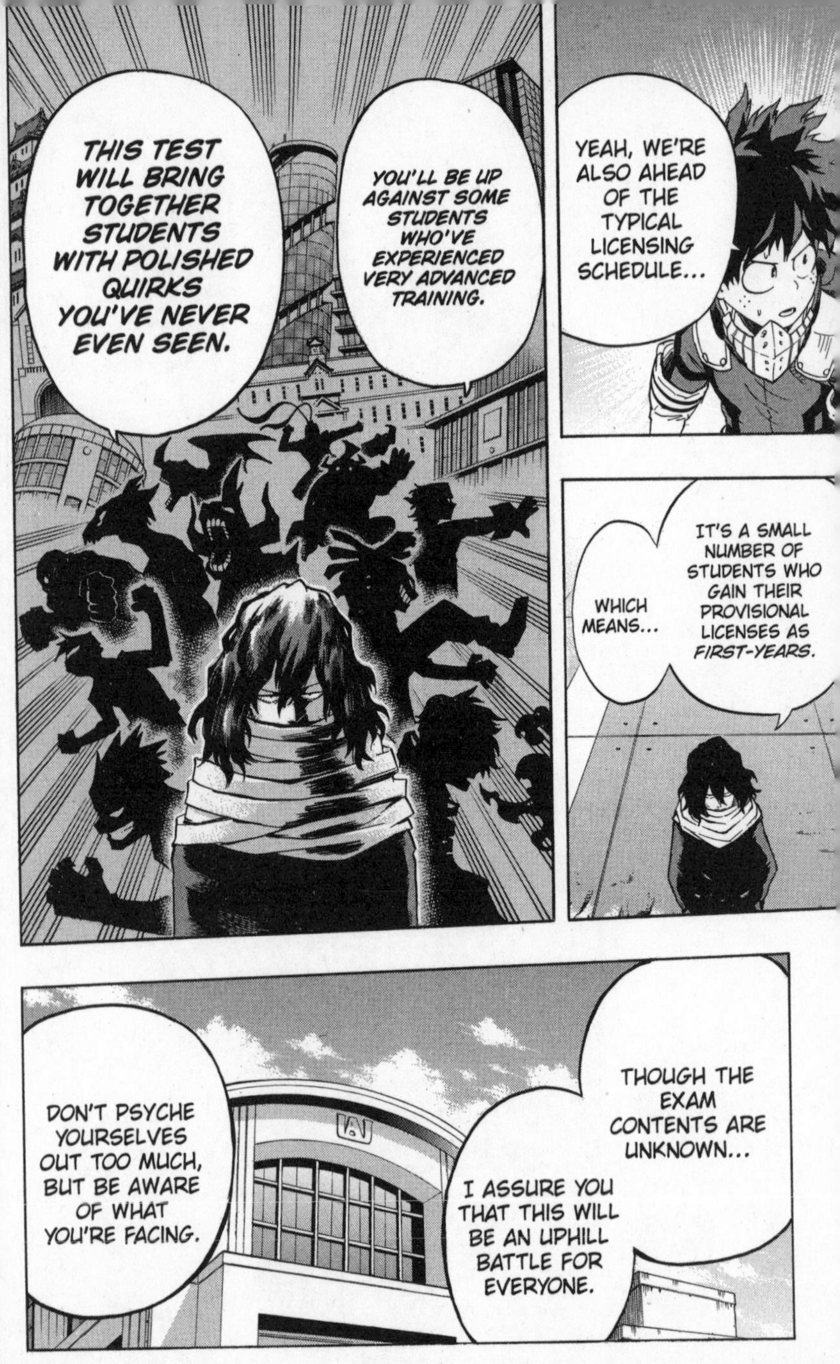
YEAH, WE'RE ALSO AHEAD OF THE TYPICAL LICENSING SCHEDULE...
IT'S A SMALL NUMBER OF STUDENTS WHO GAIN THEIR PROVISIONAL LICENSES AS *FIRST-YEARS*.
WHICH MEANS...
YOU'LL BE UP AGAINST SOME STUDENTS WHO'VE EXPERIENCED VERY ADVANCED TRAINING.
THIS TEST WILL BRING TOGETHER STUDENTS WITH POLISHED QUIRKS YOU'VE NEVER EVEN SEEN.
THOUGH THE EXAM CONTENTS ARE UNKNOWN...
I ASSURE YOU THAT THIS WILL BE AN UPHILL BATTLE FOR EVERYONE.
DON'T PSYCHE YOURSELVES OUT TOO MUCH, BUT BE AWARE OF WHAT YOU'RE FACING.

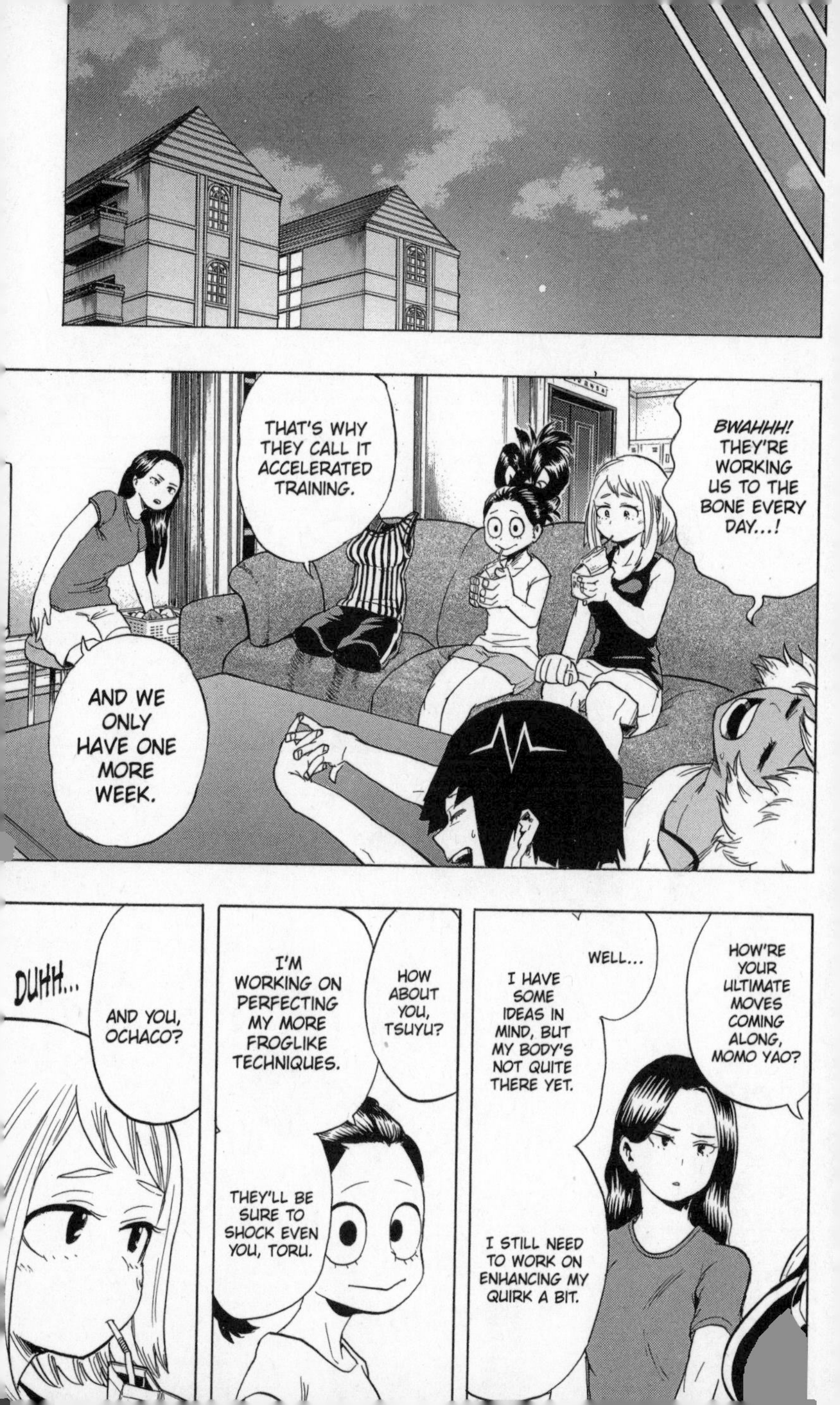

BWAHHH! THEY'RE WORKING US TO THE BONE EVERY DAY...!
THAT'S WHY THEY CALL IT ACCELERATED TRAINING.
AND WE ONLY HAVE ONE MORE WEEK.
HOW'RE YOUR ULTIMATE MOVES COMING ALONG, MOMO YAO?
WELL...
I HAVE SOME IDEAS IN MIND, BUT MY BODY'S NOT QUITE THERE YET.
I STILL NEED TO WORK ON ENHANCING MY QUIRK A BIT.
HOW ABOUT YOU, TSUYU?
I'M WORKING ON PERFECTING MY MORE FROGLIKE TECHNIQUES.
THEY'LL BE SURE TO SHOCK EVEN YOU, TORU.
AND YOU, OCHACO?
DUHH...

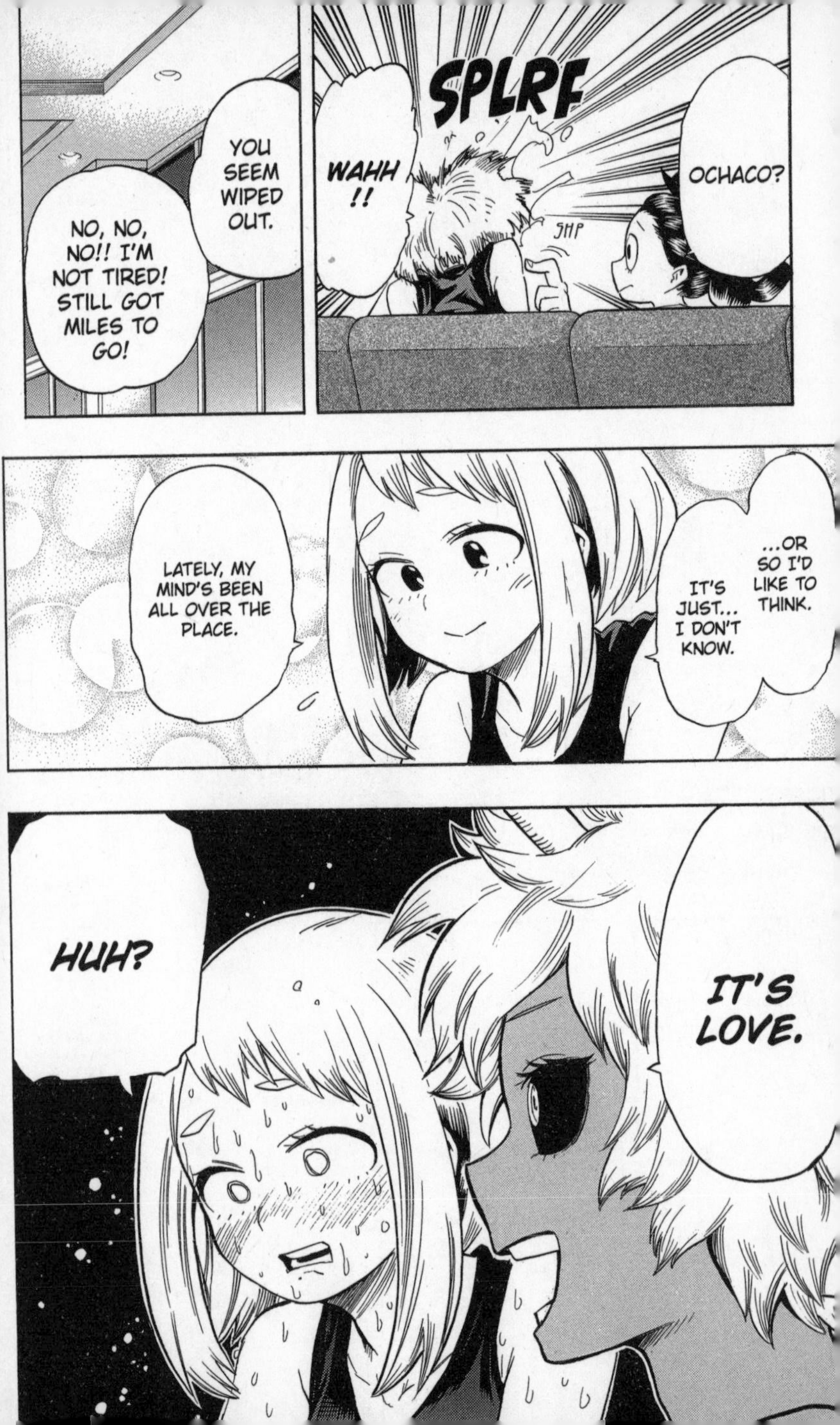
OCHACO?
SPLRF
WAHH!!
SHP
YOU SEEM WIPED OUT.
NO, NO, NO!! I'M NOT TIRED! STILL GOT MILES TO GO!
...OR SO I'D LIKE TO THINK.
IT'S JUST... I DON'T KNOW.
LATELY, MY MIND'S BEEN ALL OVER THE PLACE.
IT'S LOVE.
HUH?

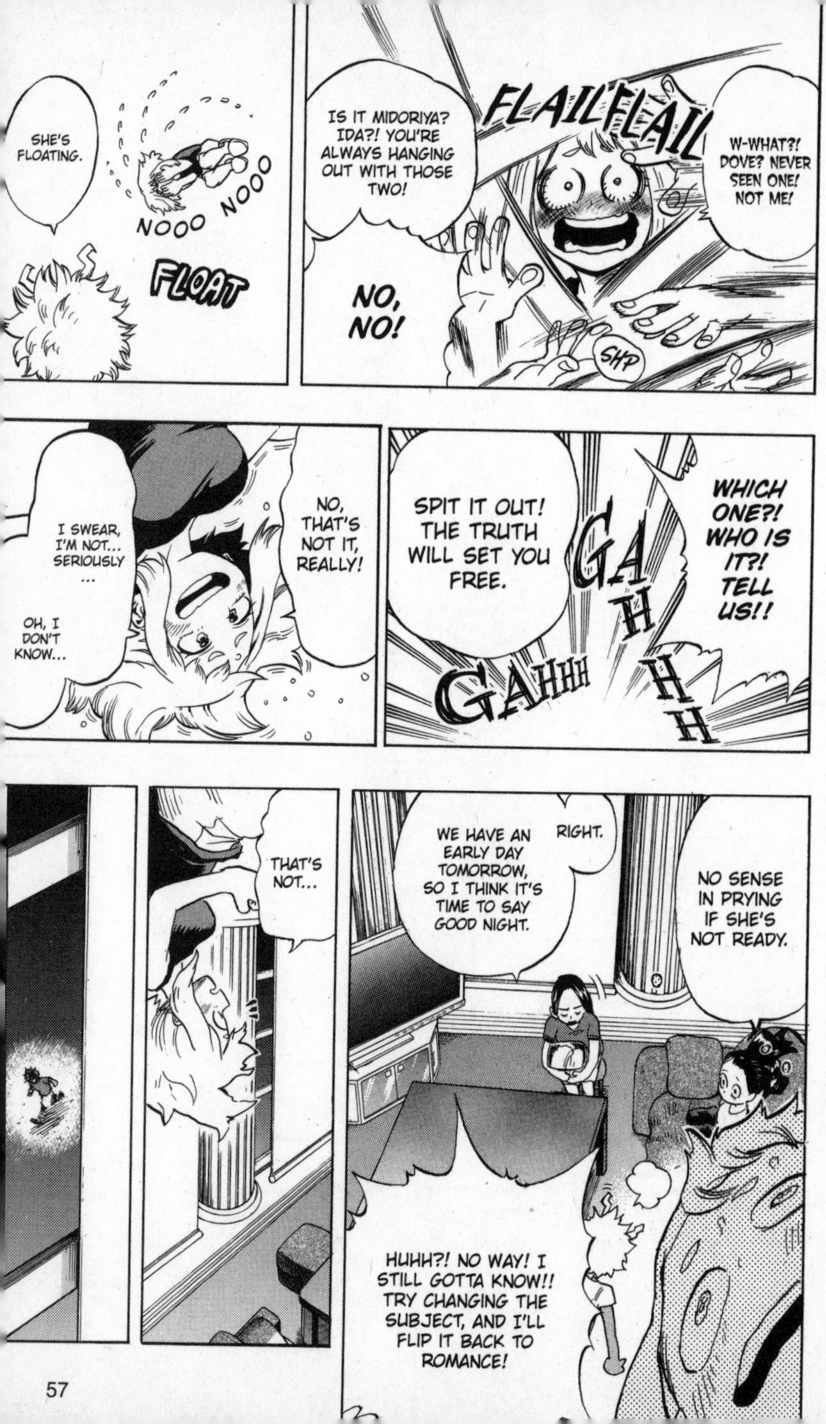
W-WHAT?! DOVE? NEVER SEEN ONE! NOT ME!
FLAILFLAIL
IS IT MIDORIYA? IDA?! YOU'RE ALWAYS HANGING OUT WITH THOSE TWO!
NO, NO!
SHP
SHE'S FLOATING.
NOOO NOOO
FLOAT
WHICH ONE?! WHO IS IT?! TELL US!!
GAHHH
SPIT IT OUT! THE TRUTH WILL SET YOU FREE.
GAHHH
NO, THAT'S NOT IT, REALLY!
I SWEAR, I'M NOT... SERIOUSLY ...
OH, I DON'T KNOW...
NO SENSE IN PRYING IF SHE'S NOT READY.
RIGHT.
WE HAVE AN EARLY DAY TOMORROW, SO I THINK IT'S TIME TO SAY GOOD NIGHT.
HUHH?! NO WAY! I STILL GOTTA KNOW!! TRY CHANGING THE SUBJECT, AND I'LL FLIP IT BACK TO ROMANCE!
THAT'S NOT...

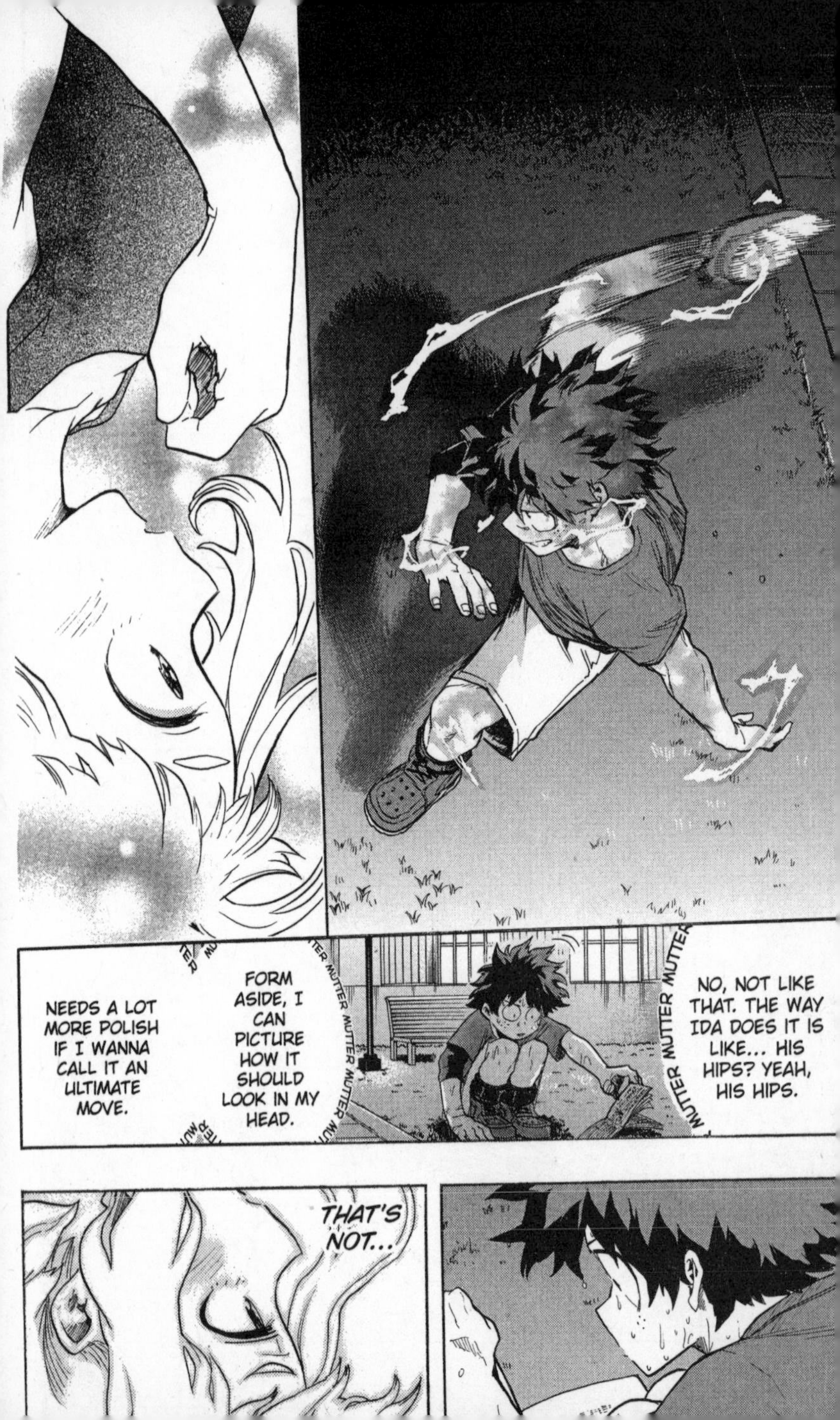
NO, NOT LIKE THAT. THE WAY IDA DOES IT IS LIKE... HIS HIPS? YEAH, HIS HIPS.
MUTTER MUTTER
FORM ASIDE, I CAN PICTURE HOW IT SHOULD LOOK IN MY HEAD.
MUTTER MUTTER
NEEDS A LOT MORE POLISH IF I WANNA CALL IT AN ULTIMATE MOVE.
THAT'S NOT...

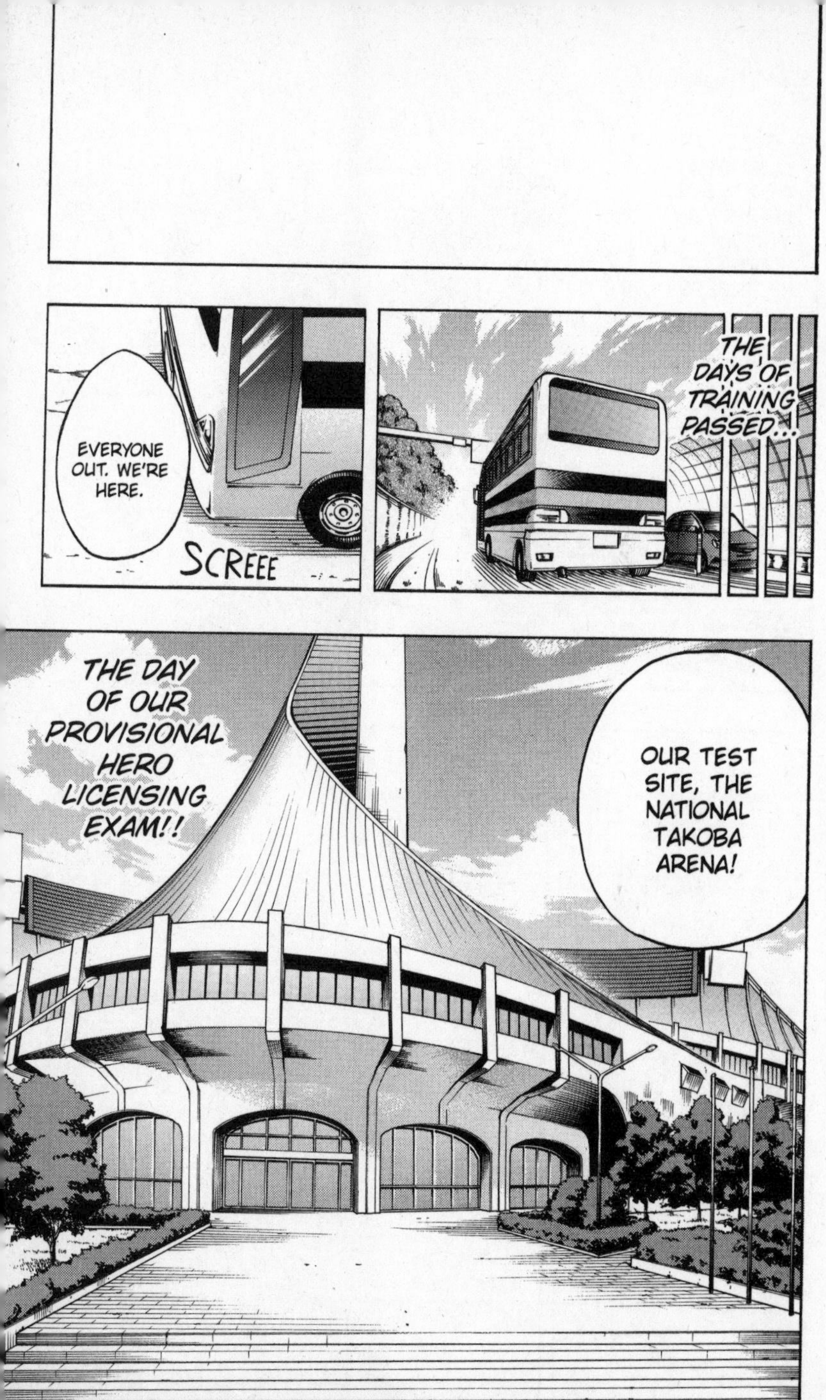
THE DAYS OF TRAINING PASSED...
EVERYONE OUT. WE'RE HERE.
SCREEE
OUR TEST SITE, THE NATIONAL TAKOBA ARENA!
THE DAY OF OUR PROVISIONAL HERO LICENSING EXAM!!

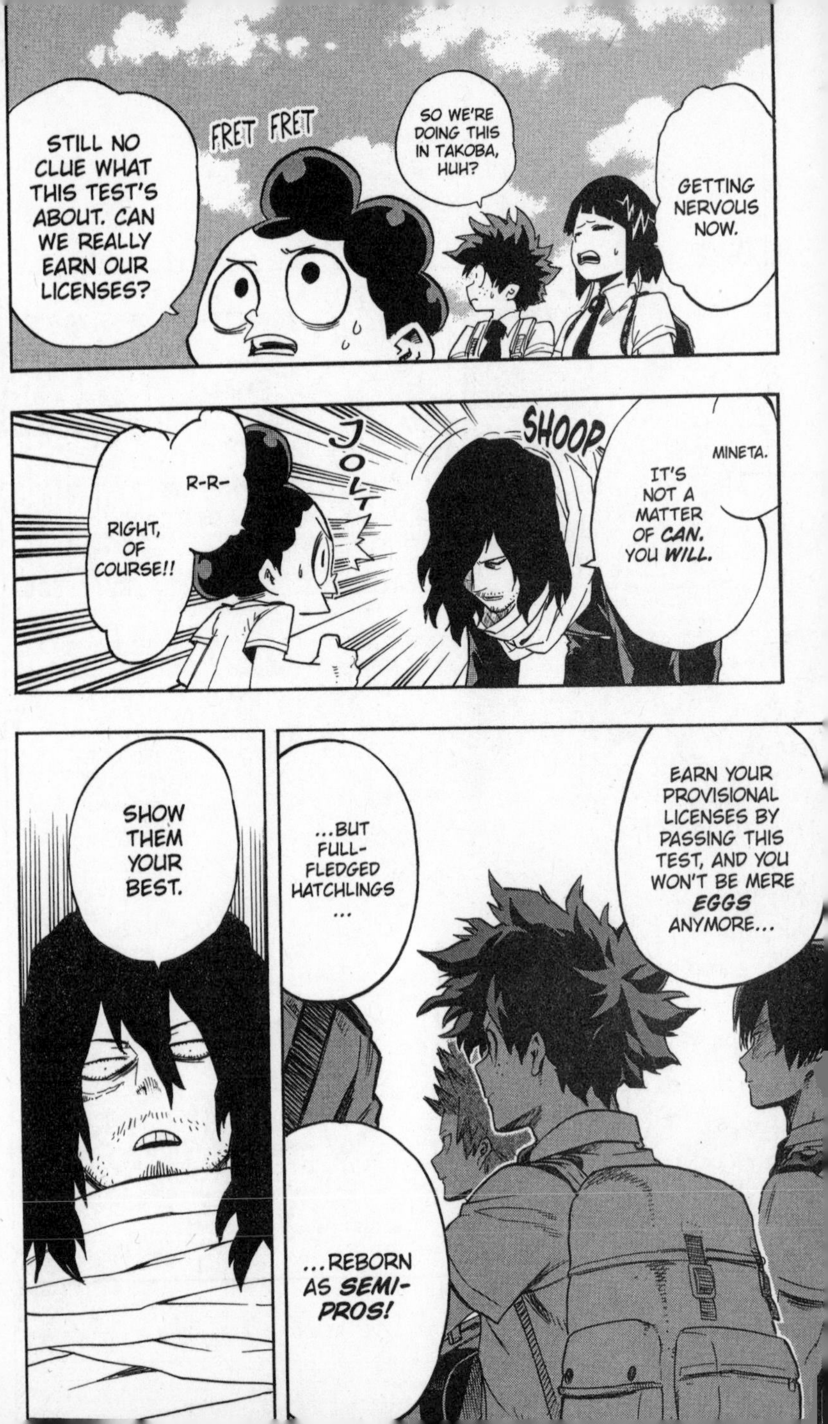
GETTING NERVOUS NOW.
SO WE'RE DOING THIS IN TAKOBA, HUH?
FRET FRET
STILL NO CLUE WHAT THIS TEST'S ABOUT. CAN WE REALLY EARN OUR LICENSES?
MINETA.
IT'S NOT A MATTER OF **CAN.** YOU **WILL.**
SHOOP
JOLT
R-R-
RIGHT, OF COURSE!!
EARN YOUR PROVISIONAL LICENSES BY PASSING THIS TEST, AND YOU WON'T BE MERE ***EGGS*** ANYMORE...
...BUT FULL-FLEDGED HATCHLINGS...
...REBORN AS ***SEMI-PROS!***
SHOW THEM YOUR BEST.

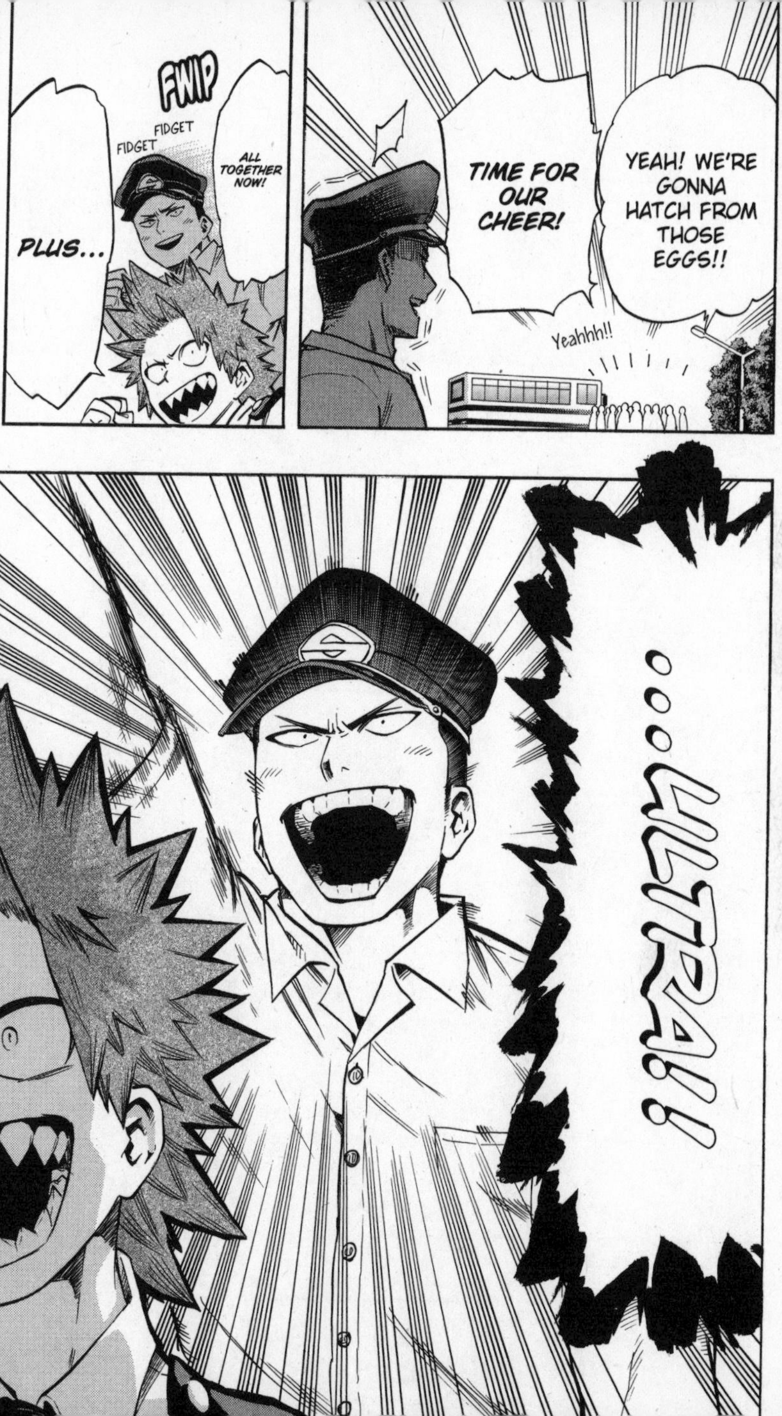
YEAH! WE'RE GONNA HATCH FROM THOSE EGGS!!
TIME FOR OUR CHEER!
Yeahhh!!
ALL TOGETHER NOW!
FWIP
FIDGET
FIDGET
PLUS...
...ULTRA!!

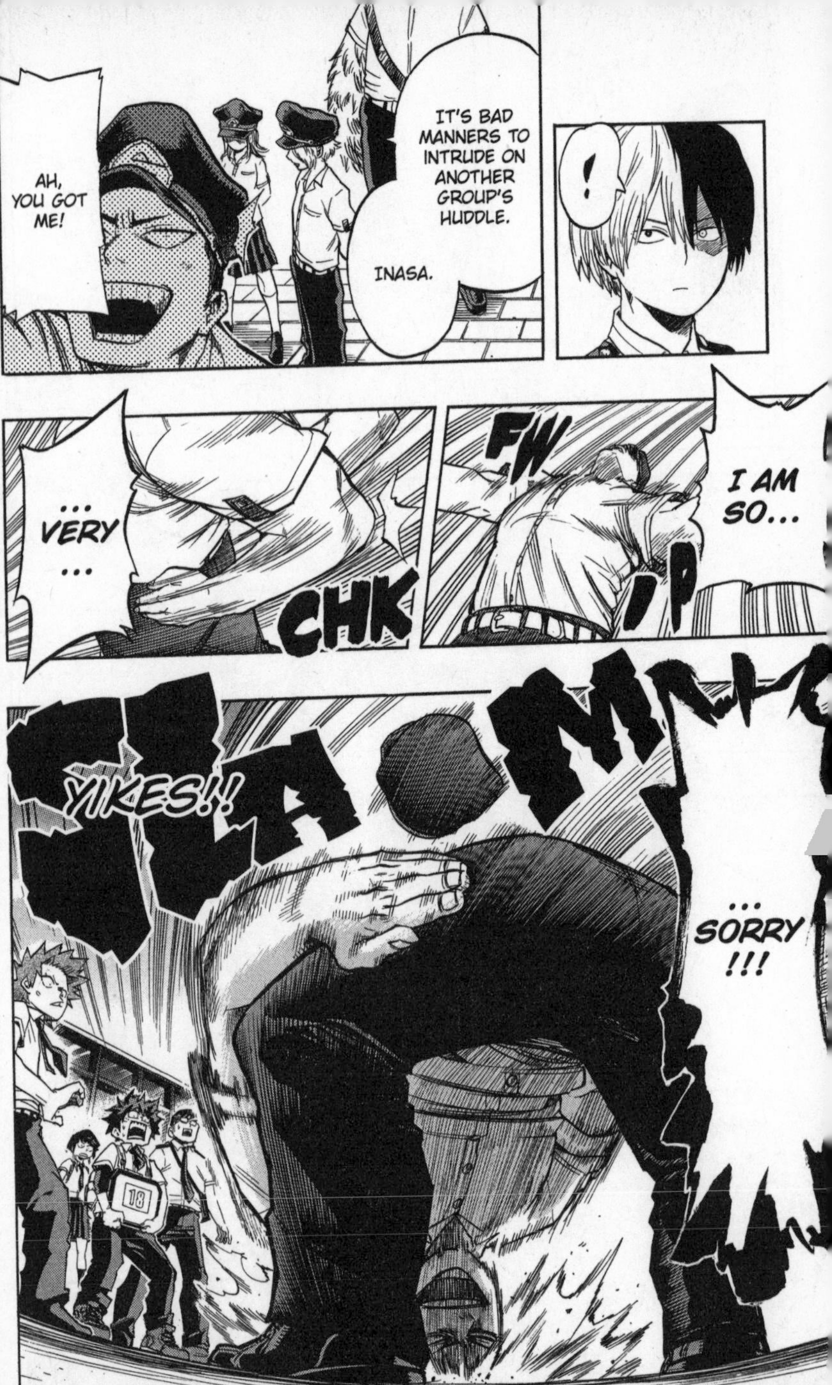
!
IT'S BAD MANNERS TO INTRUDE ON ANOTHER GROUP'S HUDDLE.
INASA.
AH, YOU GOT ME!
I AM SO...
FW
IP
... VERY ...
CHK
... SORRY !!!
YIKES!!
18

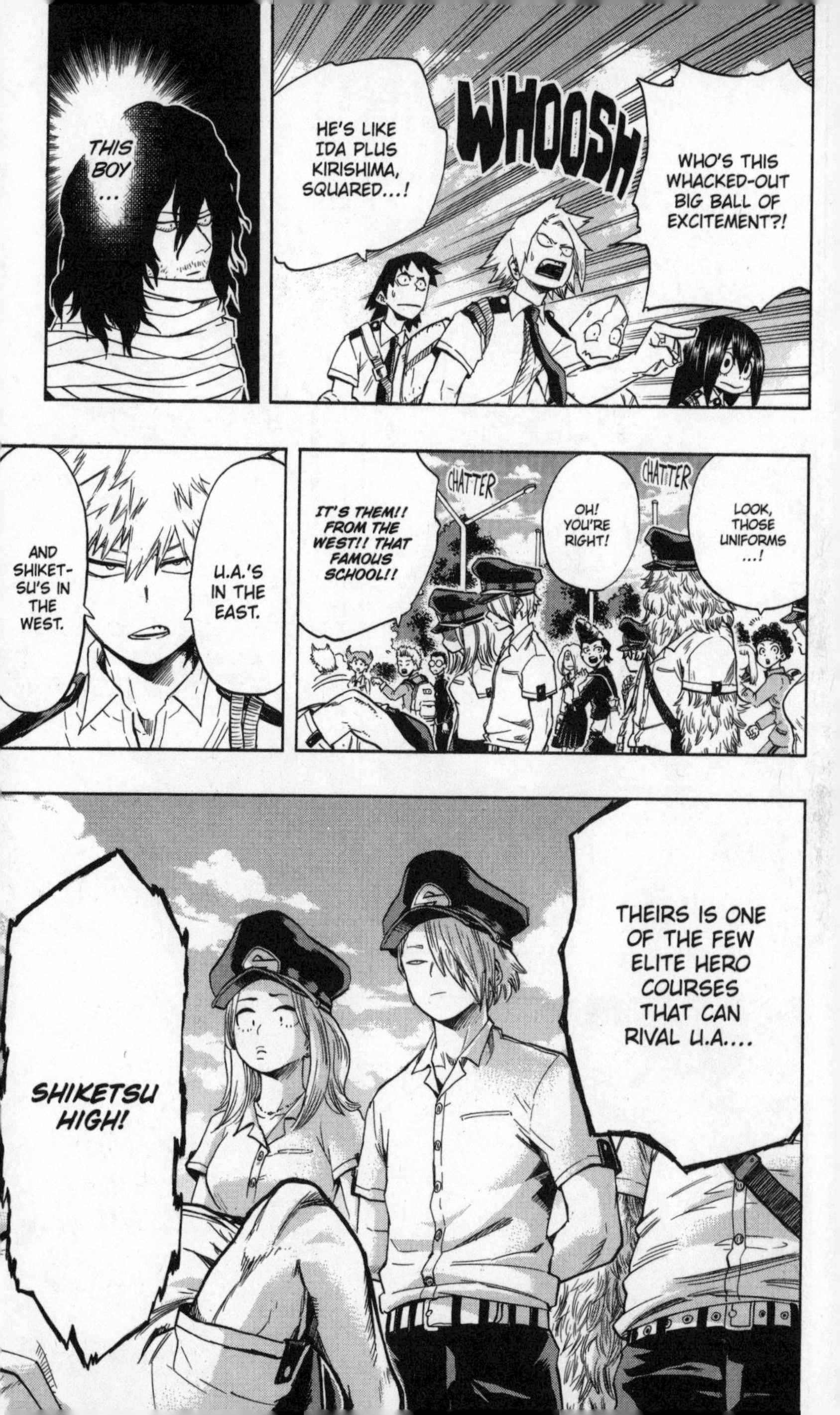
WHO'S THIS WHACKED-OUT BIG BALL OF EXCITEMENT?!
WHOOSH
HE'S LIKE IDA PLUS KIRISHIMA, SQUARED...!
THIS BOY ...
LOOK, THOSE UNIFORMS ...!
CHATTER
OH! YOU'RE RIGHT!
CHATTER
IT'S THEM!! FROM THE WEST!! THAT FAMOUS SCHOOL!!
U.A.'S IN THE EAST.
AND SHIKET-SU'S IN THE WEST.
THEIRS IS ONE OF THE FEW ELITE HERO COURSES THAT CAN RIVAL U.A....
SHIKETSU HIGH!

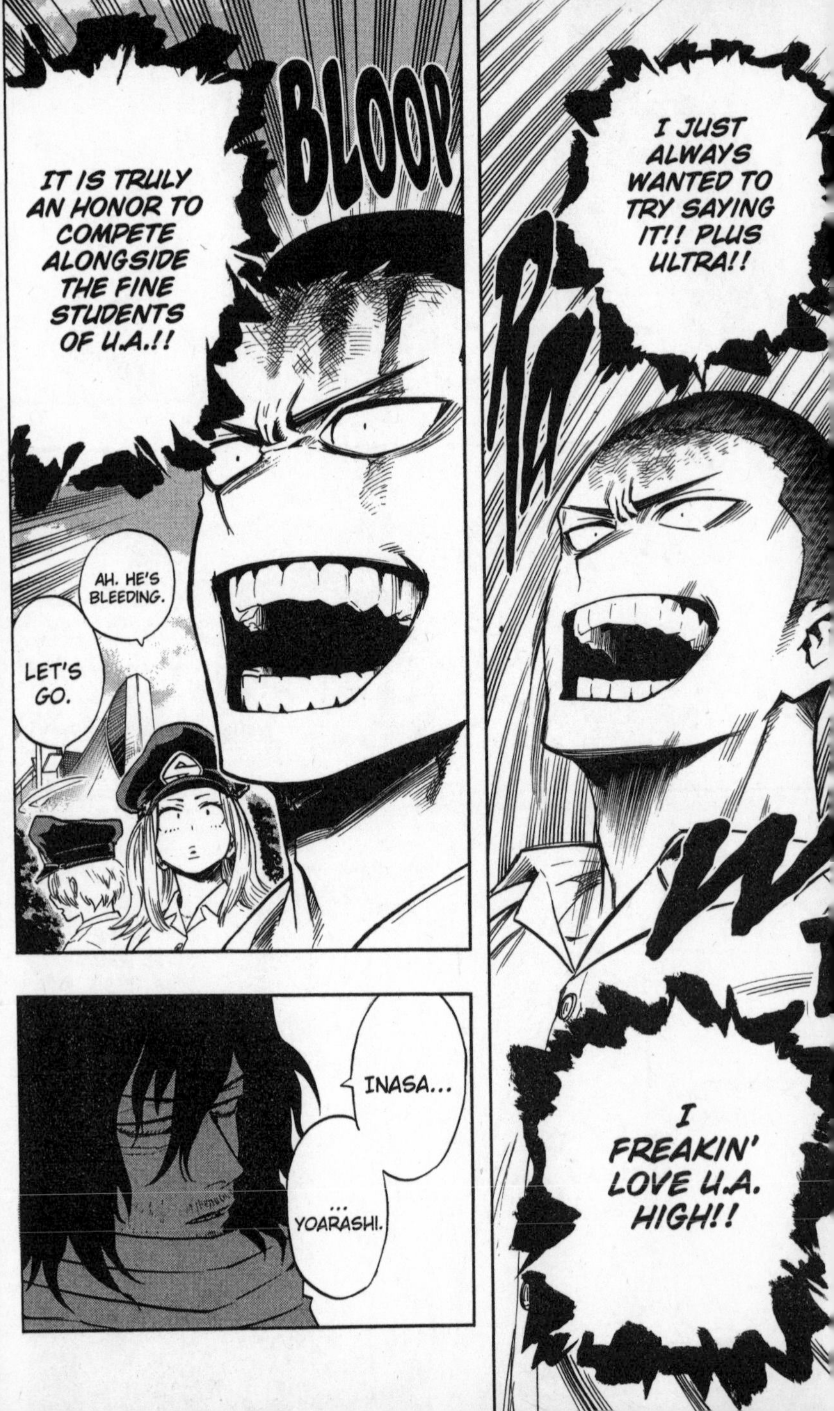
I JUST ALWAYS WANTED TO TRY SAYING IT!! PLUS ULTRA!!
I FREAKIN' LOVE U.A. HIGH!!
BLOOP
IT IS TRULY AN HONOR TO COMPETE ALONGSIDE THE FINE STUDENTS OF U.A.!!
AH. HE'S BLEEDING.
LET'S GO.
INASA...
...YOARASHI.

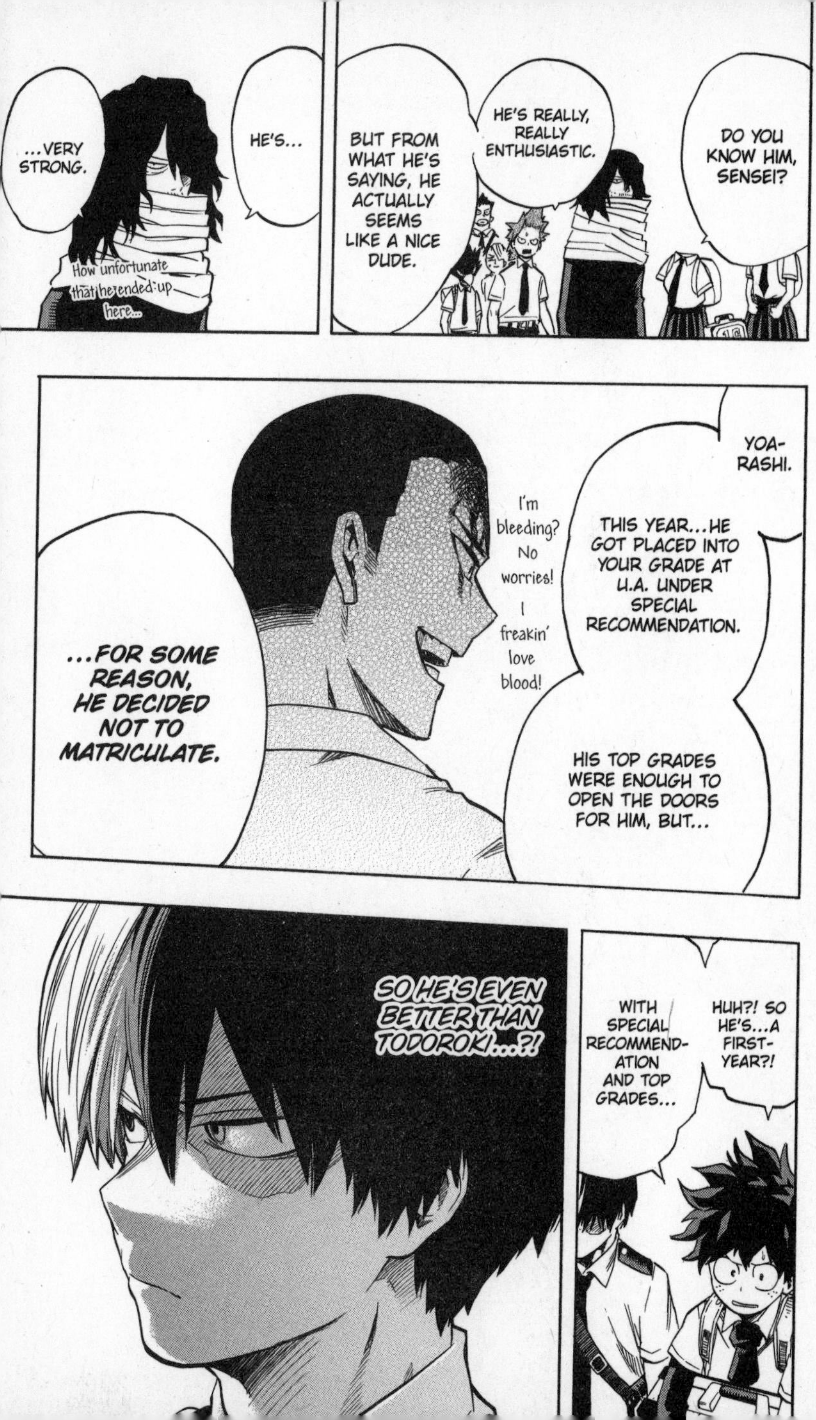
DO YOU KNOW HIM, SENSEI?
HE'S REALLY, REALLY ENTHUSIASTIC.
BUT FROM WHAT HE'S SAYING, HE ACTUALLY SEEMS LIKE A NICE DUDE.
HE'S...
...VERY STRONG.
How unfortunate that he ended up here...
YOA-RASHI.
THIS YEAR...HE GOT PLACED INTO YOUR GRADE AT U.A. UNDER SPECIAL RECOMMENDATION.
I'm bleeding? No worries! I freakin' love blood!
HIS TOP GRADES WERE ENOUGH TO OPEN THE DOORS FOR HIM, BUT...
...FOR SOME REASON, HE DECIDED NOT TO MATRICULATE.
HUH?! SO HE'S...A FIRST-YEAR?!
WITH SPECIAL RECOMMEND-ATION AND TOP GRADES...
SO HE'S EVEN BETTER THAN TODOROKI...?!

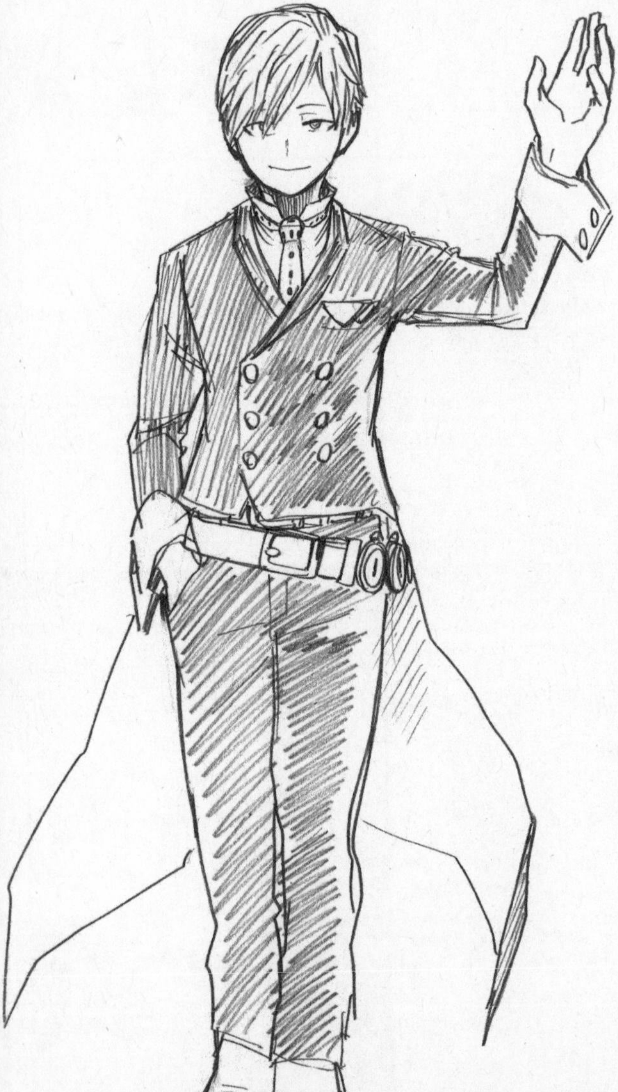

No one can claim to be unique after meeting me.

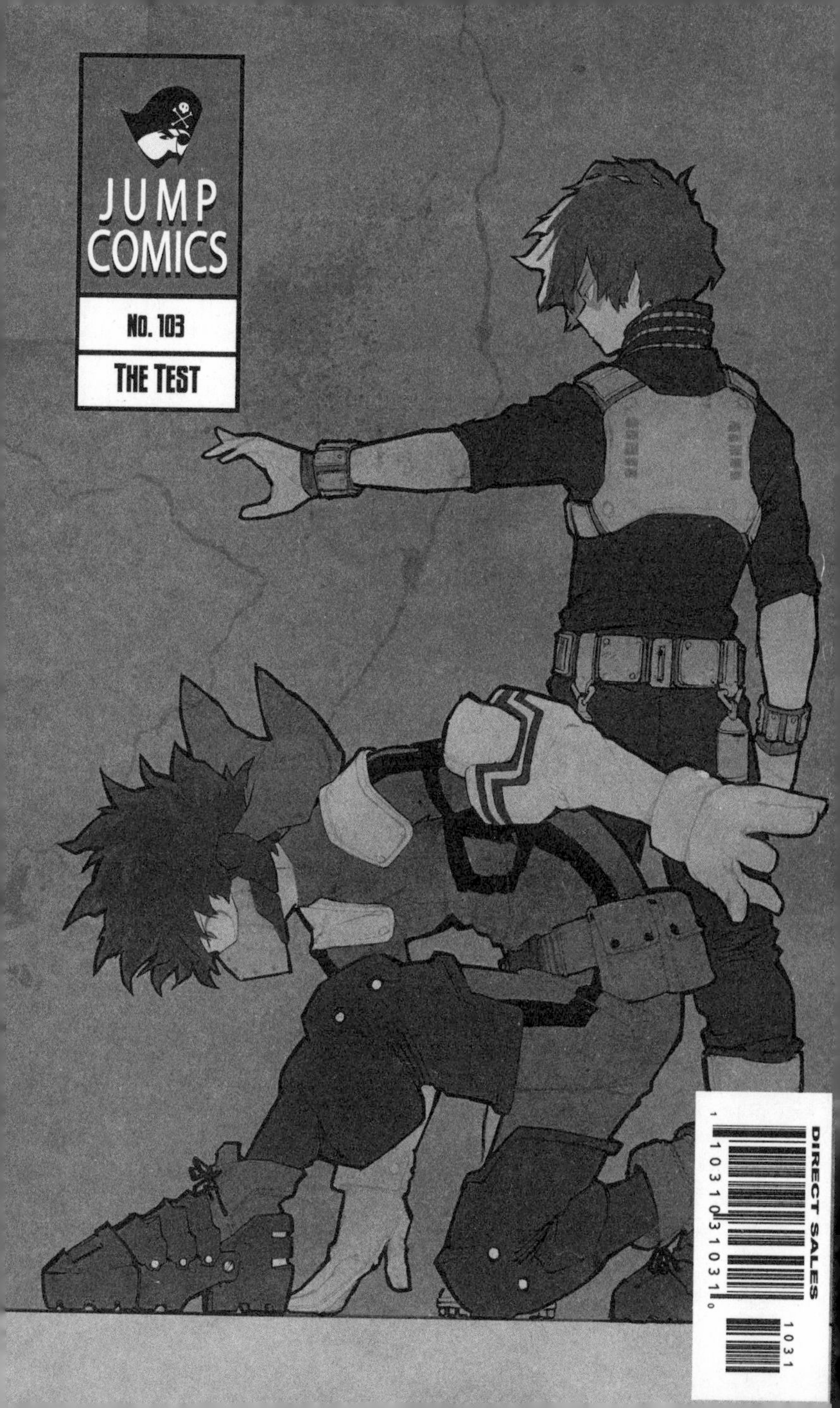
JUMP
COMICS
No. 103
THE TEST
DIRECT SALES

MY HERO
ACADEMIA

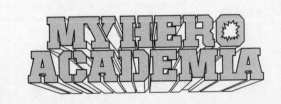

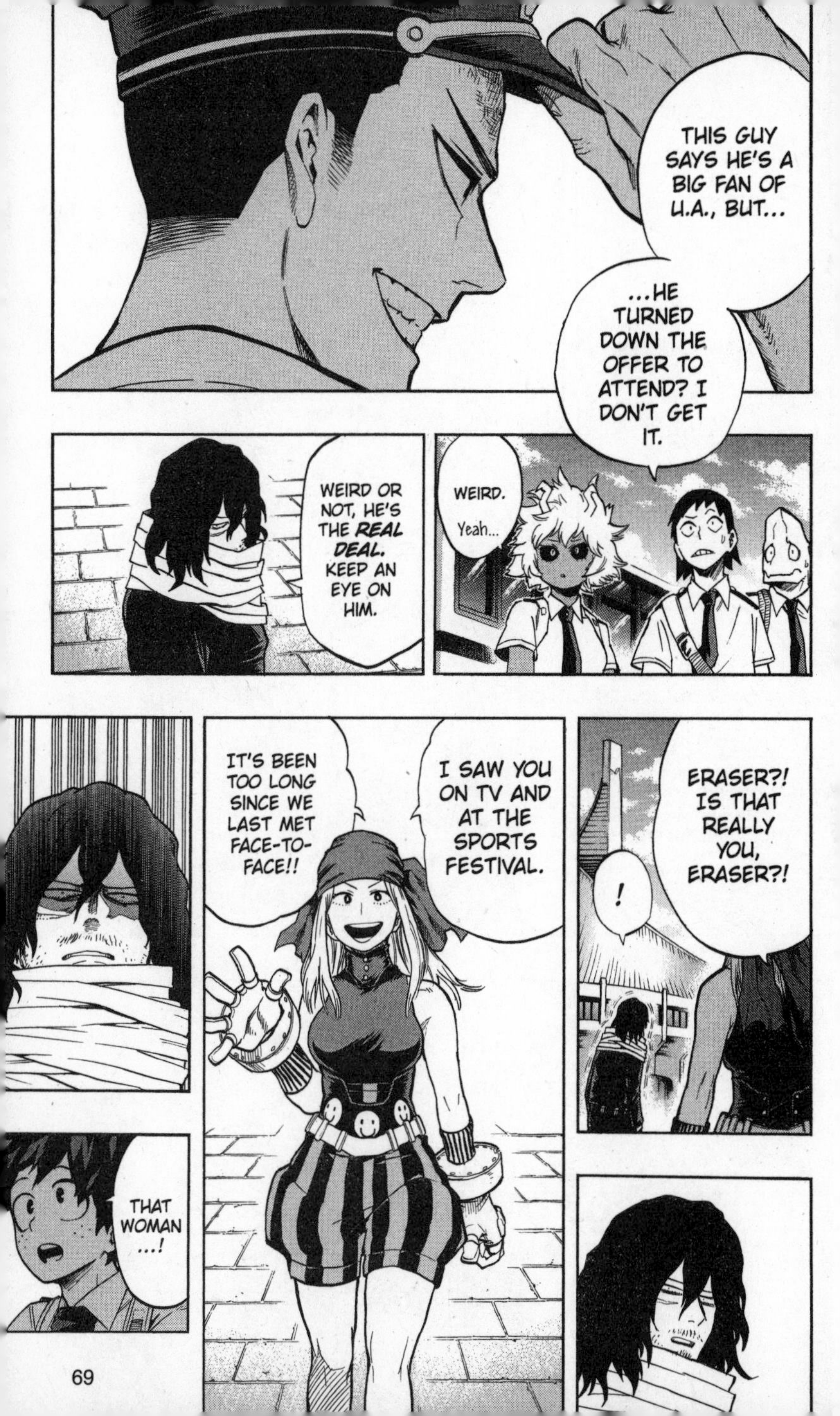

THIS GUY SAYS HE'S A BIG FAN OF U.A., BUT...
...HE TURNED DOWN THE OFFER TO ATTEND? I DON'T GET IT.
WEIRD.
Yeah...
WEIRD OR NOT, HE'S THE *REAL DEAL.* KEEP AN EYE ON HIM.
ERASER?! IS THAT REALLY YOU, ERASER?!
!
I SAW YOU ON TV AND AT THE SPORTS FESTIVAL.
IT'S BEEN TOO LONG SINCE WE LAST MET FACE-TO-FACE!!
THAT WOMAN ...!

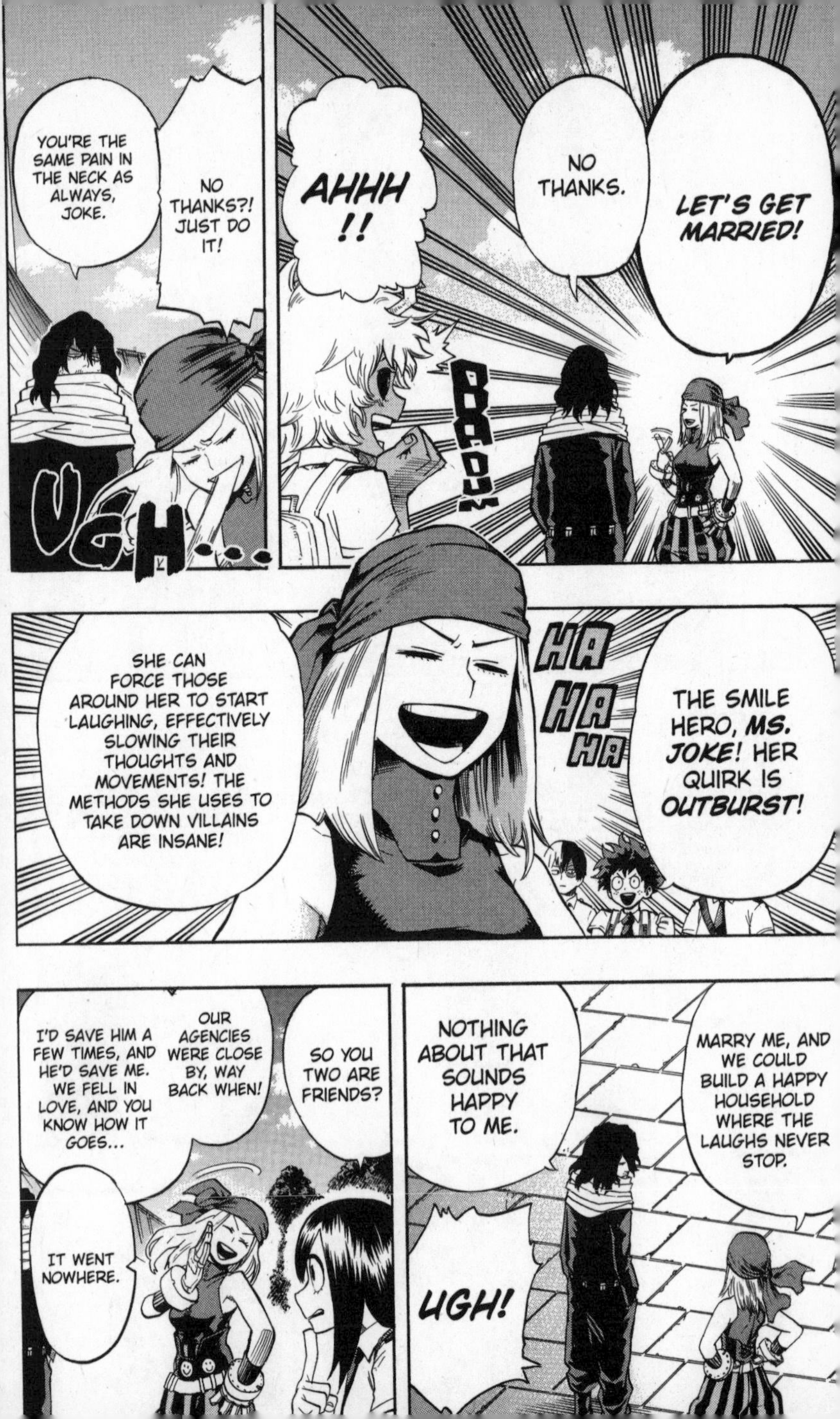
LET'S GET MARRIED!
NO THANKS.
AHHH!!
BADUM
NO THANKS?! JUST DO IT!
YOU'RE THE SAME PAIN IN THE NECK AS ALWAYS, JOKE.
UGH...
THE SMILE HERO, MS. JOKE! HER QUIRK IS OUTBURST!
HA HA HA
SHE CAN FORCE THOSE AROUND HER TO START LAUGHING, EFFECTIVELY SLOWING THEIR THOUGHTS AND MOVEMENTS! THE METHODS SHE USES TO TAKE DOWN VILLAINS ARE INSANE!
MARRY ME, AND WE COULD BUILD A HAPPY HOUSEHOLD WHERE THE LAUGHS NEVER STOP.
NOTHING ABOUT THAT SOUNDS HAPPY TO ME.
UGH!
SO YOU TWO ARE FRIENDS?
OUR AGENCIES WERE CLOSE BY, WAY BACK WHEN!
I'D SAVE HIM A FEW TIMES, AND HE'D SAVE ME. WE FELL IN LOVE, AND YOU KNOW HOW IT GOES...
IT WENT NOWHERE.

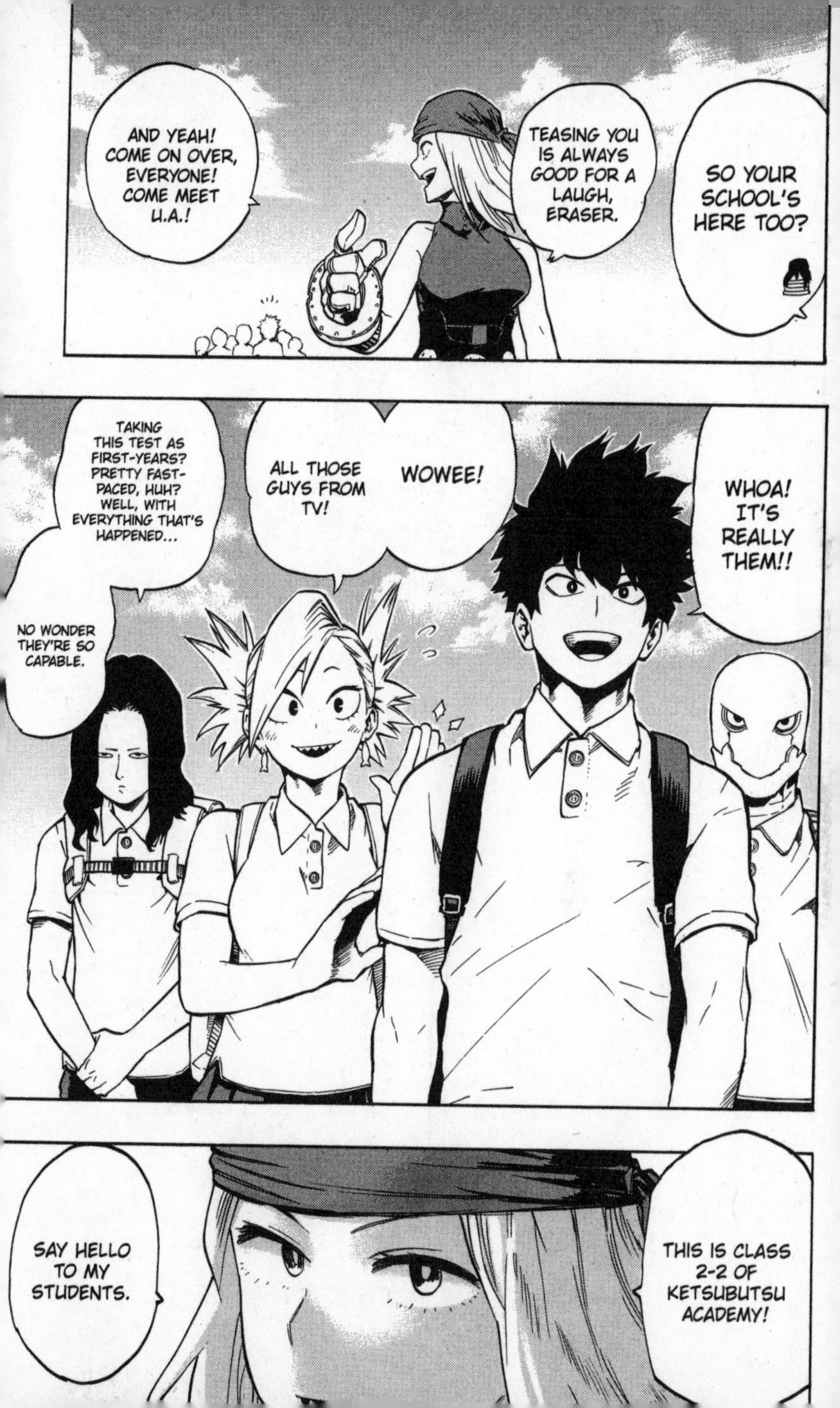
SO YOUR SCHOOL'S HERE TOO?
TEASING YOU IS ALWAYS GOOD FOR A LAUGH, ERASER.
AND YEAH! COME ON OVER, EVERYONE! COME MEET U.A.!
WHOA! IT'S REALLY THEM!!
WOWEE!
ALL THOSE GUYS FROM TV!
TAKING THIS TEST AS FIRST-YEARS? PRETTY FAST-PACED, HUH? WELL, WITH EVERYTHING THAT'S HAPPENED...
NO WONDER THEY'RE SO CAPABLE.
THIS IS CLASS 2-2 OF KETSUBUTSU ACADEMY!
SAY HELLO TO MY STUDENTS.

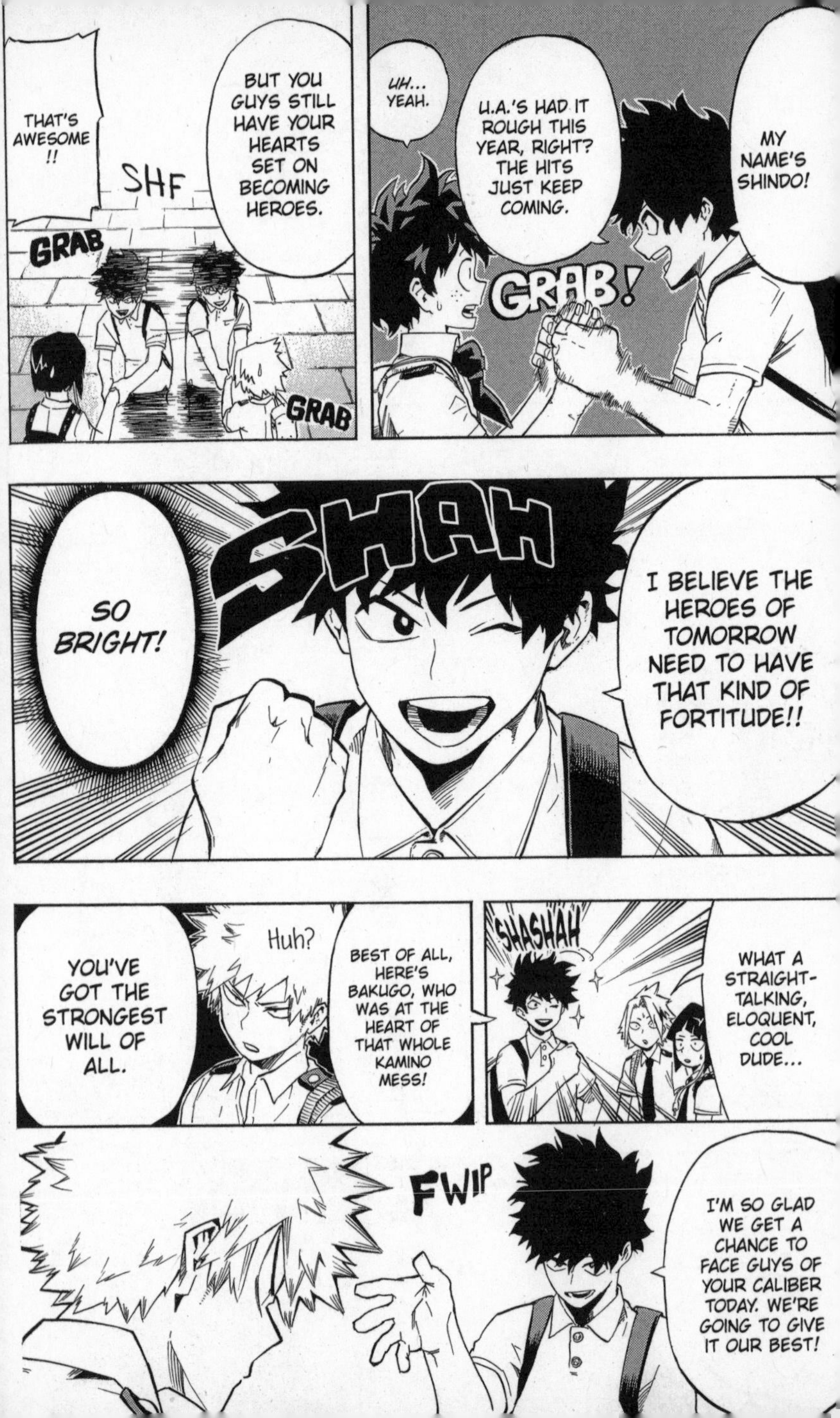
MY NAME'S SHINDO!
U.A.'S HAD IT ROUGH THIS YEAR, RIGHT? THE HITS JUST KEEP COMING.
UH... YEAH.
GRAB!
BUT YOU GUYS STILL HAVE YOUR HEARTS SET ON BECOMING HEROES.
THAT'S AWESOME!!
SHF
GRAB
GRAB
I BELIEVE THE HEROES OF TOMORROW NEED TO HAVE THAT KIND OF FORTITUDE!!
SHAH
SO BRIGHT!
WHAT A STRAIGHT-TALKING, ELOQUENT, COOL DUDE...
SHASHAH
BEST OF ALL, HERE'S BAKUGO, WHO WAS AT THE HEART OF THAT WHOLE KAMINO MESS!
Huh?
YOU'VE GOT THE STRONGEST WILL OF ALL.
I'M SO GLAD WE GET A CHANCE TO FACE GUYS OF YOUR CALIBER TODAY. WE'RE GOING TO GIVE IT OUR BEST!
FWIP

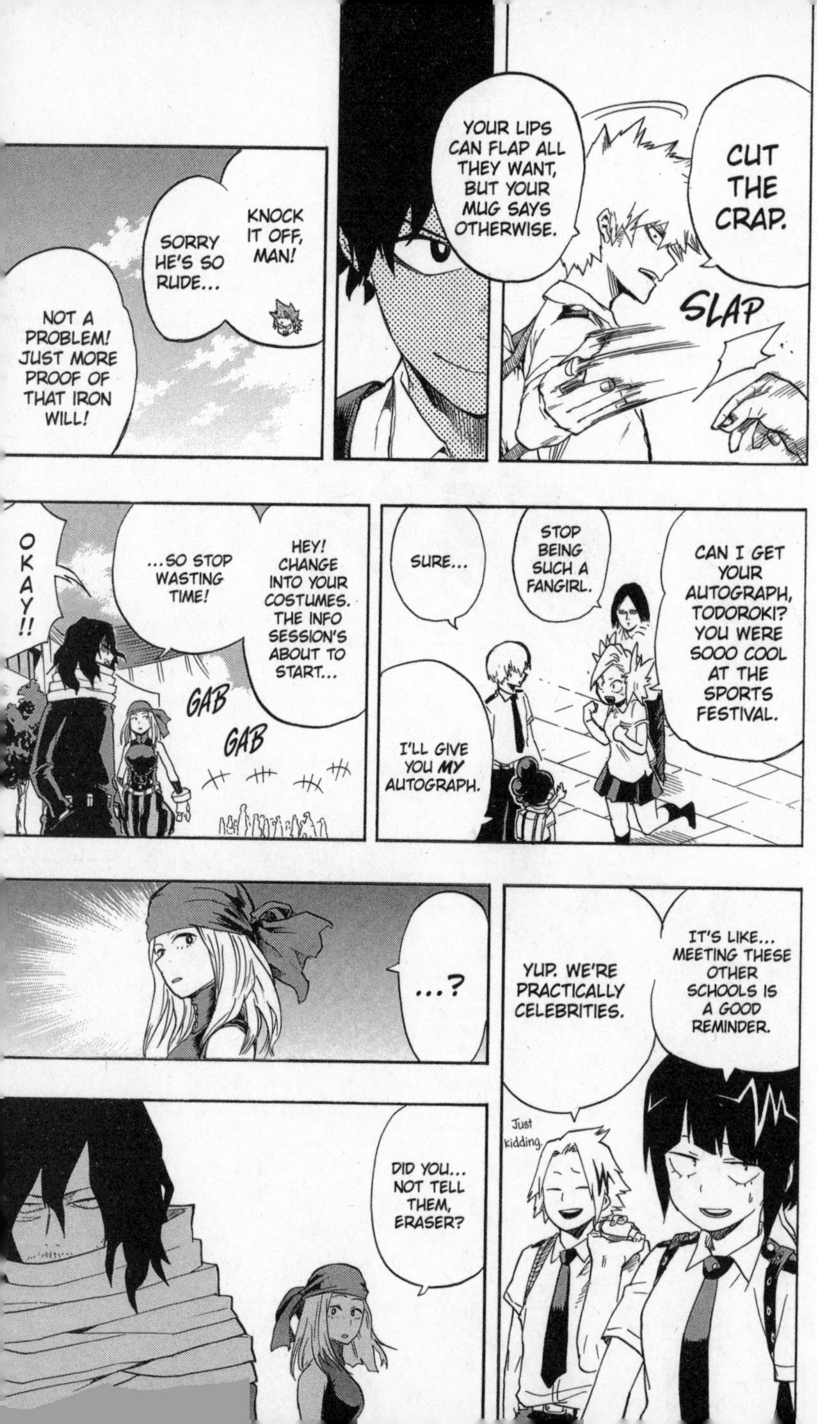
CUT THE CRAP.
SLAP
YOUR LIPS CAN FLAP ALL THEY WANT, BUT YOUR MUG SAYS OTHERWISE.
KNOCK IT OFF, MAN!
SORRY HE'S SO RUDE...
NOT A PROBLEM! JUST MORE PROOF OF THAT IRON WILL!
CAN I GET YOUR AUTOGRAPH, TODOROKI? YOU WERE SOOO COOL AT THE SPORTS FESTIVAL.
STOP BEING SUCH A FANGIRL.
SURE...
I'LL GIVE YOU MY AUTOGRAPH.
HEY! CHANGE INTO YOUR COSTUMES. THE INFO SESSION'S ABOUT TO START...
...SO STOP WASTING TIME!
OKAY!!
GAB
GAB
IT'S LIKE... MEETING THESE OTHER SCHOOLS IS A GOOD REMINDER.
YUP. WE'RE PRACTICALLY CELEBRITIES.
Just kidding.
...?
DID YOU... NOT TELL THEM, ERASER?

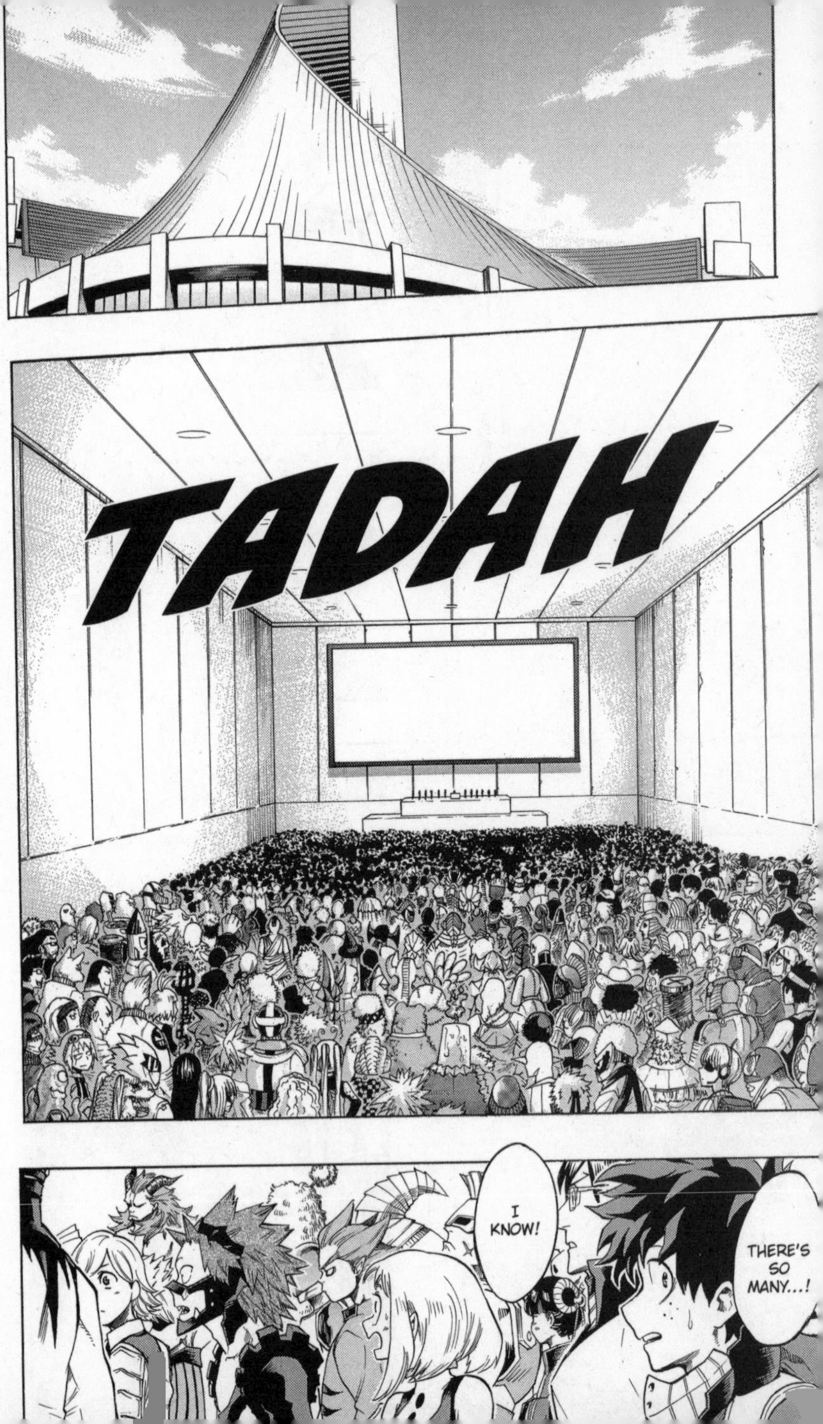
TADAH
THERE'S SO MANY...!
I KNOW!

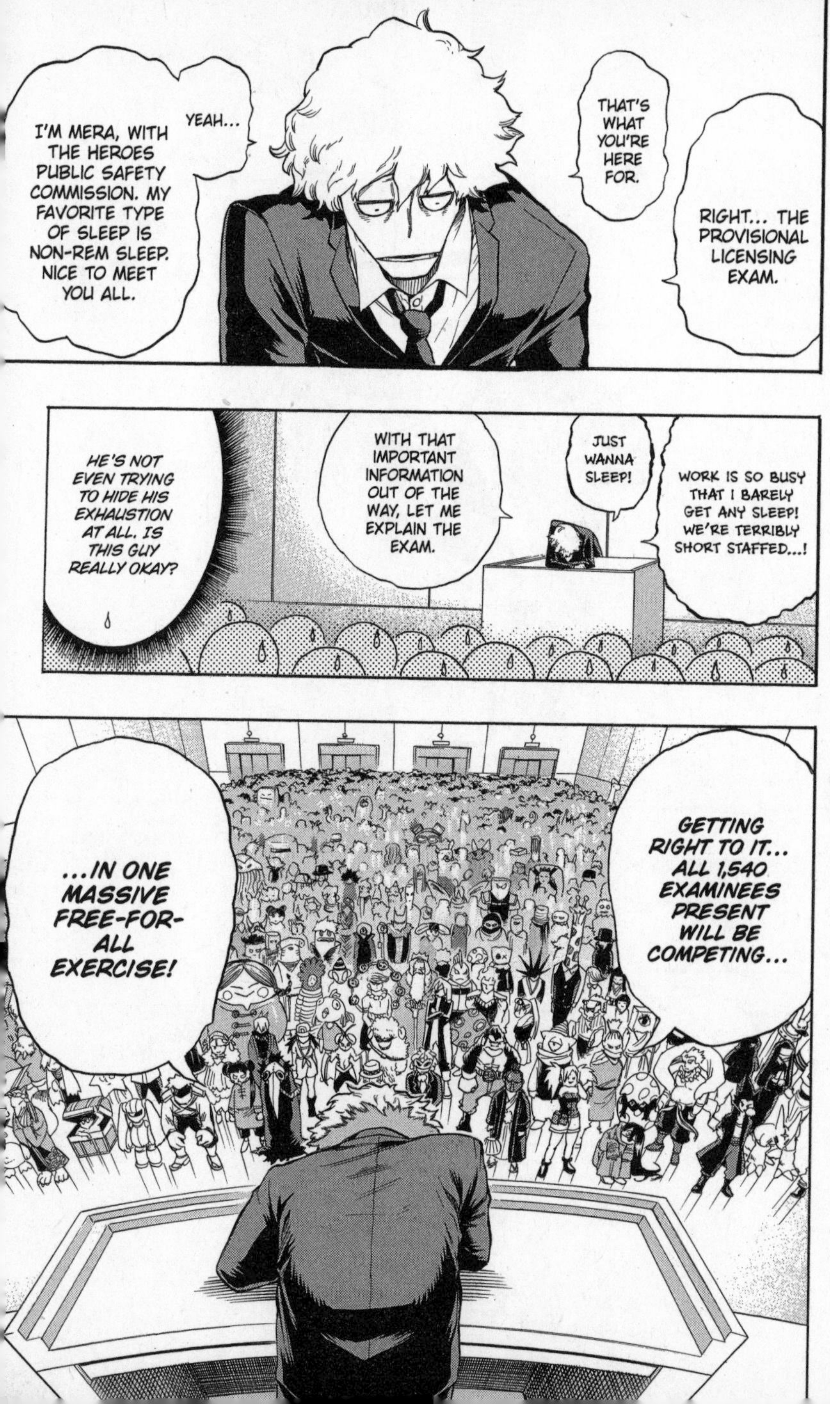
RIGHT... THE PROVISIONAL LICENSING EXAM.
THAT'S WHAT YOU'RE HERE FOR.
YEAH...
I'M MERA, WITH THE HEROES PUBLIC SAFETY COMMISSION. MY FAVORITE TYPE OF SLEEP IS NON-REM SLEEP. NICE TO MEET YOU ALL.
WORK IS SO BUSY THAT I BARELY GET ANY SLEEP! WE'RE TERRIBLY SHORT STAFFED...!
JUST WANNA SLEEP!
WITH THAT IMPORTANT INFORMATION OUT OF THE WAY, LET ME EXPLAIN THE EXAM.
HE'S NOT EVEN TRYING TO HIDE HIS EXHAUSTION AT ALL. IS THIS GUY REALLY OKAY?
GETTING RIGHT TO IT... ALL 1,540 EXAMINEES PRESENT WILL BE COMPETING...
...IN ONE MASSIVE FREE-FOR-ALL EXERCISE!

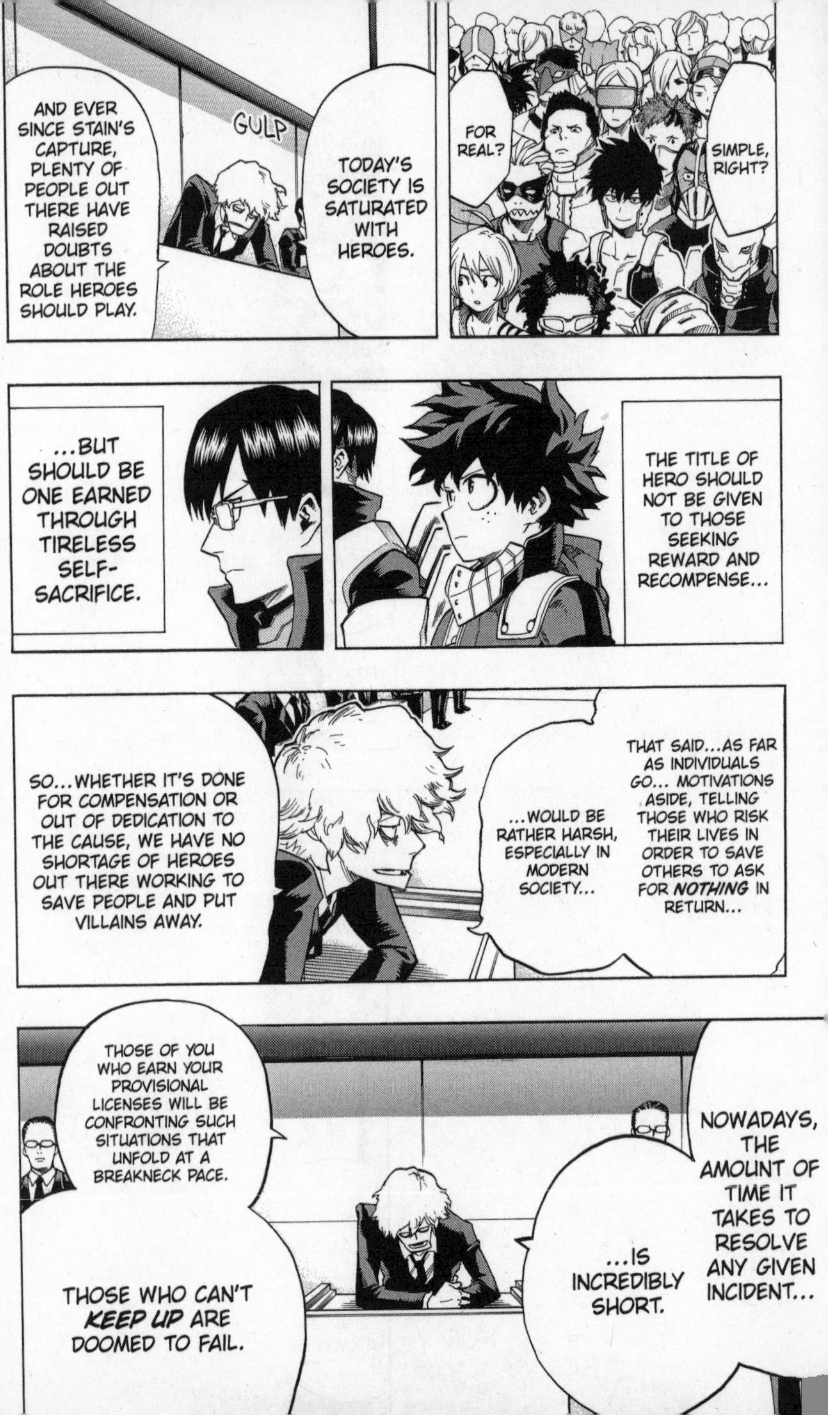
SIMPLE, RIGHT?
FOR REAL?
TODAY'S SOCIETY IS SATURATED WITH HEROES.
GULP
AND EVER SINCE STAIN'S CAPTURE, PLENTY OF PEOPLE OUT THERE HAVE RAISED DOUBTS ABOUT THE ROLE HEROES SHOULD PLAY.
THE TITLE OF HERO SHOULD NOT BE GIVEN TO THOSE SEEKING REWARD AND RECOMPENSE...
...BUT SHOULD BE ONE EARNED THROUGH TIRELESS SELF-SACRIFICE.
THAT SAID...AS FAR AS INDIVIDUALS GO... MOTIVATIONS ASIDE, TELLING THOSE WHO RISK THEIR LIVES IN ORDER TO SAVE OTHERS TO ASK FOR *NOTHING* IN RETURN...
...WOULD BE RATHER HARSH, ESPECIALLY IN MODERN SOCIETY...
SO...WHETHER IT'S DONE FOR COMPENSATION OR OUT OF DEDICATION TO THE CAUSE, WE HAVE NO SHORTAGE OF HEROES OUT THERE WORKING TO SAVE PEOPLE AND PUT VILLAINS AWAY.
NOWADAYS, THE AMOUNT OF TIME IT TAKES TO RESOLVE ANY GIVEN INCIDENT...
...IS INCREDIBLY SHORT.
THOSE OF YOU WHO EARN YOUR PROVISIONAL LICENSES WILL BE CONFRONTING SUCH SITUATIONS THAT UNFOLD AT A BREAKNECK PACE.
THOSE WHO CAN'T *KEEP UP* ARE DOOMED TO FAIL.

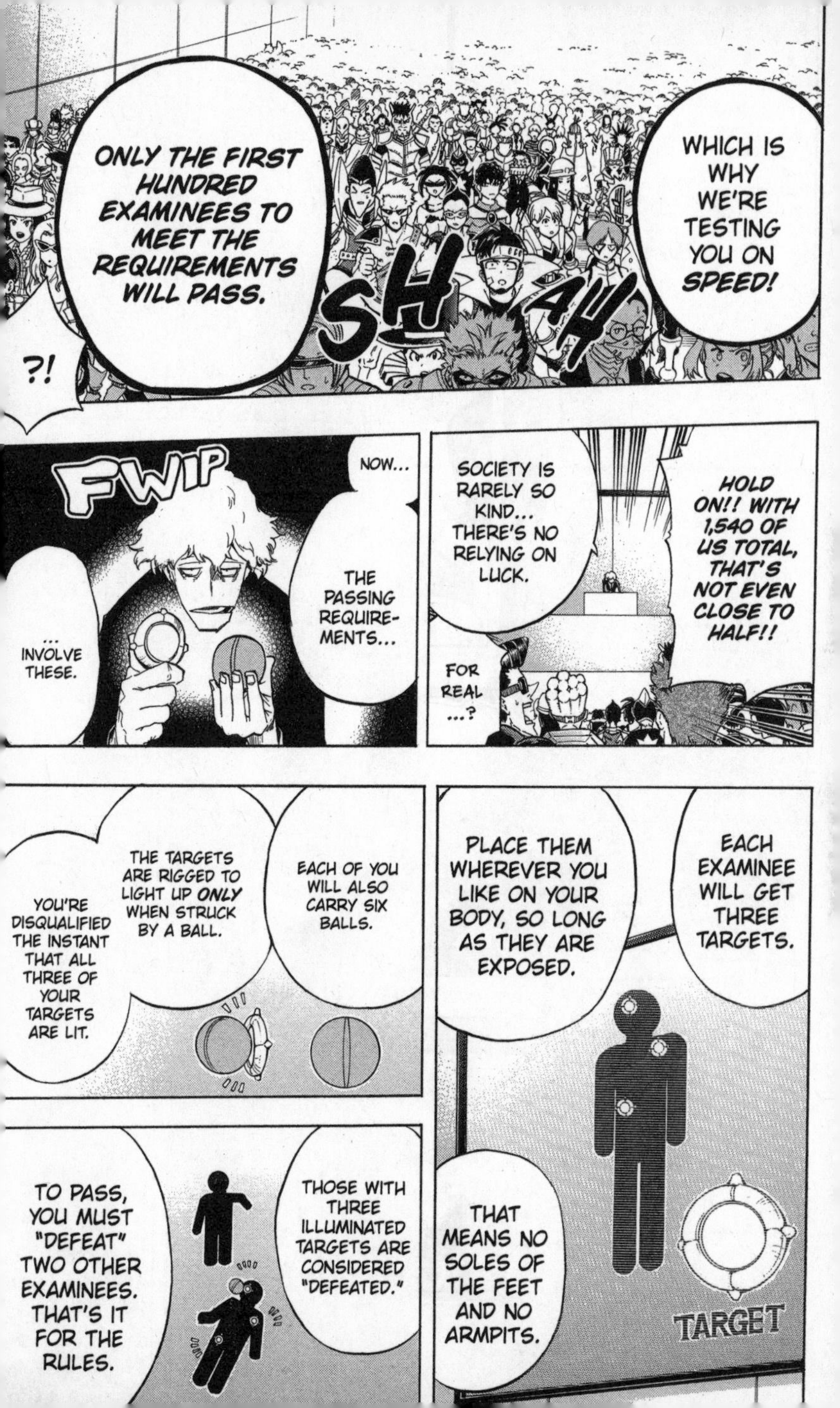
WHICH IS WHY WE'RE TESTING YOU ON SPEED!
SHAH
ONLY THE FIRST HUNDRED EXAMINEES TO MEET THE REQUIREMENTS WILL PASS.
?!
HOLD ON!! WITH 1,540 OF US TOTAL, THAT'S NOT EVEN CLOSE TO HALF!!
SOCIETY IS RARELY SO KIND... THERE'S NO RELYING ON LUCK.
FOR REAL ...?
NOW...
FWIP
THE PASSING REQUIRE-MENTS...
... INVOLVE THESE.
EACH EXAMINEE WILL GET THREE TARGETS.
PLACE THEM WHEREVER YOU LIKE ON YOUR BODY, SO LONG AS THEY ARE EXPOSED.
THAT MEANS NO SOLES OF THE FEET AND NO ARMPITS.
TARGET
EACH OF YOU WILL ALSO CARRY SIX BALLS.
THE TARGETS ARE RIGGED TO LIGHT UP *ONLY* WHEN STRUCK BY A BALL.
YOU'RE DISQUALIFIED THE INSTANT THAT ALL THREE OF YOUR TARGETS ARE LIT.
THOSE WITH THREE ILLUMINATED TARGETS ARE CONSIDERED "DEFEATED."
TO PASS, YOU MUST "DEFEAT" TWO OTHER EXAMINEES. THAT'S IT FOR THE RULES.

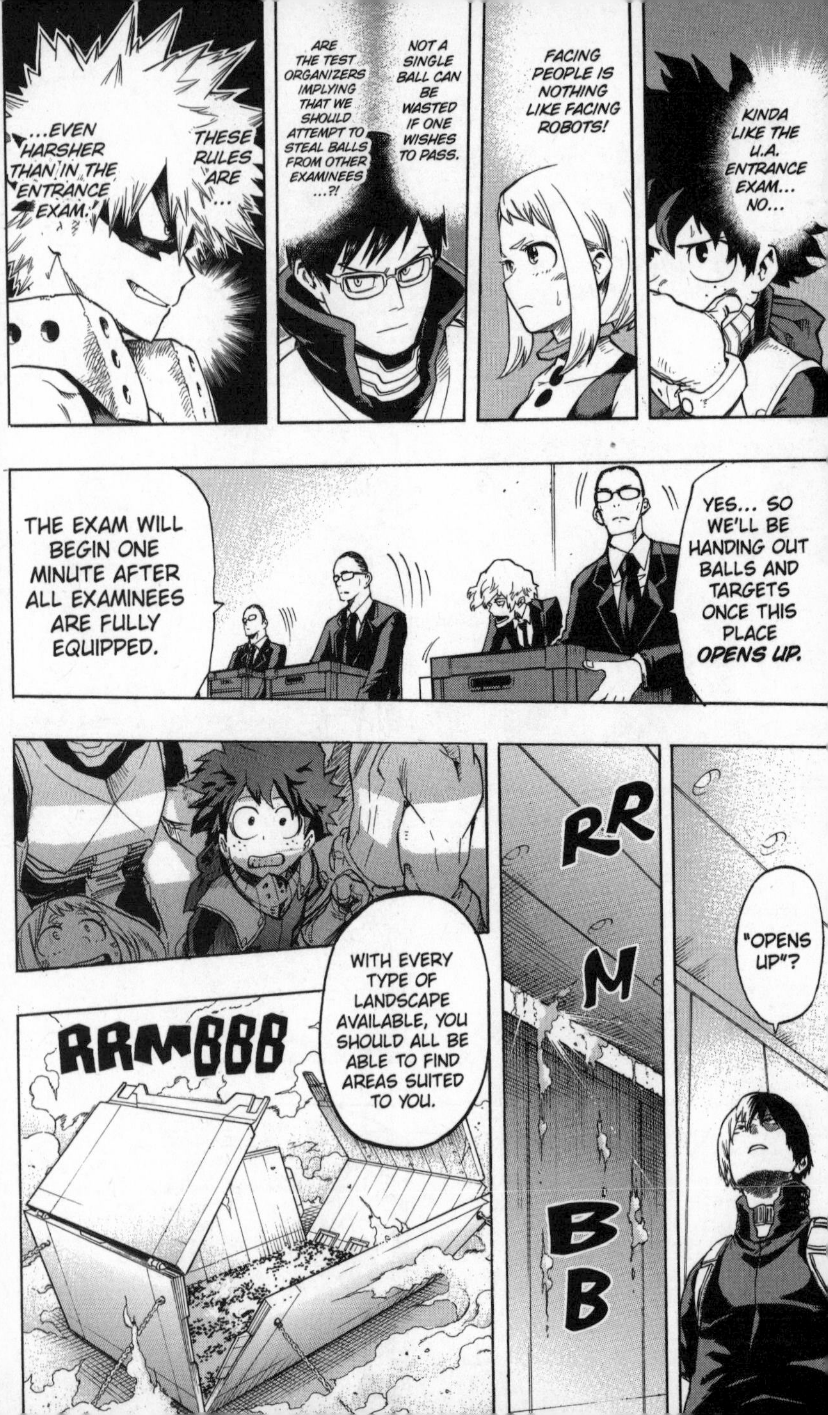
KINDA LIKE THE U.A. ENTRANCE EXAM... NO...
FACING PEOPLE IS NOTHING LIKE FACING ROBOTS!
NOT A SINGLE BALL CAN BE WASTED IF ONE WISHES TO PASS.
ARE THE TEST ORGANIZERS IMPLYING THAT WE SHOULD ATTEMPT TO STEAL BALLS FROM OTHER EXAMINEES ...?!
THESE RULES ARE...
...EVEN HARSHER THAN IN THE ENTRANCE EXAM.
YES... SO WE'LL BE HANDING OUT BALLS AND TARGETS ONCE THIS PLACE OPENS UP.
THE EXAM WILL BEGIN ONE MINUTE AFTER ALL EXAMINEES ARE FULLY EQUIPPED.
"OPENS UP"?
RRMBB
WITH EVERY TYPE OF LANDSCAPE AVAILABLE, YOU SHOULD ALL BE ABLE TO FIND AREAS SUITED TO YOU.
RRMBBB

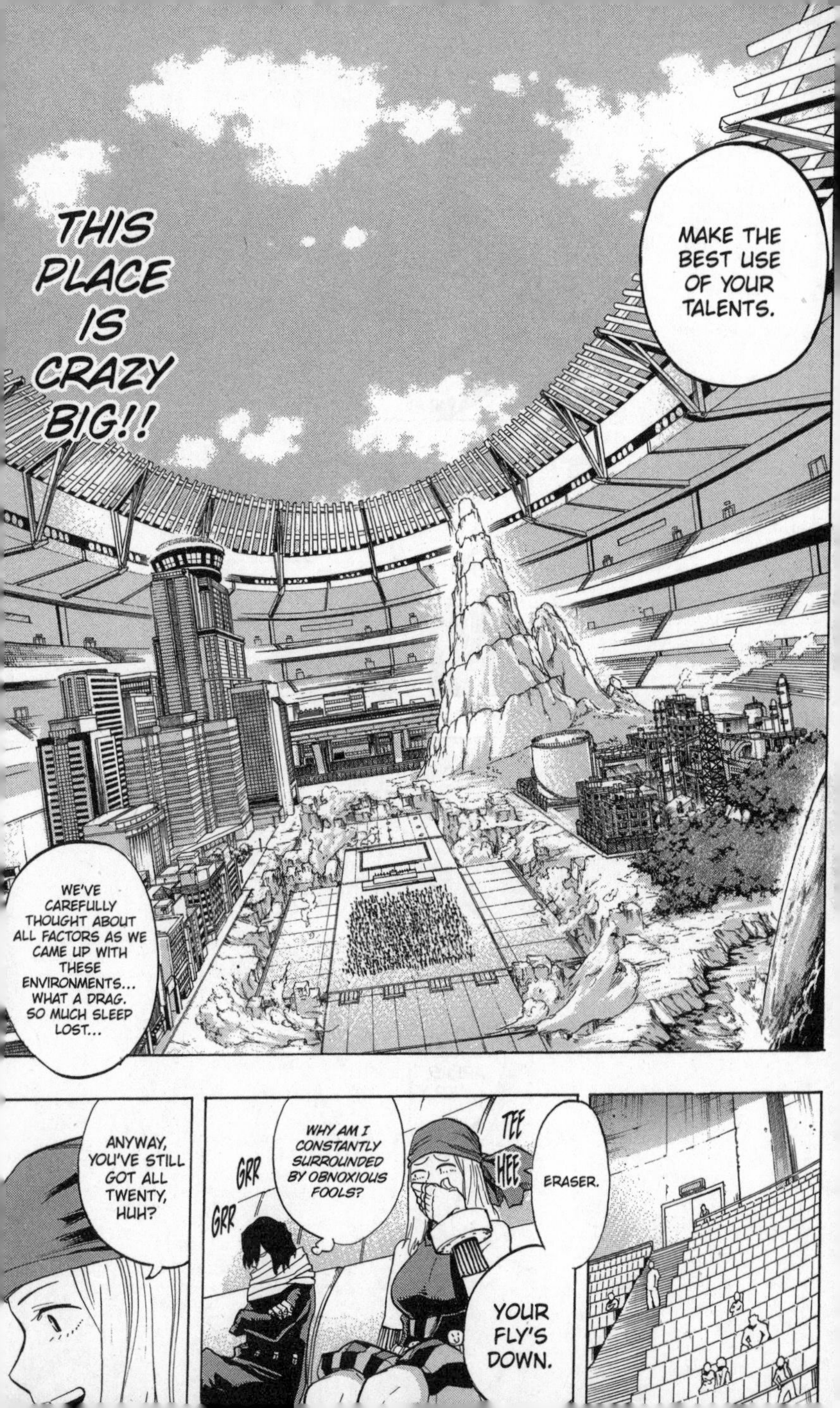
MAKE THE BEST USE OF YOUR TALENTS.
THIS PLACE IS CRAZY BIG!!
WE'VE CAREFULLY THOUGHT ABOUT ALL FACTORS AS WE CAME UP WITH THESE ENVIRONMENTS... WHAT A DRAG. SO MUCH SLEEP LOST...
ERASER.
YOUR FLY'S DOWN.
TEE HEE
WHY AM I CONSTANTLY SURROUNDED BY OBNOXIOUS FOOLS?
GRR GRR
ANYWAY, YOU'VE STILL GOT ALL TWENTY, HUH?

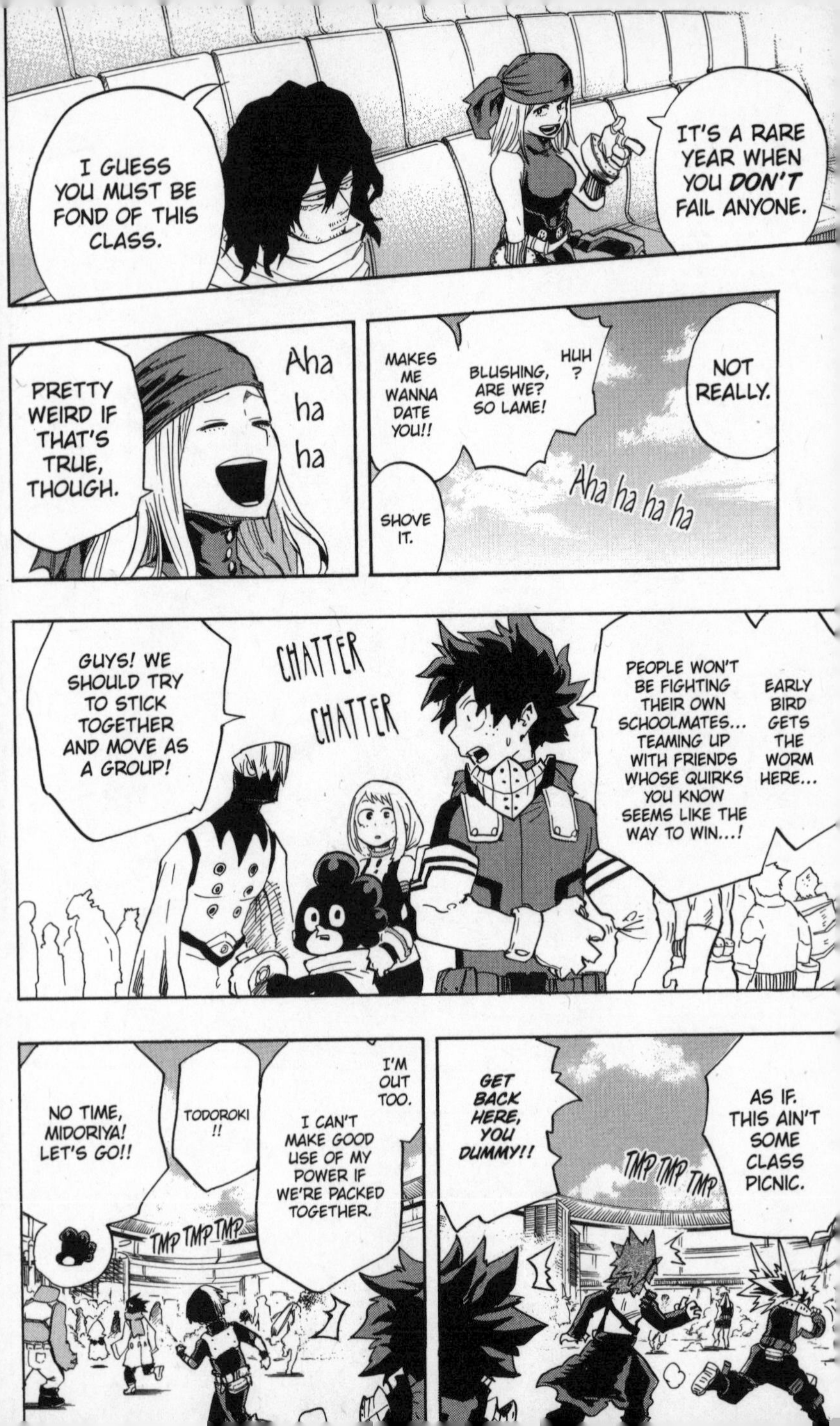

IT'S A RARE YEAR WHEN YOU **DON'T** FAIL ANYONE.
I GUESS YOU MUST BE FOND OF THIS CLASS.
NOT REALLY.
HUH?
BLUSHING, ARE WE? SO LAME!
MAKES ME WANNA DATE YOU!!
Aha ha ha ha
SHOVE IT.
Aha ha ha
PRETTY WEIRD IF THAT'S TRUE, THOUGH.
EARLY BIRD GETS THE WORM HERE...
PEOPLE WON'T BE FIGHTING THEIR OWN SCHOOLMATES... TEAMING UP WITH FRIENDS WHOSE QUIRKS YOU KNOW SEEMS LIKE THE WAY TO WIN...!
CHATTER
CHATTER
GUYS! WE SHOULD TRY TO STICK TOGETHER AND MOVE AS A GROUP!
AS IF. THIS AIN'T SOME CLASS PICNIC.
TMP TMP TMP
GET BACK HERE, YOU DUMMY!!
I'M OUT TOO.
I CAN'T MAKE GOOD USE OF MY POWER IF WE'RE PACKED TOGETHER.
TODOROKI!!
NO TIME, MIDORIYA! LET'S GO!!
TMP TMP TMP

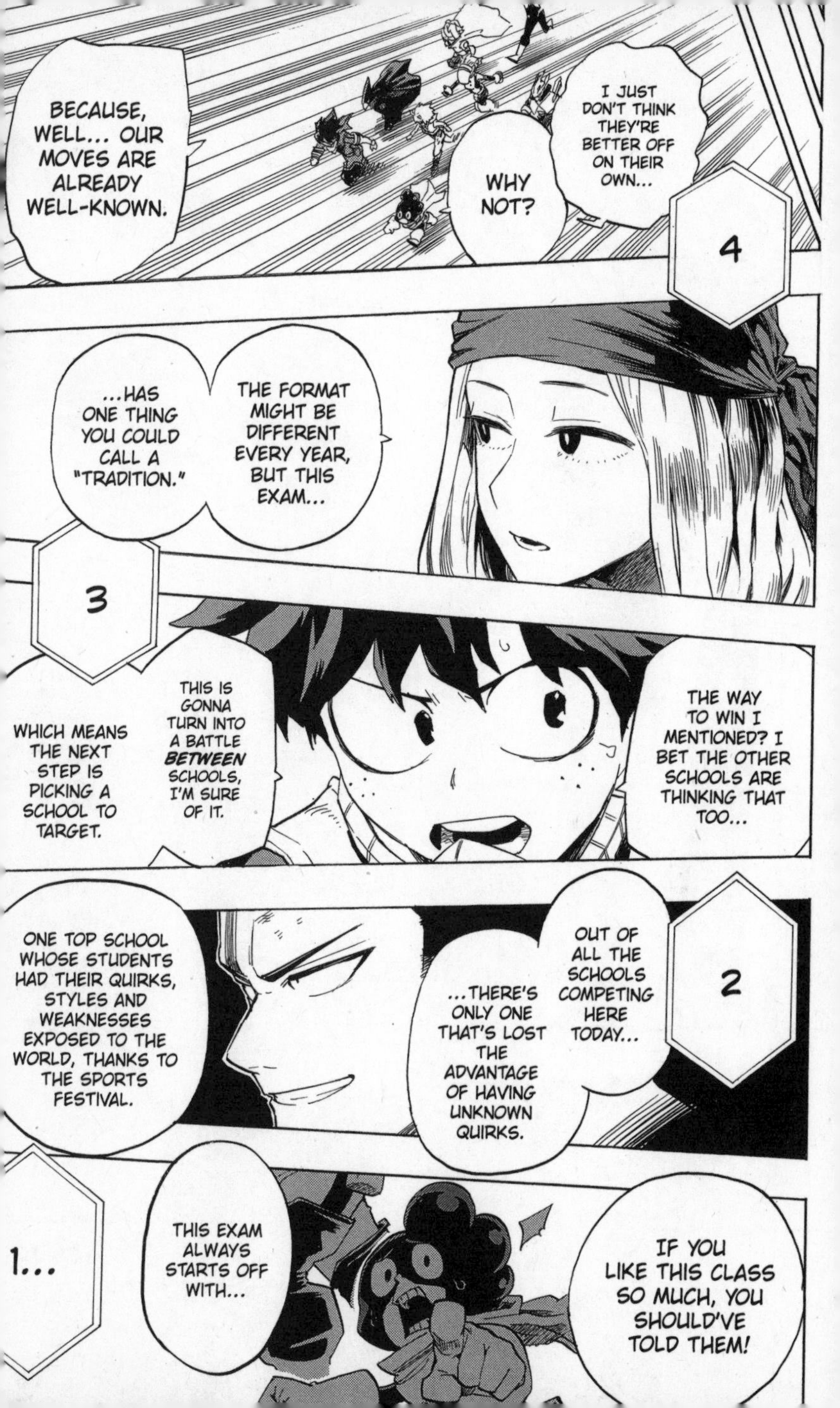

I JUST DON'T THINK THEY'RE BETTER OFF ON THEIR OWN...
WHY NOT?
BECAUSE, WELL... OUR MOVES ARE ALREADY WELL-KNOWN.
4
THE FORMAT MIGHT BE DIFFERENT EVERY YEAR, BUT THIS EXAM...
...HAS ONE THING YOU COULD CALL A "TRADITION."
3
THE WAY TO WIN I MENTIONED? I BET THE OTHER SCHOOLS ARE THINKING THAT TOO...
THIS IS GONNA TURN INTO A BATTLE *BETWEEN* SCHOOLS, I'M SURE OF IT.
WHICH MEANS THE NEXT STEP IS PICKING A SCHOOL TO TARGET.
2
OUT OF ALL THE SCHOOLS COMPETING HERE TODAY...
...THERE'S ONLY ONE THAT'S LOST THE ADVANTAGE OF HAVING UNKNOWN QUIRKS.
ONE TOP SCHOOL WHOSE STUDENTS HAD THEIR QUIRKS, STYLES AND WEAKNESSES EXPOSED TO THE WORLD, THANKS TO THE SPORTS FESTIVAL.
IF YOU LIKE THIS CLASS SO MUCH, YOU SHOULD'VE TOLD THEM!
THIS EXAM ALWAYS STARTS OFF WITH...
1...

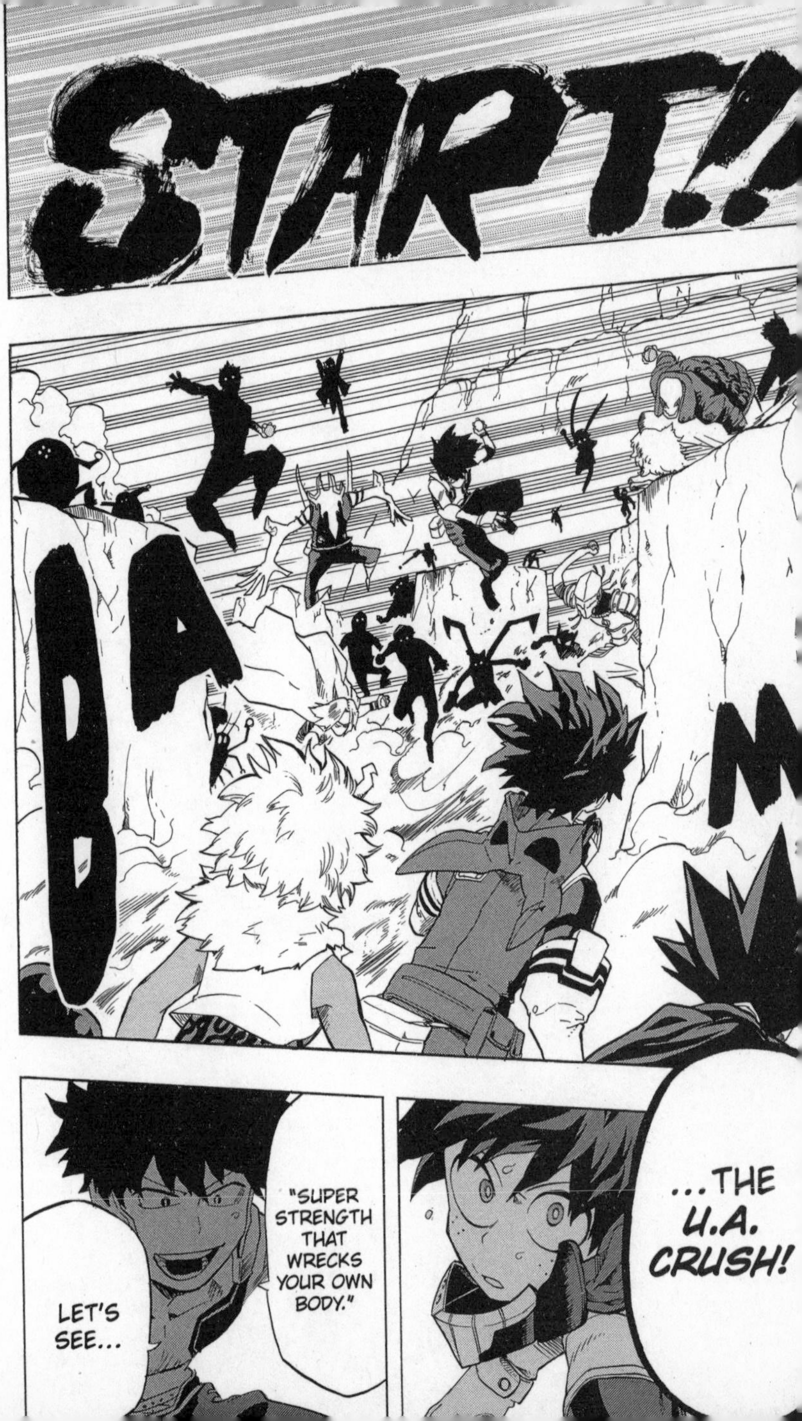
START!!
BAM
...THE U.A. CRUSH!
"SUPER STRENGTH THAT WRECKS YOUR OWN BODY."
LET'S SEE...

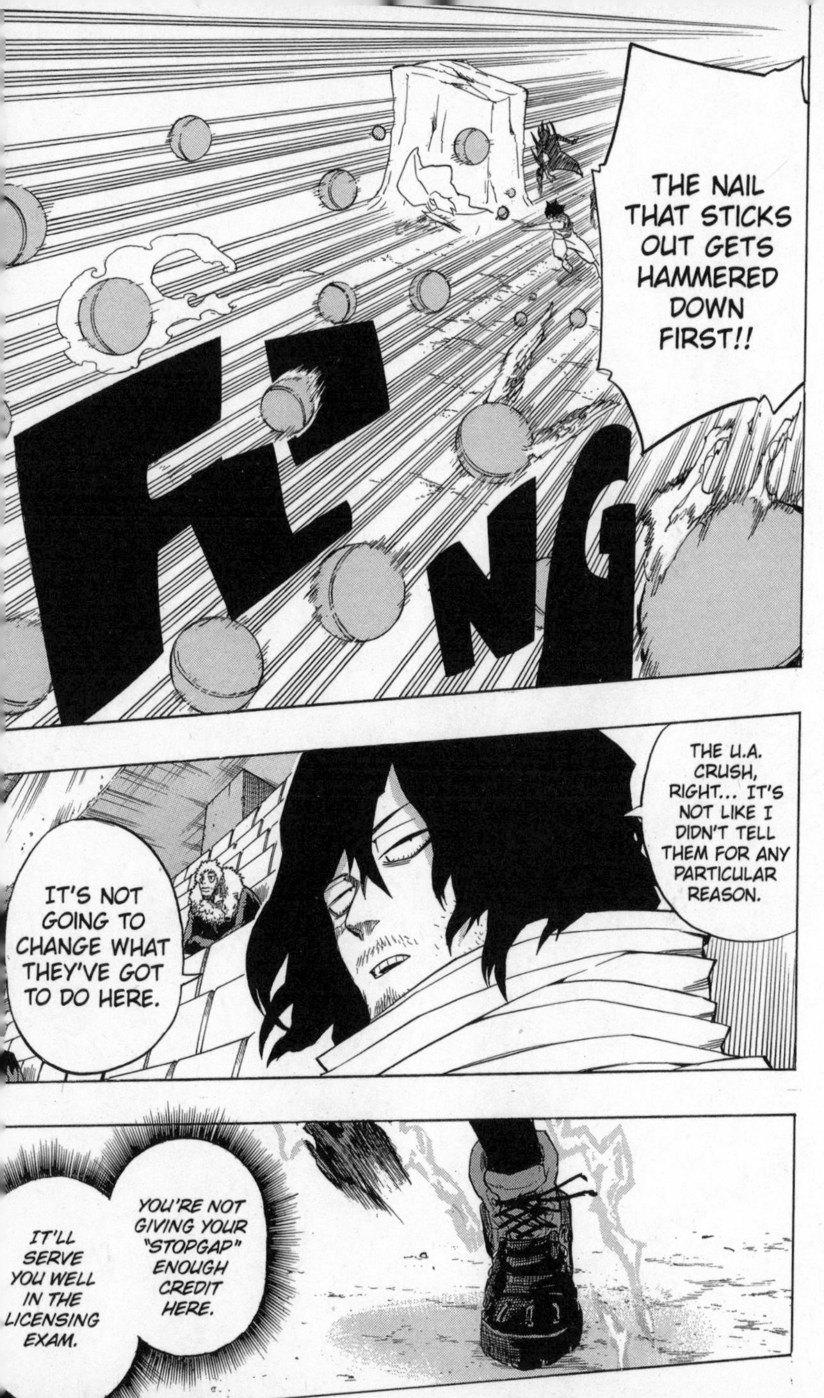

THE NAIL THAT STICKS OUT GETS HAMMERED DOWN FIRST!!
FZ NG
THE U.A. CRUSH, RIGHT... IT'S NOT LIKE I DIDN'T TELL THEM FOR ANY PARTICULAR REASON.
IT'S NOT GOING TO CHANGE WHAT THEY'VE GOT TO DO HERE.
YOU'RE NOT GIVING YOUR "STOPGAP" ENOUGH CREDIT HERE.
IT'LL SERVE YOU WELL IN THE LICENSING EXAM.

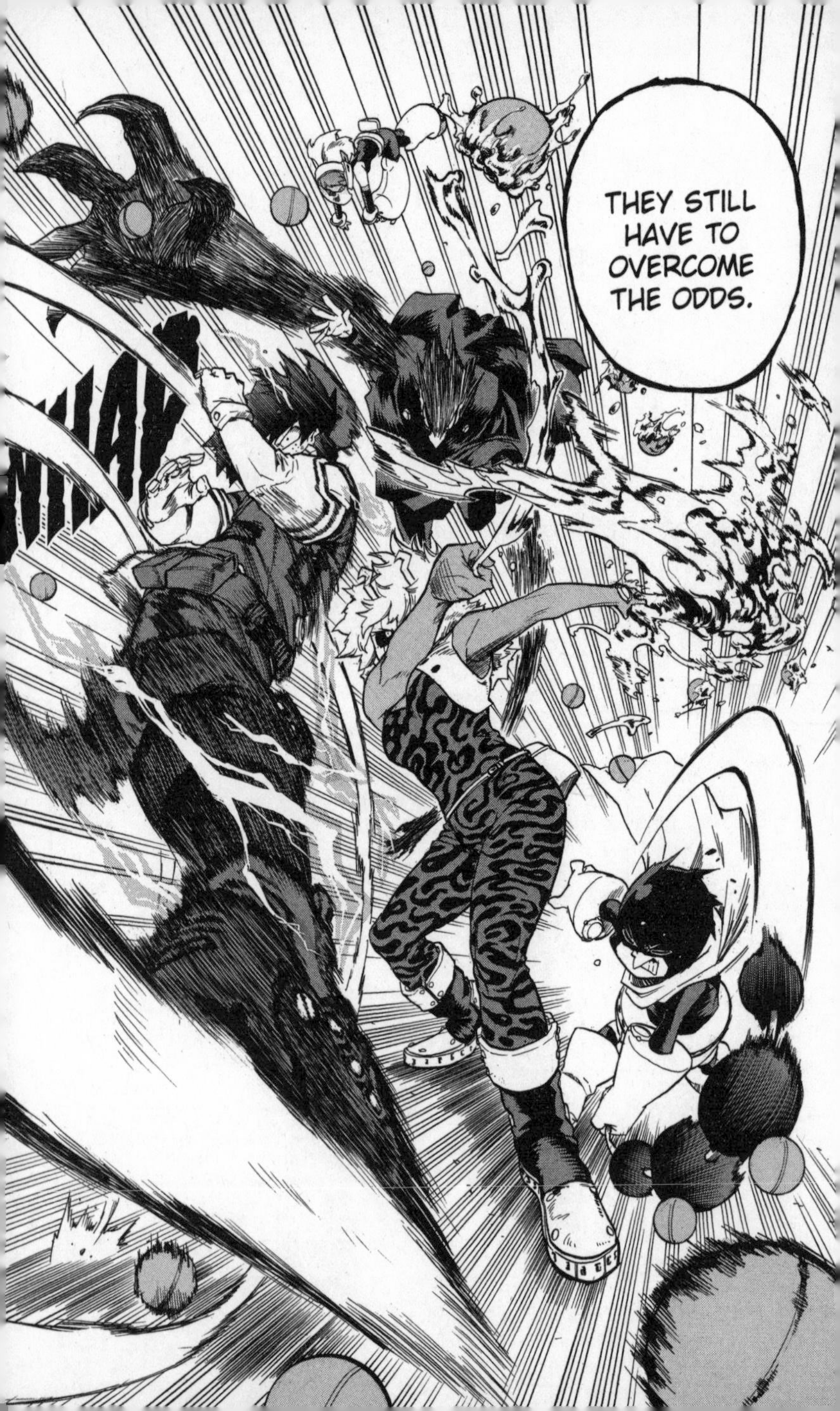
THEY STILL HAVE TO OVERCOME THE ODDS.

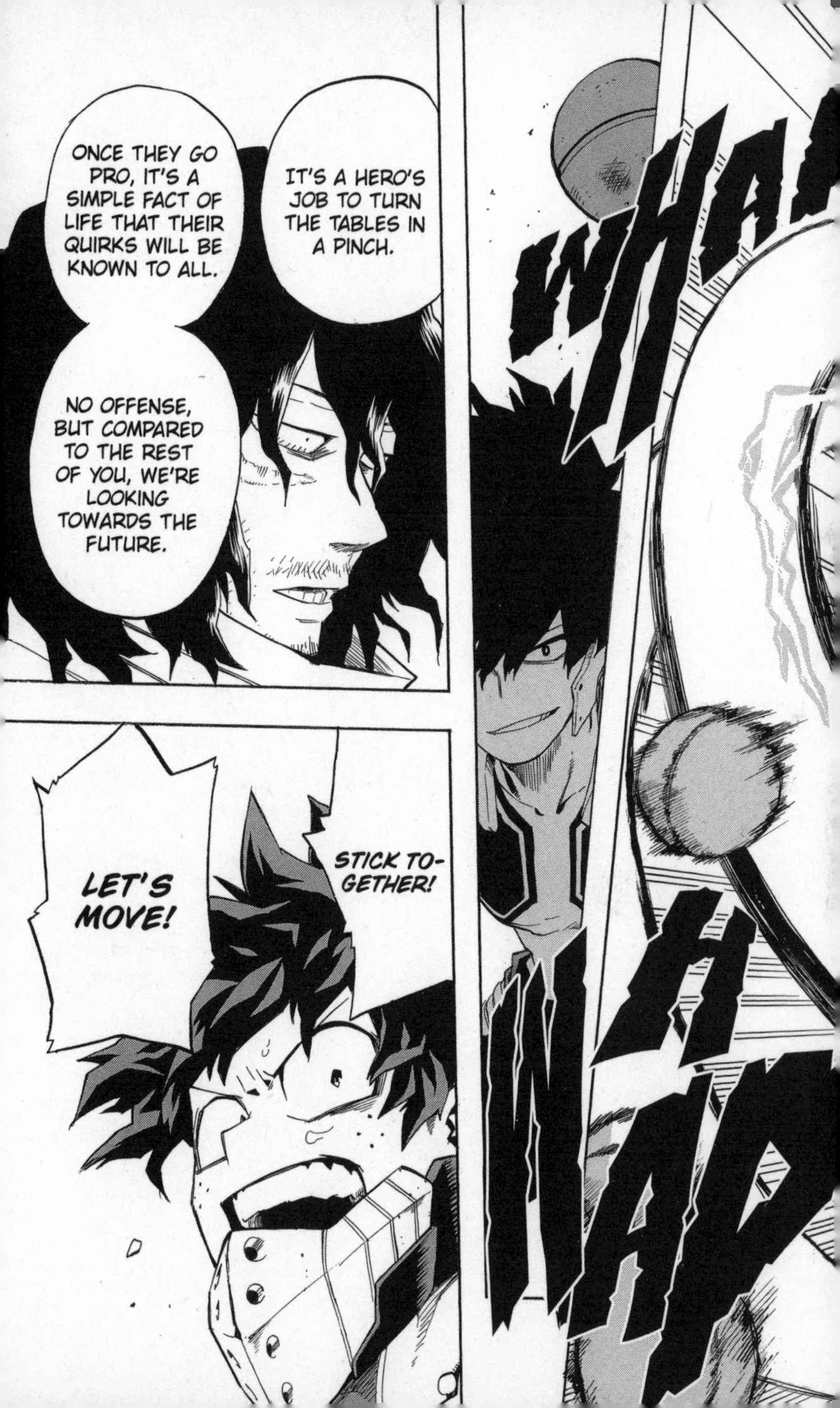
IT'S A HERO'S JOB TO TURN THE TABLES IN A PINCH.
ONCE THEY GO PRO, IT'S A SIMPLE FACT OF LIFE THAT THEIR QUIRKS WILL BE KNOWN TO ALL.
NO OFFENSE, BUT COMPARED TO THE REST OF YOU, WE'RE LOOKING TOWARDS THE FUTURE.
STICK TO-GETHER!
LET'S MOVE!

傑物学園

MS. JOKE (28)
(EMI FUKUKADO)

STREET CLOTHES

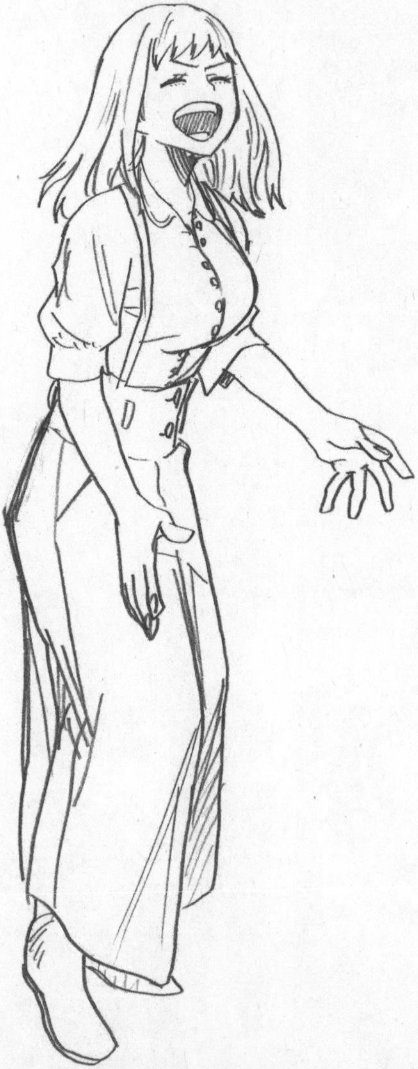

Birthday: 2/5
Height: 166 cm
Favorite Thing: Comedy

THE SUPPLEMENT

She's tried countless times to get a laugh out of Aizawa, but every time he was one step ahead in erasing her Quirk, so she never succeeded.

There's nothing like a great smile, huh?

She actually came to watch the first-years at the sports festival. For those of you out there bored enough to count your own leg hairs, try finding her in the crowd shots back in volume 4.

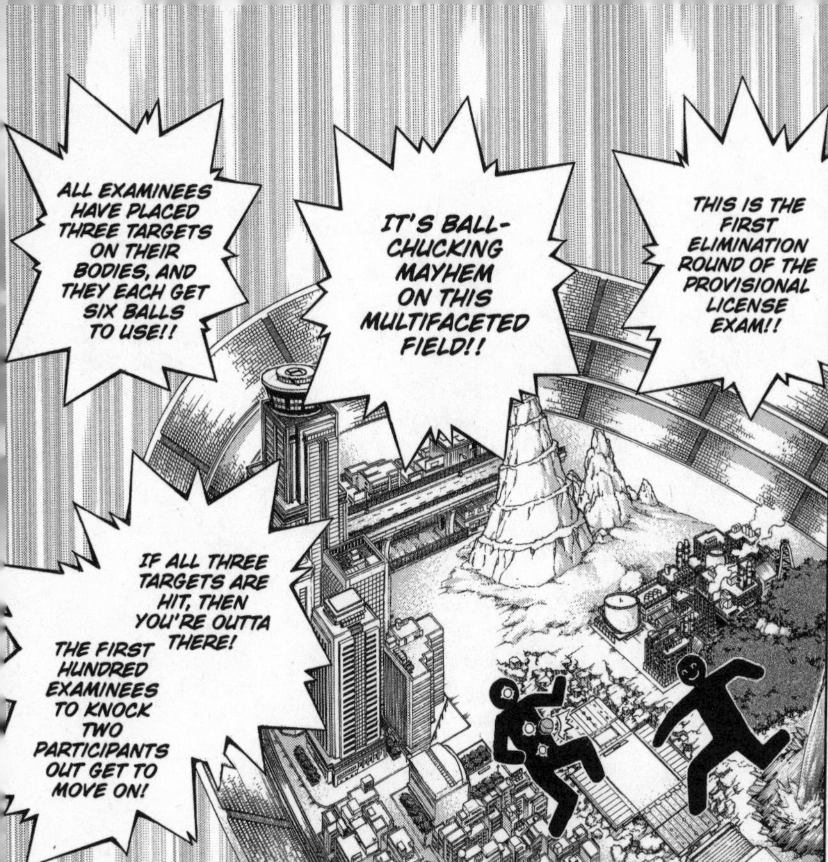
THIS IS THE FIRST ELIMINATION ROUND OF THE PROVISIONAL LICENSE EXAM!!
IT'S BALL-CHUCKING MAYHEM ON THIS MULTIFACETED FIELD!!
ALL EXAMINEES HAVE PLACED THREE TARGETS ON THEIR BODIES, AND THEY EACH GET SIX BALLS TO USE!!
IF ALL THREE TARGETS ARE HIT, THEN YOU'RE OUTTA THERE!
THE FIRST HUNDRED EXAMINEES TO KNOCK TWO PARTICIPANTS OUT GET TO MOVE ON!

No. 104 - White-Hot Battle! To Each Their Own Strengths!

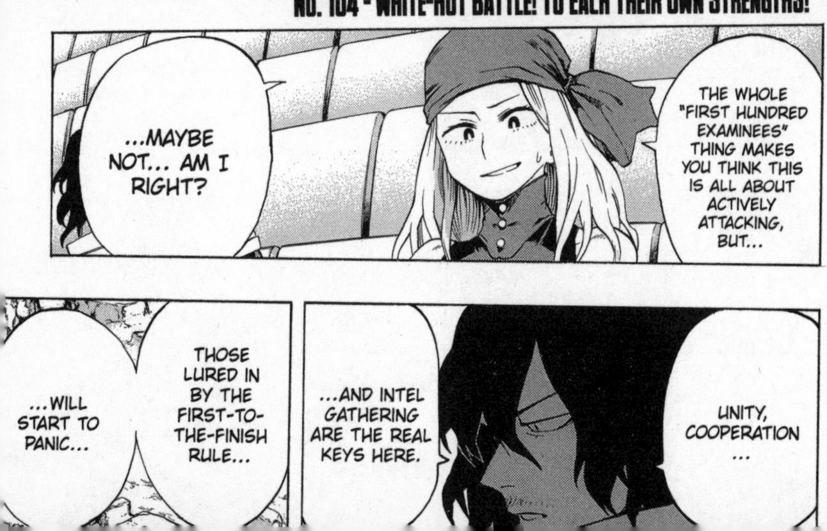
THE WHOLE "FIRST HUNDRED EXAMINEES" THING MAKES YOU THINK THIS IS ALL ABOUT ACTIVELY ATTACKING, BUT...
...MAYBE NOT... AM I RIGHT?
UNITY, COOPERATION ...
...AND INTEL GATHERING ARE THE REAL KEYS HERE.
THOSE LURED IN BY THE FIRST-TO-THE-FINISH RULE...
...WILL START TO PANIC...

No. 104 - White-Hot Battle! To Each Their Own Strengths!

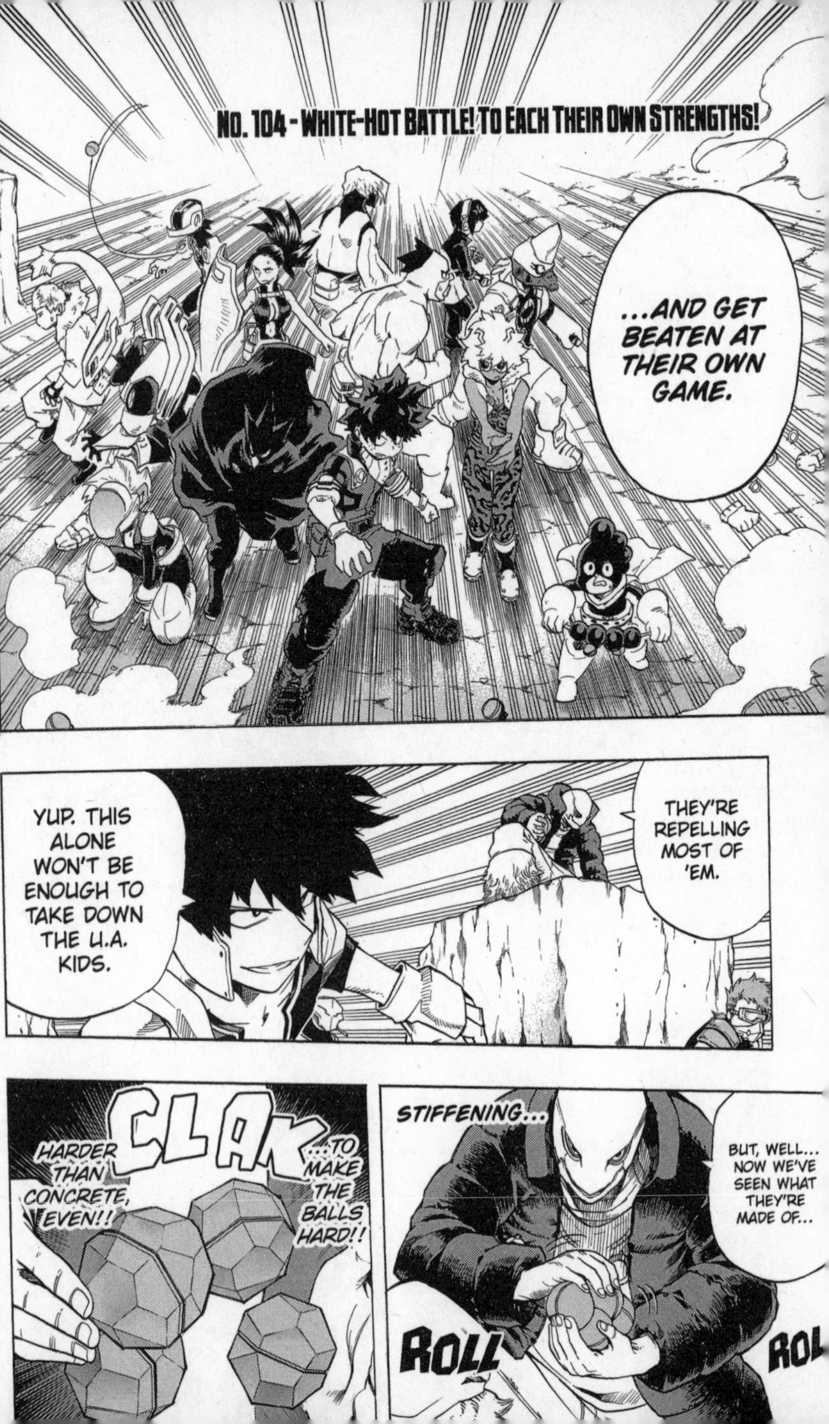
...AND GET BEATEN AT THEIR OWN GAME.
THEY'RE REPELLING MOST OF 'EM.
YUP. THIS ALONE WON'T BE ENOUGH TO TAKE DOWN THE U.A. KIDS.
BUT, WELL... NOW WE'VE SEEN WHAT THEY'RE MADE OF...
STIFFENING...
ROL
ROLL
CLAK
...TO MAKE THE BALLS HARD!!
HARDER THAN CONCRETE, EVEN!!

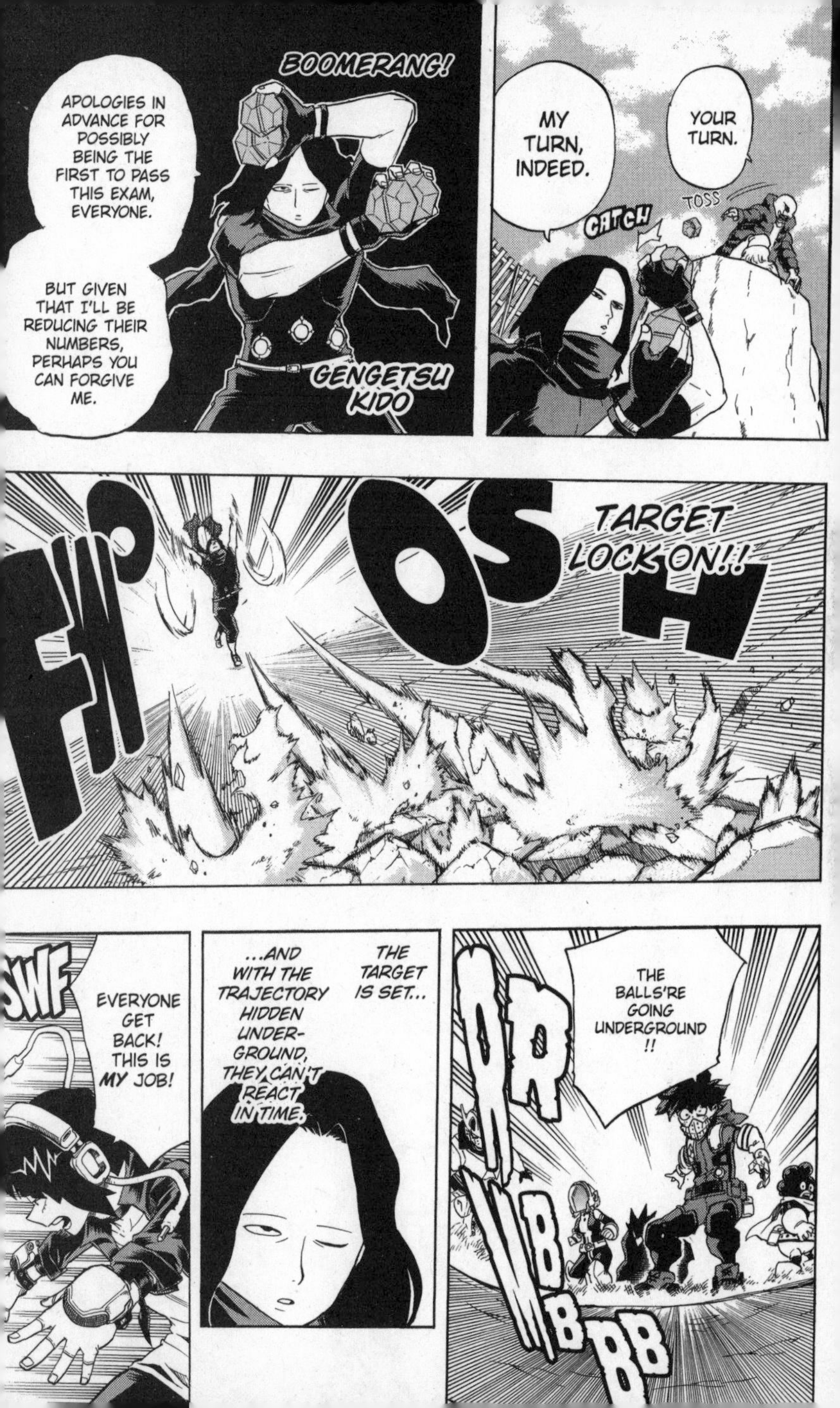
YOUR TURN.
TOSS
MY TURN, INDEED.
CATCH
BOOMERANG!
APOLOGIES IN ADVANCE FOR POSSIBLY BEING THE FIRST TO PASS THIS EXAM, EVERYONE.
BUT GIVEN THAT I'LL BE REDUCING THEIR NUMBERS, PERHAPS YOU CAN FORGIVE ME.
GENGETSU KIDO
TARGET LOCK ON!!
FWOOSH
THE BALLS'RE GOING UNDERGROUND!!
THE TARGET IS SET...
...AND WITH THE TRAJECTORY HIDDEN UNDERGROUND, THEY CAN'T REACT IN TIME.
SWF
EVERYONE GET BACK! THIS IS *MY* JOB!

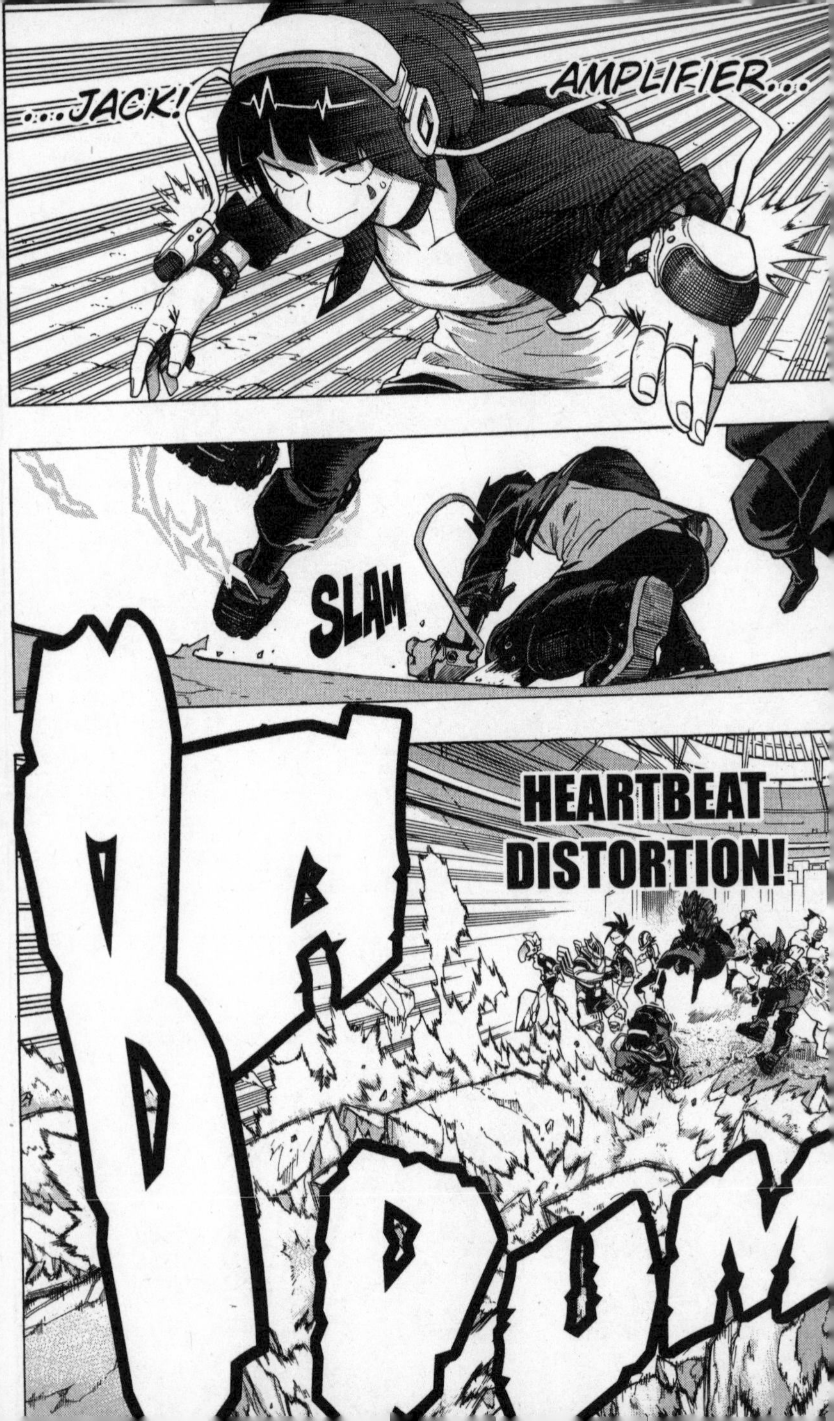
AMPLIFIER...
...JACK!
SLAM
HEARTBEAT DISTORTION!

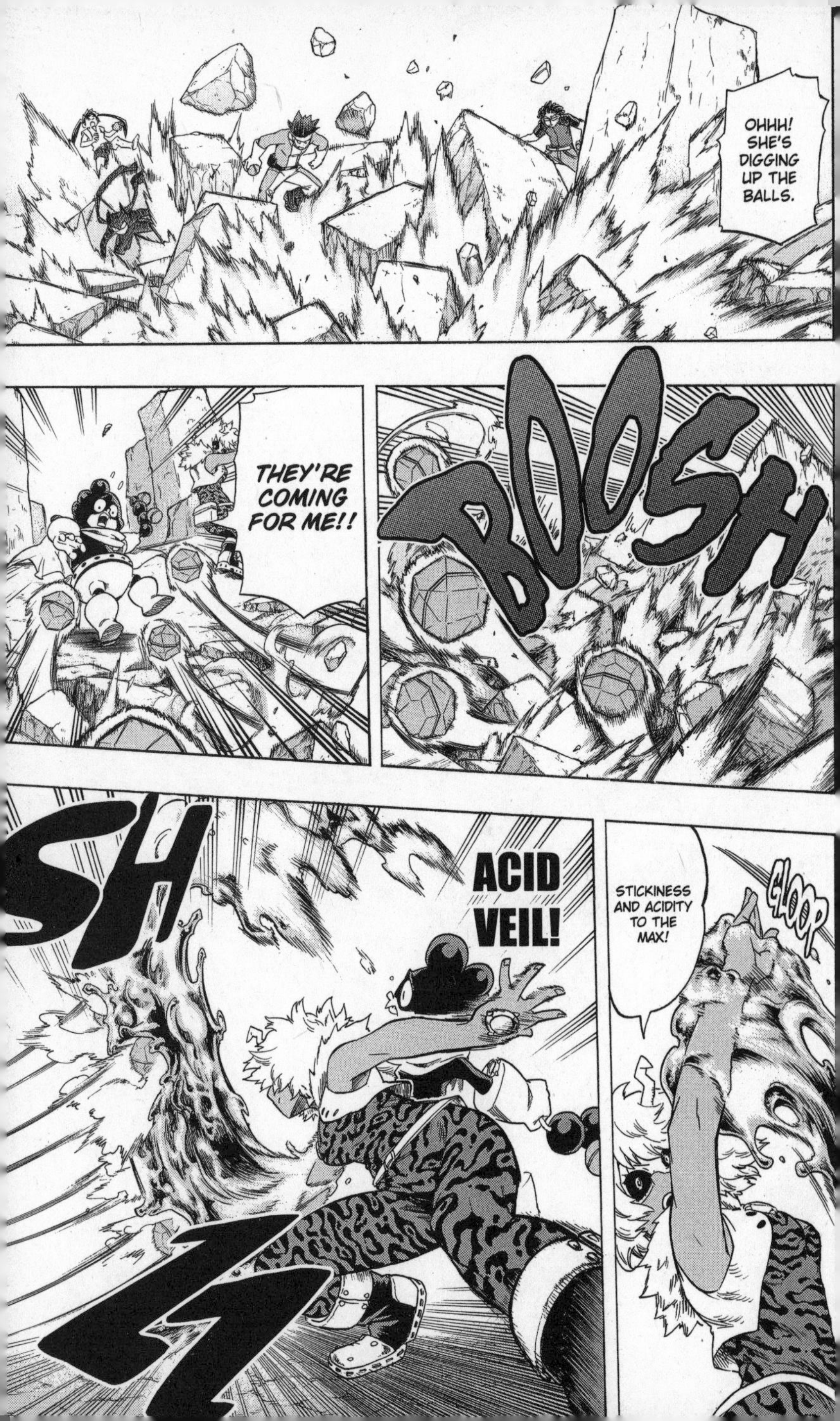
OHHH! SHE'S DIGGING UP THE BALLS.
BOOSH
THEY'RE COMING FOR ME!!
STICKINESS AND ACIDITY TO THE MAX!
GLOOP
ACID VEIL!

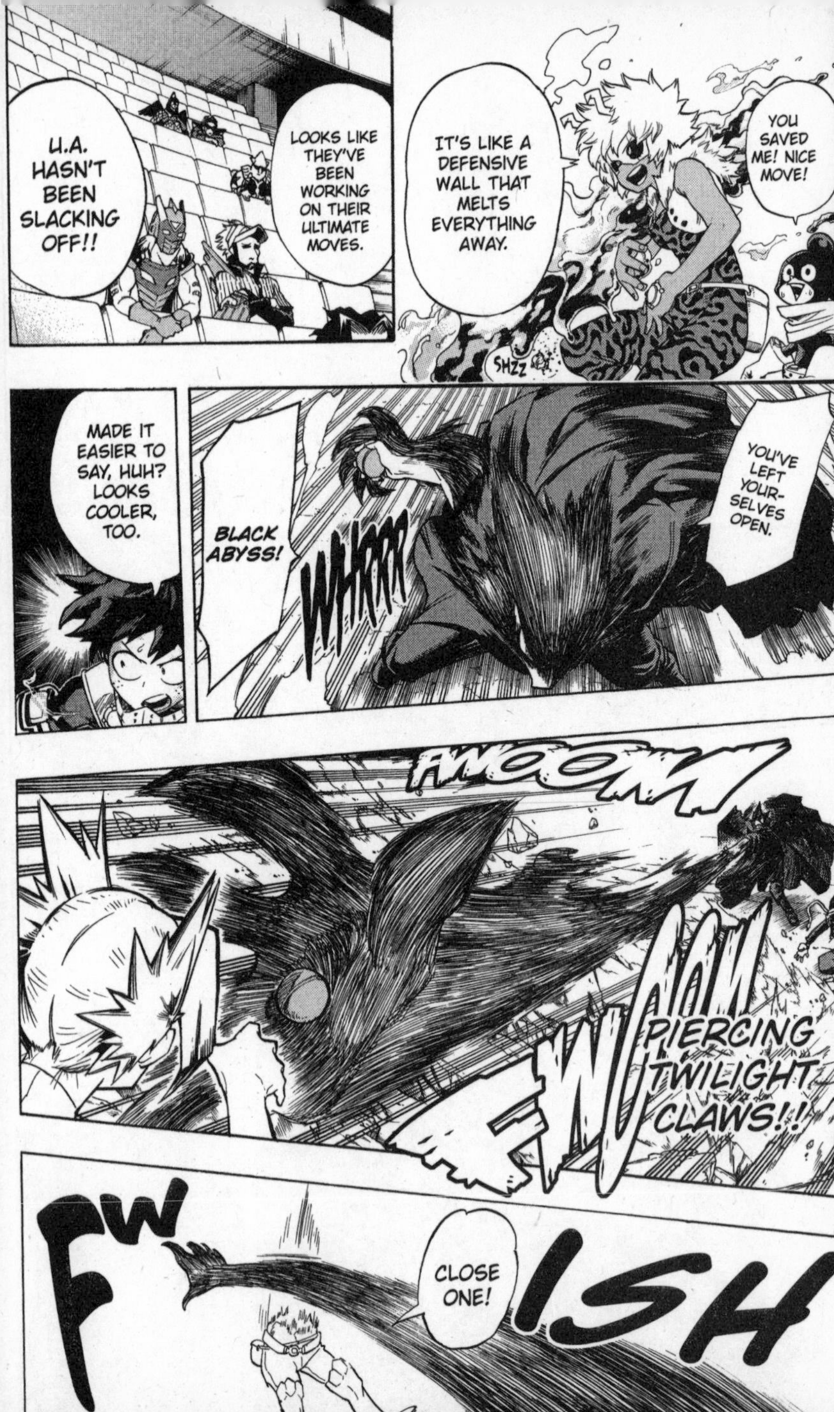
YOU SAVED ME! NICE MOVE!
IT'S LIKE A DEFENSIVE WALL THAT MELTS EVERYTHING AWAY.
SHZZ
LOOKS LIKE THEY'VE BEEN WORKING ON THEIR ULTIMATE MOVES.
U.A. HASN'T BEEN SLACKING OFF!!
YOU'VE LEFT YOURSELVES OPEN.
BLACK ABYSS!
WHRRR
MADE IT EASIER TO SAY, HUH? LOOKS COOLER, TOO.
FWOOM
PIERCING TWILIGHT CLAWS!!
CLOSE ONE!
FWISH

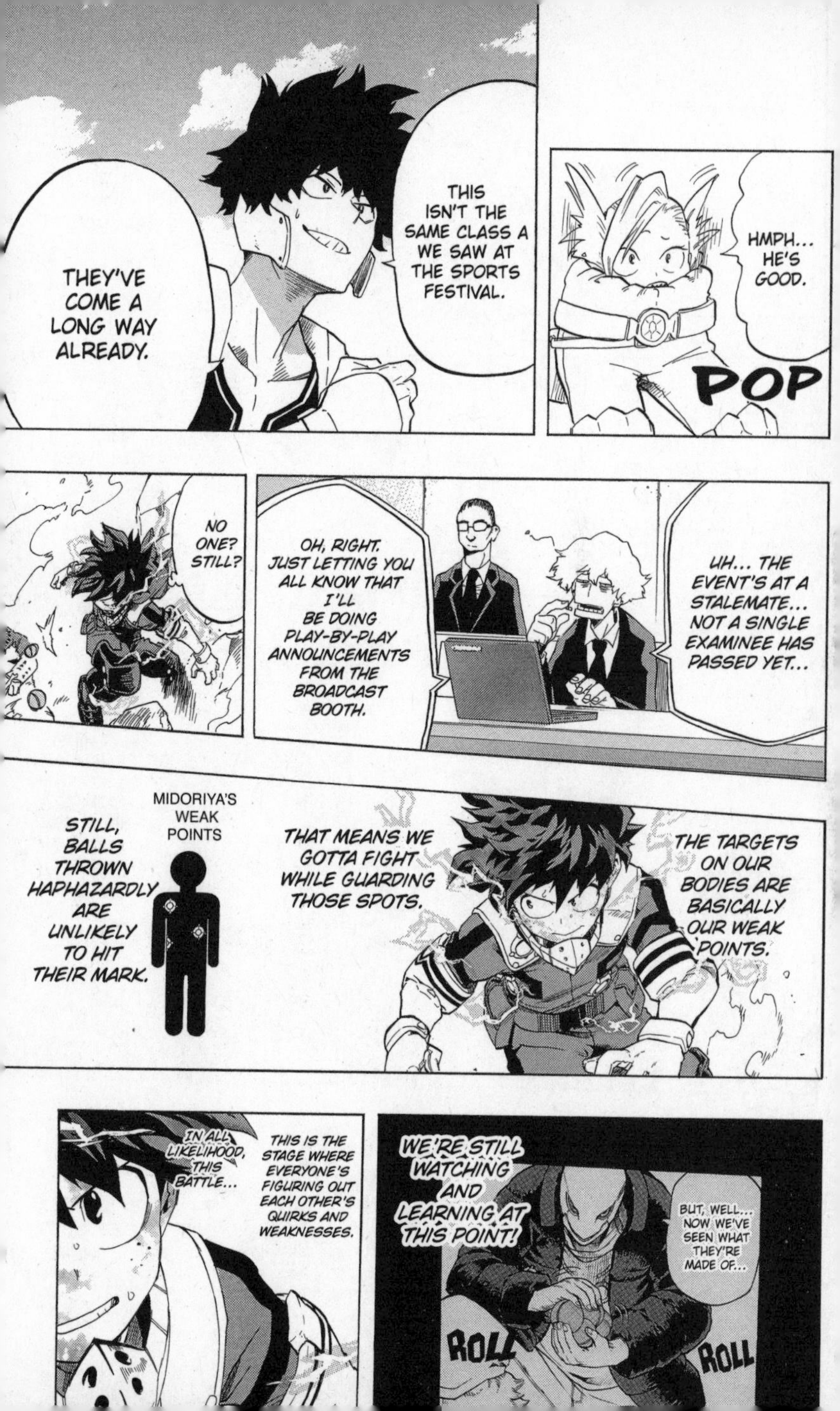

HMPH... HE'S GOOD.
POP
THIS ISN'T THE SAME CLASS A WE SAW AT THE SPORTS FESTIVAL.
THEY'VE COME A LONG WAY ALREADY.
UH... THE EVENT'S AT A STALEMATE... NOT A SINGLE EXAMINEE HAS PASSED YET...
OH, RIGHT. JUST LETTING YOU ALL KNOW THAT I'LL BE DOING PLAY-BY-PLAY ANNOUNCEMENTS FROM THE BROADCAST BOOTH.
NO ONE? STILL?
THE TARGETS ON OUR BODIES ARE BASICALLY OUR WEAK POINTS.
THAT MEANS WE GOTTA FIGHT WHILE GUARDING THOSE SPOTS.
MIDORIYA'S WEAK POINTS
STILL, BALLS THROWN HAPHAZARDLY ARE UNLIKELY TO HIT THEIR MARK.
BUT, WELL... NOW WE'VE SEEN WHAT THEY'RE MADE OF...
WE'RE STILL WATCHING AND LEARNING AT THIS POINT!
ROLL
ROLL
THIS IS THE STAGE WHERE EVERYONE'S FIGURING OUT EACH OTHER'S QUIRKS AND WEAKNESSES.
IN ALL LIKELIHOOD, THIS BATTLE...

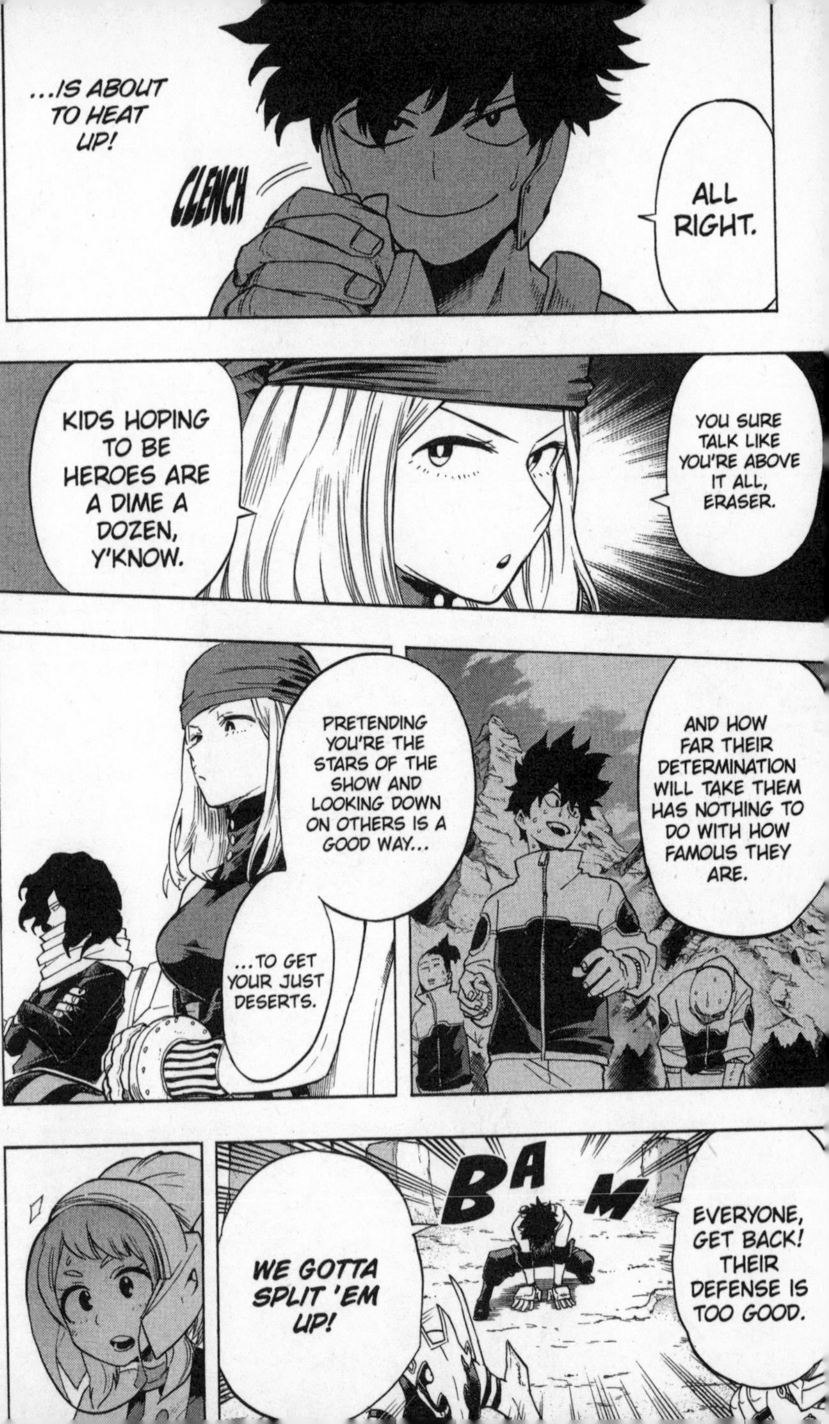
ALL RIGHT.
...IS ABOUT TO HEAT UP!
CLENCH
YOU SURE TALK LIKE YOU'RE ABOVE IT ALL, ERASER.
KIDS HOPING TO BE HEROES ARE A DIME A DOZEN, Y'KNOW.
AND HOW FAR THEIR DETERMINATION WILL TAKE THEM HAS NOTHING TO DO WITH HOW FAMOUS THEY ARE.
PRETENDING YOU'RE THE STARS OF THE SHOW AND LOOKING DOWN ON OTHERS IS A GOOD WAY...
...TO GET YOUR JUST DESERTS.
EVERYONE, GET BACK! THEIR DEFENSE IS TOO GOOD.
BAM
WE GOTTA SPLIT 'EM UP!

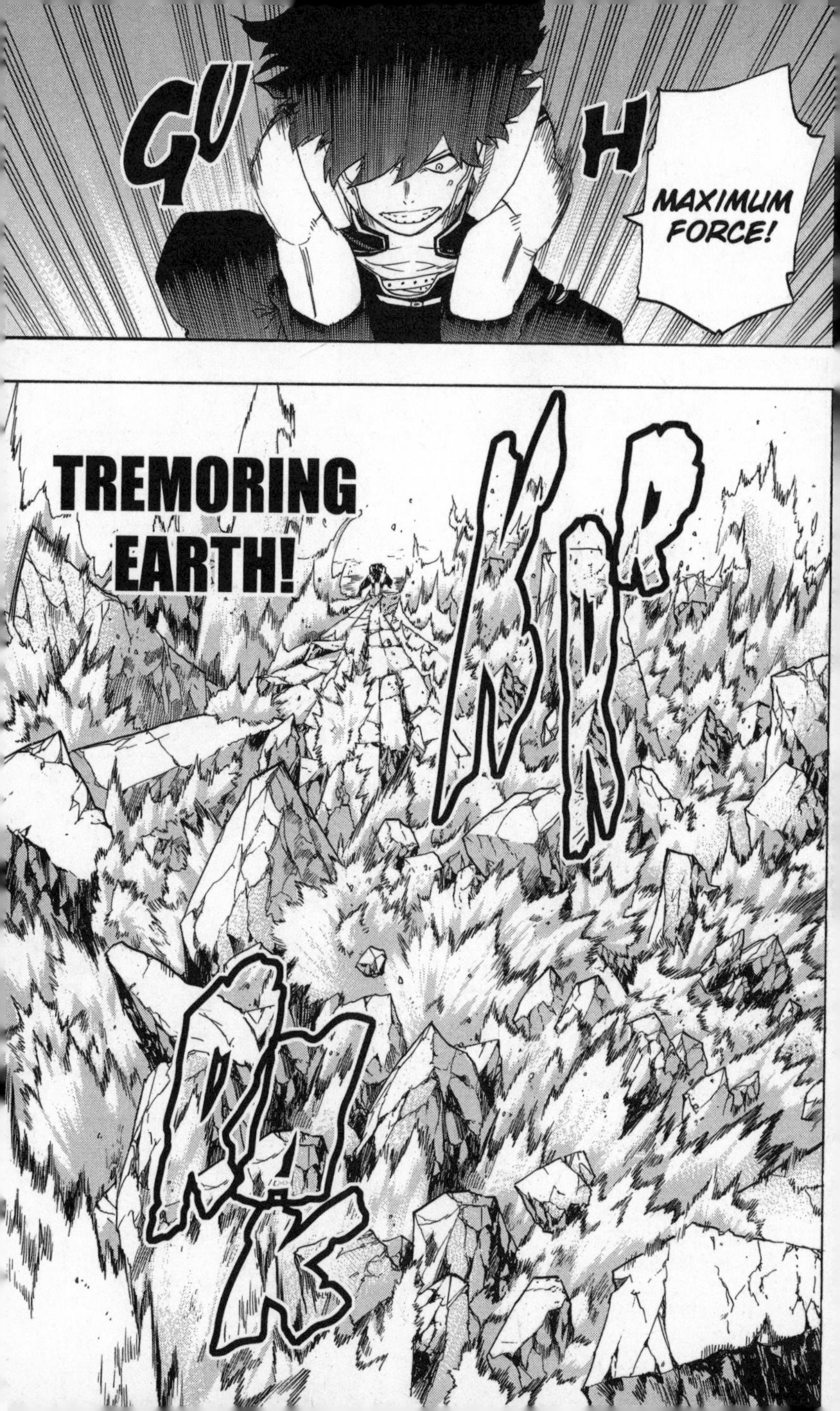
MAXIMUM FORCE!
GUH
TREMORING EARTH!

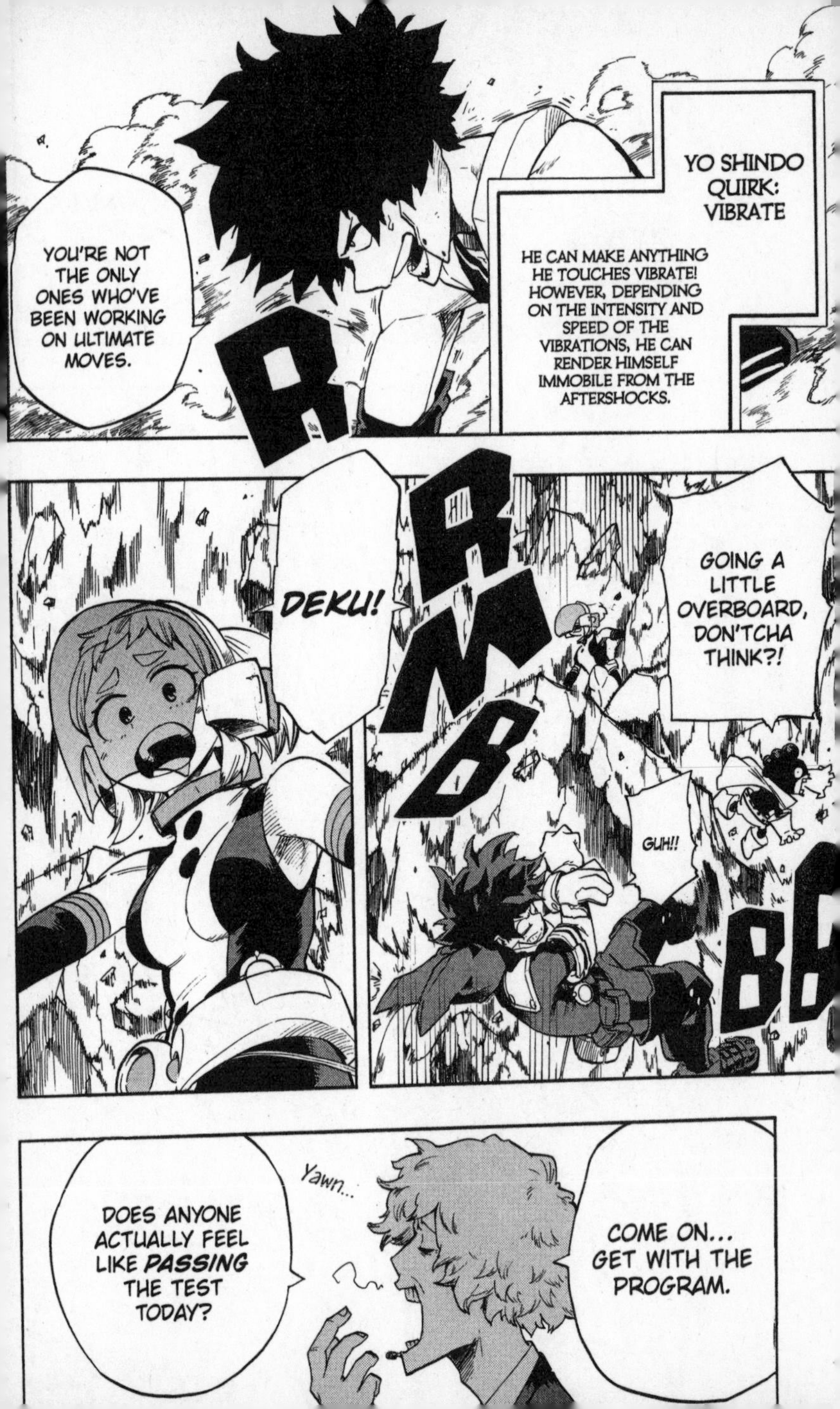

YO SHINDO QUIRK: VIBRATE
HE CAN MAKE ANYTHING HE TOUCHES VIBRATE! HOWEVER, DEPENDING ON THE INTENSITY AND SPEED OF THE VIBRATIONS, HE CAN RENDER HIMSELF IMMOBILE FROM THE AFTERSHOCKS.
YOU'RE NOT THE ONLY ONES WHO'VE BEEN WORKING ON ULTIMATE MOVES.
R
GOING A LITTLE OVERBOARD, DON'TCHA THINK?!
RMB
GUH!!
BB
DEKU!
COME ON... GET WITH THE PROGRAM.
Yawn...
DOES ANYONE ACTUALLY FEEL LIKE *PASSING* THE TEST TODAY?

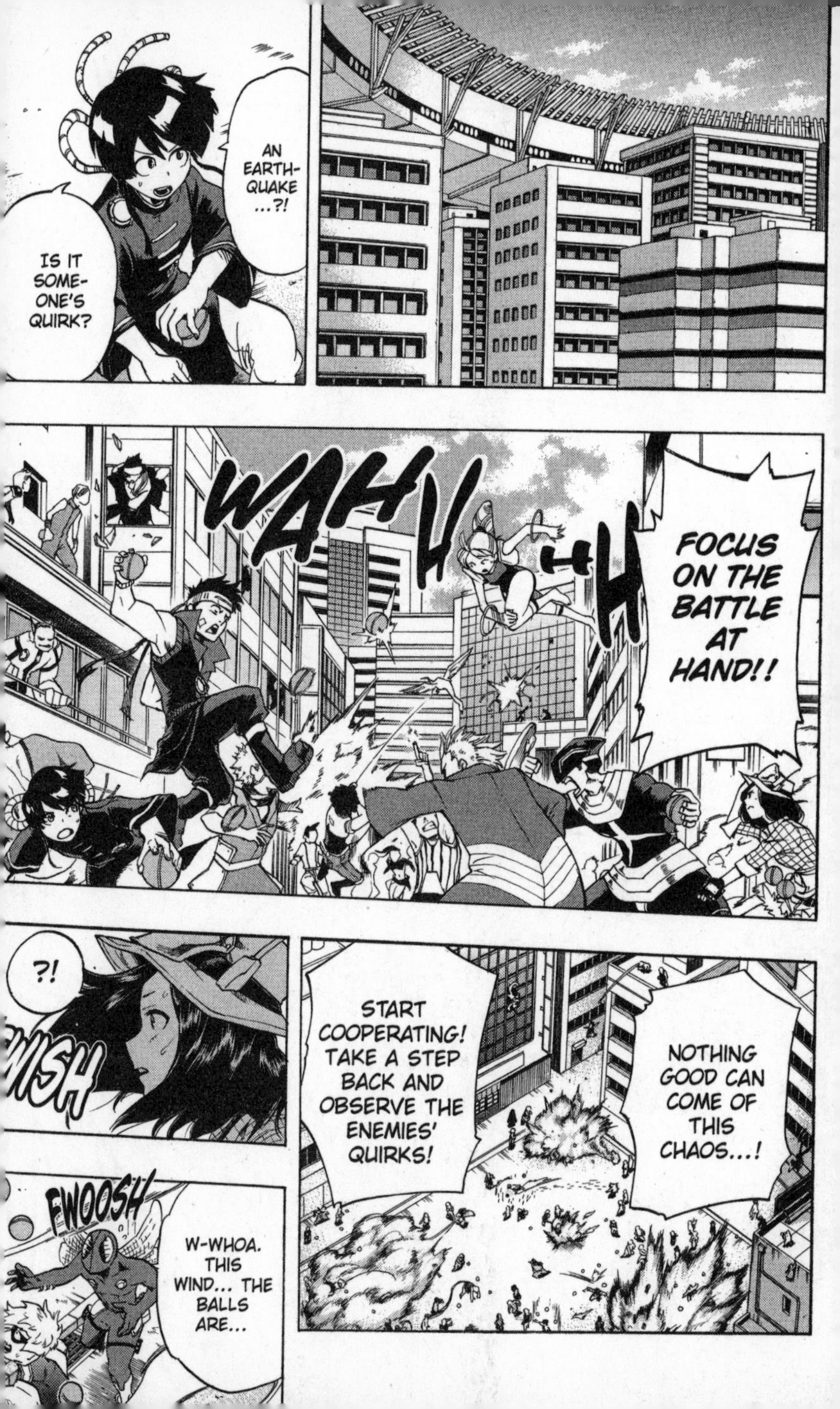

AN EARTH-QUAKE ...?!
IS IT SOME-ONE'S QUIRK?
WAHHHH
FOCUS ON THE BATTLE AT HAND!!
NOTHING GOOD CAN COME OF THIS CHAOS...!
START COOPERATING! TAKE A STEP BACK AND OBSERVE THE ENEMIES' QUIRKS!
?!
WISH
FWOOSH
W-WHOA. THIS WIND... THE BALLS ARE...

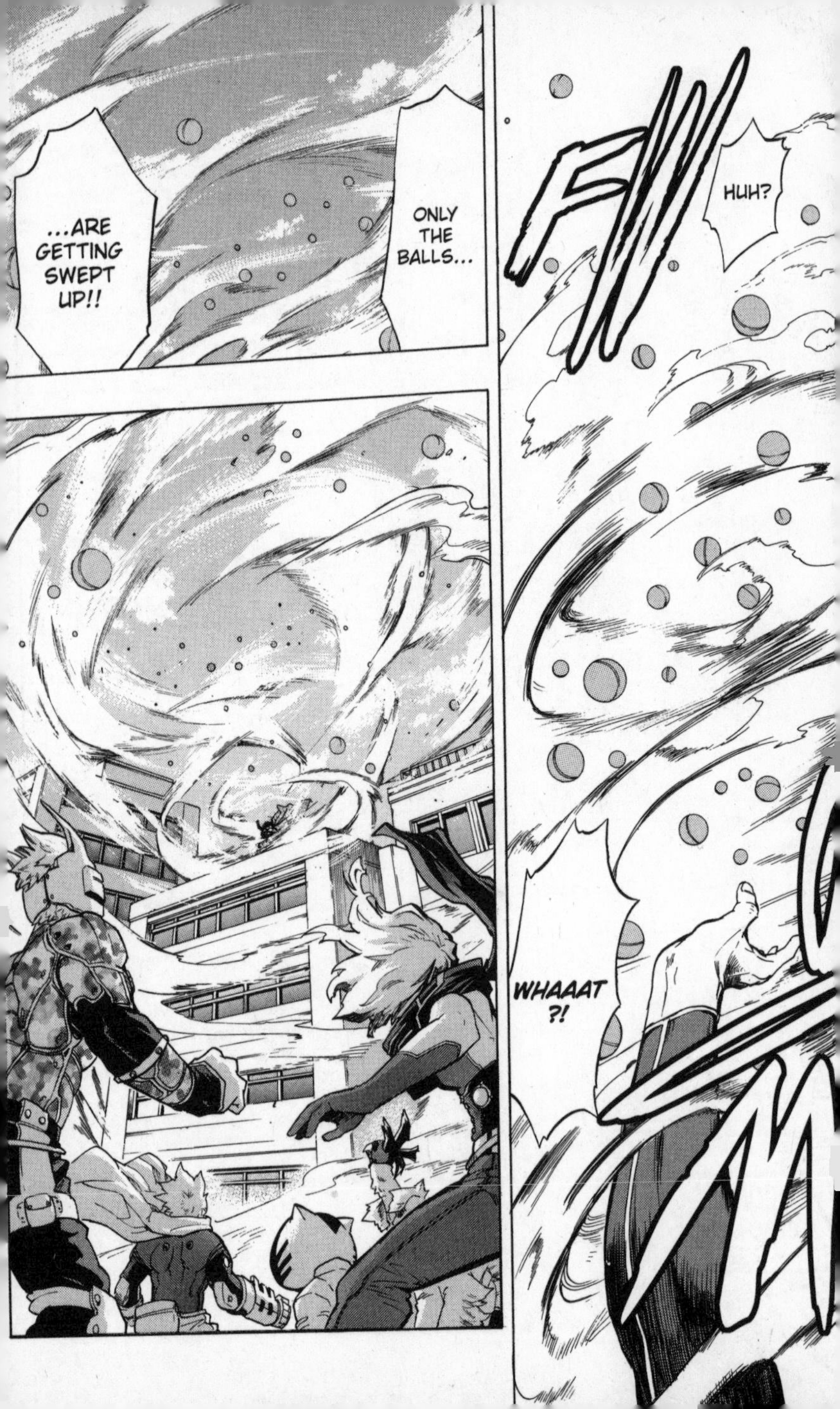
HUH?
WHAAAT?!
ONLY THE BALLS...
...ARE GETTING SWEPT UP!!

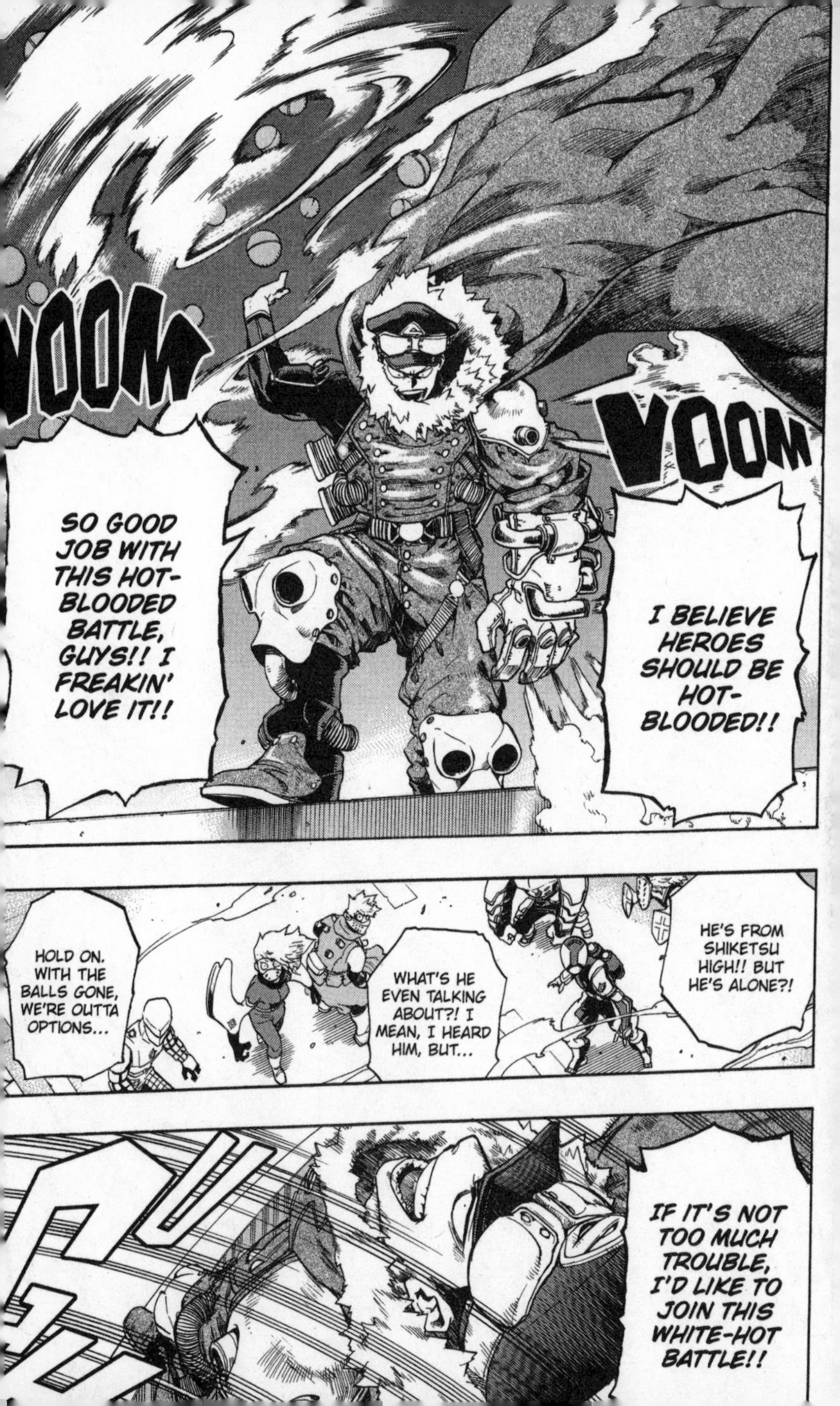
VOOM
VOOM
I BELIEVE HEROES SHOULD BE HOT-BLOODED!!
SO GOOD JOB WITH THIS HOT-BLOODED BATTLE, GUYS!! I FREAKIN' LOVE IT!!
HE'S FROM SHIKETSU HIGH!! BUT HE'S ALONE?!
WHAT'S HE EVEN TALKING ABOUT?! I MEAN, I HEARD HIM, BUT...
HOLD ON. WITH THE BALLS GONE, WE'RE OUTTA OPTIONS...
IF IT'S NOT TOO MUCH TROUBLE, I'D LIKE TO JOIN THIS WHITE-HOT BATTLE!!

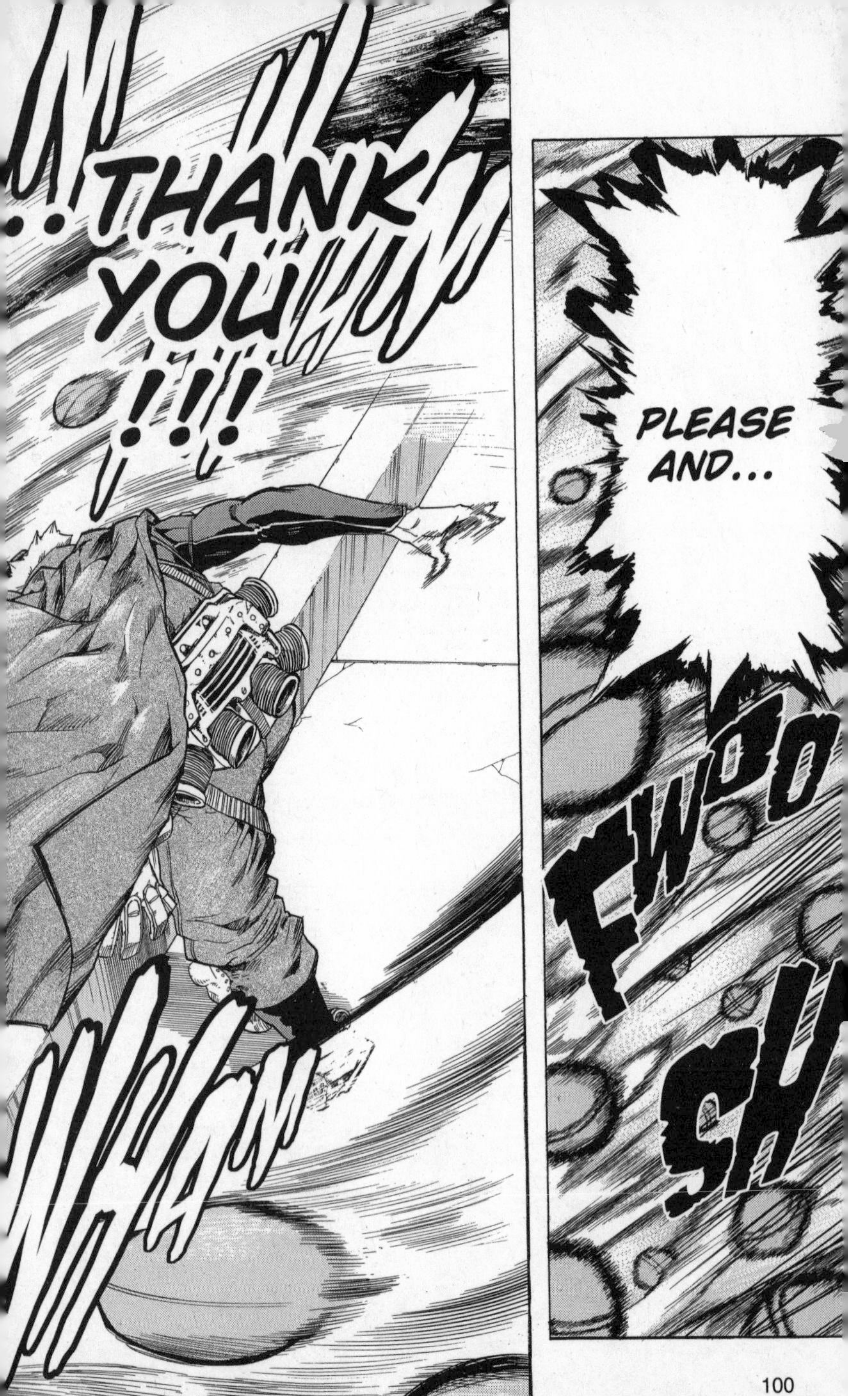
PLEASE AND...
FWOO
SH
..!! THANK YOU!!!!

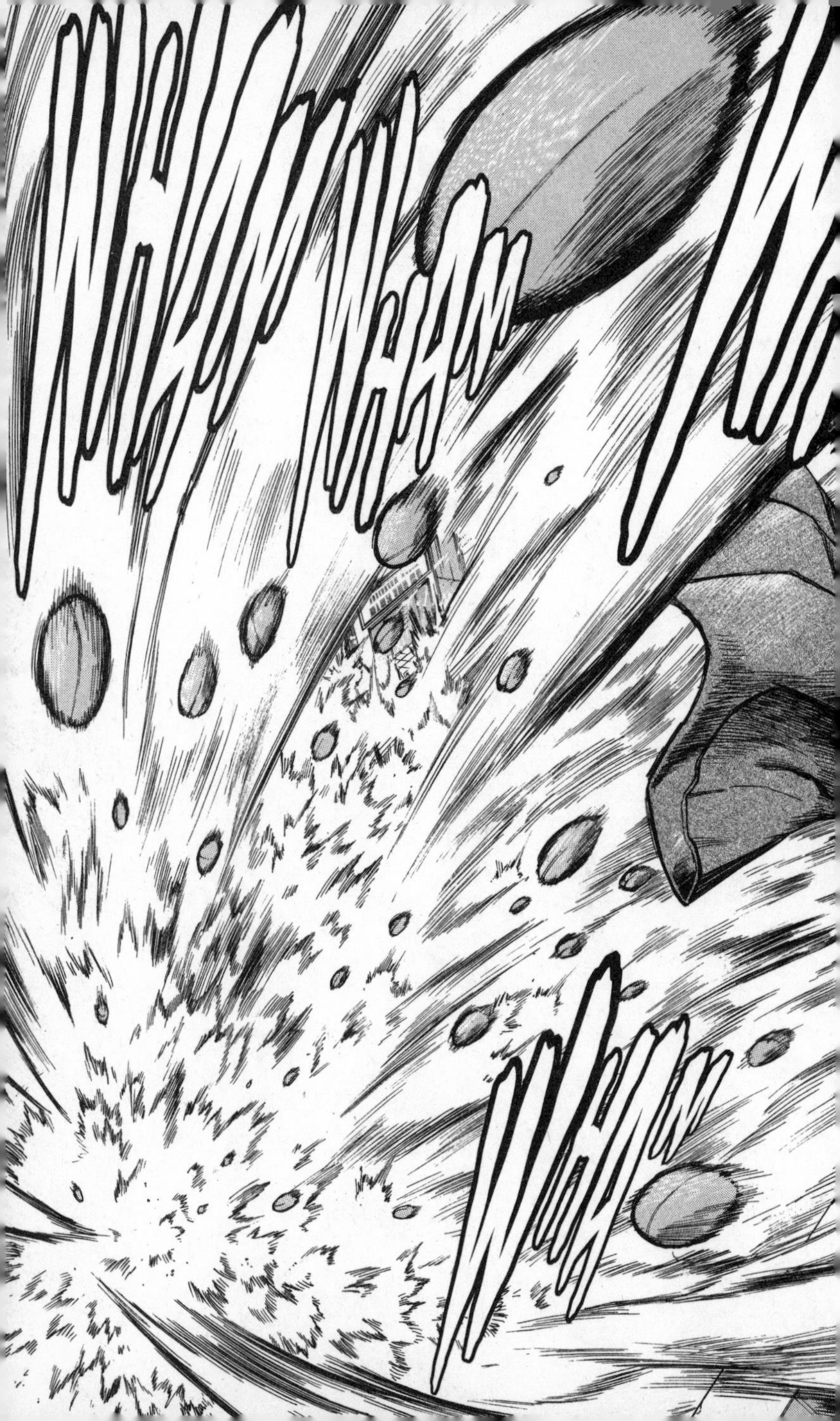

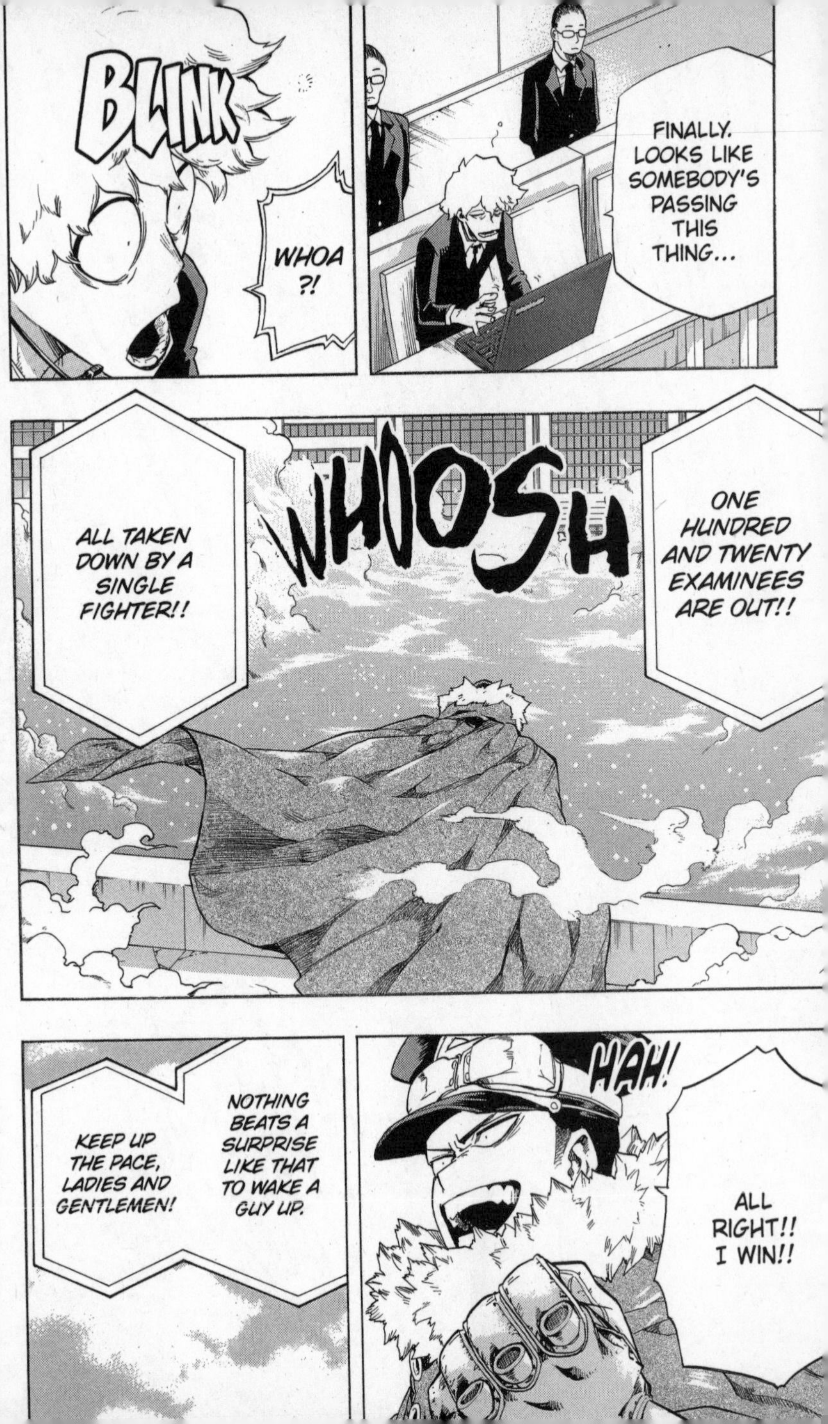
FINALLY. LOOKS LIKE SOMEBODY'S PASSING THIS THING...
BLINK
WHOA ?!
ONE HUNDRED AND TWENTY EXAMINEES ARE OUT!!
WHOOSH
ALL TAKEN DOWN BY A SINGLE FIGHTER!!
HAH!
ALL RIGHT!! I WIN!!
NOTHING BEATS A SURPRISE LIKE THAT TO WAKE A GUY UP.
KEEP UP THE PACE, LADIES AND GENTLEMEN!

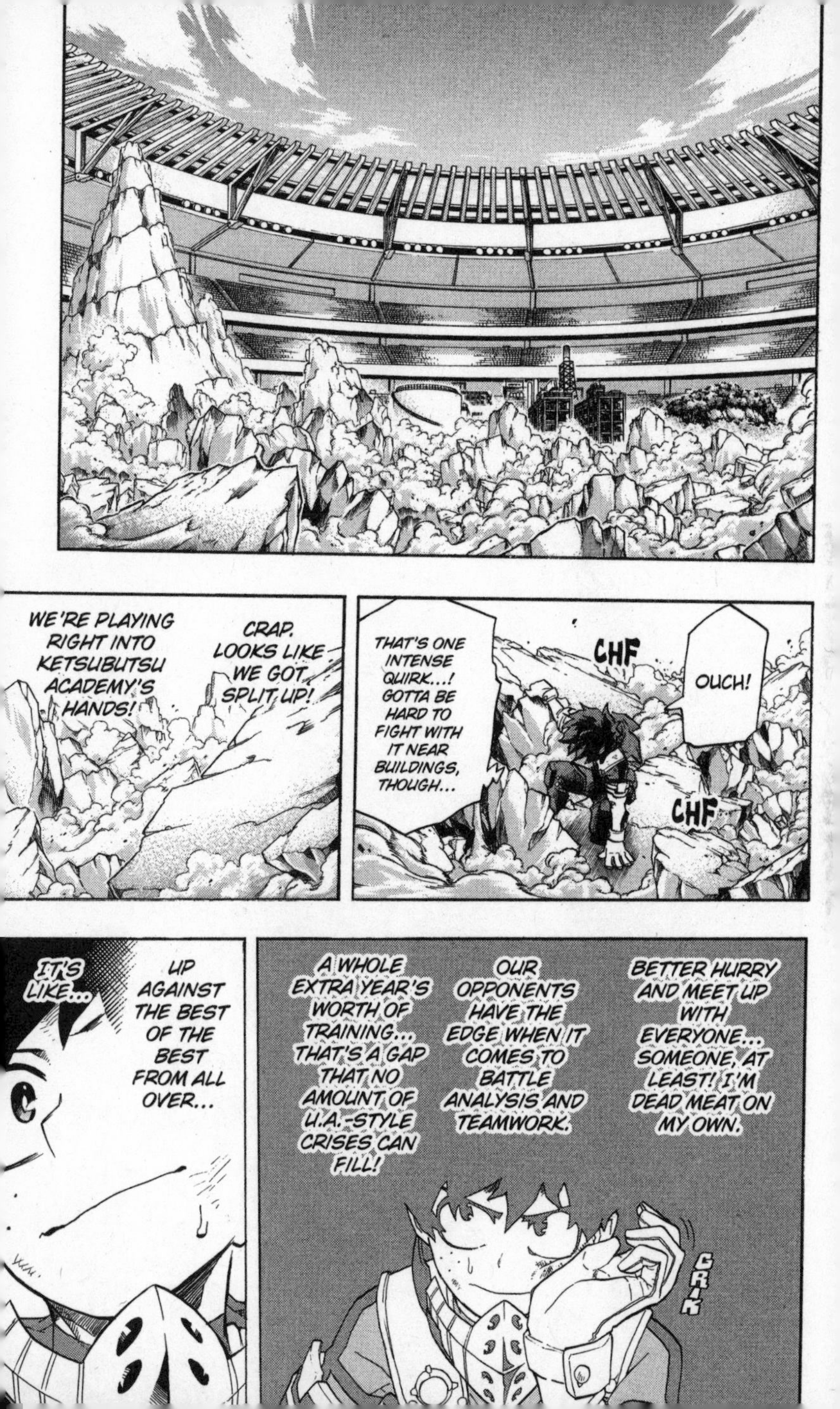
OUCH!
CHF
THAT'S ONE INTENSE QUIRK...! GOTTA BE HARD TO FIGHT WITH IT NEAR BUILDINGS, THOUGH...
CHF
CRAP. LOOKS LIKE WE GOT SPLIT UP!
WE'RE PLAYING RIGHT INTO KETSUBUTSU ACADEMY'S HANDS!
BETTER HURRY AND MEET UP WITH EVERYONE... SOMEONE, AT LEAST! I'M DEAD MEAT ON MY OWN.
OUR OPPONENTS HAVE THE EDGE WHEN IT COMES TO BATTLE ANALYSIS AND TEAMWORK.
A WHOLE EXTRA YEAR'S WORTH OF TRAINING... THAT'S A GAP THAT NO AMOUNT OF U.A.-STYLE CRISES CAN FILL!
CRIK
IT'S LIKE...
UP AGAINST THE BEST OF THE BEST FROM ALL OVER...

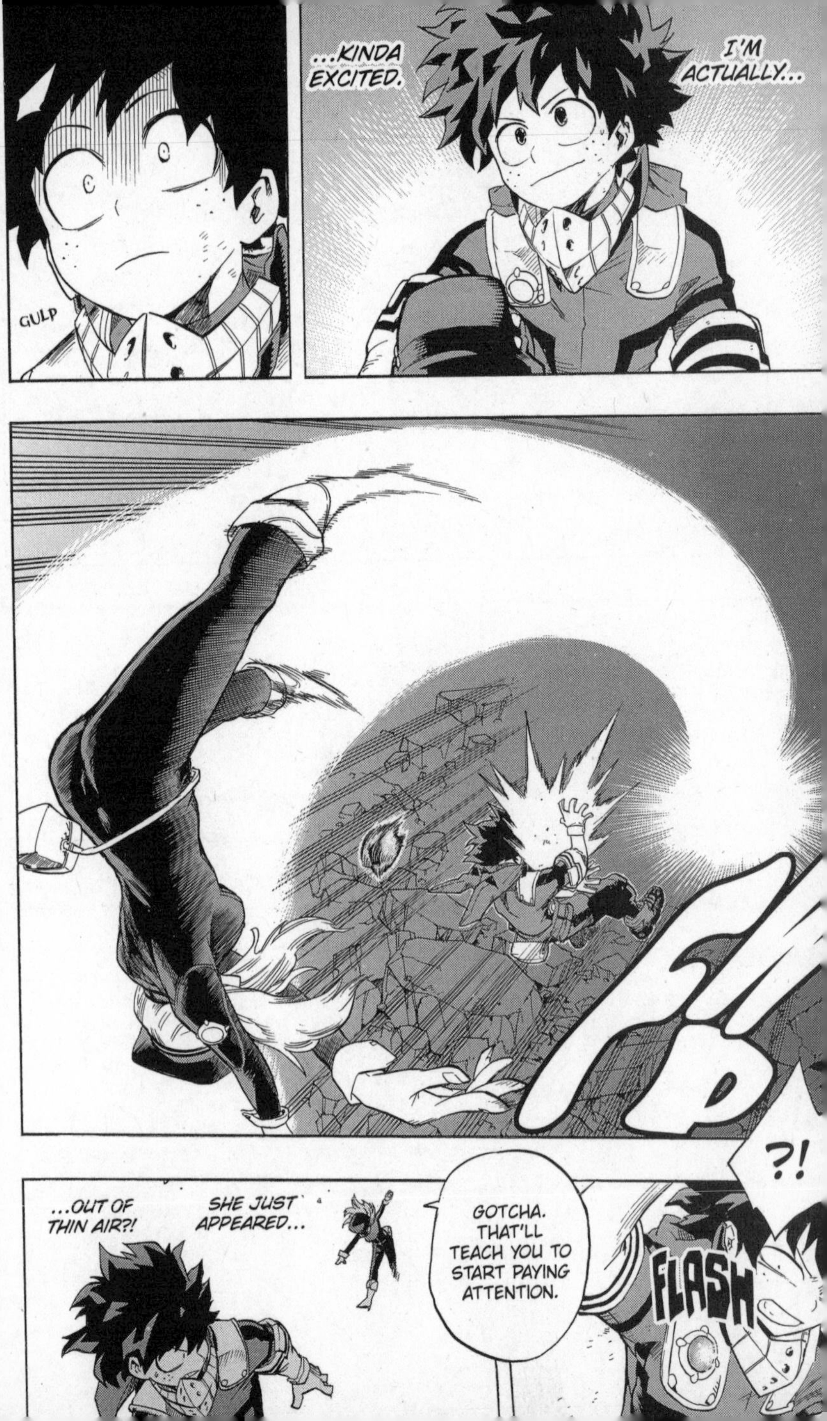

I'M ACTUALLY...
...KINDA EXCITED.
GULP
?!
FLASH
GOTCHA. THAT'LL TEACH YOU TO START PAYING ATTENTION.
SHE JUST APPEARED...
...OUT OF THIN AIR?!

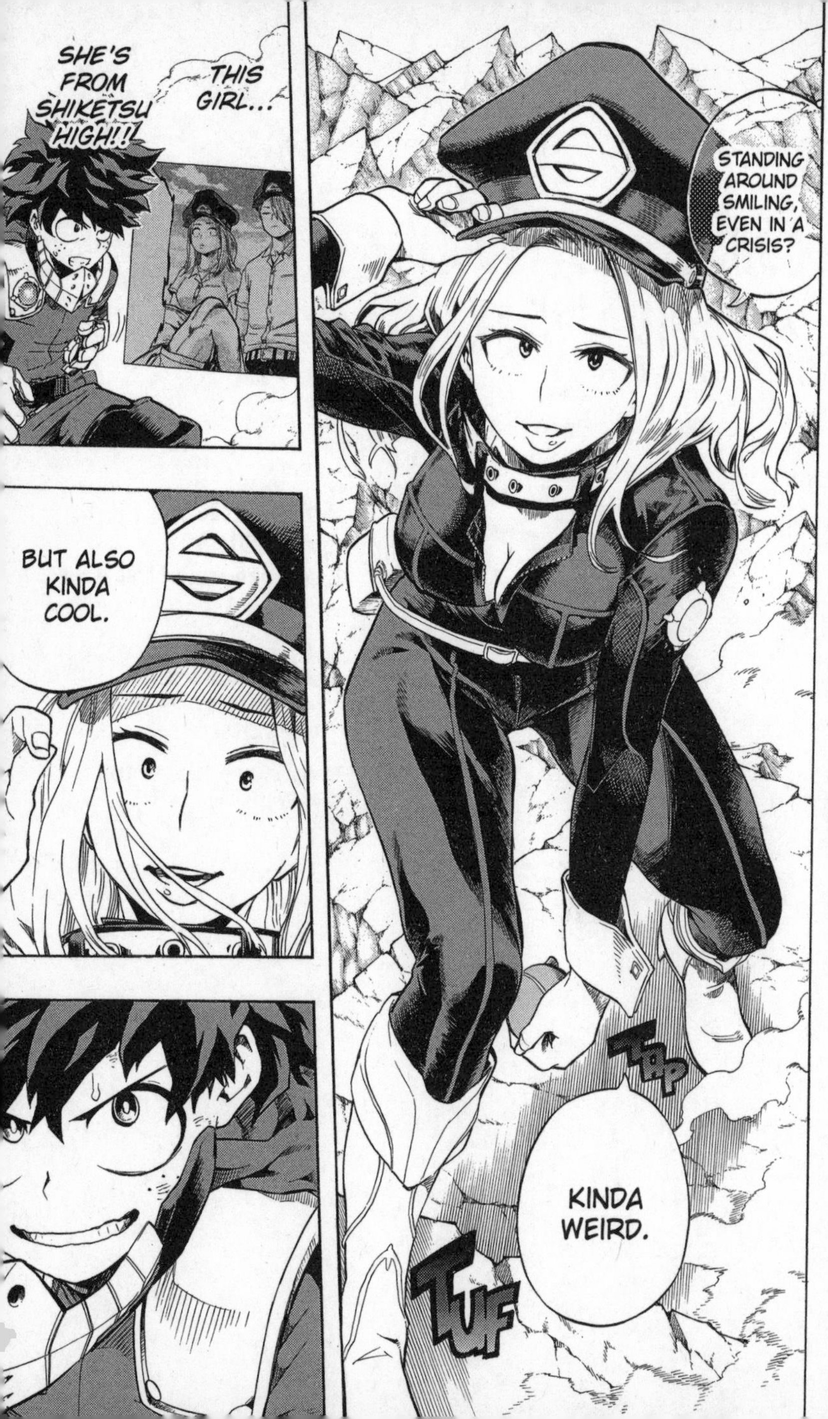
STANDING AROUND SMILING, EVEN IN A CRISIS?
TAP
KINDA WEIRD.
TUF
THIS GIRL...
SHE'S FROM SHIKETSU HIGH!!
BUT ALSO KINDA COOL.

SHORT SLEEVES EVEN IN WINTER

Birthday: 9/26
Height: 190 cm
Favorite Thing: Hot-bloodedness

THE SUPPLEMENT
The overall feel of his costume paints him as an amazing guy.

IT'S A PAIN IN THE *** TO DRAW!!!

No. 105 - Shiketsu High Lurking

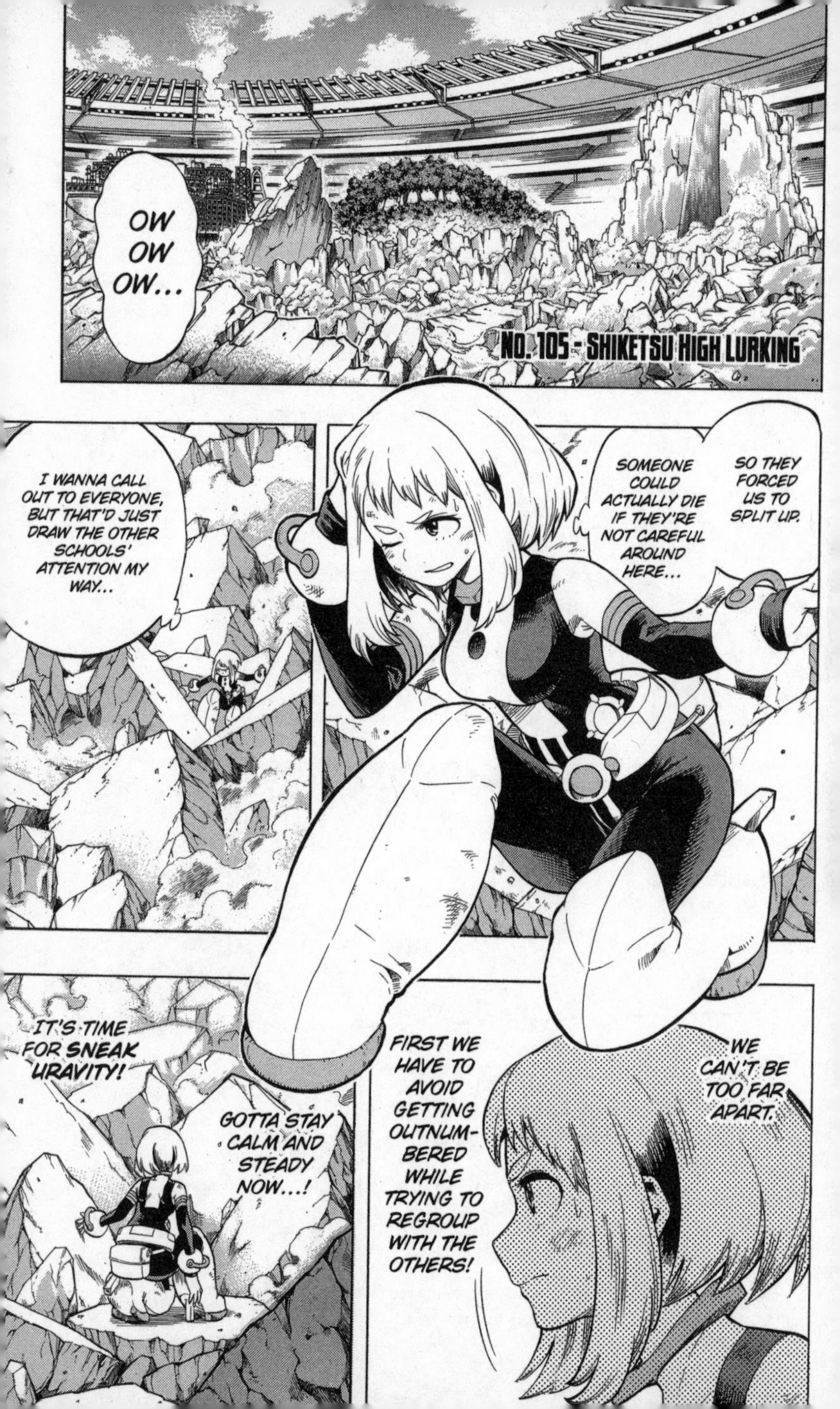
OW OW OW...
SO THEY FORCED US TO SPLIT UP.
SOMEONE COULD ACTUALLY DIE IF THEY'RE NOT CAREFUL AROUND HERE...
I WANNA CALL OUT TO EVERYONE, BUT THAT'D JUST DRAW THE OTHER SCHOOLS' ATTENTION MY WAY...
WE CAN'T BE TOO FAR APART.
FIRST WE HAVE TO AVOID GETTING OUTNUM-BERED WHILE TRYING TO REGROUP WITH THE OTHERS!
IT'S TIME FOR **SNEAK URAVITY!**
GOTTA STAY CALM AND STEADY NOW...!

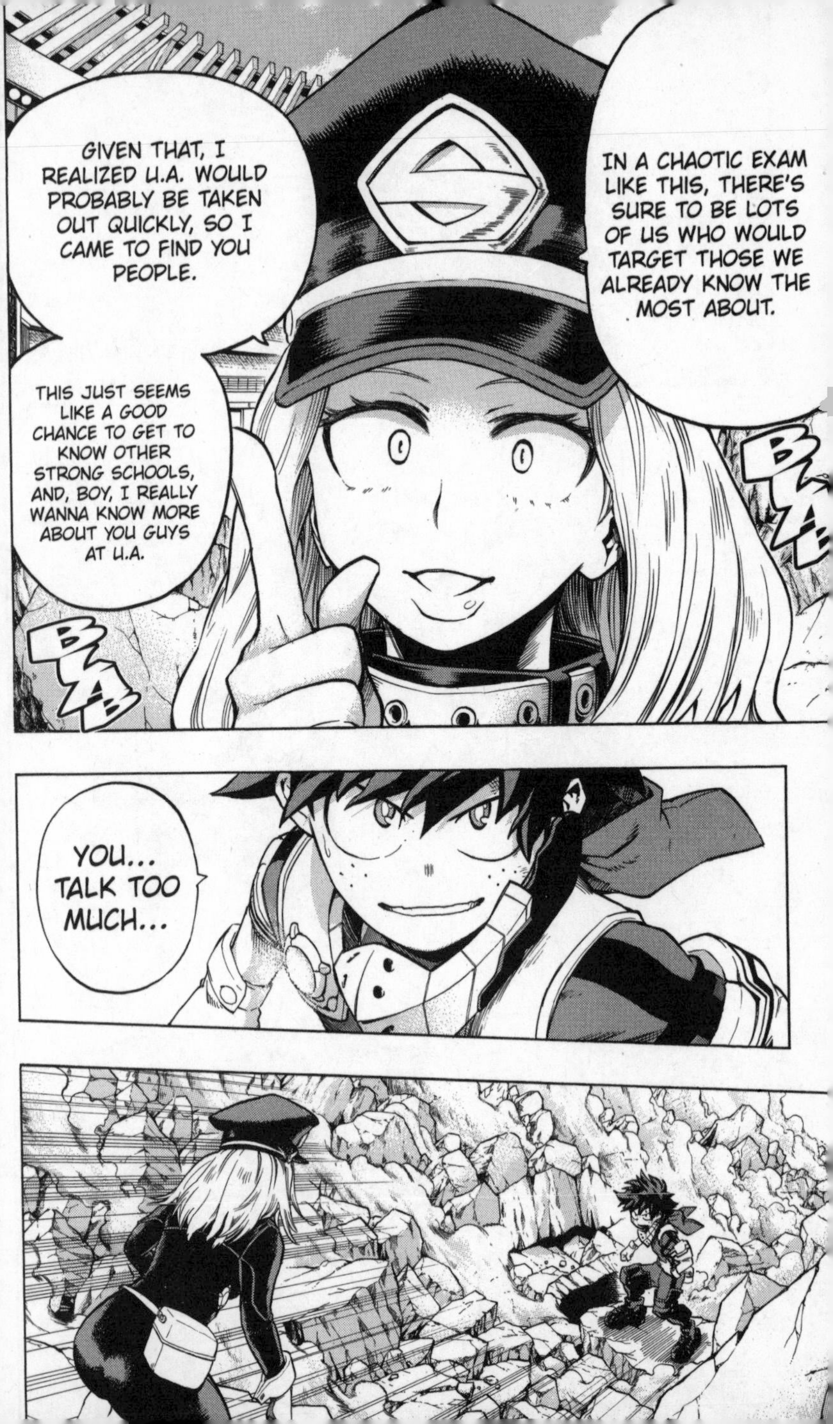
IN A CHAOTIC EXAM LIKE THIS, THERE'S SURE TO BE LOTS OF US WHO WOULD TARGET THOSE WE ALREADY KNOW THE MOST ABOUT.
GIVEN THAT, I REALIZED U.A. WOULD PROBABLY BE TAKEN OUT QUICKLY, SO I CAME TO FIND YOU PEOPLE.
THIS JUST SEEMS LIKE A GOOD CHANCE TO GET TO KNOW OTHER STRONG SCHOOLS, AND, BOY, I REALLY WANNA KNOW MORE ABOUT YOU GUYS AT U.A.
YOU... TALK TOO MUCH...

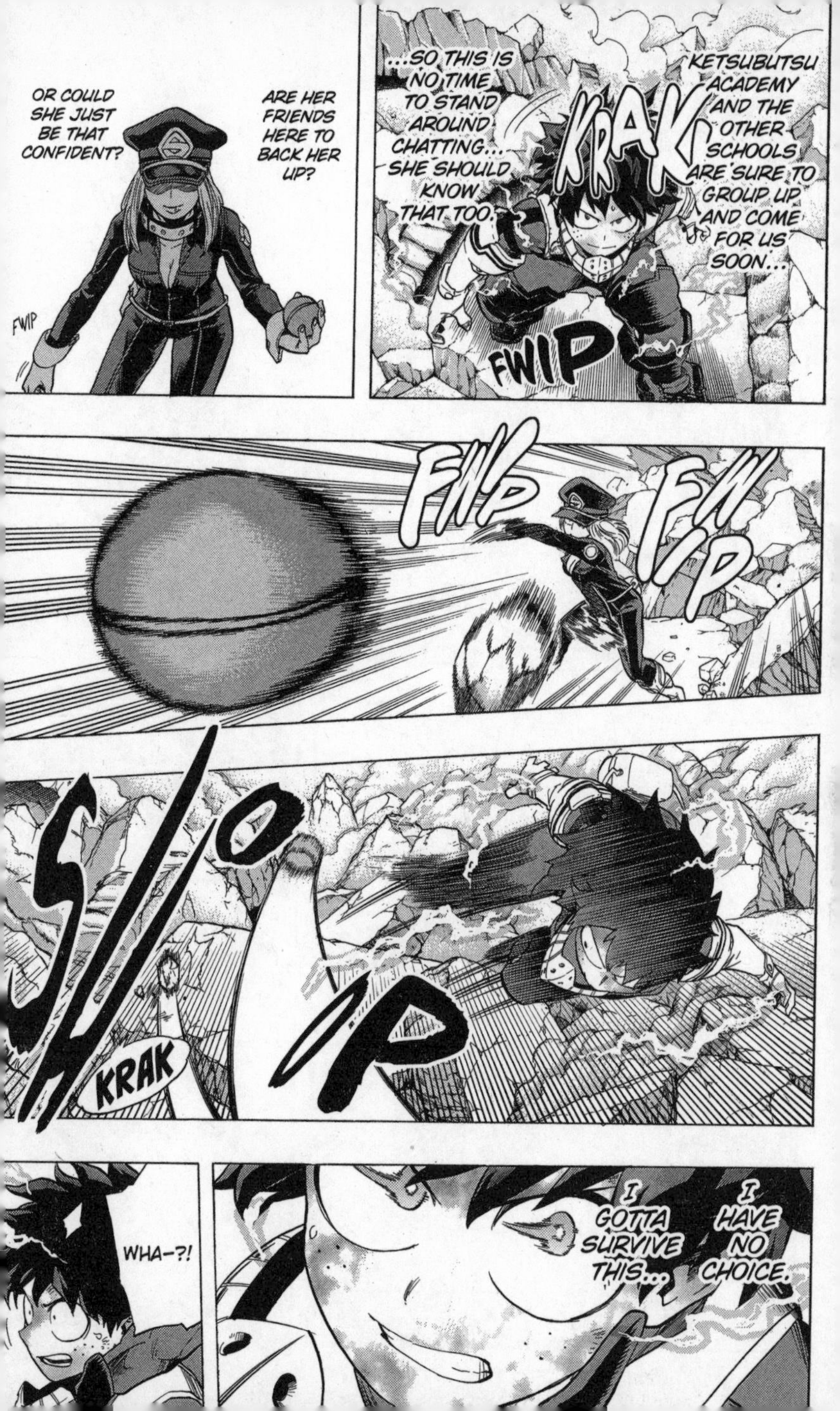
KETSUBUTSU ACADEMY AND THE OTHER SCHOOLS ARE SURE TO GROUP UP AND COME FOR US SOON...
...SO THIS IS NO TIME TO STAND AROUND CHATTING... SHE SHOULD KNOW THAT TOO.
KRAK
FWIP
ARE HER FRIENDS HERE TO BACK HER UP?
OR COULD SHE JUST BE THAT CONFIDENT?
FWIP
FWIP
FWIP
KRAK
I HAVE NO CHOICE.
I GOTTA SURVIVE THIS...
WHA-?!

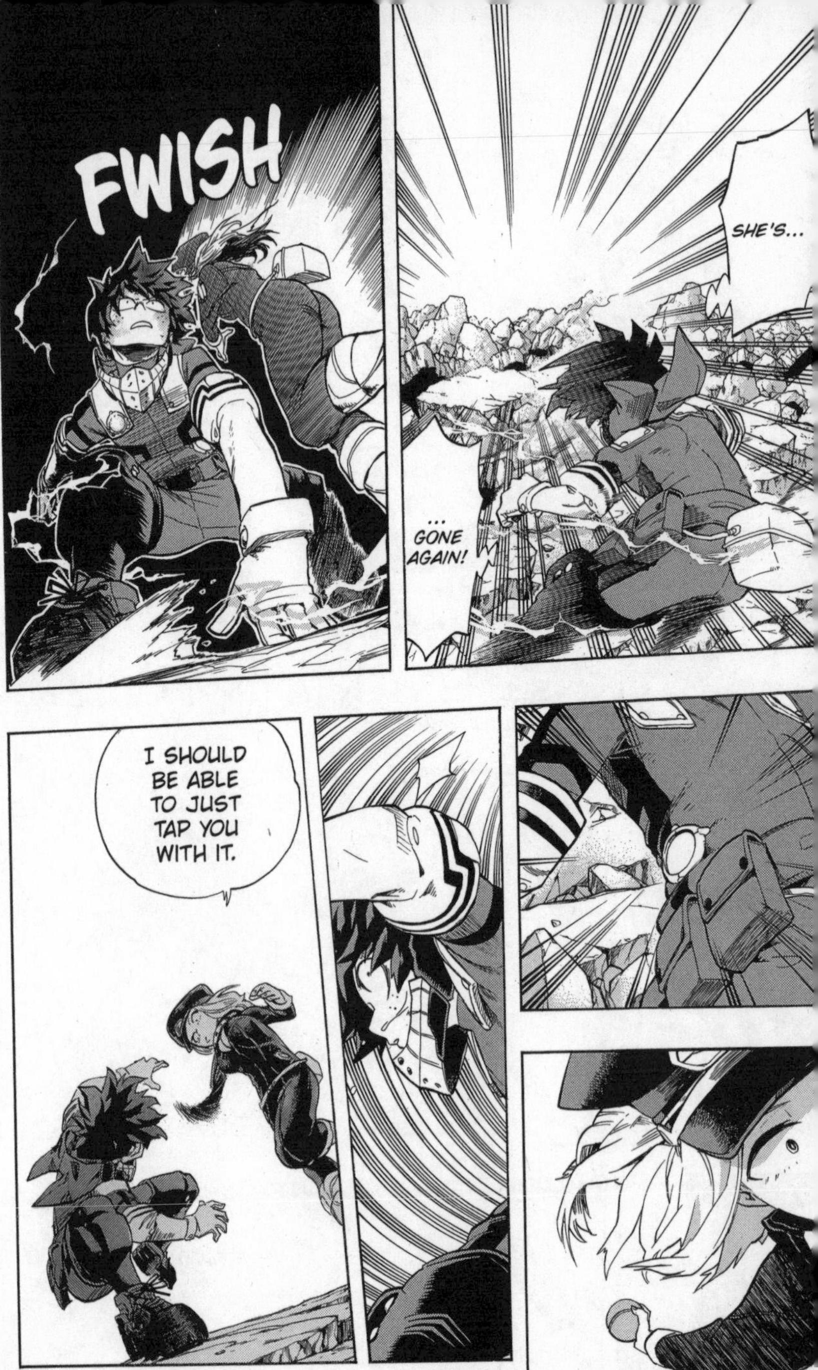
SHE'S...
... GONE AGAIN!
FWISH
I SHOULD BE ABLE TO JUST TAP YOU WITH IT.

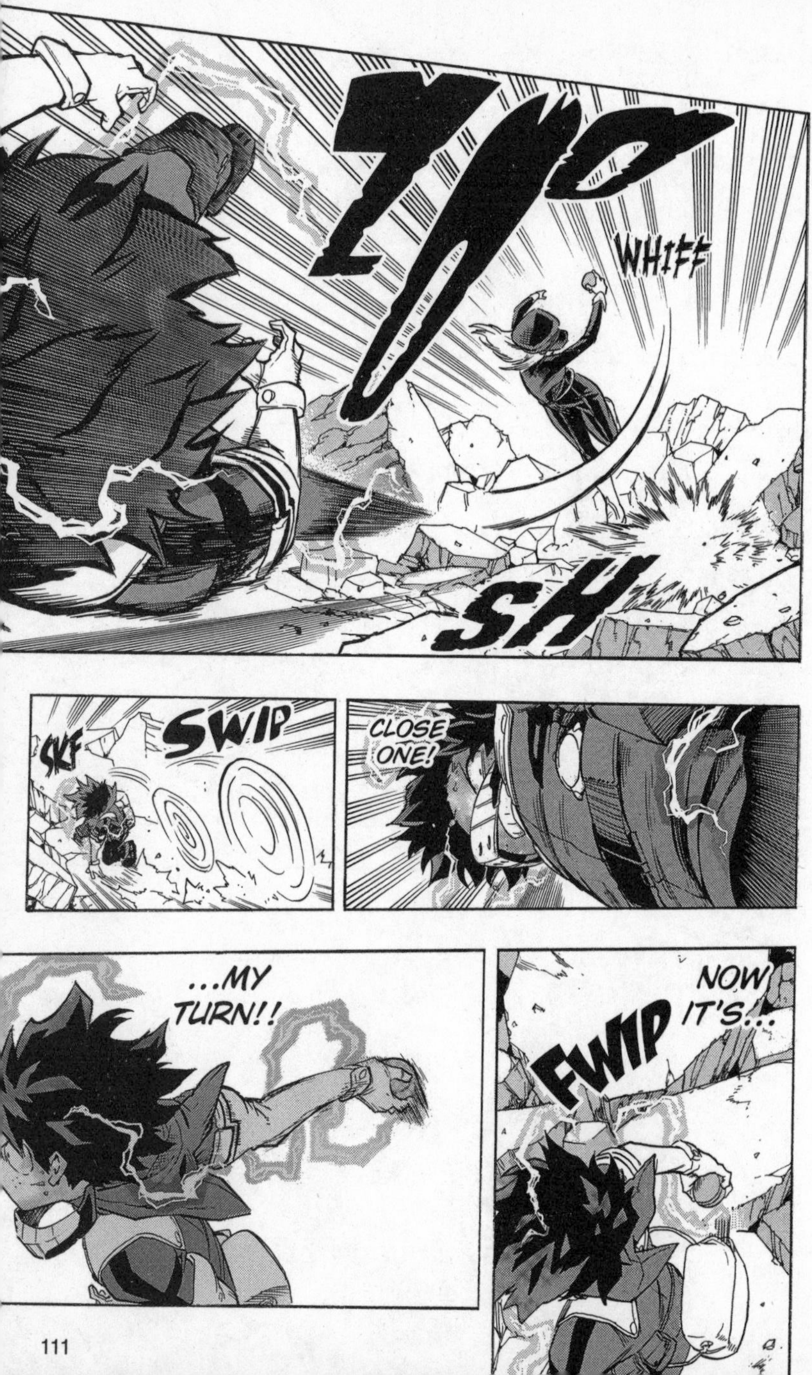
WHIFF
SH
CLOSE ONE!
SWIP
SKF
NOW IT'S...
FWIP
...MY TURN!!

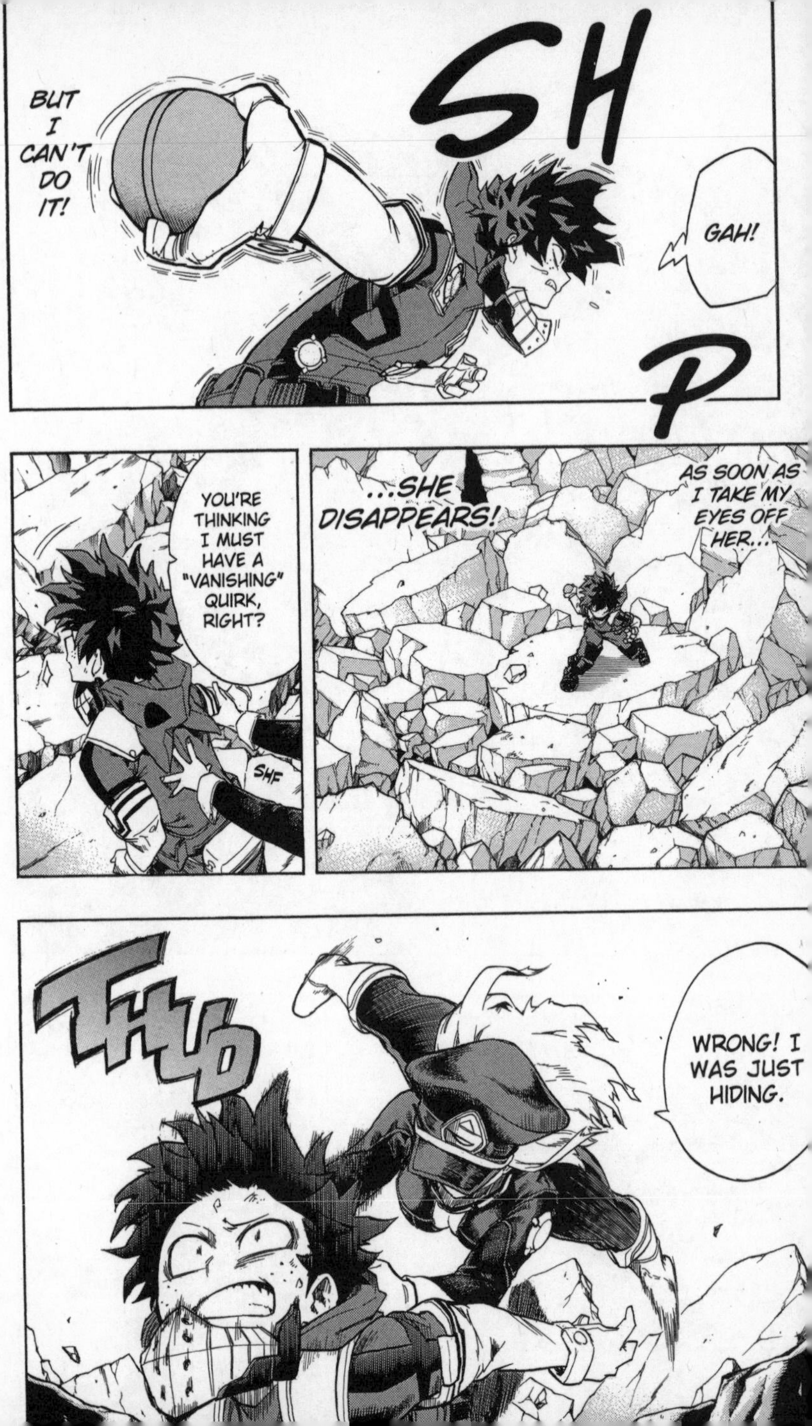
SHP
GAH!
BUT I CAN'T DO IT!
AS SOON AS I TAKE MY EYES OFF HER...
...SHE DISAPPEARS!
YOU'RE THINKING I MUST HAVE A "VANISHING" QUIRK, RIGHT?
SHF
WRONG! I WAS JUST HIDING.
THUD

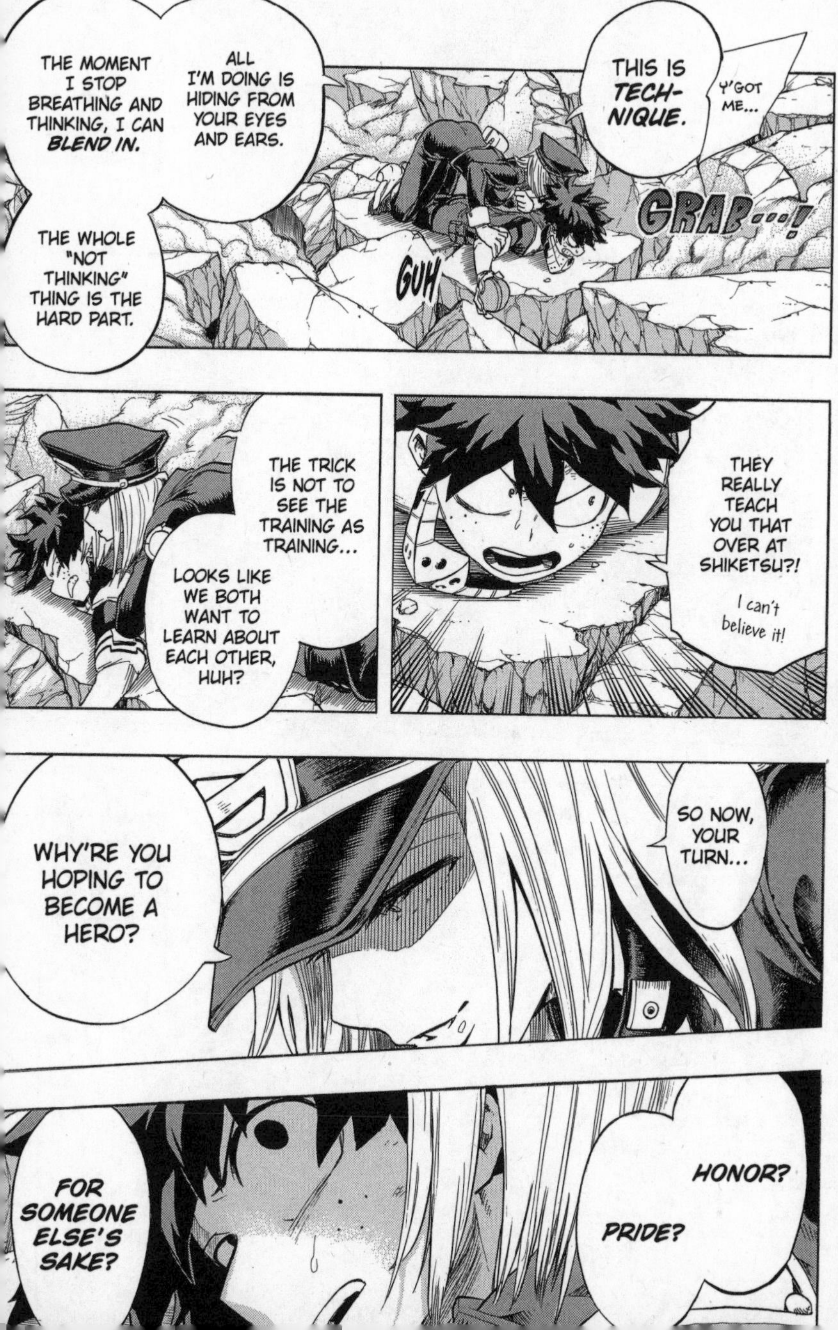
Y'GOT ME...
THIS IS TECHNIQUE.
GRAB...!
ALL I'M DOING IS HIDING FROM YOUR EYES AND EARS.
THE MOMENT I STOP BREATHING AND THINKING, I CAN BLEND IN.
GUH
THE WHOLE "NOT THINKING" THING IS THE HARD PART.
THEY REALLY TEACH YOU THAT OVER AT SHIKETSU?!
I can't believe it!
THE TRICK IS NOT TO SEE THE TRAINING AS TRAINING...
LOOKS LIKE WE BOTH WANT TO LEARN ABOUT EACH OTHER, HUH?
SO NOW, YOUR TURN...
WHY'RE YOU HOPING TO BECOME A HERO?
HONOR?
PRIDE?
FOR SOMEONE ELSE'S SAKE?

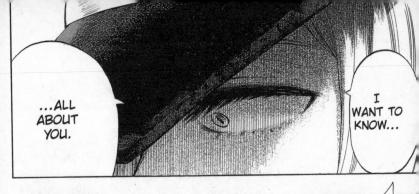

...ALL ABOUT YOU.

I WANT TO KNOW...

WHOA!

NGH!

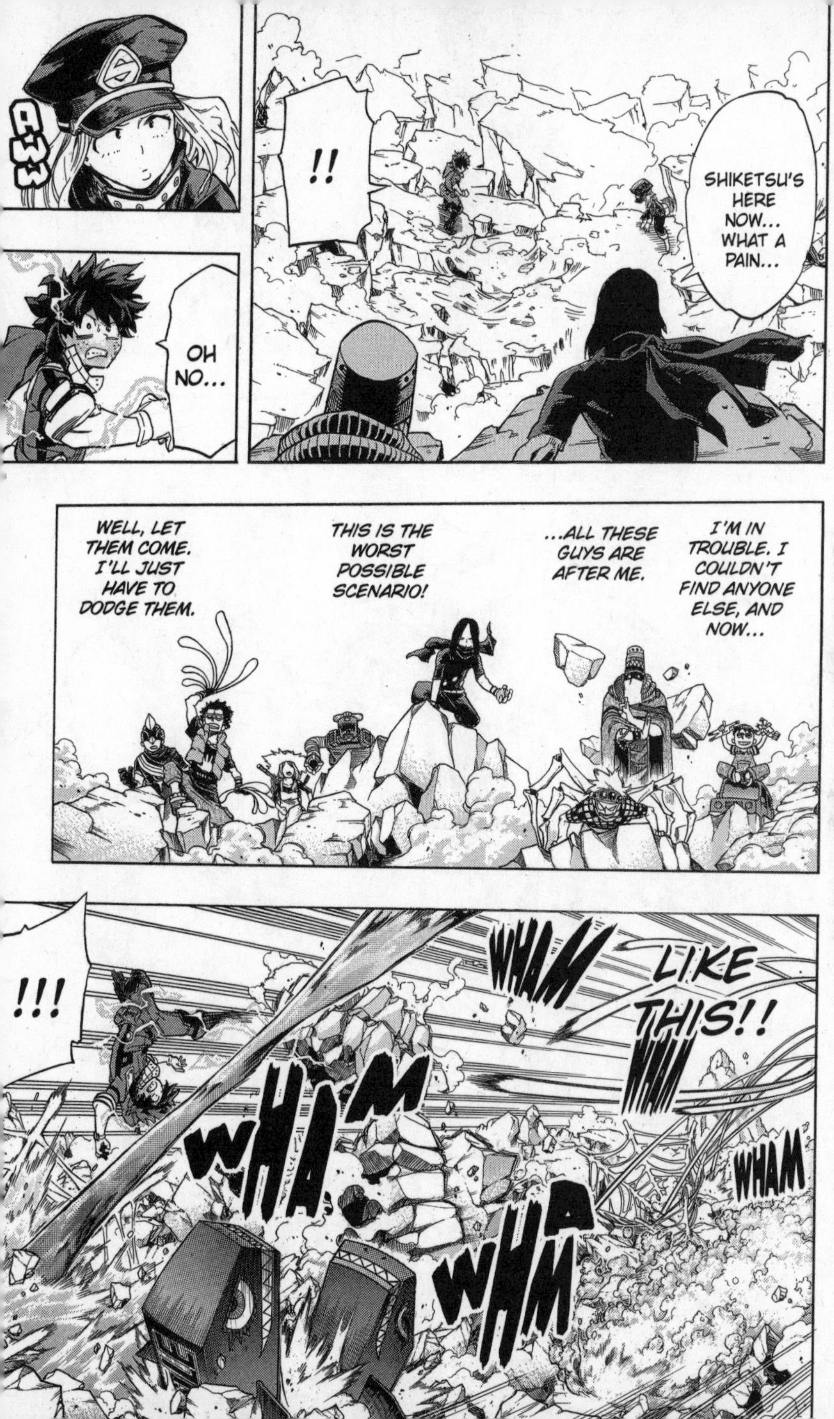
SHIKETSU'S HERE NOW... WHAT A PAIN...
!!
AWW
OH NO...
I'M IN TROUBLE. I COULDN'T FIND ANYONE ELSE, AND NOW...
...ALL THESE GUYS ARE AFTER ME.
THIS IS THE WORST POSSIBLE SCENARIO!
WELL, LET THEM COME. I'LL JUST HAVE TO DODGE THEM.
LIKE THIS!!
WHAM
WHAM
WHAM
WHAM
WHAM
!!!

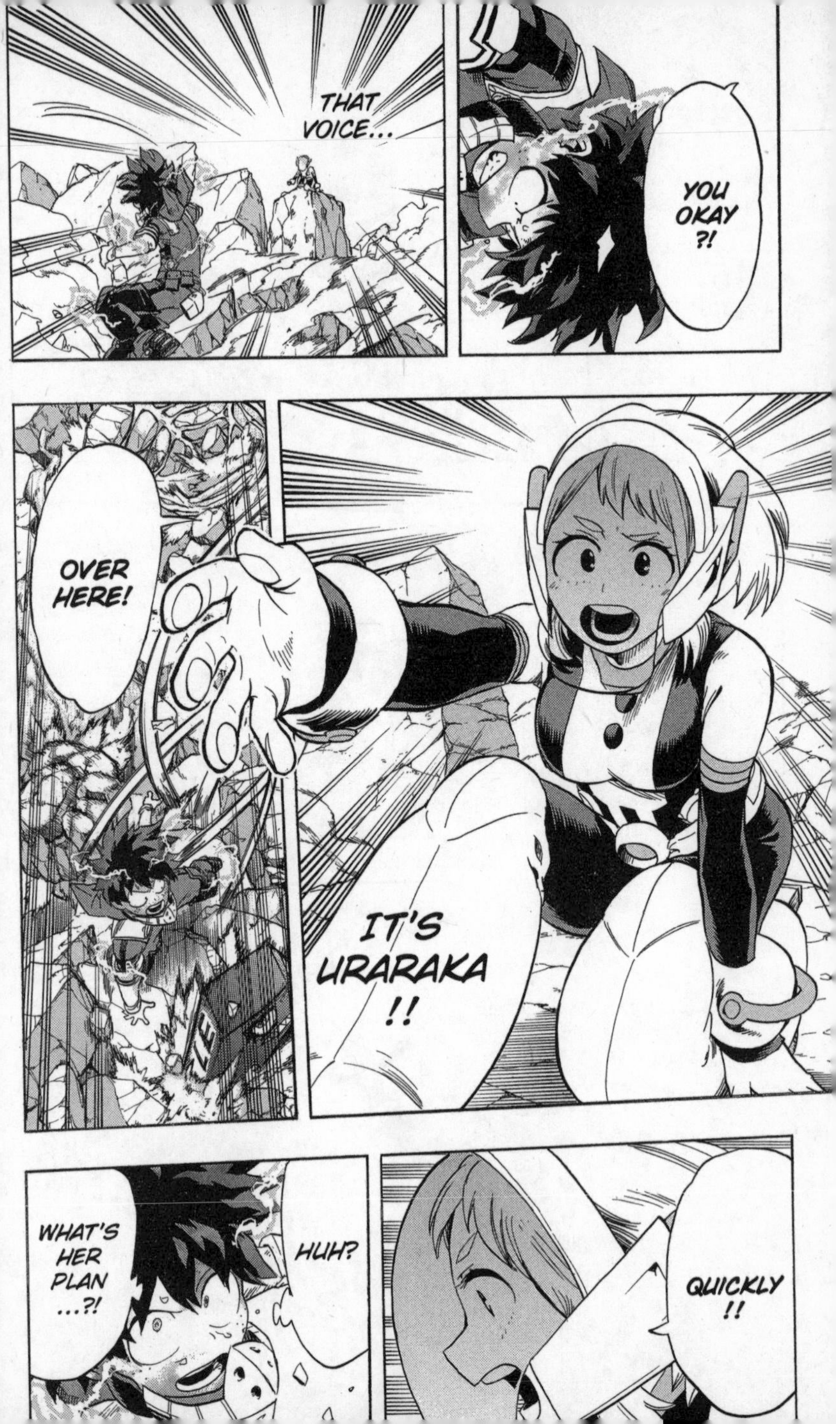
YOU OKAY ?!
THAT VOICE...
IT'S URARAKA !!
OVER HERE!
QUICKLY !!
HUH?
WHAT'S HER PLAN ...?!

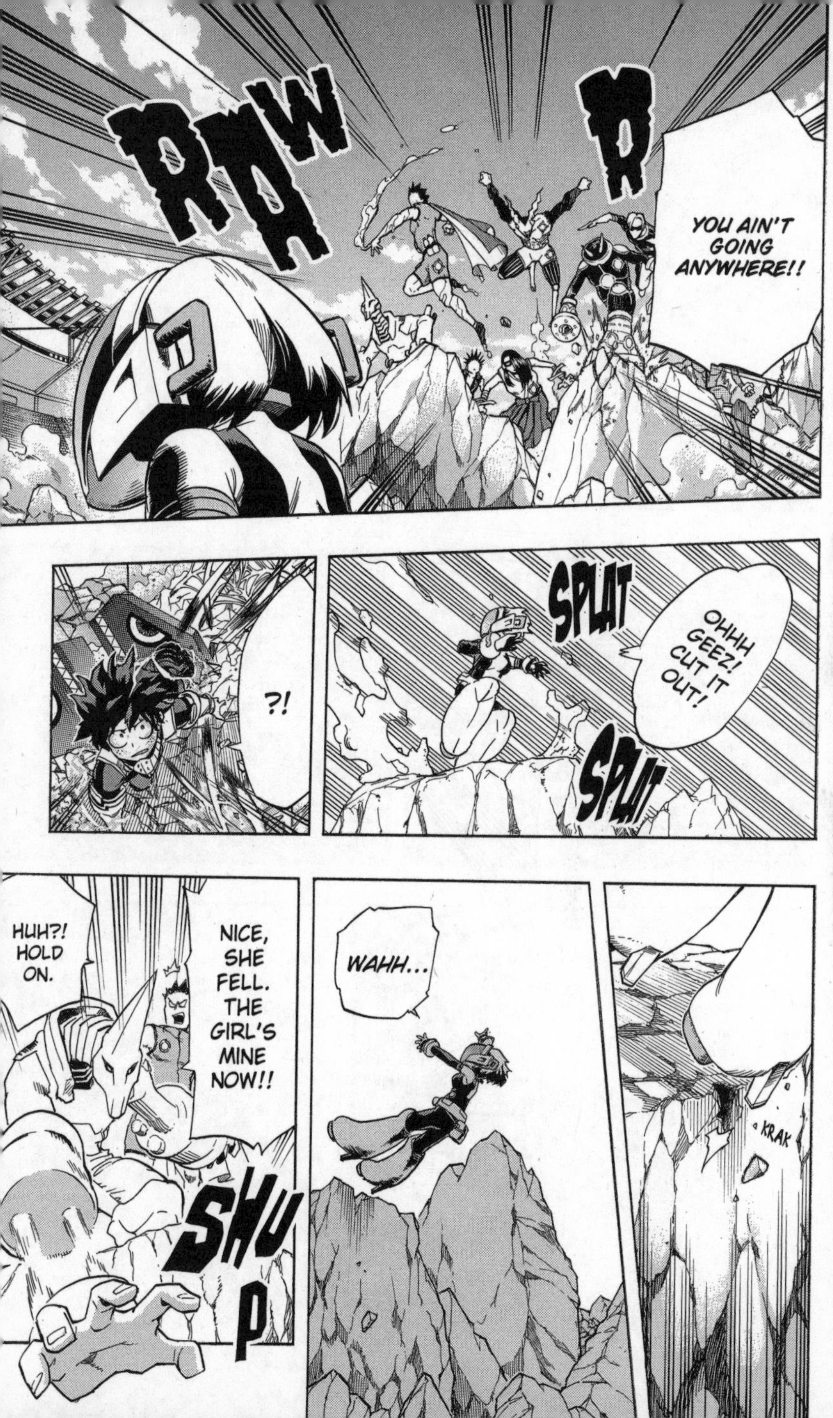
RAWR
YOU AIN'T GOING ANYWHERE!!
OHHH GEEZ! CUT IT OUT!
SPLAT
SPLAT
?!
KRAK
WAHH...
NICE, SHE FELL. THE GIRL'S MINE NOW!!
HUH?! HOLD ON.
SHUP

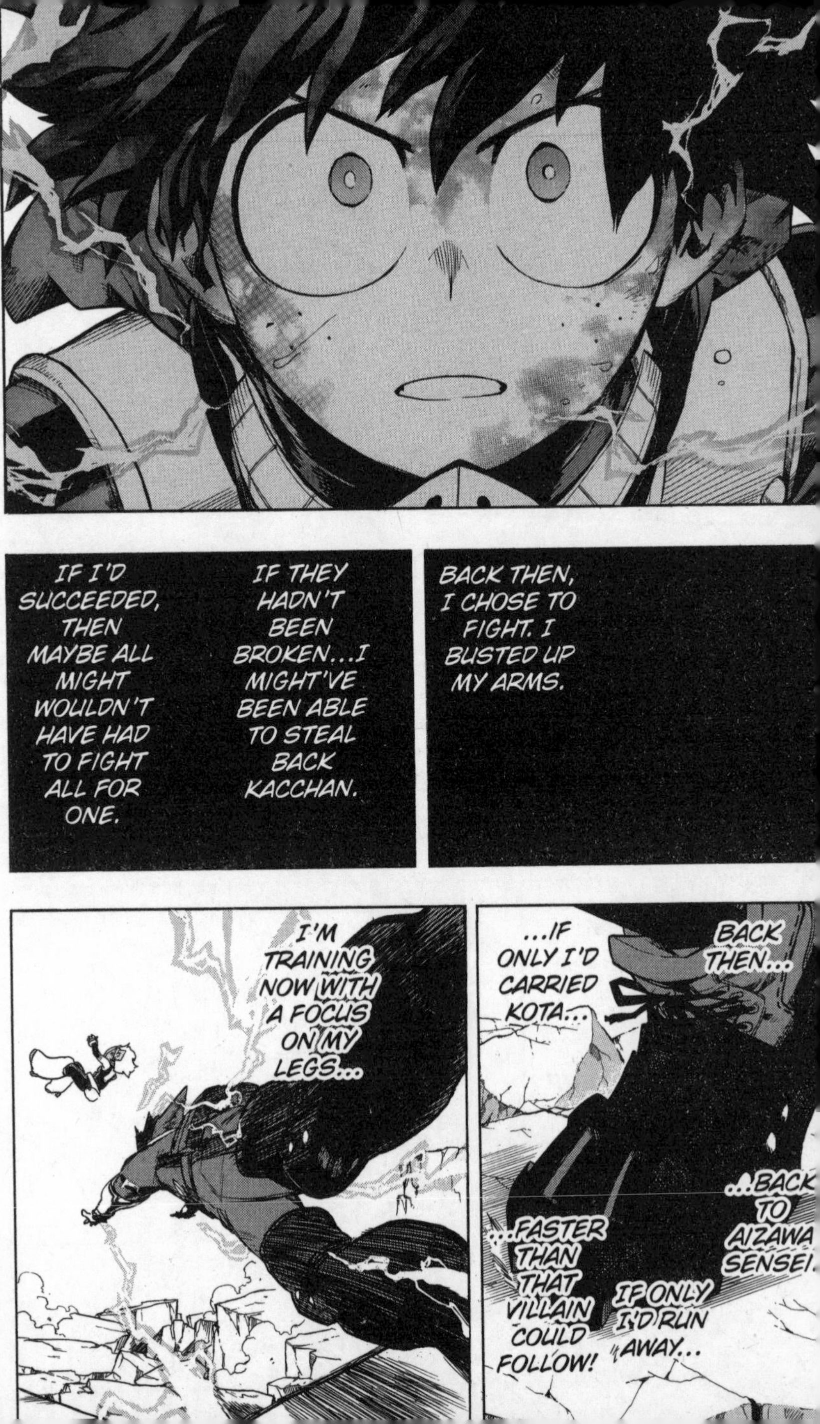
BACK THEN, I CHOSE TO FIGHT. I BUSTED UP MY ARMS.
IF THEY HADN'T BEEN BROKEN...I MIGHT'VE BEEN ABLE TO STEAL BACK KACCHAN.
IF I'D SUCCEEDED, THEN MAYBE ALL MIGHT WOULDN'T HAVE HAD TO FIGHT ALL FOR ONE.
BACK THEN...
...IF ONLY I'D CARRIED KOTA...
...BACK TO AIZAWA SENSEI.
IF ONLY I'D RUN AWAY...
...FASTER THAN THAT VILLAIN COULD FOLLOW!
I'M TRAINING NOW WITH A FOCUS ON MY LEGS...

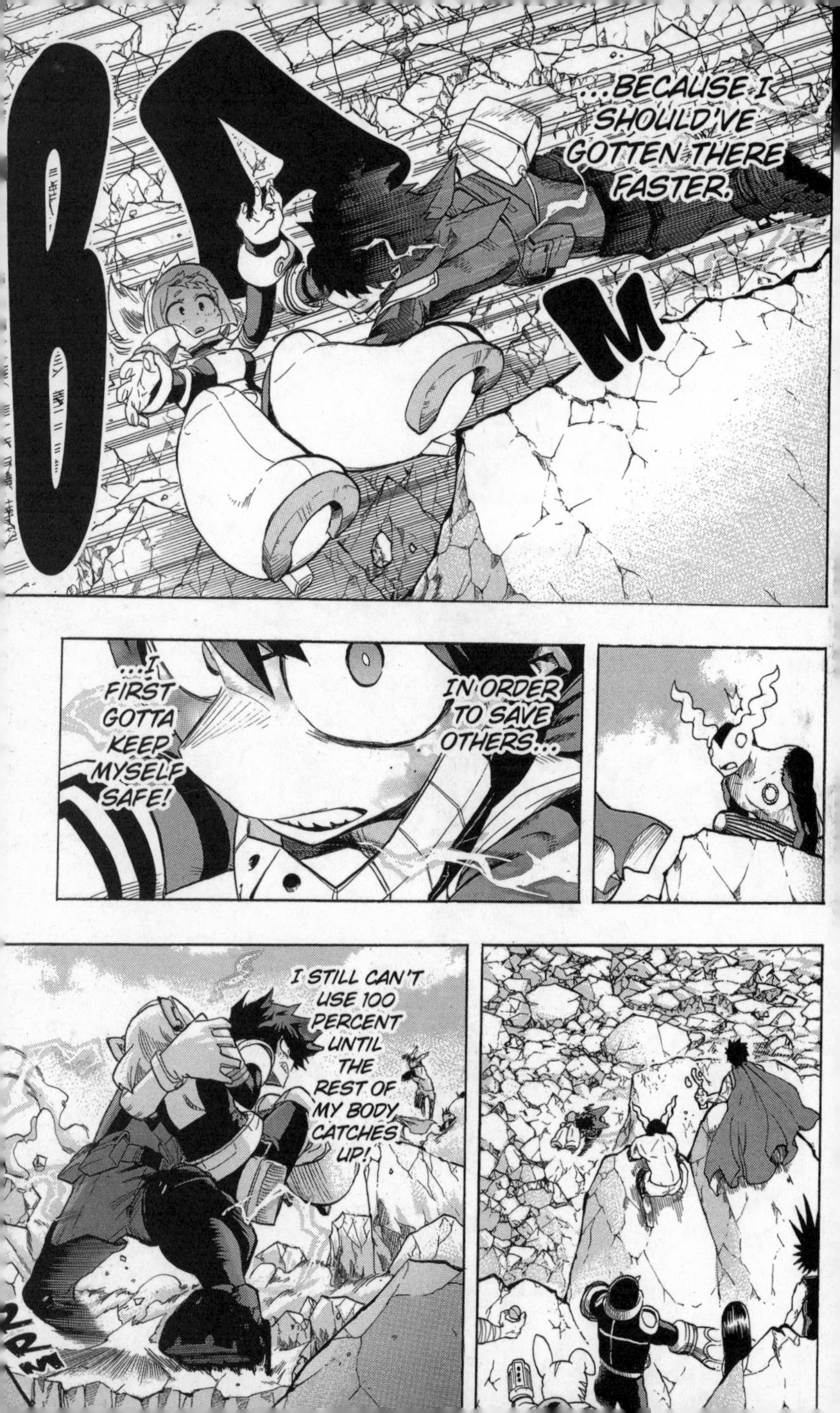
...BECAUSE I SHOULD'VE GOTTEN THERE FASTER.
BAM
IN ORDER TO SAVE OTHERS...
...I FIRST GOTTA KEEP MYSELF SAFE!
I STILL CAN'T USE 100 PERCENT UNTIL THE REST OF MY BODY CATCHES UP!

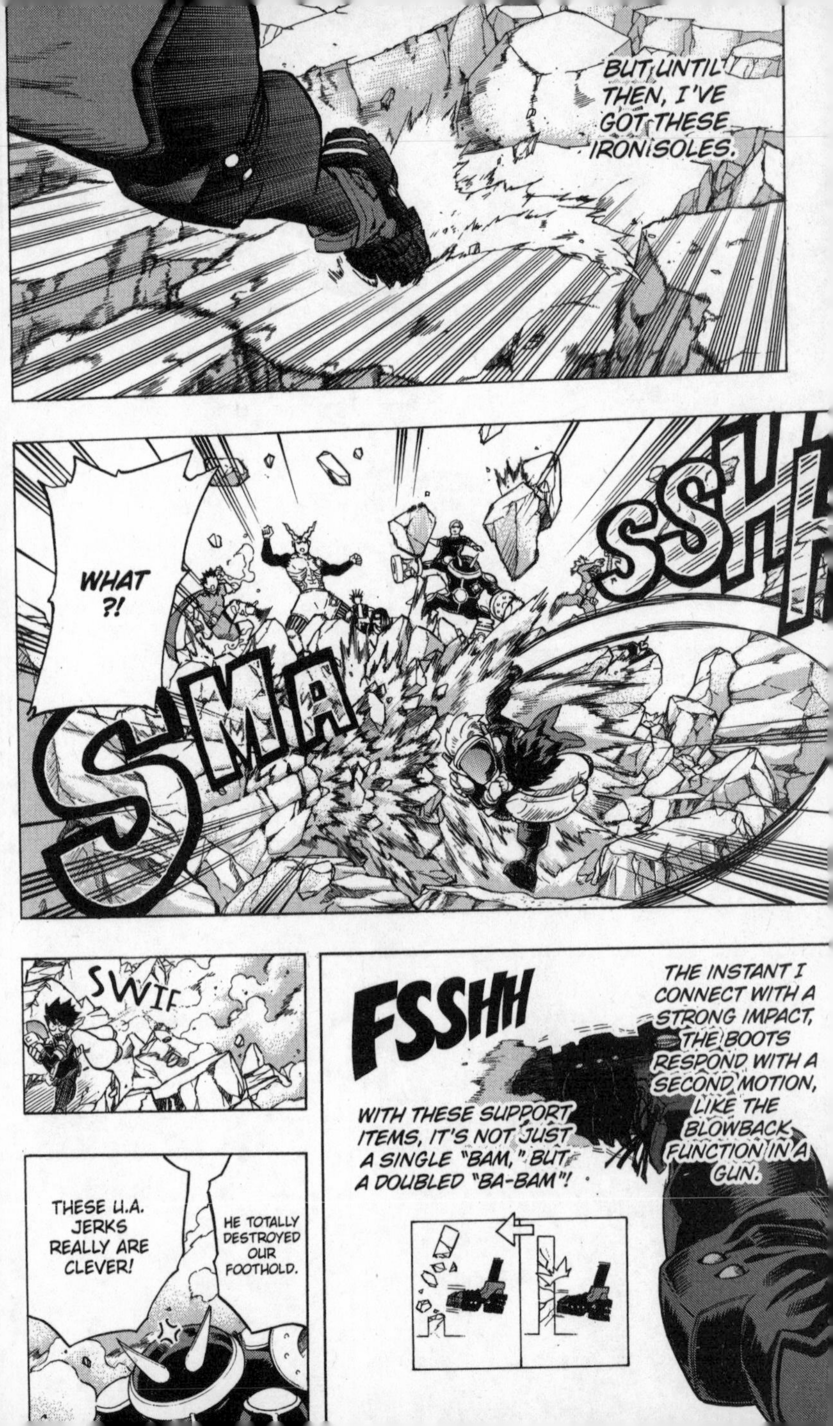
BUT UNTIL THEN, I'VE GOT THESE IRON SOLES.
SSH
WHAT ?!
SMA
THE INSTANT I CONNECT WITH A STRONG IMPACT, THE BOOTS RESPOND WITH A SECOND MOTION, LIKE THE BLOWBACK FUNCTION IN A GUN.
FSSHH
WITH THESE SUPPORT ITEMS, IT'S NOT JUST A SINGLE "BAM," BUT A DOUBLED "BA-BAM"!
SWIF
HE TOTALLY DESTROYED OUR FOOTHOLD.
THESE U.A. JERKS REALLY ARE CLEVER!

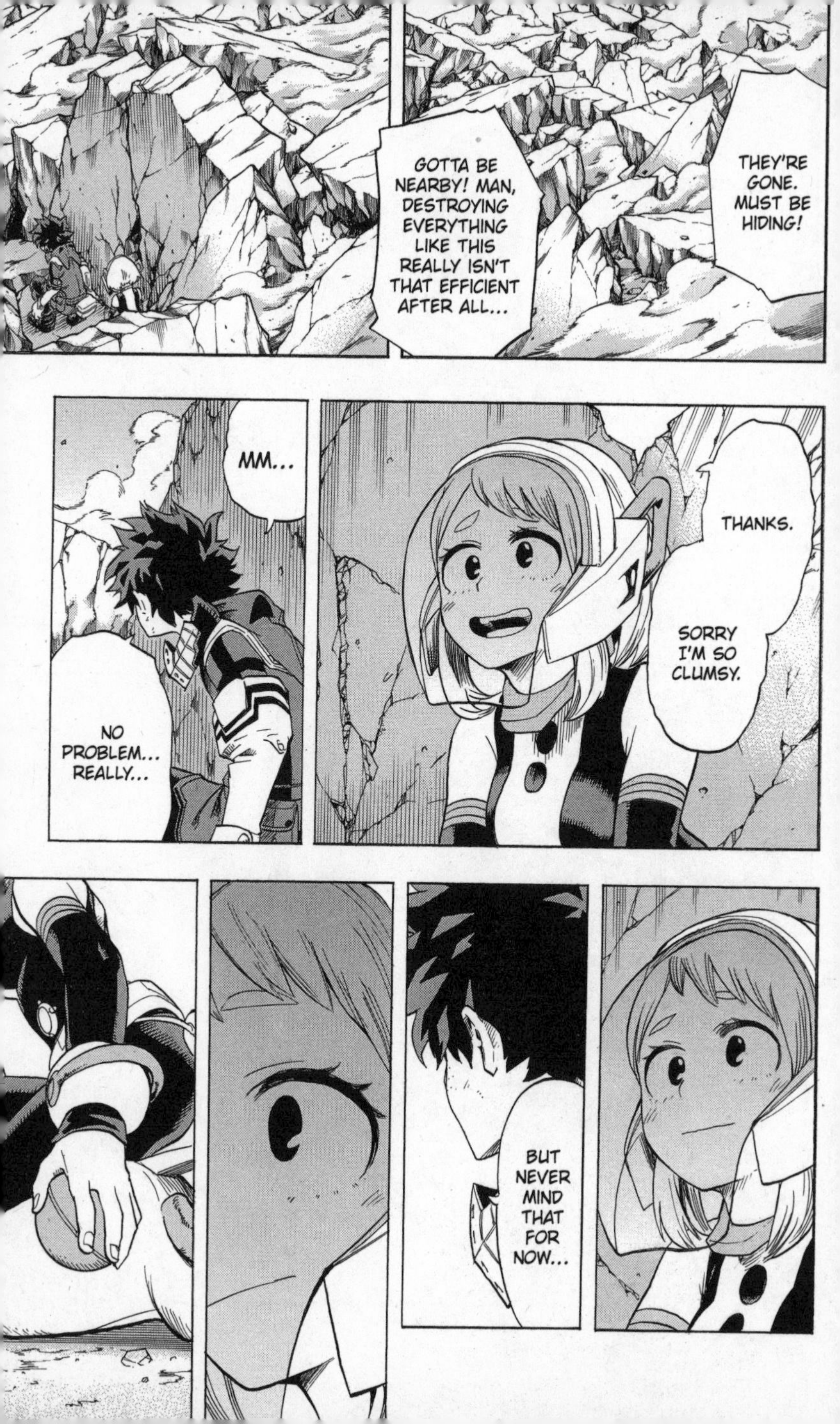
THEY'RE GONE. MUST BE HIDING!
GOTTA BE NEARBY! MAN, DESTROYING EVERYTHING LIKE THIS REALLY ISN'T THAT EFFICIENT AFTER ALL...
THANKS.
SORRY I'M SO CLUMSY.
MM...
NO PROBLEM... REALLY...
BUT NEVER MIND THAT FOR NOW...

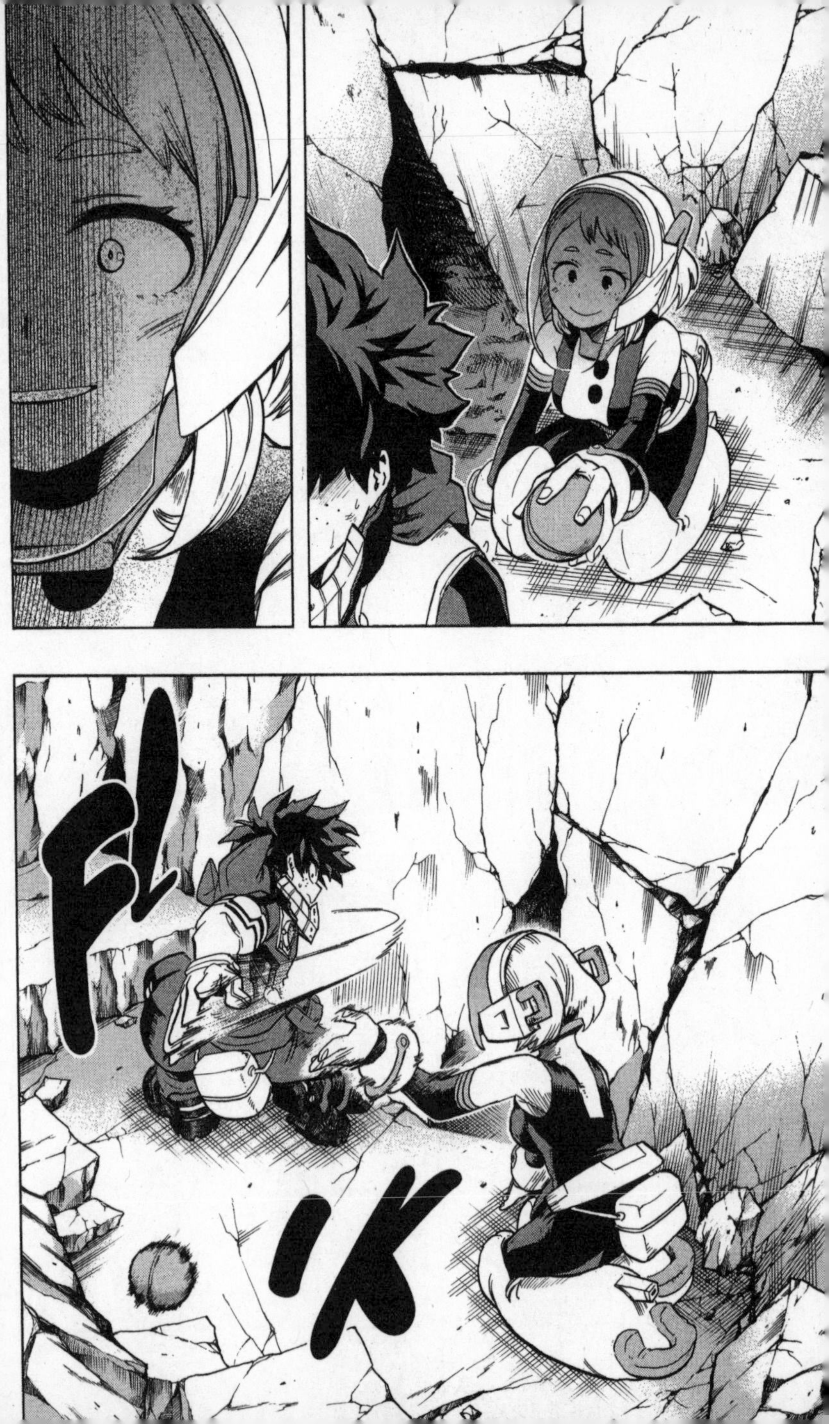
FL
IK

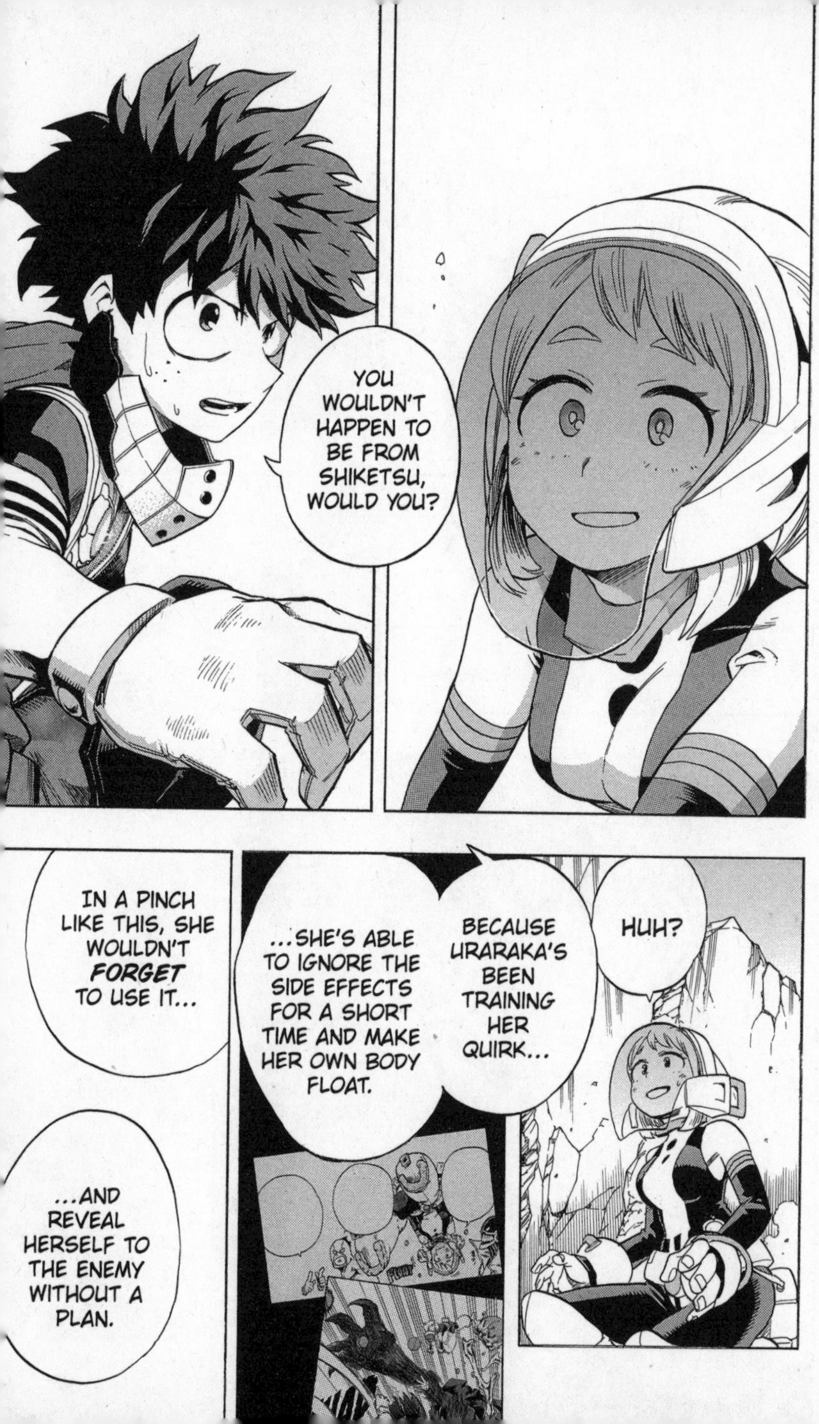
YOU WOULDN'T HAPPEN TO BE FROM SHIKETSU, WOULD YOU?
HUH?
BECAUSE URARAKA'S BEEN TRAINING HER QUIRK...
...SHE'S ABLE TO IGNORE THE SIDE EFFECTS FOR A SHORT TIME AND MAKE HER OWN BODY FLOAT.
IN A PINCH LIKE THIS, SHE WOULDN'T *FORGET* TO USE IT...
...AND REVEAL HERSELF TO THE ENEMY WITHOUT A PLAN.

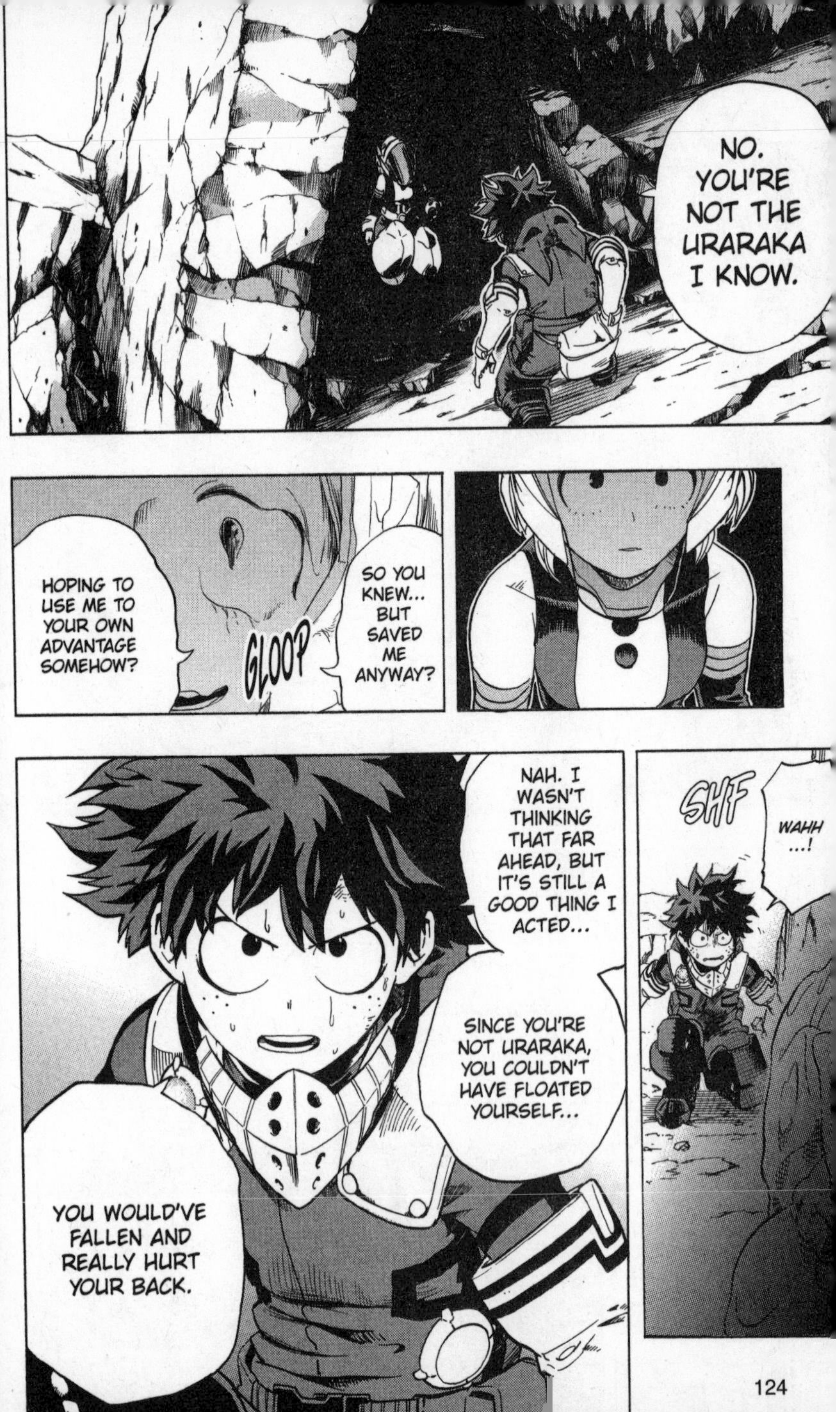
NO. YOU'RE NOT THE URARAKA I KNOW.
SO YOU KNEW... BUT SAVED ME ANYWAY?
GLOOP
HOPING TO USE ME TO YOUR OWN ADVANTAGE SOMEHOW?
SHF
WAHH ...!
NAH. I WASN'T THINKING THAT FAR AHEAD, BUT IT'S STILL A GOOD THING I ACTED...
SINCE YOU'RE NOT URARAKA, YOU COULDN'T HAVE FLOATED YOURSELF...
YOU WOULD'VE FALLEN AND REALLY HURT YOUR BACK.

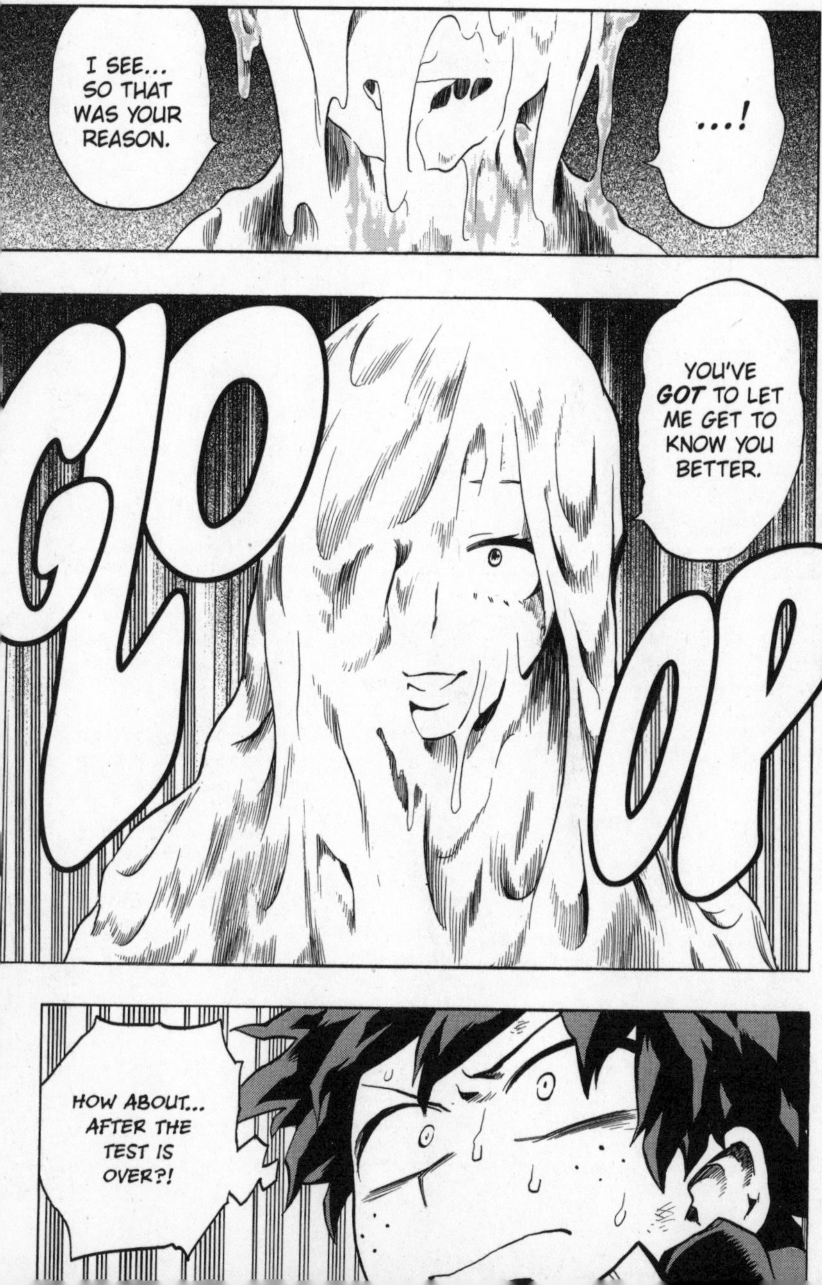
...!
I SEE... SO THAT WAS YOUR REASON.
YOU'VE *GOT* TO LET ME GET TO KNOW YOU BETTER.
GLOOP
HOW ABOUT... AFTER THE TEST IS OVER?!

傑物学園
YO SHINDO (17)

STREET CLOTHES

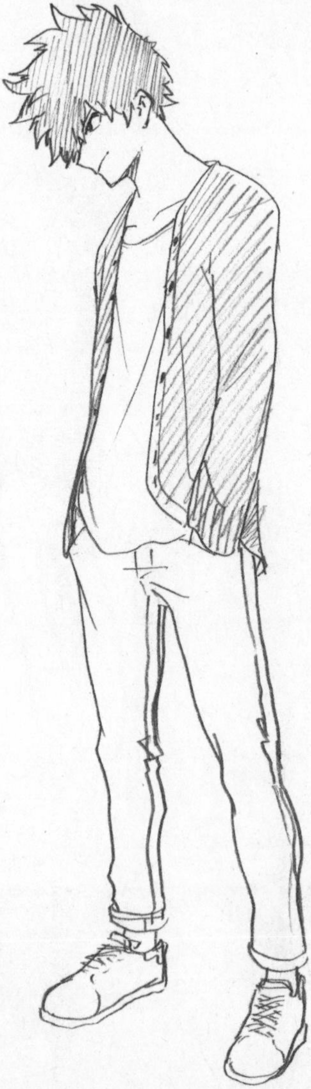

Birthday: 5/13
Height: 176 cm
Favorite Thing: Trolling

THE SUPPLEMENT

A pretty boy.

When I decided to introduce a pretty boy, I found myself at a loss for how to create such a character. What makes a pretty boy a pretty boy? I thought real hard about it and came to the conclusion that the hairstyle is really all you need to make him look the part. It took about five minutes to reach that conclusion, from start to finish.

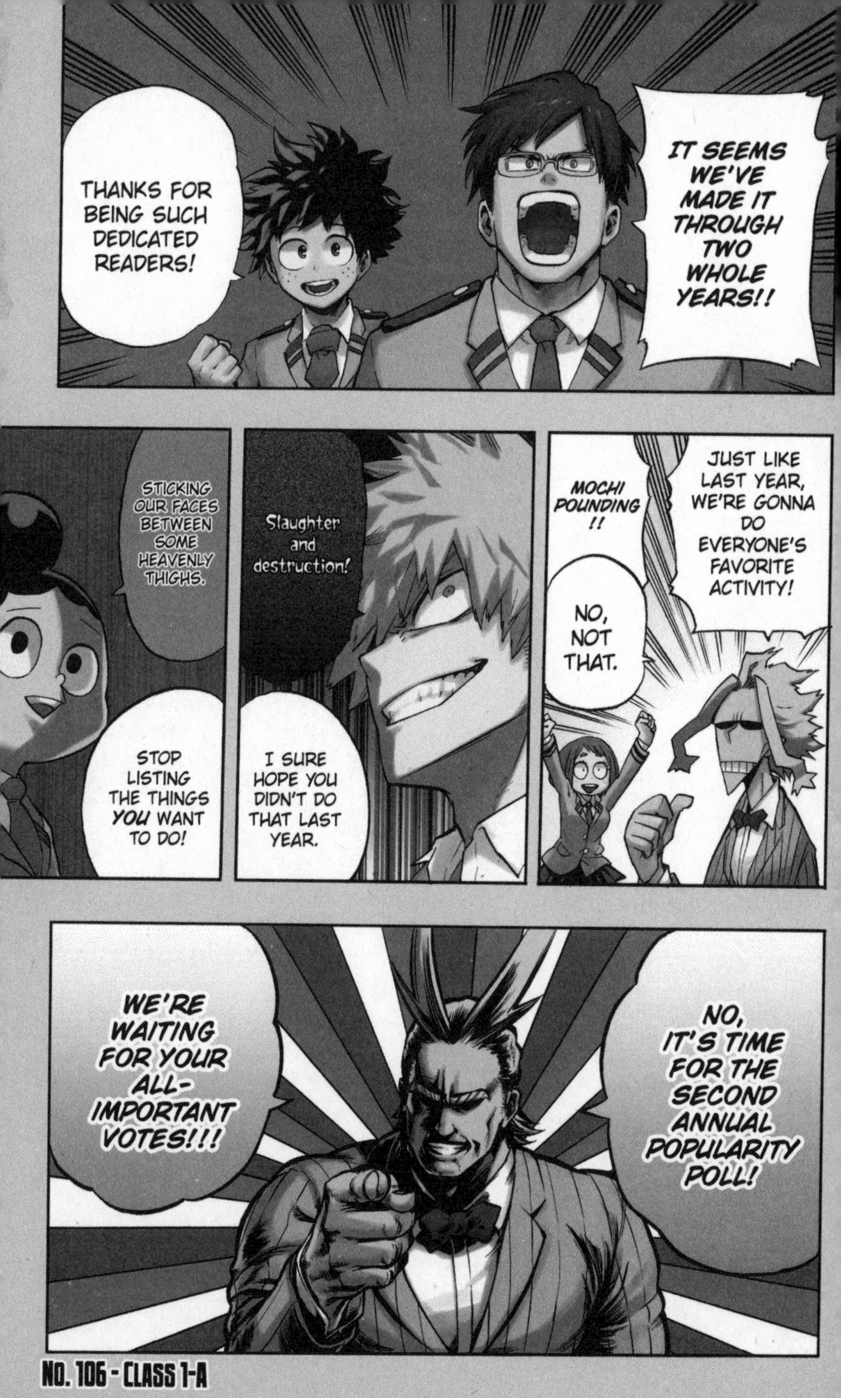
IT SEEMS WE'VE MADE IT THROUGH TWO WHOLE YEARS!!
THANKS FOR BEING SUCH DEDICATED READERS!
JUST LIKE LAST YEAR, WE'RE GONNA DO EVERYONE'S FAVORITE ACTIVITY!
MOCHI POUNDING !!
NO, NOT THAT.
Slaughter and destruction!
I SURE HOPE YOU DIDN'T DO THAT LAST YEAR.
STICKING OUR FACES BETWEEN SOME HEAVENLY THIGHS.
STOP LISTING THE THINGS *YOU* WANT TO DO!
NO, IT'S TIME FOR THE SECOND ANNUAL POPULARITY POLL!
WE'RE WAITING FOR YOUR ALL-IMPORTANT VOTES!!!

NO. 106 - CLASS 1-A

No. 106 - Class 1-A

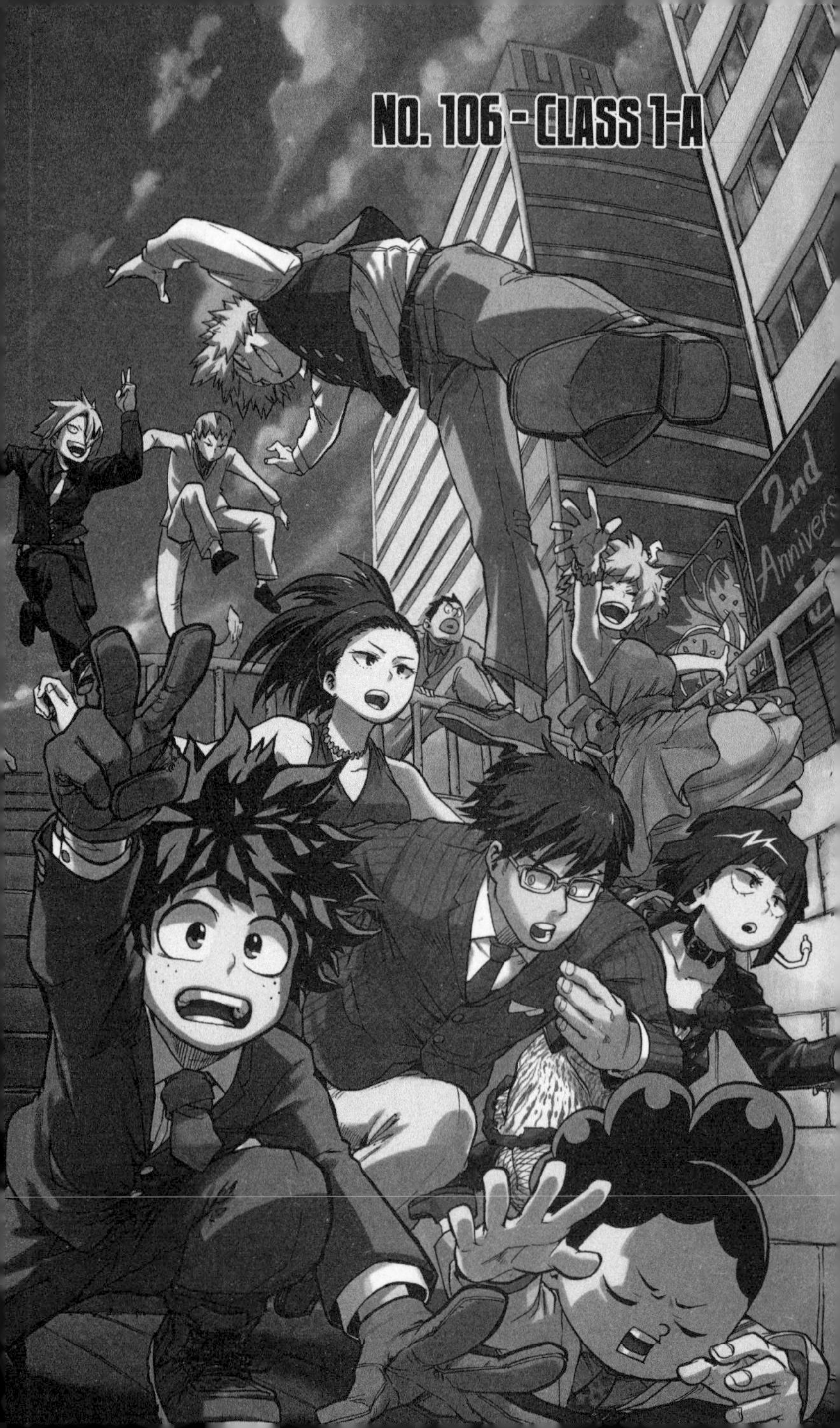

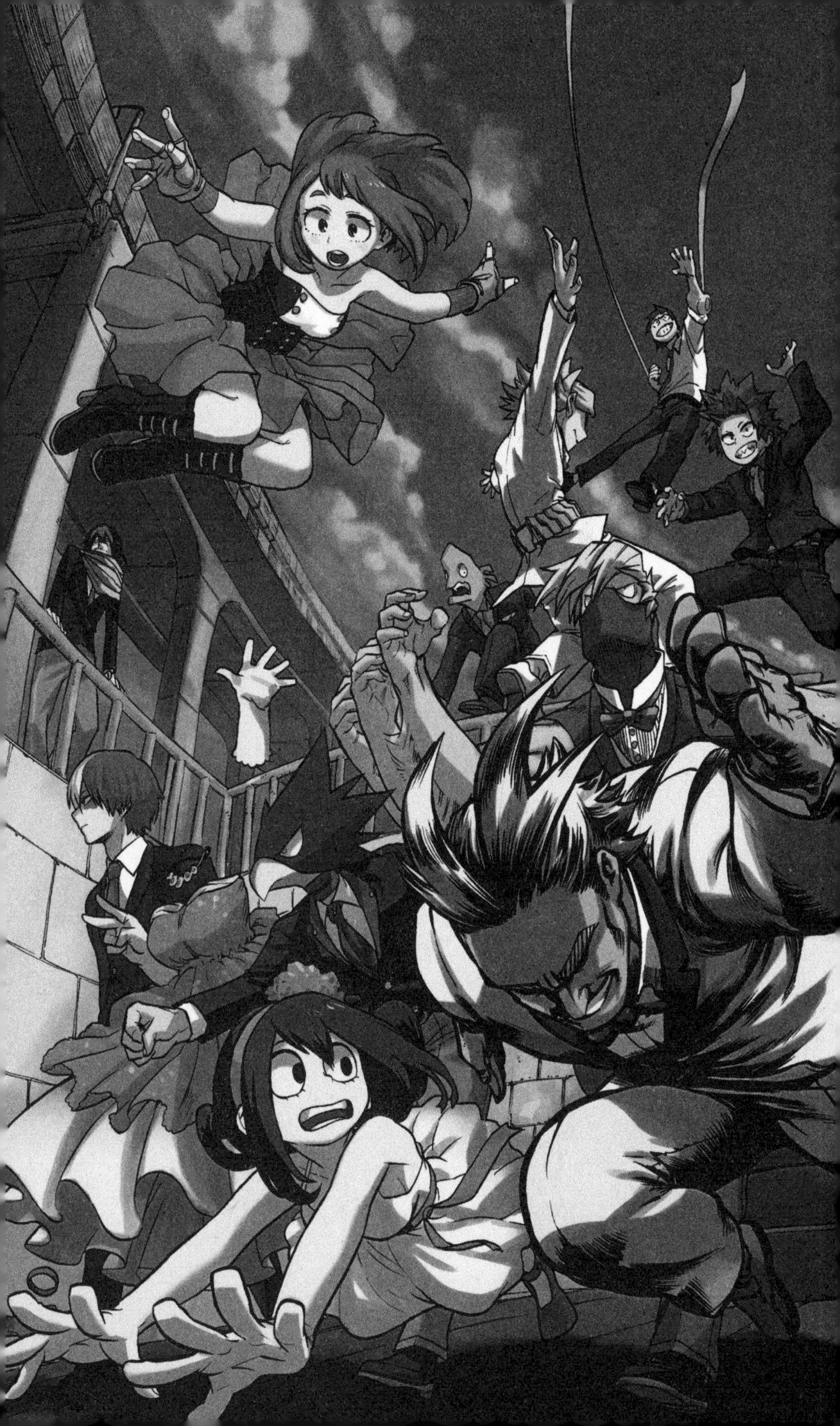

MY HERO ACADEMIA

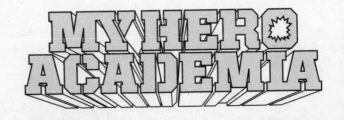

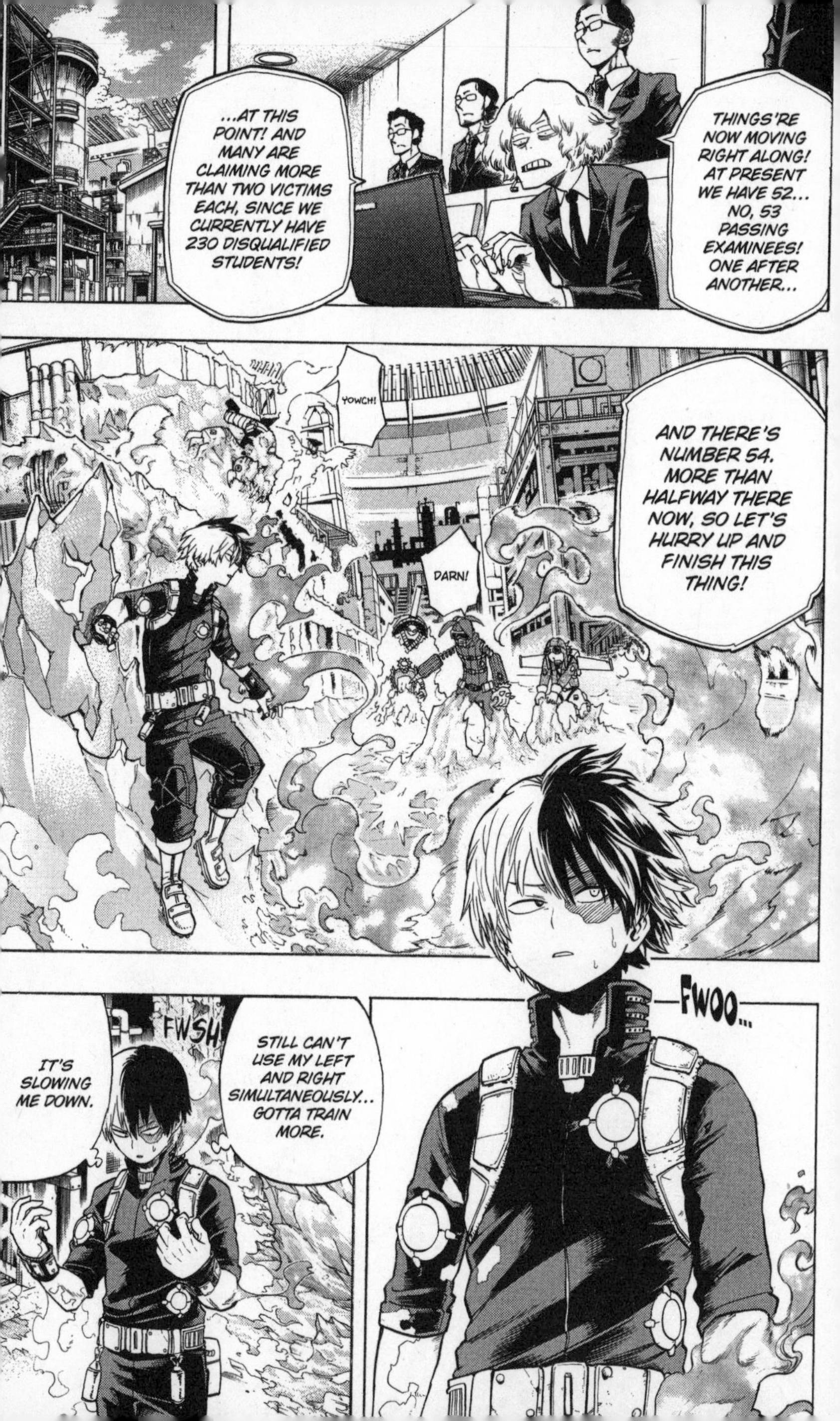
THINGS'RE NOW MOVING RIGHT ALONG! AT PRESENT WE HAVE 52... NO, 53 PASSING EXAMINEES! ONE AFTER ANOTHER...
...AT THIS POINT! AND MANY ARE CLAIMING MORE THAN TWO VICTIMS EACH, SINCE WE CURRENTLY HAVE 230 DISQUALIFIED STUDENTS!
AND THERE'S NUMBER 54. MORE THAN HALFWAY THERE NOW, SO LET'S HURRY UP AND FINISH THIS THING!
YOWCH!
DARN!
FWOO...
FWSH
STILL CAN'T USE MY LEFT AND RIGHT SIMULTANEOUSLY... GOTTA TRAIN MORE.
IT'S SLOWING ME DOWN.

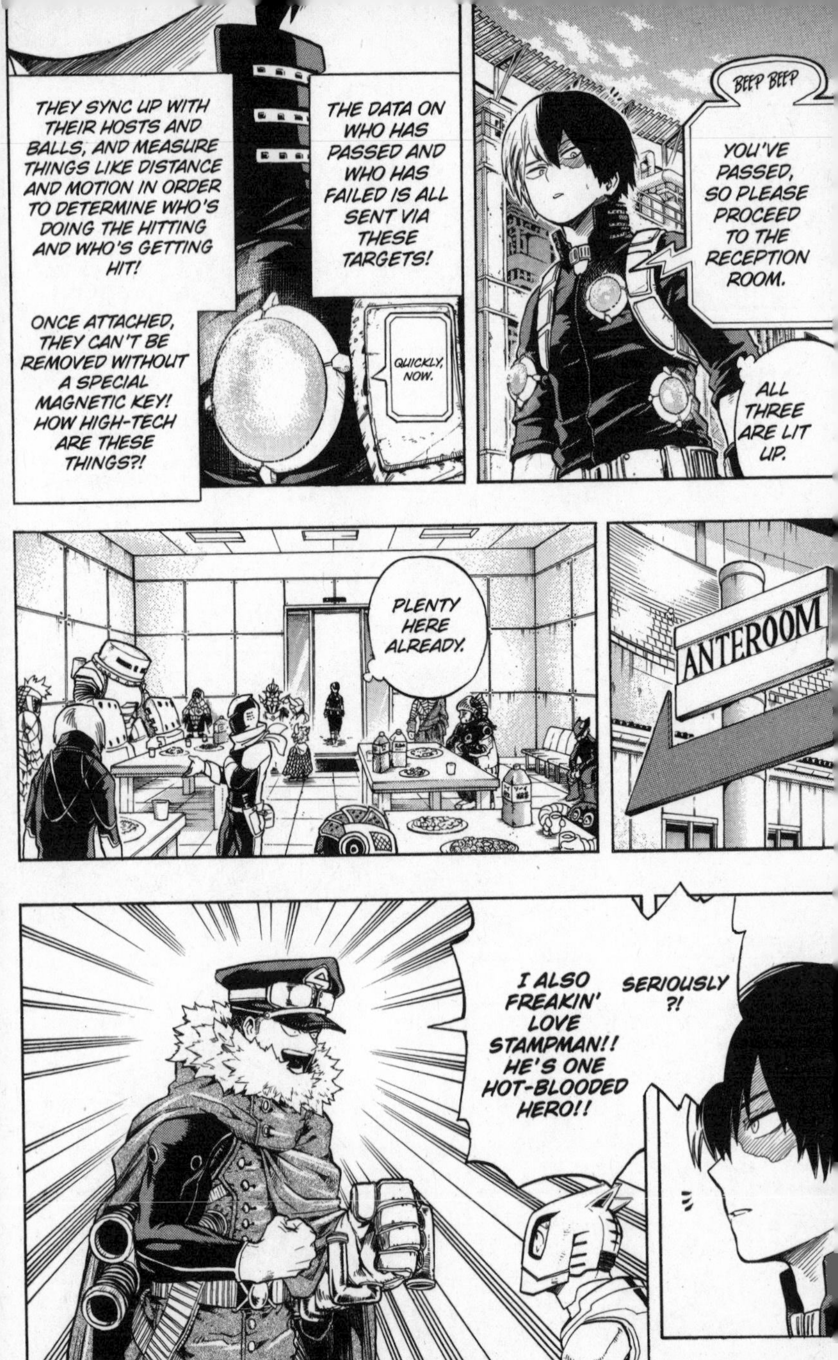
BEEP BEEP
YOU'VE PASSED, SO PLEASE PROCEED TO THE RECEPTION ROOM.
ALL THREE ARE LIT UP.
THE DATA ON WHO HAS PASSED AND WHO HAS FAILED IS ALL SENT VIA THESE TARGETS!
THEY SYNC UP WITH THEIR HOSTS AND BALLS, AND MEASURE THINGS LIKE DISTANCE AND MOTION IN ORDER TO DETERMINE WHO'S DOING THE HITTING AND WHO'S GETTING HIT!
QUICKLY, NOW.
ONCE ATTACHED, THEY CAN'T BE REMOVED WITHOUT A SPECIAL MAGNETIC KEY! HOW HIGH-TECH ARE THESE THINGS?!
ANTEROOM
PLENTY HERE ALREADY.
SERIOUSLY?!
I ALSO FREAKIN' LOVE STAMPMAN!! HE'S ONE HOT-BLOODED HERO!!

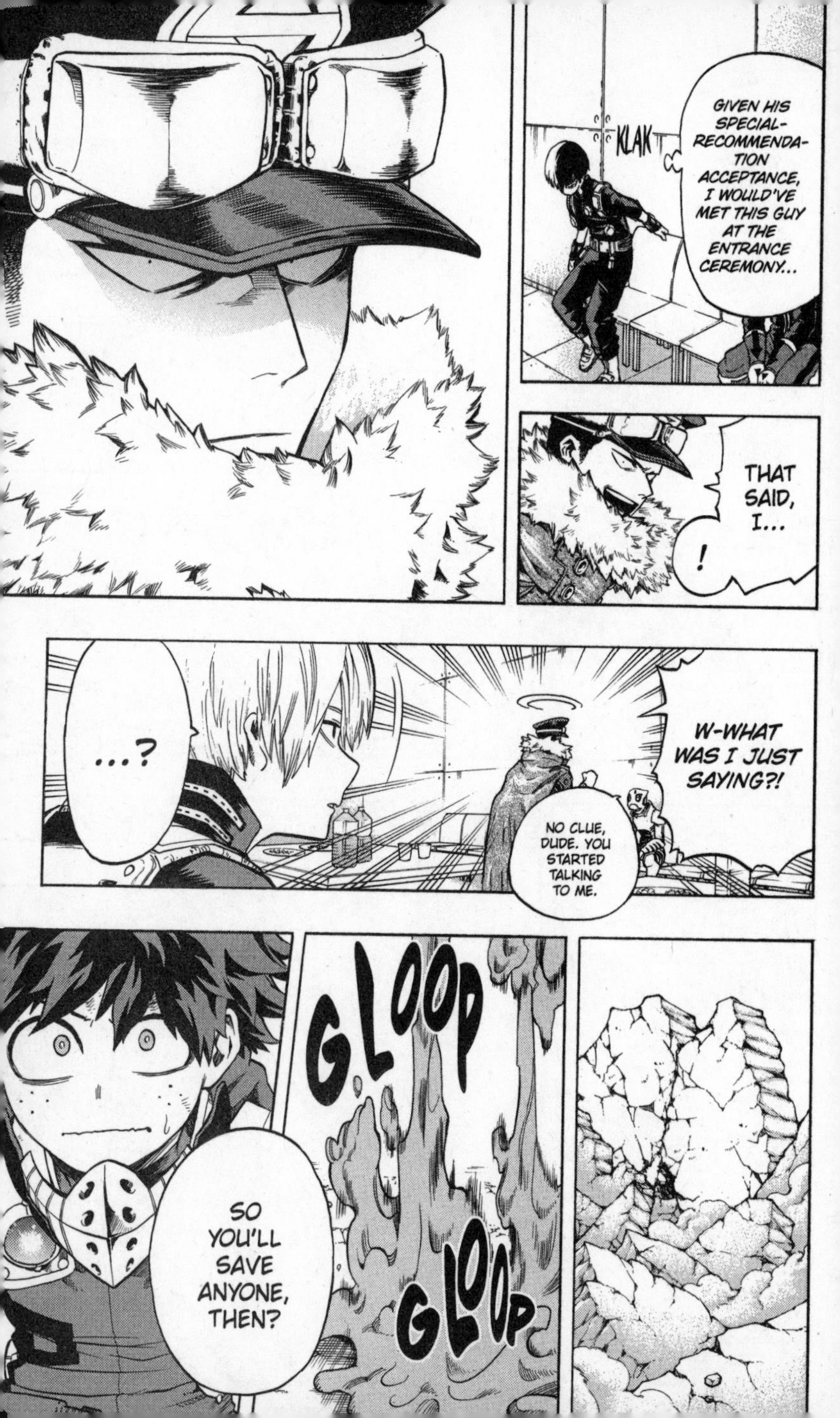
KLAK
GIVEN HIS SPECIAL-RECOMMENDATION ACCEPTANCE, I WOULD'VE MET THIS GUY AT THE ENTRANCE CEREMONY...
THAT SAID, I...
!
W-WHAT WAS I JUST SAYING?!
NO CLUE, DUDE. YOU STARTED TALKING TO ME.
...?
GLOOP
GLOOP
SO YOU'LL SAVE ANYONE, THEN?

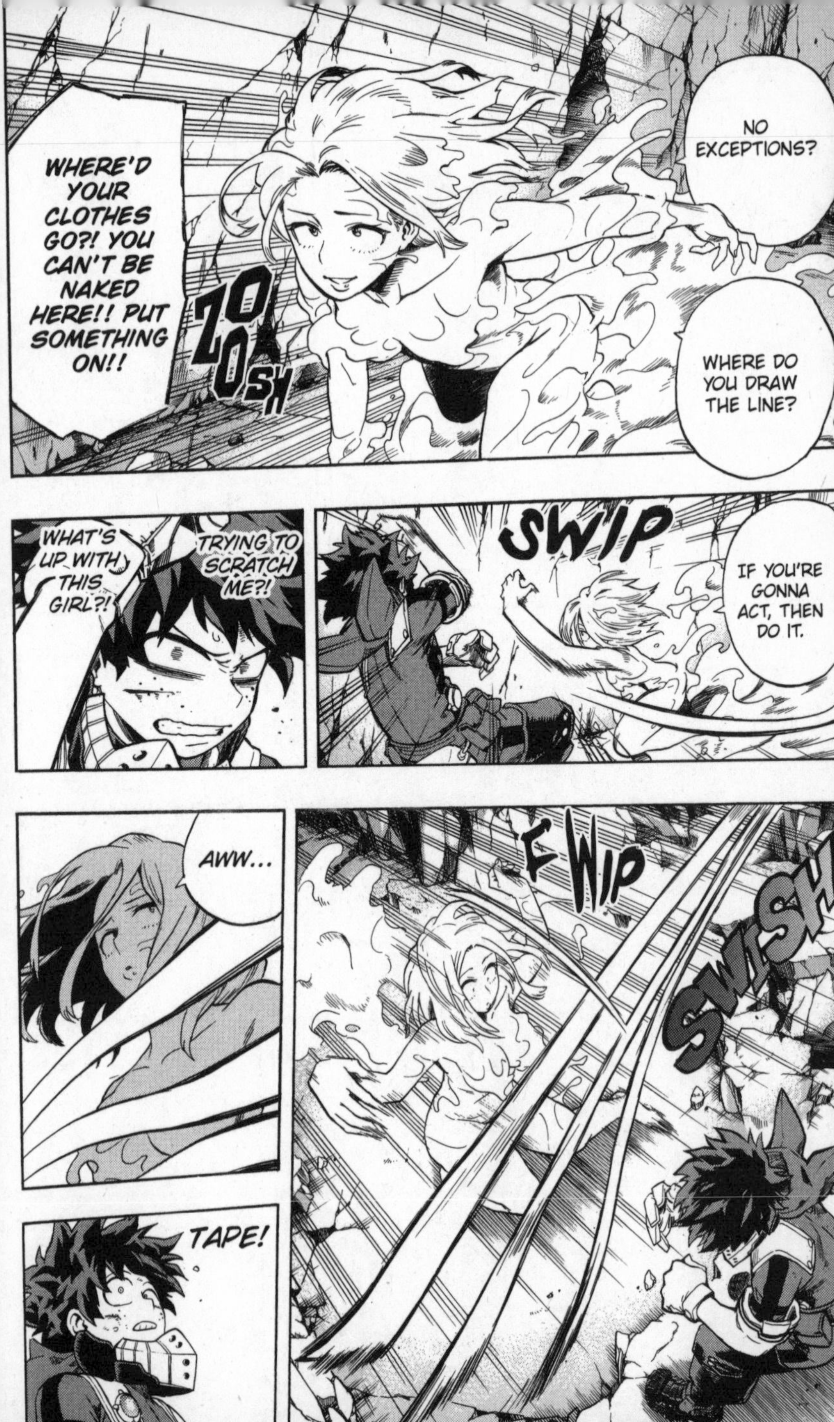
NO EXCEPTIONS?
WHERE DO YOU DRAW THE LINE?
WHERE'D YOUR CLOTHES GO?! YOU CAN'T BE NAKED HERE!! PUT SOMETHING ON!!
ZOOSH
IF YOU'RE GONNA ACT, THEN DO IT.
SWIP
TRYING TO SCRATCH ME?!
WHAT'S UP WITH THIS GIRL?!
FWIP
SWISH
AWW...
TAPE!

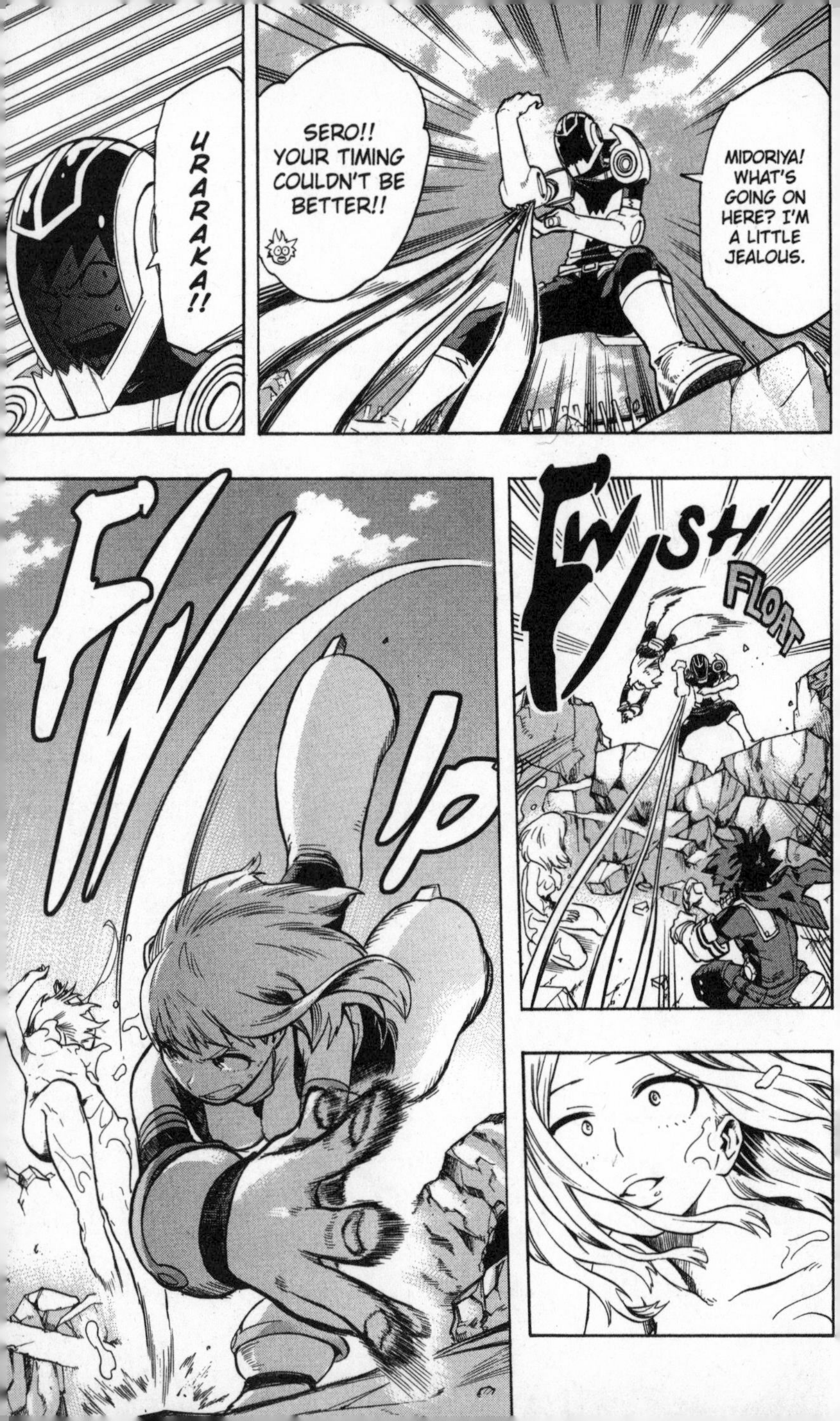
MIDORIYA! WHAT'S GOING ON HERE? I'M A LITTLE JEALOUS.
SERO!! YOUR TIMING COULDN'T BE BETTER!!
URARAKA!!
FWSH
FLOAT
FWIP

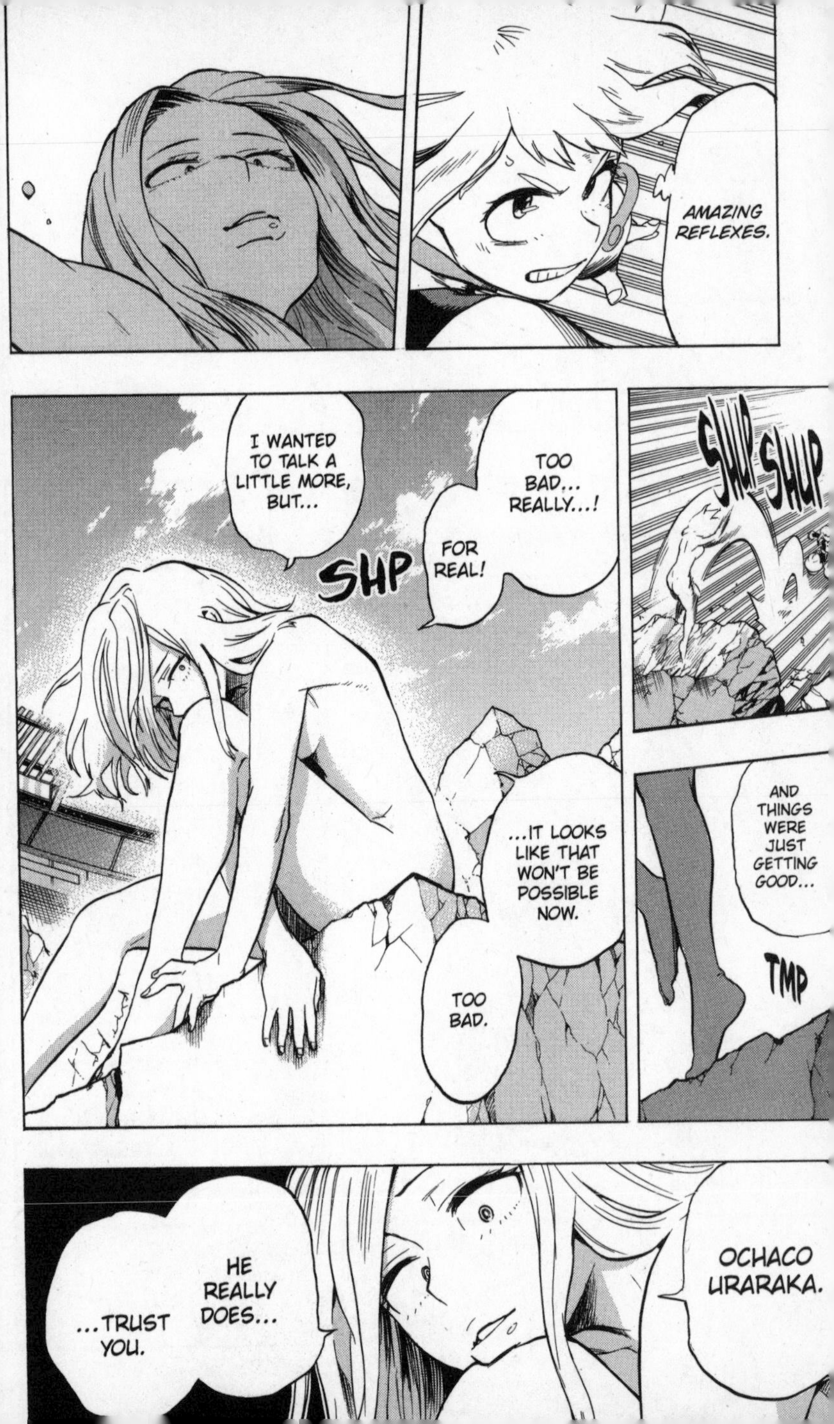
AMAZING REFLEXES.
SHUP SHUP
AND THINGS WERE JUST GETTING GOOD...
TMP
TOO BAD... REALLY...!
FOR REAL!
I WANTED TO TALK A LITTLE MORE, BUT...
SHP
...IT LOOKS LIKE THAT WON'T BE POSSIBLE NOW.
TOO BAD.
OCHACO URARAKA.
HE REALLY DOES...
...TRUST YOU.

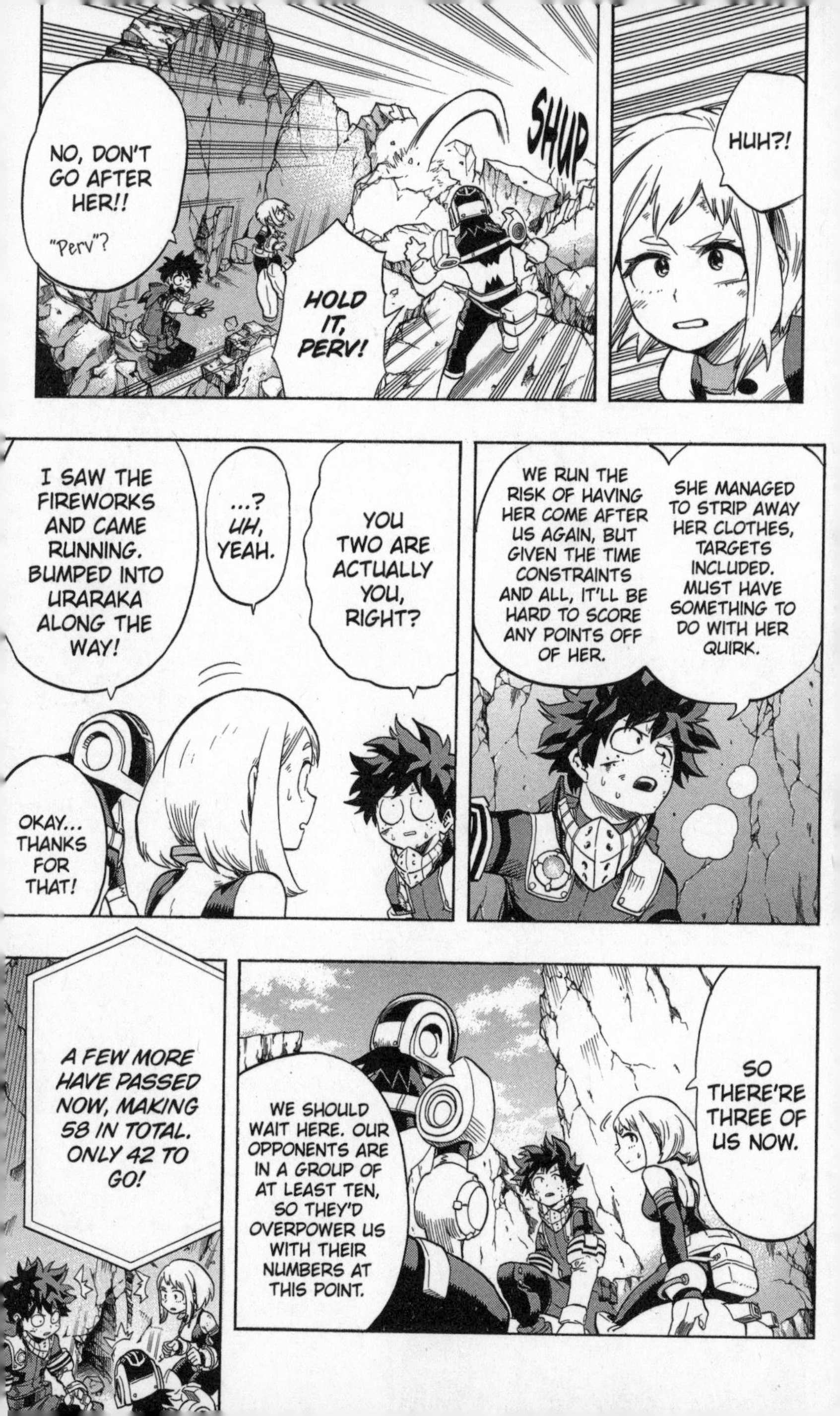
HUH?!
SHUP
HOLD IT, PERV!
NO, DON'T GO AFTER HER!!
"Perv"?
SHE MANAGED TO STRIP AWAY HER CLOTHES, TARGETS INCLUDED. MUST HAVE SOMETHING TO DO WITH HER QUIRK.
WE RUN THE RISK OF HAVING HER COME AFTER US AGAIN, BUT GIVEN THE TIME CONSTRAINTS AND ALL, IT'LL BE HARD TO SCORE ANY POINTS OFF OF HER.
YOU TWO ARE ACTUALLY YOU, RIGHT?
...? UH, YEAH.
I SAW THE FIREWORKS AND CAME RUNNING. BUMPED INTO URARAKA ALONG THE WAY!
OKAY... THANKS FOR THAT!
SO THERE'RE THREE OF US NOW.
WE SHOULD WAIT HERE. OUR OPPONENTS ARE IN A GROUP OF AT LEAST TEN, SO THEY'D OVERPOWER US WITH THEIR NUMBERS AT THIS POINT.
A FEW MORE HAVE PASSED NOW, MAKING 58 IN TOTAL. ONLY 42 TO GO!

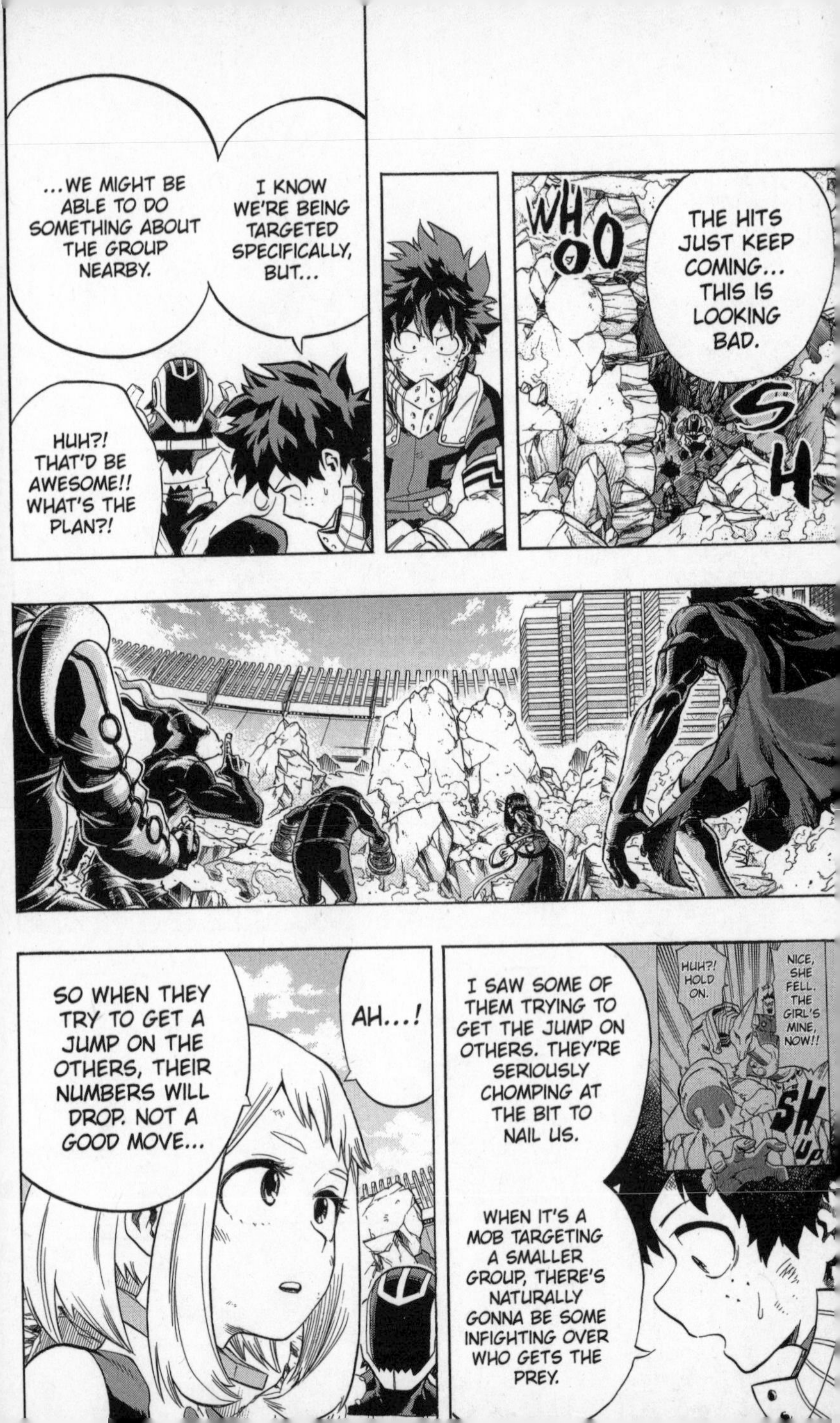
WHOOO
THE HITS JUST KEEP COMING... THIS IS LOOKING BAD.
SH
I KNOW WE'RE BEING TARGETED SPECIFICALLY, BUT...
...WE MIGHT BE ABLE TO DO SOMETHING ABOUT THE GROUP NEARBY.
HUH?! THAT'D BE AWESOME!! WHAT'S THE PLAN?!
NICE, SHE FELL. THE GIRL'S MINE, NOW!!
HUH?! HOLD ON.
SHUP
I SAW SOME OF THEM TRYING TO GET THE JUMP ON OTHERS. THEY'RE SERIOUSLY CHOMPING AT THE BIT TO NAIL US.
WHEN IT'S A MOB TARGETING A SMALLER GROUP, THERE'S NATURALLY GONNA BE SOME INFIGHTING OVER WHO GETS THE PREY.
AH...!
SO WHEN THEY TRY TO GET A JUMP ON THE OTHERS, THEIR NUMBERS WILL DROP. NOT A GOOD MOVE...

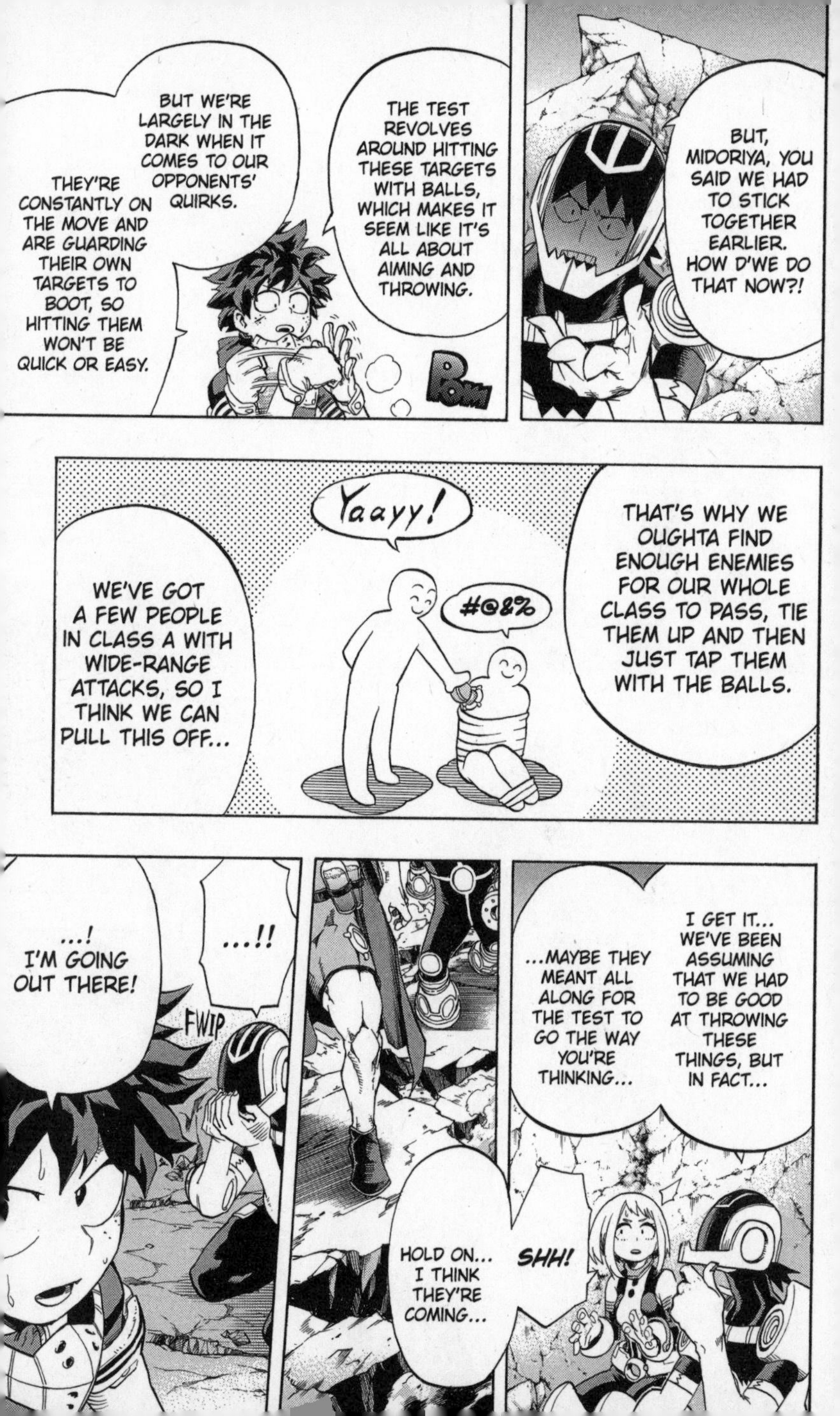
BUT, MIDORIYA, YOU SAID WE HAD TO STICK TOGETHER EARLIER. HOW D'WE DO THAT NOW?!
THE TEST REVOLVES AROUND HITTING THESE TARGETS WITH BALLS, WHICH MAKES IT SEEM LIKE IT'S ALL ABOUT AIMING AND THROWING.
BUT WE'RE LARGELY IN THE DARK WHEN IT COMES TO OUR OPPONENTS' QUIRKS.
THEY'RE CONSTANTLY ON THE MOVE AND ARE GUARDING THEIR OWN TARGETS TO BOOT, SO HITTING THEM WON'T BE QUICK OR EASY.
POM
THAT'S WHY WE OUGHTA FIND ENOUGH ENEMIES FOR OUR WHOLE CLASS TO PASS, TIE THEM UP AND THEN JUST TAP THEM WITH THE BALLS.
Yaayy!
#@&%
WE'VE GOT A FEW PEOPLE IN CLASS A WITH WIDE-RANGE ATTACKS, SO I THINK WE CAN PULL THIS OFF...
I GET IT... WE'VE BEEN ASSUMING THAT WE HAD TO BE GOOD AT THROWING THESE THINGS, BUT IN FACT...
...MAYBE THEY MEANT ALL ALONG FOR THE TEST TO GO THE WAY YOU'RE THINKING...
SHH!
HOLD ON... I THINK THEY'RE COMING...
...!!
...! I'M GOING OUT THERE!
FWIP

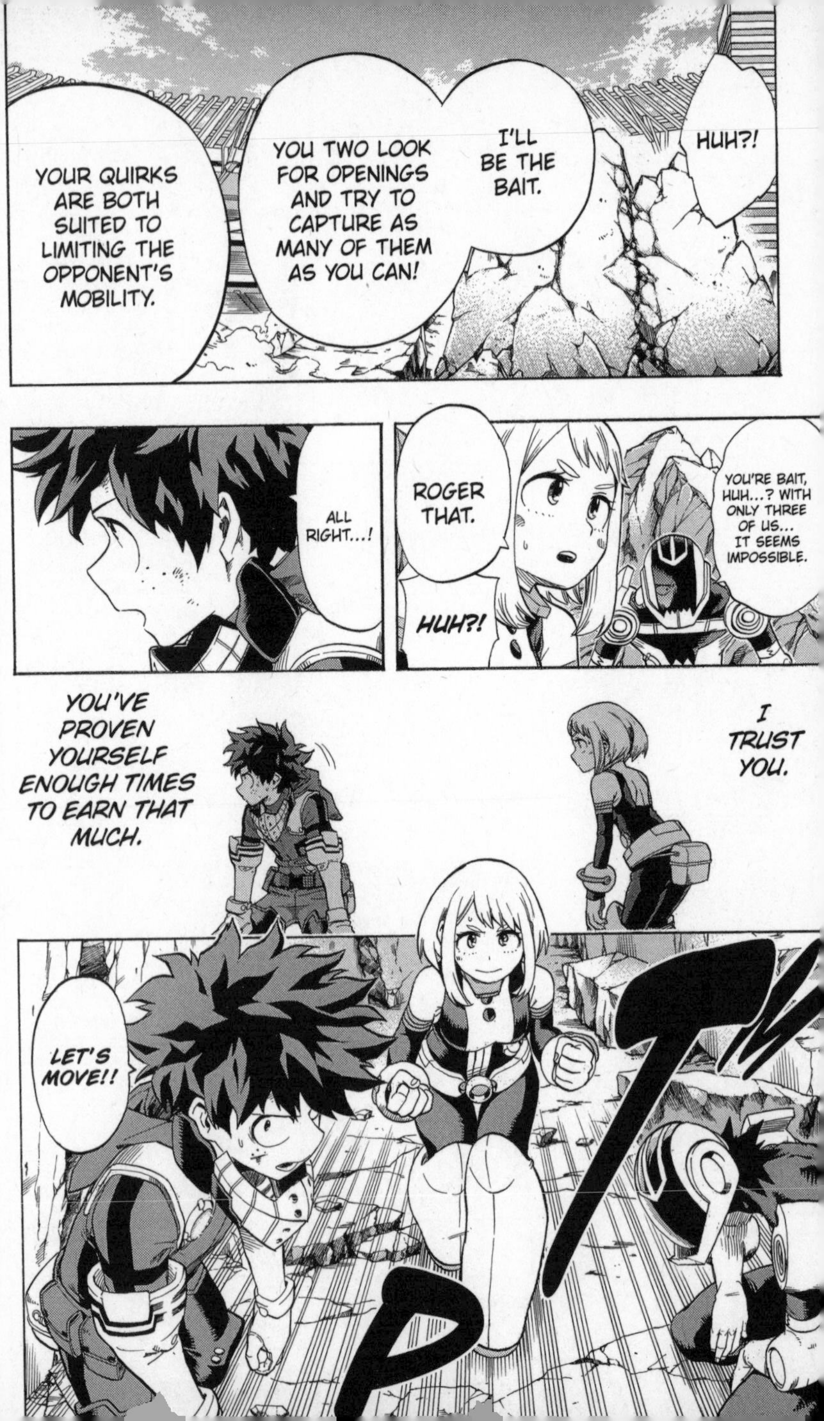
HUH?!
I'LL BE THE BAIT.
YOU TWO LOOK FOR OPENINGS AND TRY TO CAPTURE AS MANY OF THEM AS YOU CAN!
YOUR QUIRKS ARE BOTH SUITED TO LIMITING THE OPPONENT'S MOBILITY.
YOU'RE BAIT, HUH...? WITH ONLY THREE OF US... IT SEEMS IMPOSSIBLE.
ROGER THAT.
HUH?!
ALL RIGHT...!
I TRUST YOU.
YOU'VE PROVEN YOURSELF ENOUGH TIMES TO EARN THAT MUCH.
LET'S MOVE!!

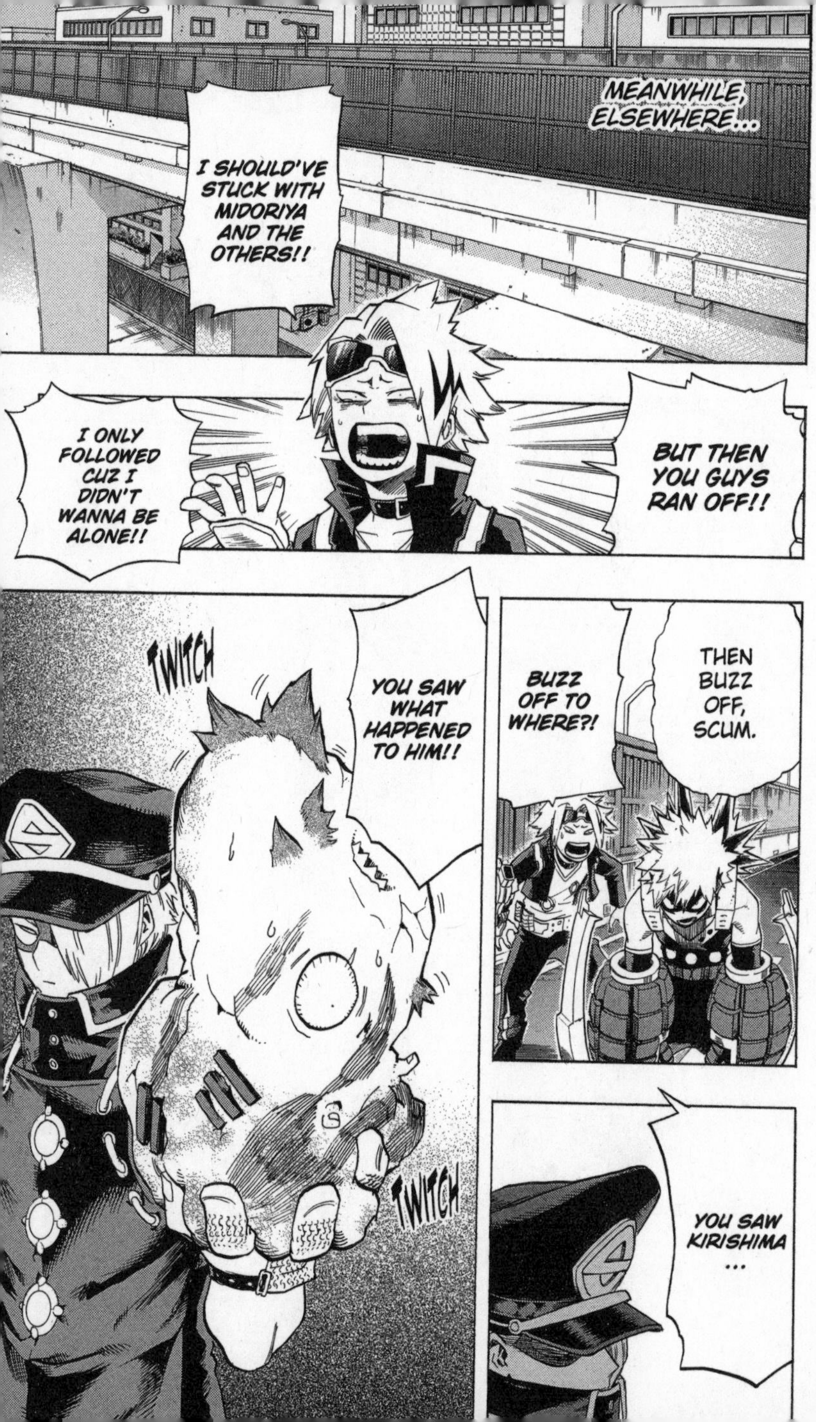
MEANWHILE, ELSEWHERE...
I SHOULD'VE STUCK WITH MIDORIYA AND THE OTHERS!!
BUT THEN YOU GUYS RAN OFF!!
I ONLY FOLLOWED CUZ I DIDN'T WANNA BE ALONE!!
THEN BUZZ OFF, SCUM.
BUZZ OFF TO WHERE?!
YOU SAW KIRISHIMA ...
TWITCH
YOU SAW WHAT HAPPENED TO HIM!!
TWITCH

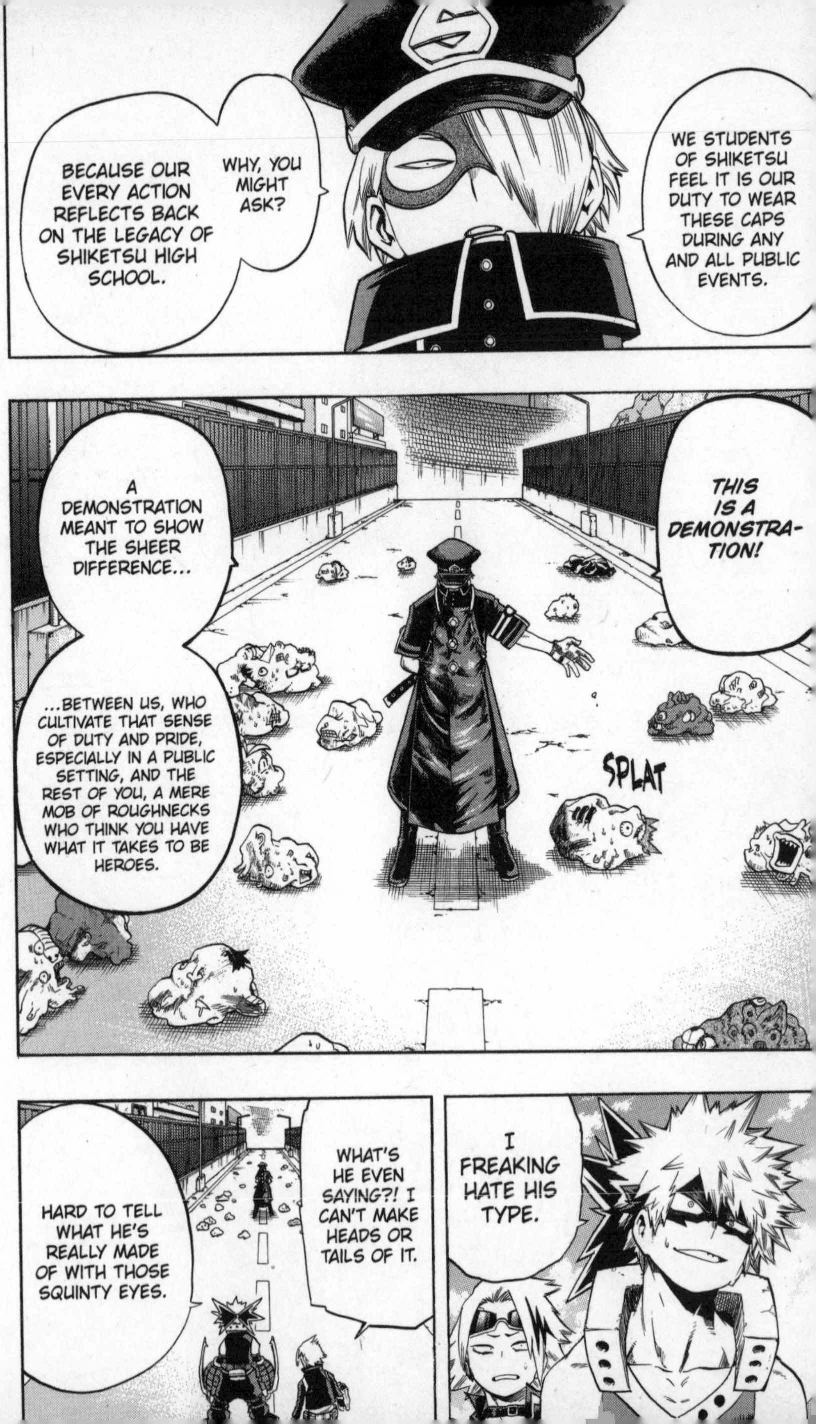
WE STUDENTS OF SHIKETSU FEEL IT IS OUR DUTY TO WEAR THESE CAPS DURING ANY AND ALL PUBLIC EVENTS.
WHY, YOU MIGHT ASK?
BECAUSE OUR EVERY ACTION REFLECTS BACK ON THE LEGACY OF SHIKETSU HIGH SCHOOL.
THIS IS A DEMONSTRATION!
A DEMONSTRATION MEANT TO SHOW THE SHEER DIFFERENCE...
...BETWEEN US, WHO CULTIVATE THAT SENSE OF DUTY AND PRIDE, ESPECIALLY IN A PUBLIC SETTING, AND THE REST OF YOU, A MERE MOB OF ROUGHNECKS WHO THINK YOU HAVE WHAT IT TAKES TO BE HEROES.
SPLAT
I FREAKING HATE HIS TYPE.
WHAT'S HE EVEN SAYING?! I CAN'T MAKE HEADS OR TAILS OF IT.
HARD TO TELL WHAT HE'S REALLY MADE OF WITH THOSE SQUINTY EYES.

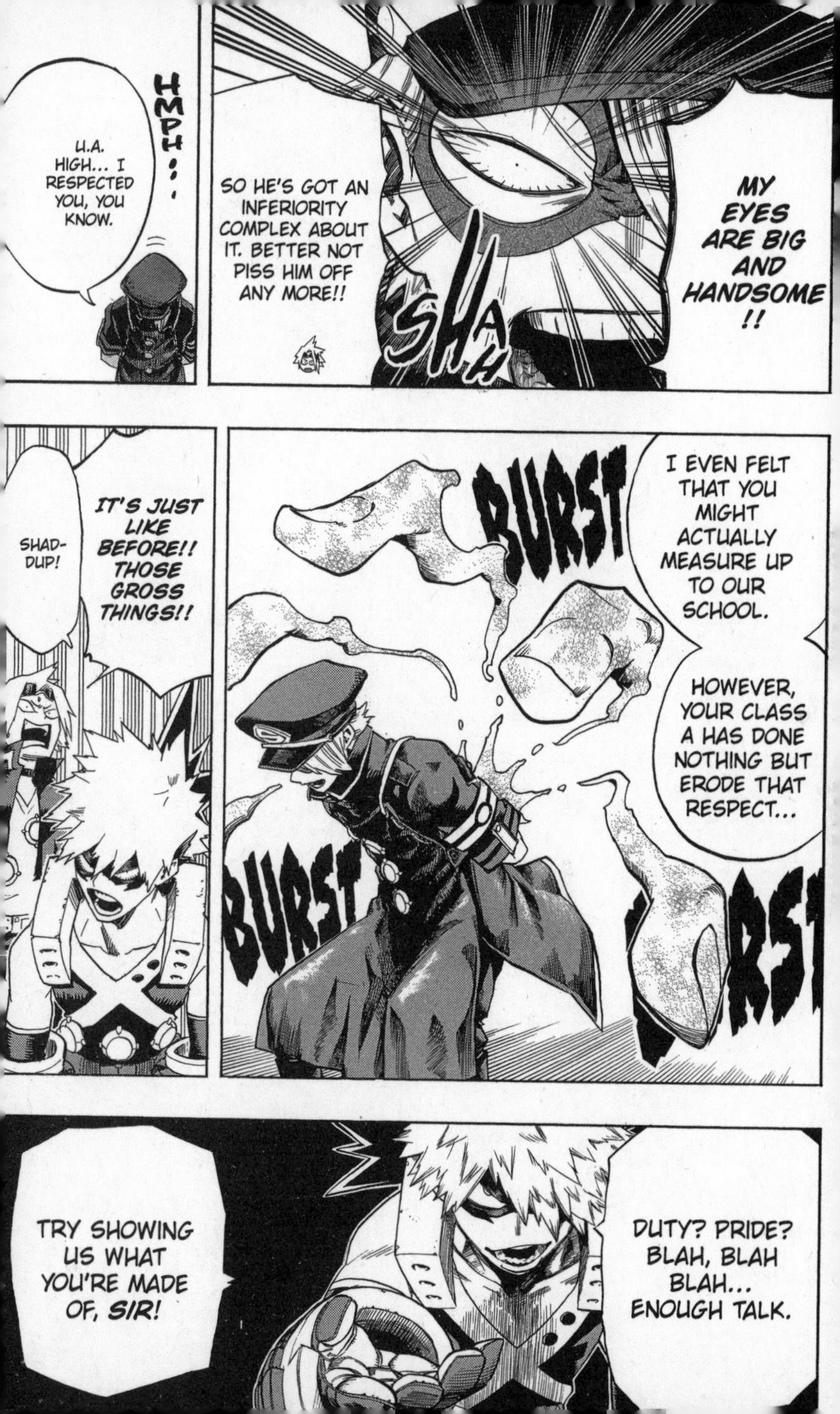
MY EYES ARE BIG AND HANDSOME!!
SHAH
SO HE'S GOT AN INFERIORITY COMPLEX ABOUT IT. BETTER NOT PISS HIM OFF ANY MORE!!
HMPH...
U.A. HIGH... I RESPECTED YOU, YOU KNOW.
I EVEN FELT THAT YOU MIGHT ACTUALLY MEASURE UP TO OUR SCHOOL.
HOWEVER, YOUR CLASS A HAS DONE NOTHING BUT ERODE THAT RESPECT...
BURST
BURST
IT'S JUST LIKE BEFORE!! THOSE GROSS THINGS!!
SHAD-DUP!
DUTY? PRIDE? BLAH, BLAH BLAH... ENOUGH TALK.
TRY SHOWING US WHAT YOU'RE MADE OF, SIR!

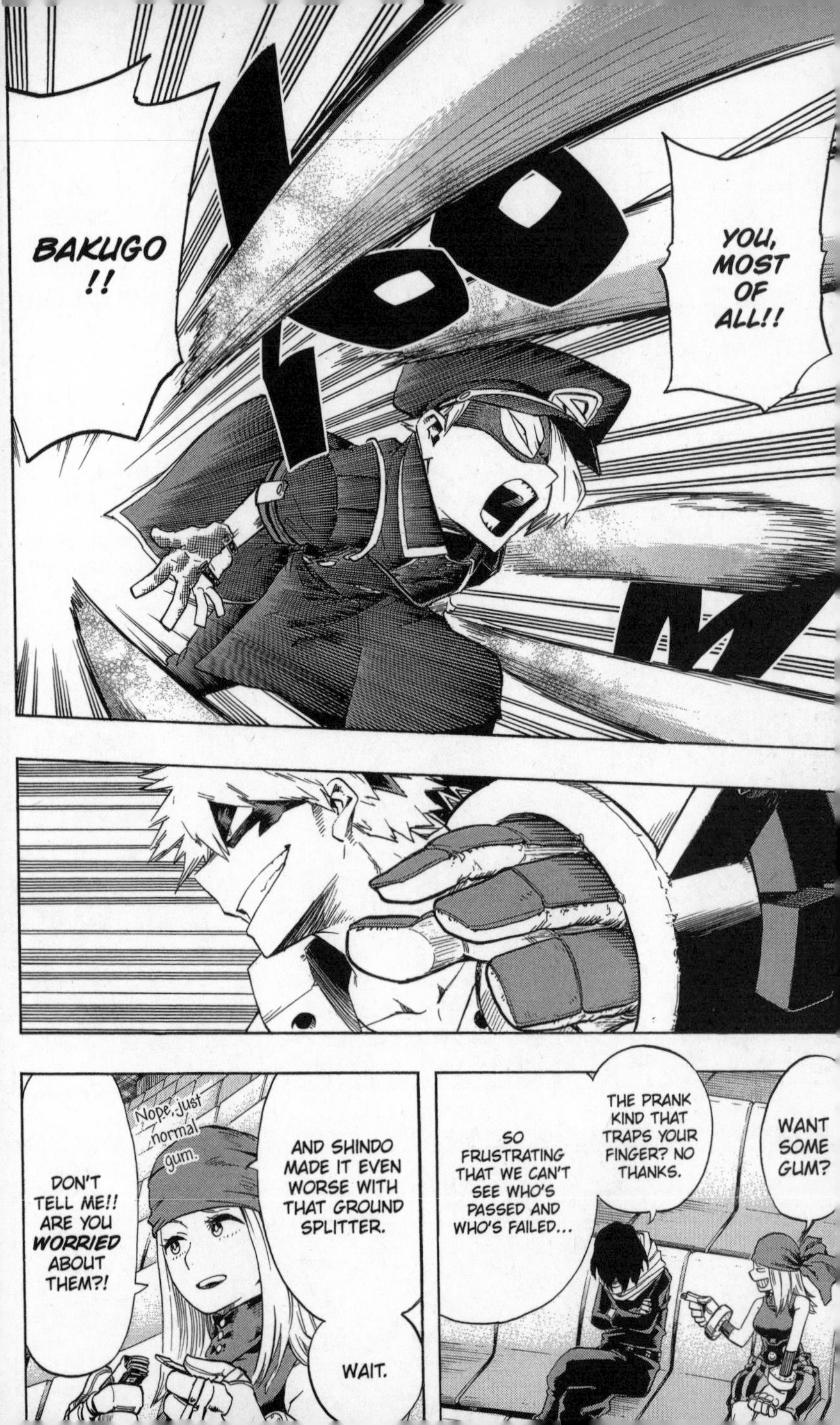
YOU, MOST OF ALL!!
BAKUGO!!
WANT SOME GUM?
THE PRANK KIND THAT TRAPS YOUR FINGER? NO THANKS.
SO FRUSTRATING THAT WE CAN'T SEE WHO'S PASSED AND WHO'S FAILED...
AND SHINDO MADE IT EVEN WORSE WITH THAT GROUND SPLITTER.
Nope, just normal gum.
WAIT.
DON'T TELL ME!! ARE YOU ***WORRIED*** ABOUT THEM?!

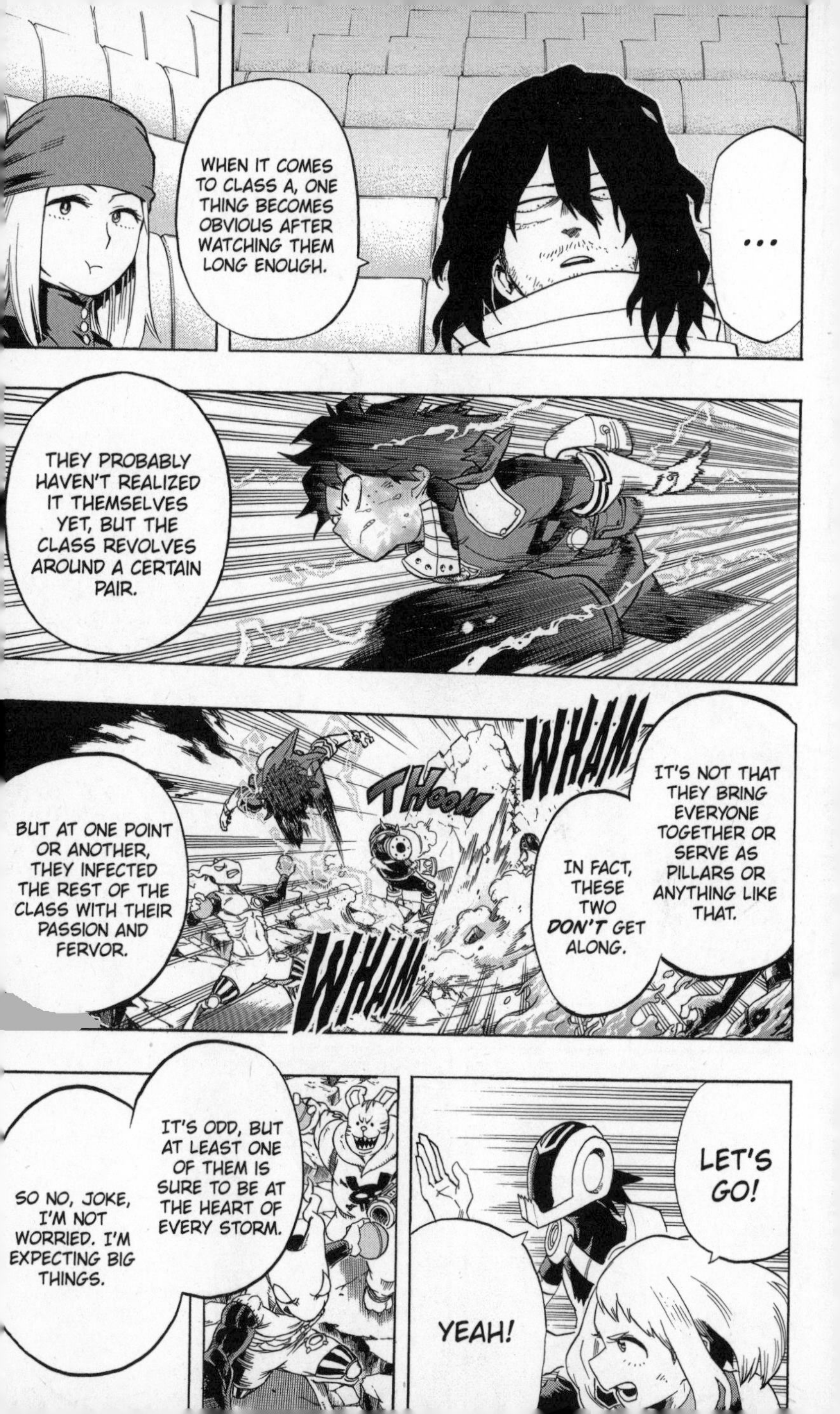
...
WHEN IT COMES TO CLASS A, ONE THING BECOMES OBVIOUS AFTER WATCHING THEM LONG ENOUGH.
THEY PROBABLY HAVEN'T REALIZED IT THEMSELVES YET, BUT THE CLASS REVOLVES AROUND A CERTAIN PAIR.
IT'S NOT THAT THEY BRING EVERYONE TOGETHER OR SERVE AS PILLARS OR ANYTHING LIKE THAT.
IN FACT, THESE TWO *DON'T* GET ALONG.
WHAM
THOOM
BUT AT ONE POINT OR ANOTHER, THEY INFECTED THE REST OF THE CLASS WITH THEIR PASSION AND FERVOR.
WHAM
LET'S GO!
YEAH!
IT'S ODD, BUT AT LEAST ONE OF THEM IS SURE TO BE AT THE HEART OF EVERY STORM.
SO NO, JOKE, I'M NOT WORRIED. I'M EXPECTING BIG THINGS.

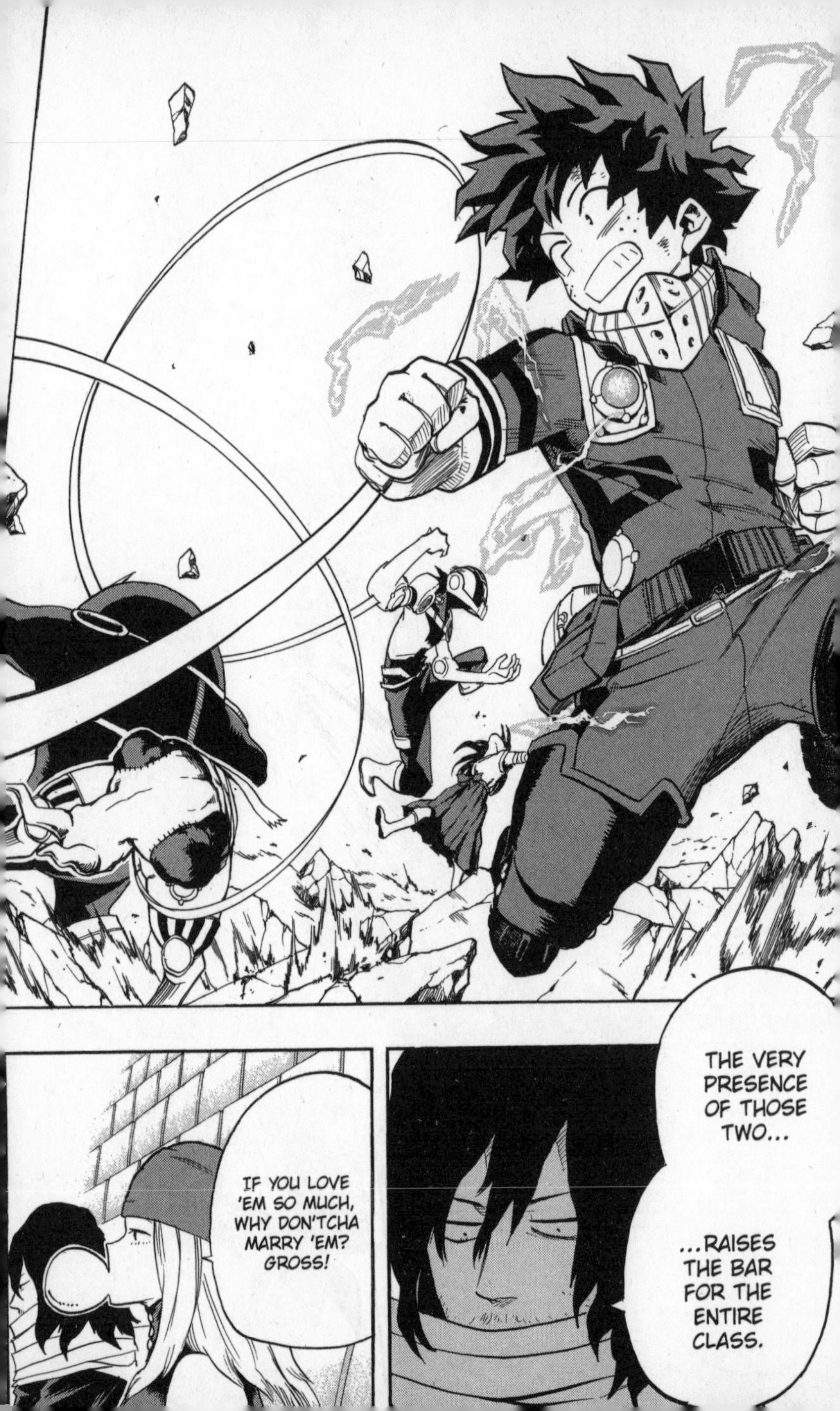
THE VERY PRESENCE OF THOSE TWO...
...RAISES THE BAR FOR THE ENTIRE CLASS.
IF YOU LOVE 'EM SO MUCH, WHY DON'TCHA MARRY 'EM? GROSS!

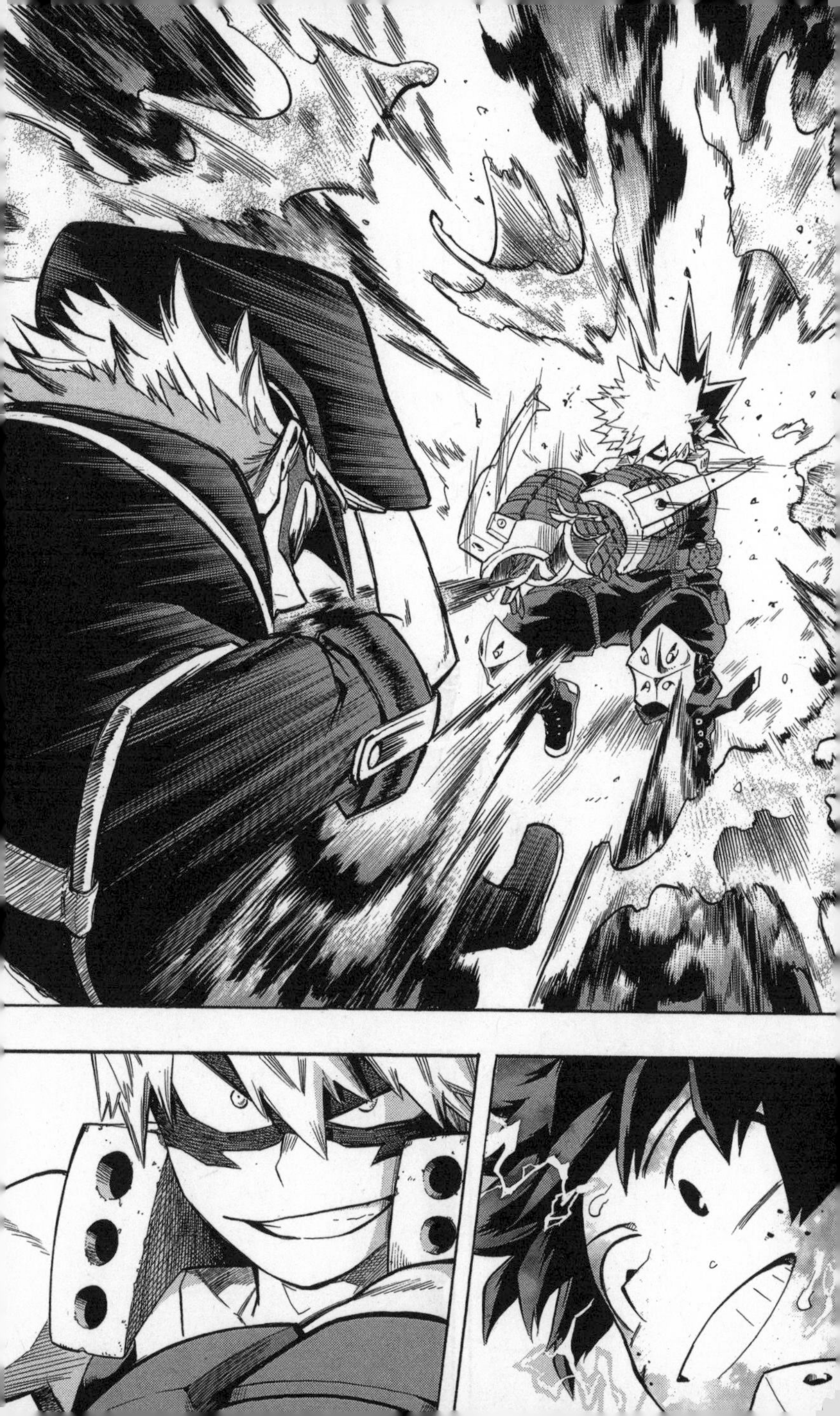

SEIJI SHISHIKURA (16)

STREET CLOTHES

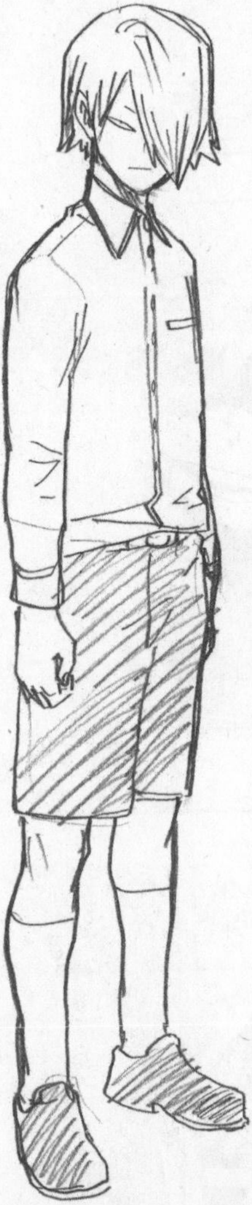

Birthday: 2/9
Height: 172 cm
Favorite Thing: Vegetables

THE SUPPLEMENT

I actually really like this guy. His Quirk is so awesomely gross. I wanna write *The Heartwarming, Comedic Times of Shishikura's Meatballs*, a story that follows him in his everyday life.

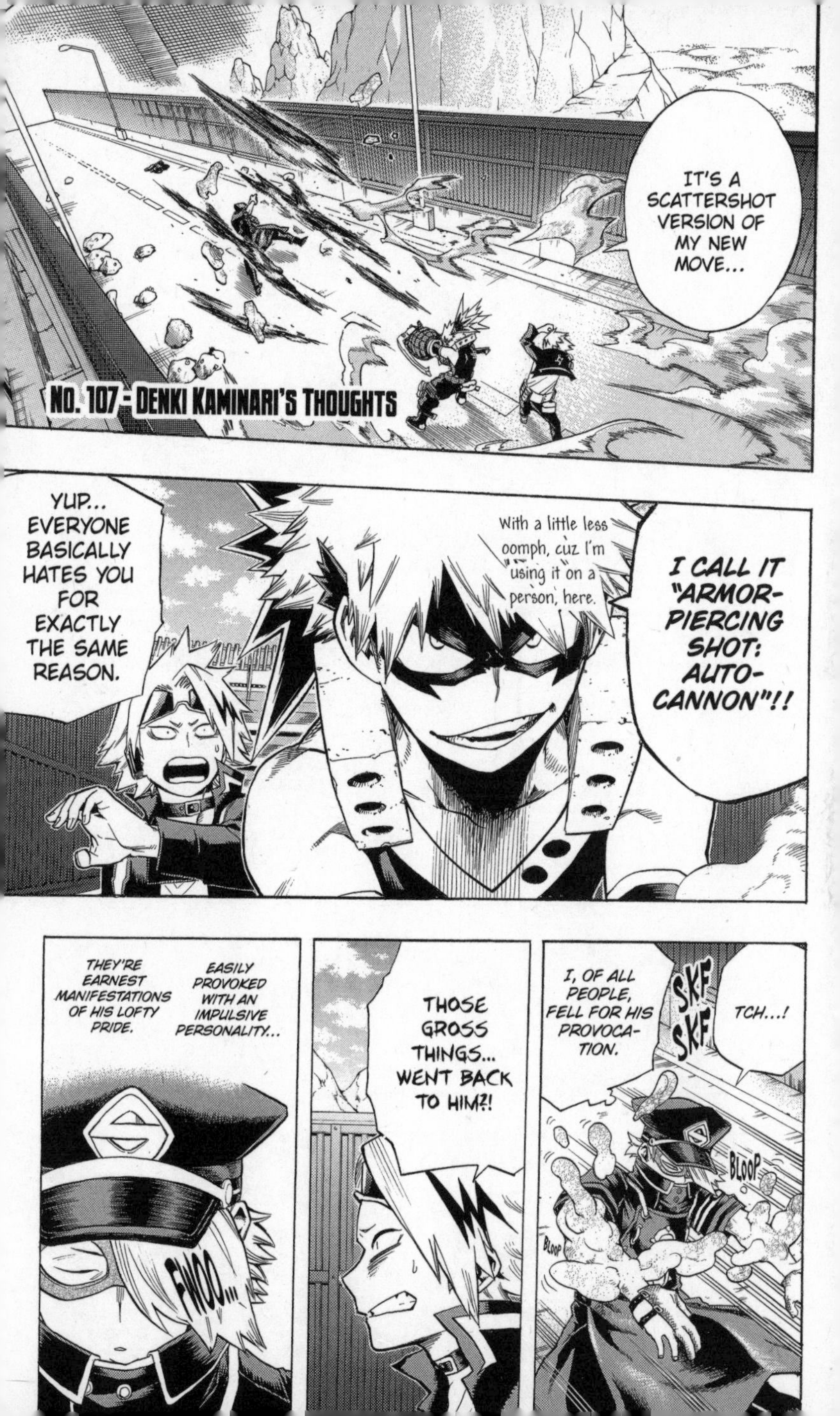
No. 107 - Denki Kaminari's Thoughts
IT'S A SCATTERSHOT VERSION OF MY NEW MOVE...
I CALL IT "ARMOR-PIERCING SHOT: AUTO-CANNON"!!
With a little less oomph, cuz I'm using it on a person, here.
YUP... EVERYONE BASICALLY HATES YOU FOR EXACTLY THE SAME REASON.
TCH...!
SKF SKF
I, OF ALL PEOPLE, FELL FOR HIS PROVOCA-TION.
BLOOP
BLOOP
THOSE GROSS THINGS... WENT BACK TO HIM?!
EASILY PROVOKED WITH AN IMPULSIVE PERSONALITY...
THEY'RE EARNEST MANIFESTATIONS OF HIS LOFTY PRIDE.
FWOO...

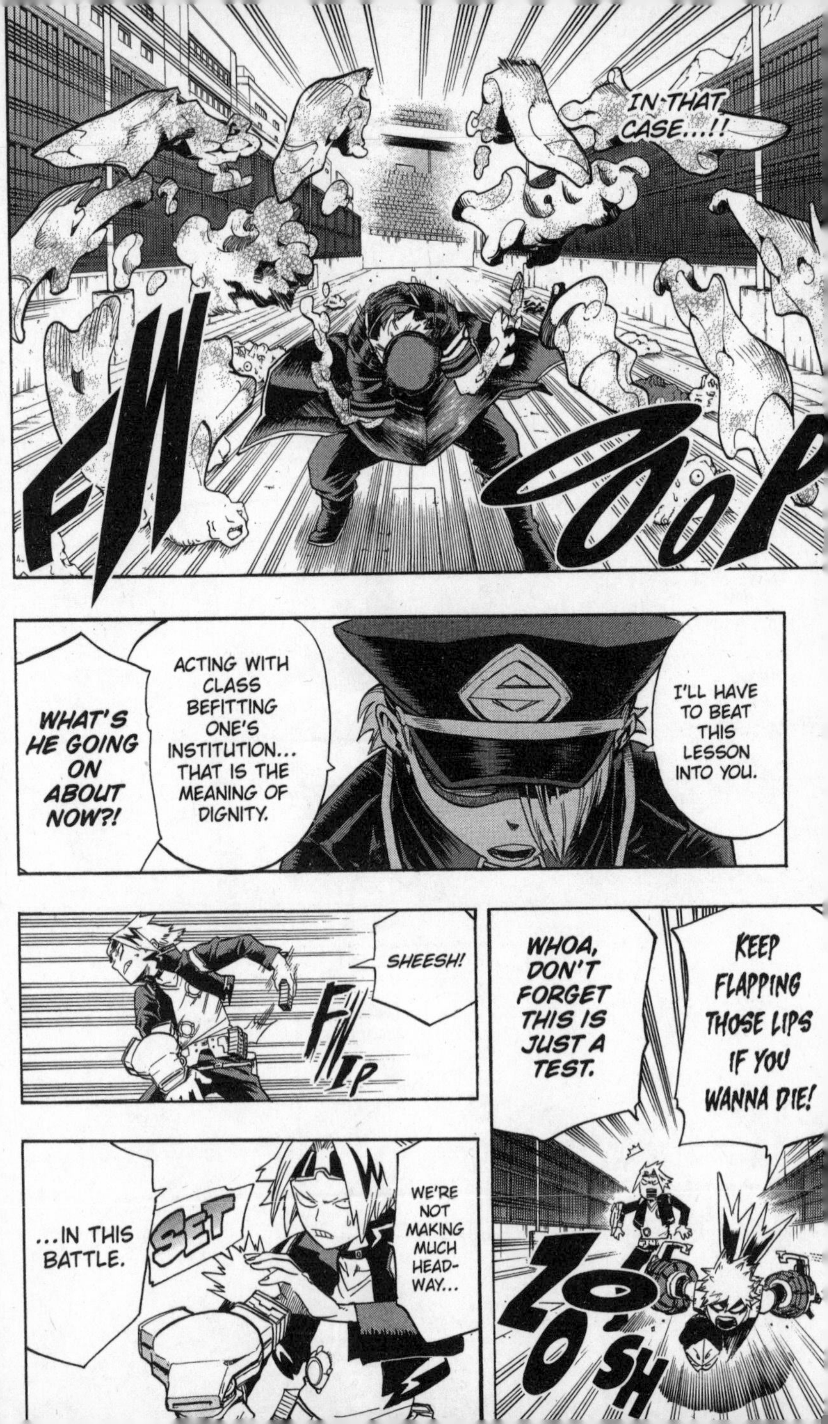
IN THAT CASE...!!
FWOOOP
I'LL HAVE TO BEAT THIS LESSON INTO YOU.
ACTING WITH CLASS BEFITTING ONE'S INSTITUTION... THAT IS THE MEANING OF DIGNITY.
WHAT'S HE GOING ON ABOUT NOW?!
KEEP FLAPPING THOSE LIPS IF YOU WANNA DIE!
WHOA, DON'T FORGET THIS IS JUST A TEST.
ZOOSH
SHEESH!
FLIP
WE'RE NOT MAKING MUCH HEADWAY...
SET
...IN THIS BATTLE.

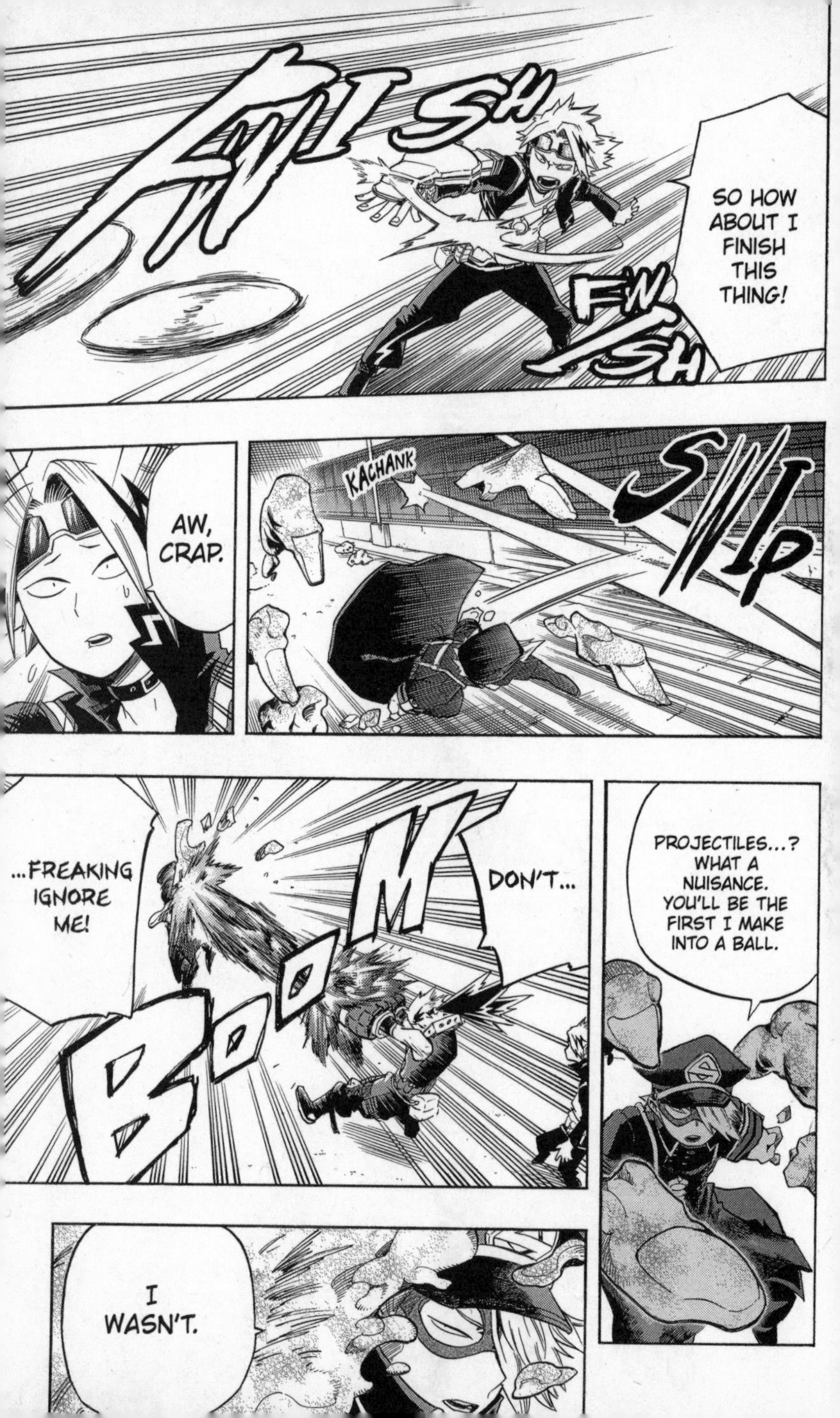
SO HOW ABOUT I FINISH THIS THING!
KACHANK
AW, CRAP.
PROJECTILES...? WHAT A NUISANCE. YOU'LL BE THE FIRST I MAKE INTO A BALL.
DON'T...
...FREAKING IGNORE ME!
BOOM
I WASN'T.

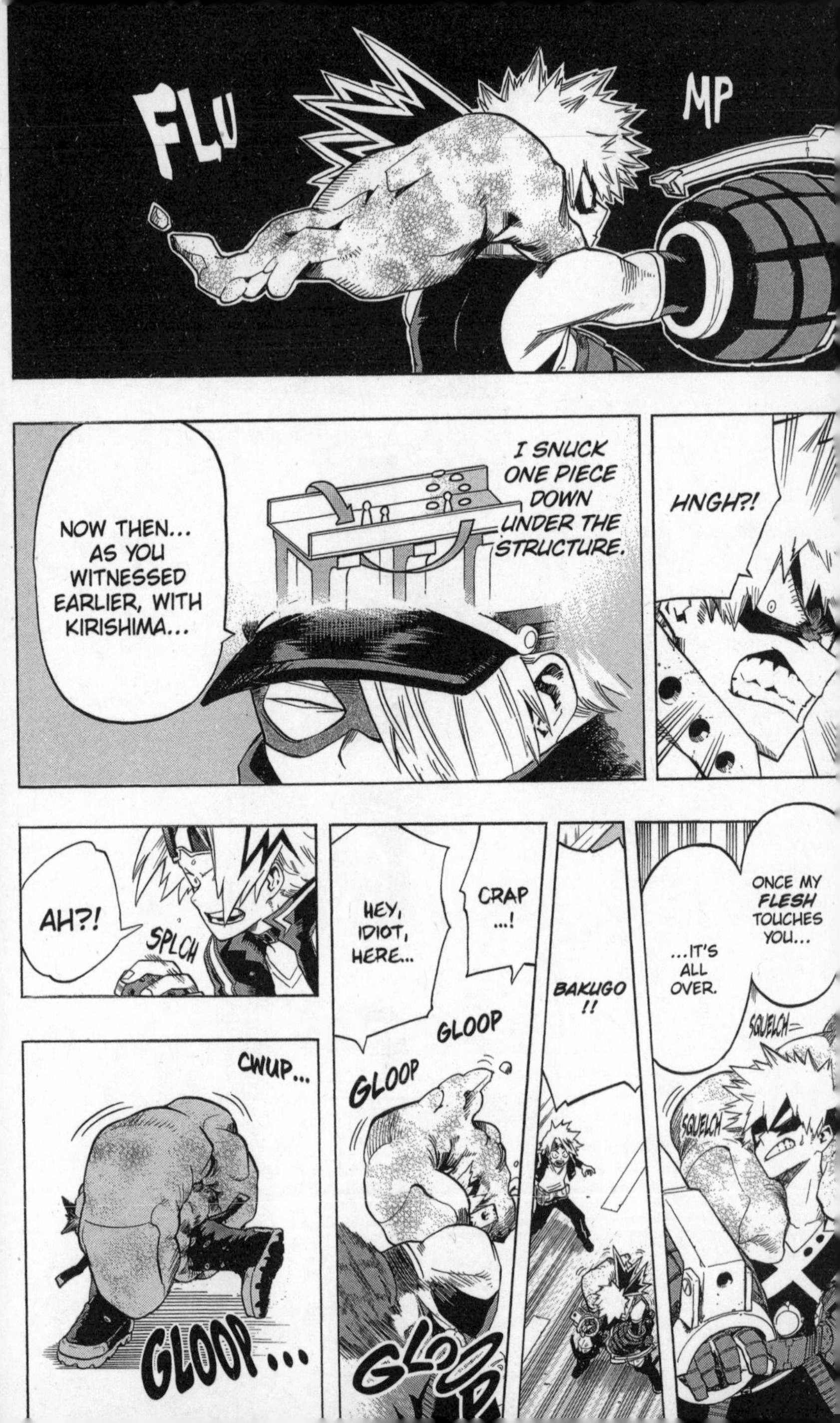

FLU
MP
HNGH?!
I SNUCK ONE PIECE DOWN UNDER THE STRUCTURE.
NOW THEN... AS YOU WITNESSED EARLIER, WITH KIRISHIMA...
ONCE MY FLESH TOUCHES YOU...
...IT'S ALL OVER.
SQUELCH
SQUELCH
BAKUGO!!
CRAP...!
HEY, IDIOT, HERE...
GLOOP
GLOOP
AH?!
SPLCH
CWUP...
GLOOP...

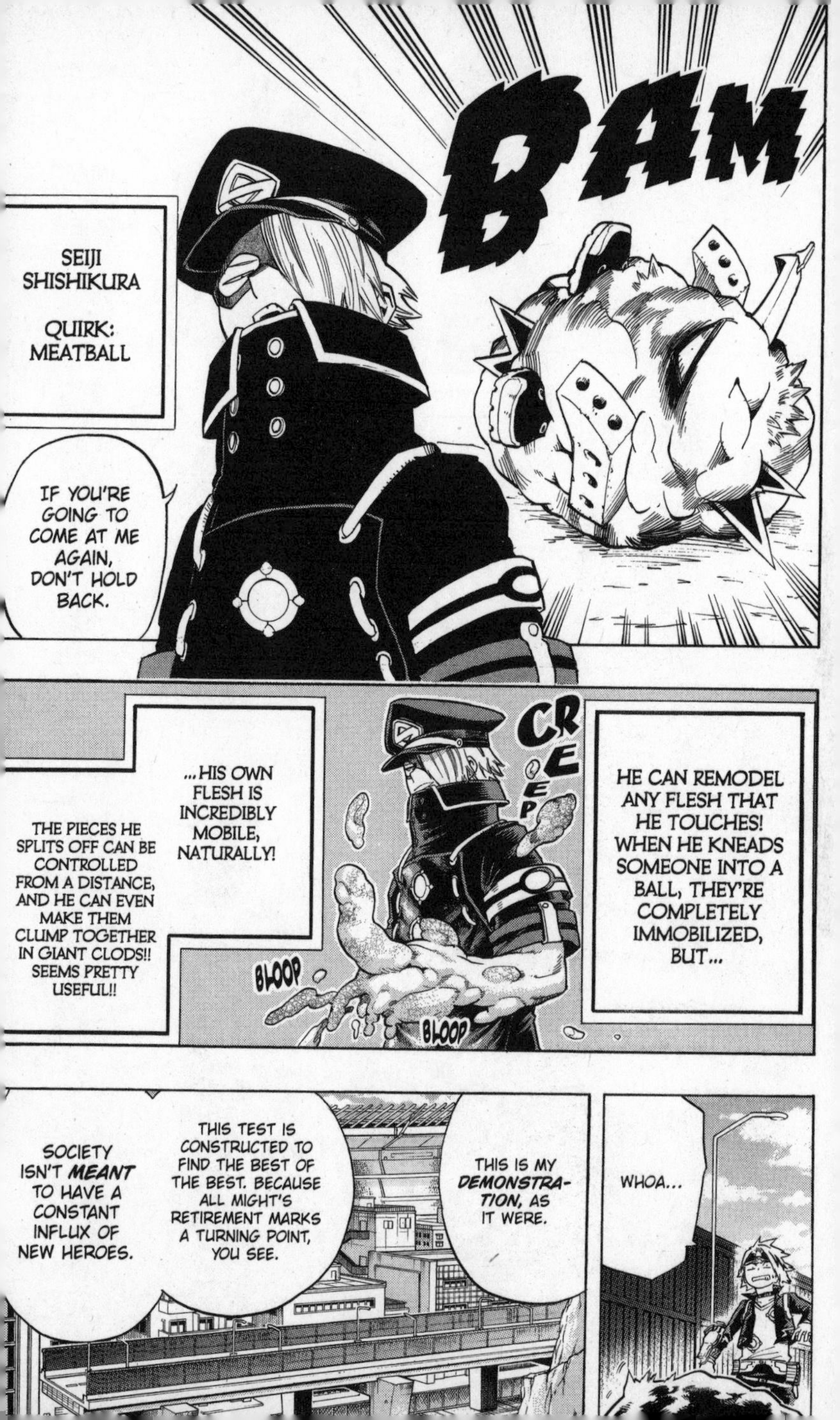
BAM
SEIJI SHISHIKURA

QUIRK: MEATBALL
IF YOU'RE GOING TO COME AT ME AGAIN, DON'T HOLD BACK.
HE CAN REMODEL ANY FLESH THAT HE TOUCHES! WHEN HE KNEADS SOMEONE INTO A BALL, THEY'RE COMPLETELY IMMOBILIZED, BUT...
CREEP
...HIS OWN FLESH IS INCREDIBLY MOBILE, NATURALLY!
THE PIECES HE SPLITS OFF CAN BE CONTROLLED FROM A DISTANCE, AND HE CAN EVEN MAKE THEM CLUMP TOGETHER IN GIANT CLODS!! SEEMS PRETTY USEFUL!!
BLOOP
BLOOP
WHOA...
THIS IS MY *DEMONSTRATION,* AS IT WERE.
THIS TEST IS CONSTRUCTED TO FIND THE BEST OF THE BEST. BECAUSE ALL MIGHT'S RETIREMENT MARKS A TURNING POINT, YOU SEE.
SOCIETY ISN'T *MEANT* TO HAVE A CONSTANT INFLUX OF NEW HEROES.

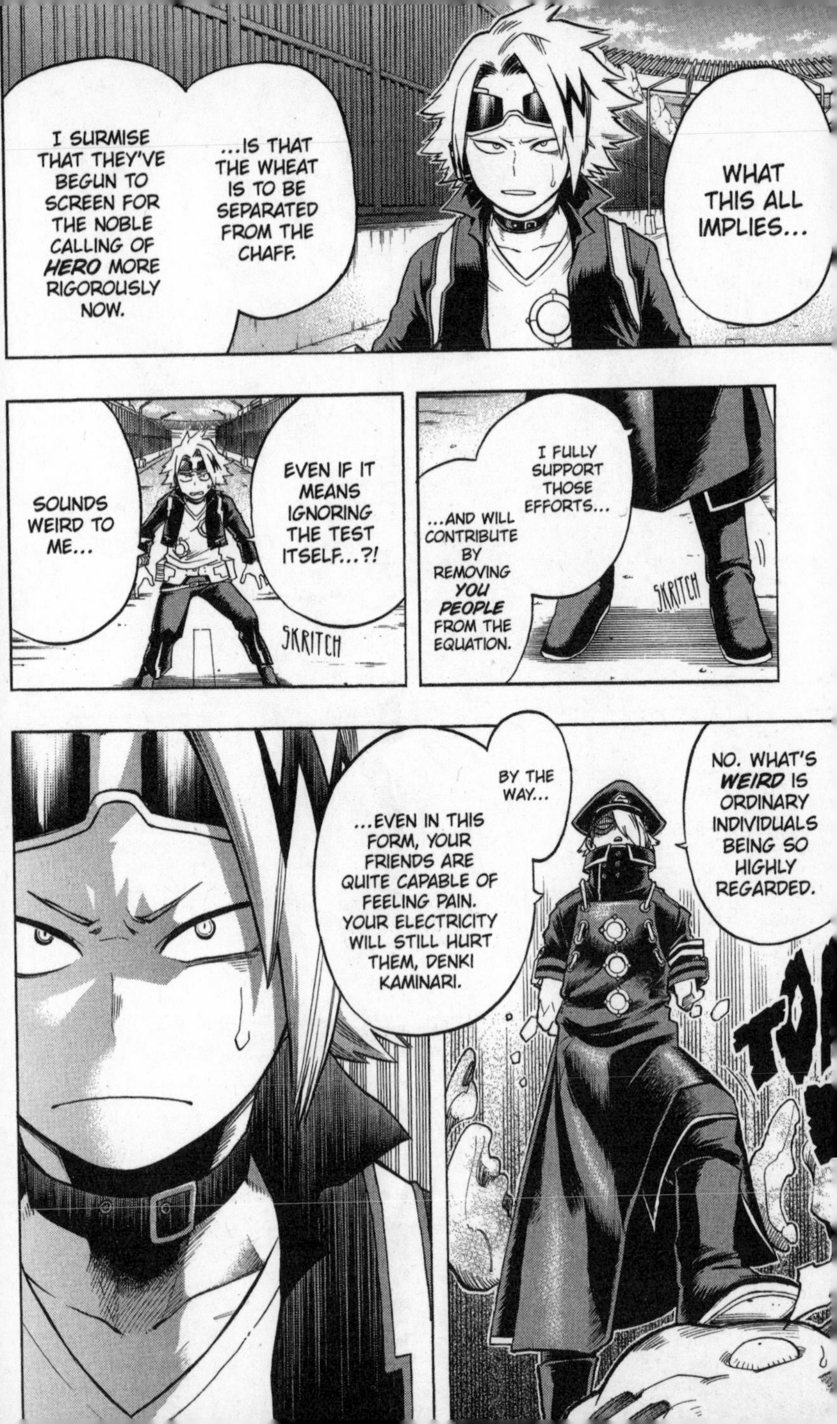
WHAT THIS ALL IMPLIES...
...IS THAT THE WHEAT IS TO BE SEPARATED FROM THE CHAFF.
I SURMISE THAT THEY'VE BEGUN TO SCREEN FOR THE NOBLE CALLING OF *HERO* MORE RIGOROUSLY NOW.
I FULLY SUPPORT THOSE EFFORTS...
...AND WILL CONTRIBUTE BY REMOVING *YOU PEOPLE* FROM THE EQUATION.
SKRITCH
EVEN IF IT MEANS IGNORING THE TEST ITSELF...?!
SOUNDS WEIRD TO ME...
SKRITCH
NO. WHAT'S *WEIRD* IS ORDINARY INDIVIDUALS BEING SO HIGHLY REGARDED.
BY THE WAY...
...EVEN IN THIS FORM, YOUR FRIENDS ARE QUITE CAPABLE OF FEELING PAIN. YOUR ELECTRICITY WILL STILL HURT THEM, DENKI KAMINARI.

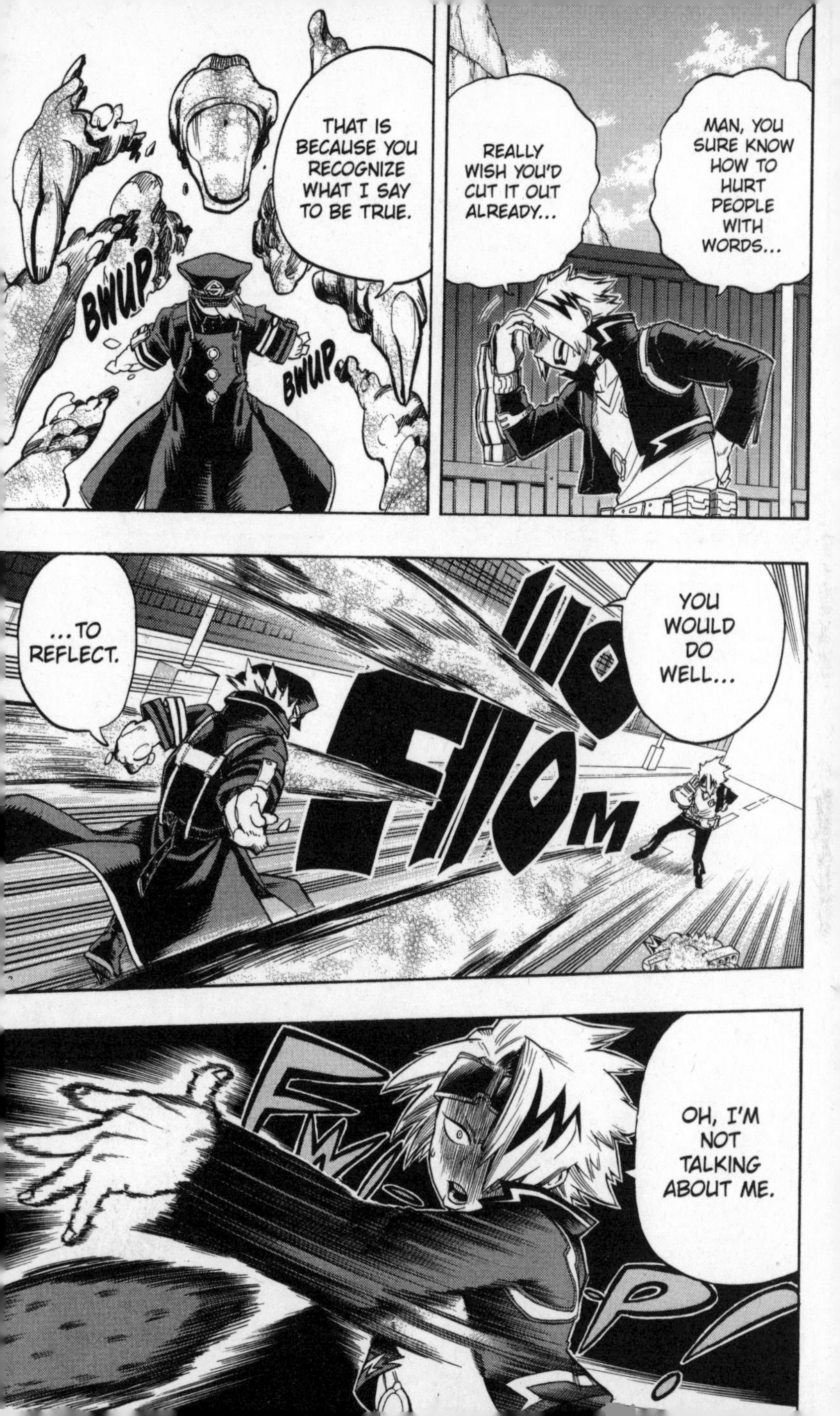
MAN, YOU SURE KNOW HOW TO HURT PEOPLE WITH WORDS...
REALLY WISH YOU'D CUT IT OUT ALREADY...
THAT IS BECAUSE YOU RECOGNIZE WHAT I SAY TO BE TRUE.
BWUP
BWUP
YOU WOULD DO WELL...
...TO REFLECT.
OH, I'M NOT TALKING ABOUT ME.

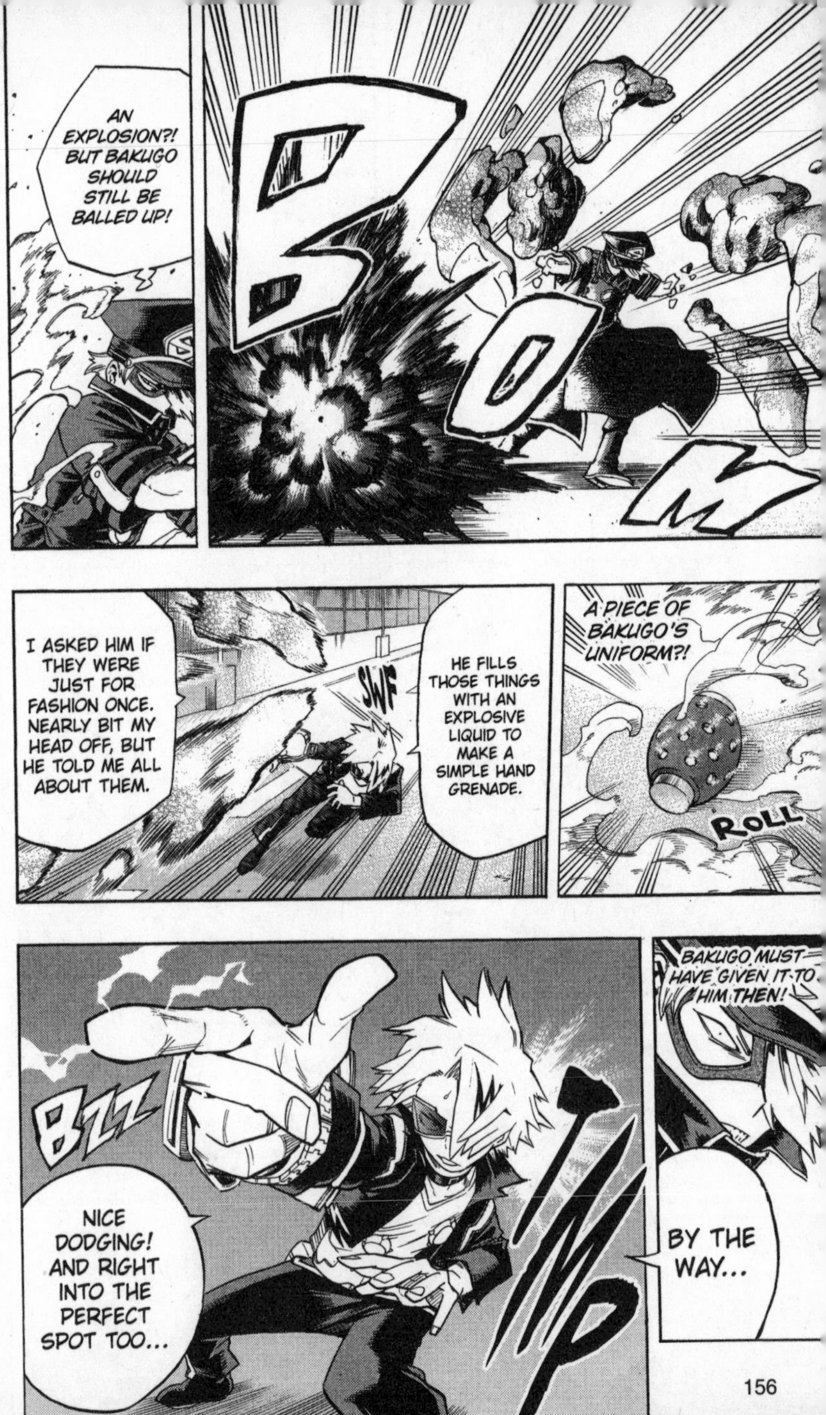
BOOM
AN EXPLOSION?! BUT BAKUGO SHOULD STILL BE BALLED UP!
A PIECE OF BAKUGO'S UNIFORM?!
ROLL
HE FILLS THOSE THINGS WITH AN EXPLOSIVE LIQUID TO MAKE A SIMPLE HAND GRENADE.
SWF
I ASKED HIM IF THEY WERE JUST FOR FASHION ONCE. NEARLY BIT MY HEAD OFF, BUT HE TOLD ME ALL ABOUT THEM.
BAKUGO MUST HAVE GIVEN IT TO HIM THEN!
BY THE WAY...
BZZZ
NICE DODGING! AND RIGHT INTO THE PERFECT SPOT TOO...

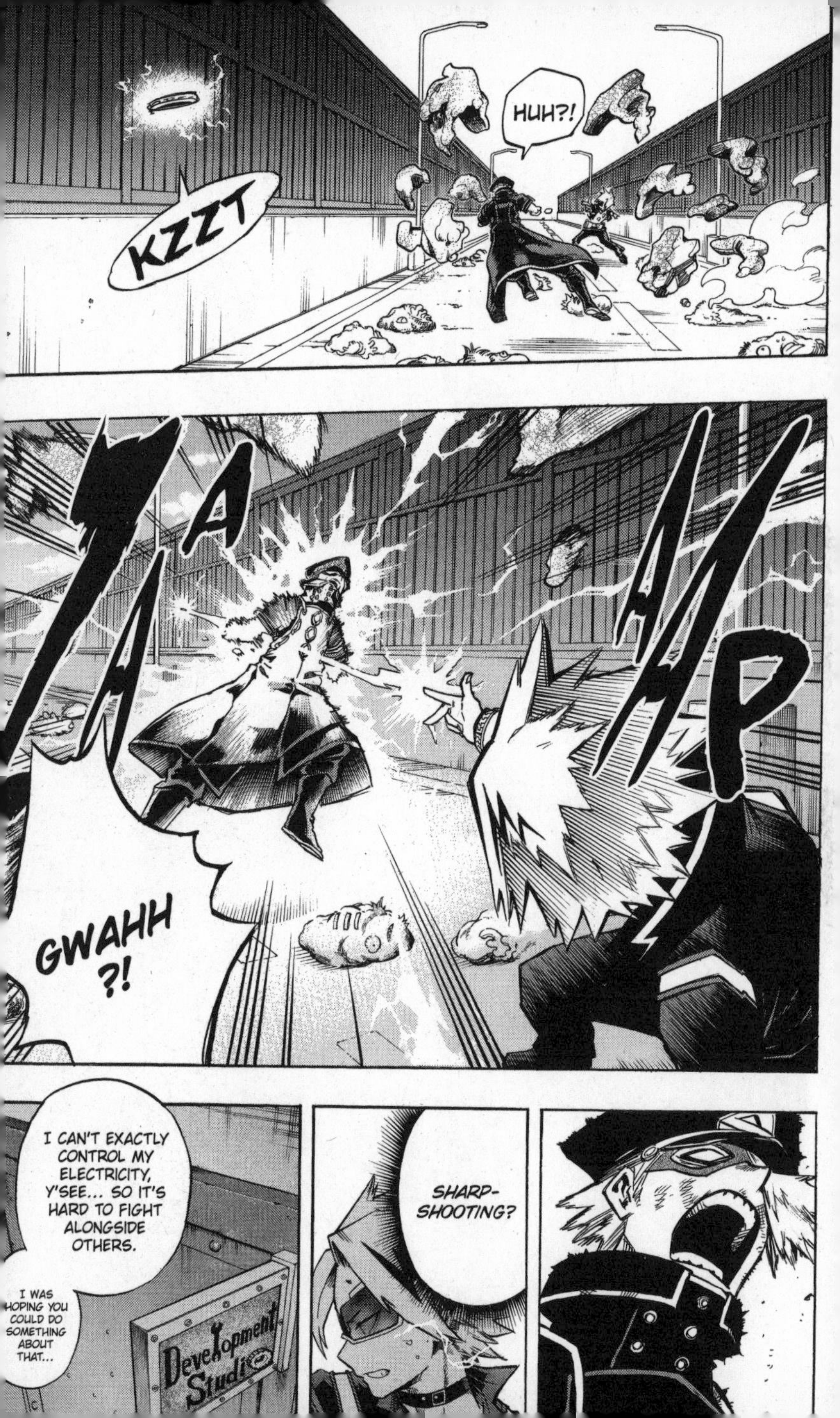
HUH?!
KZZT
ZAAAAP
GWAHH ?!
SHARP-SHOOTING?
I CAN'T EXACTLY CONTROL MY ELECTRICITY, Y'SEE... SO IT'S HARD TO FIGHT ALONGSIDE OTHERS.
I WAS HOPING YOU COULD DO SOMETHING ABOUT THAT...
Development Studio

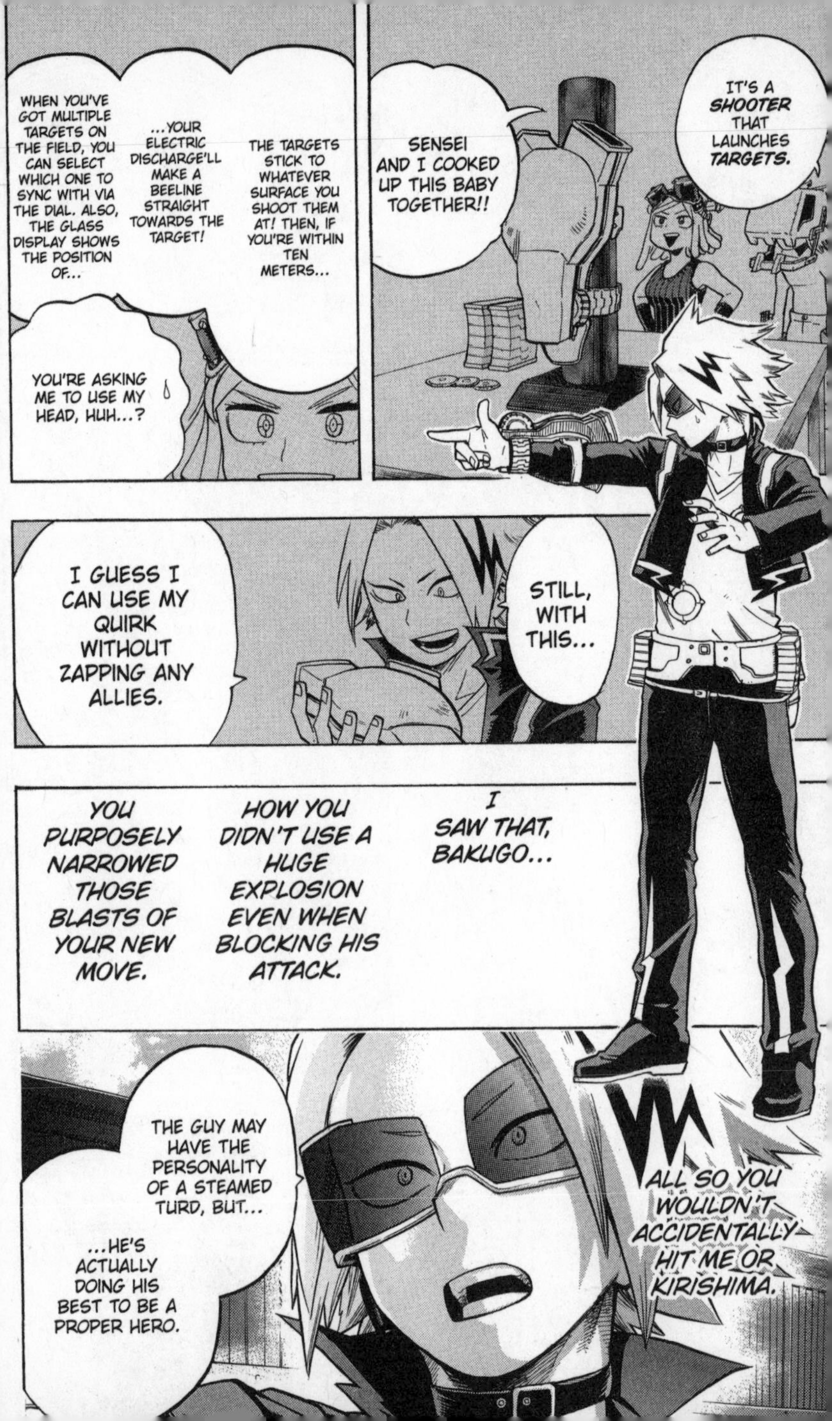
IT'S A SHOOTER THAT LAUNCHES TARGETS.
SENSEI AND I COOKED UP THIS BABY TOGETHER!!
THE TARGETS STICK TO WHATEVER SURFACE YOU SHOOT THEM AT! THEN, IF YOU'RE WITHIN TEN METERS...
...YOUR ELECTRIC DISCHARGE'LL MAKE A BEELINE STRAIGHT TOWARDS THE TARGET!
WHEN YOU'VE GOT MULTIPLE TARGETS ON THE FIELD, YOU CAN SELECT WHICH ONE TO SYNC WITH VIA THE DIAL. ALSO, THE GLASS DISPLAY SHOWS THE POSITION OF...
YOU'RE ASKING ME TO USE MY HEAD, HUH...?
STILL, WITH THIS...
I GUESS I CAN USE MY QUIRK WITHOUT ZAPPING ANY ALLIES.
I SAW THAT, BAKUGO...
HOW YOU DIDN'T USE A HUGE EXPLOSION EVEN WHEN BLOCKING HIS ATTACK.
YOU PURPOSELY NARROWED THOSE BLASTS OF YOUR NEW MOVE.
ALL SO YOU WOULDN'T ACCIDENTALLY HIT ME OR KIRISHIMA.
THE GUY MAY HAVE THE PERSONALITY OF A STEAMED TURD, BUT...
...HE'S ACTUALLY DOING HIS BEST TO BE A PROPER HERO.

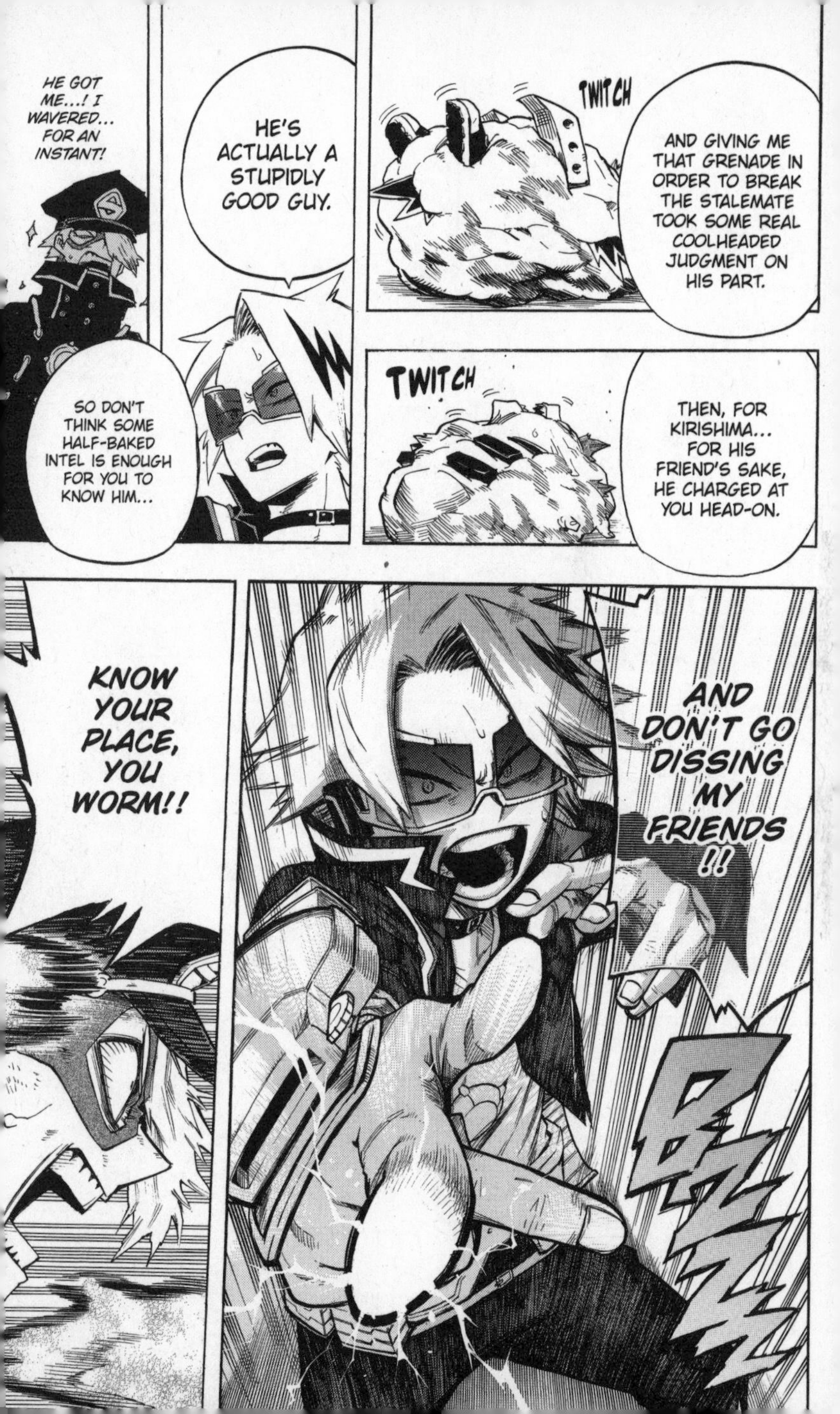
AND GIVING ME THAT GRENADE IN ORDER TO BREAK THE STALEMATE TOOK SOME REAL COOLHEADED JUDGMENT ON HIS PART.
TWITCH
THEN, FOR KIRISHIMA... FOR HIS FRIEND'S SAKE, HE CHARGED AT YOU HEAD-ON.
TWITCH
HE'S ACTUALLY A STUPIDLY GOOD GUY.
SO DON'T THINK SOME HALF-BAKED INTEL IS ENOUGH FOR YOU TO KNOW HIM...
HE GOT ME...! I WAVERED... FOR AN INSTANT!
AND DON'T GO DISSING MY FRIENDS!!
KNOW YOUR PLACE, YOU WORM!!

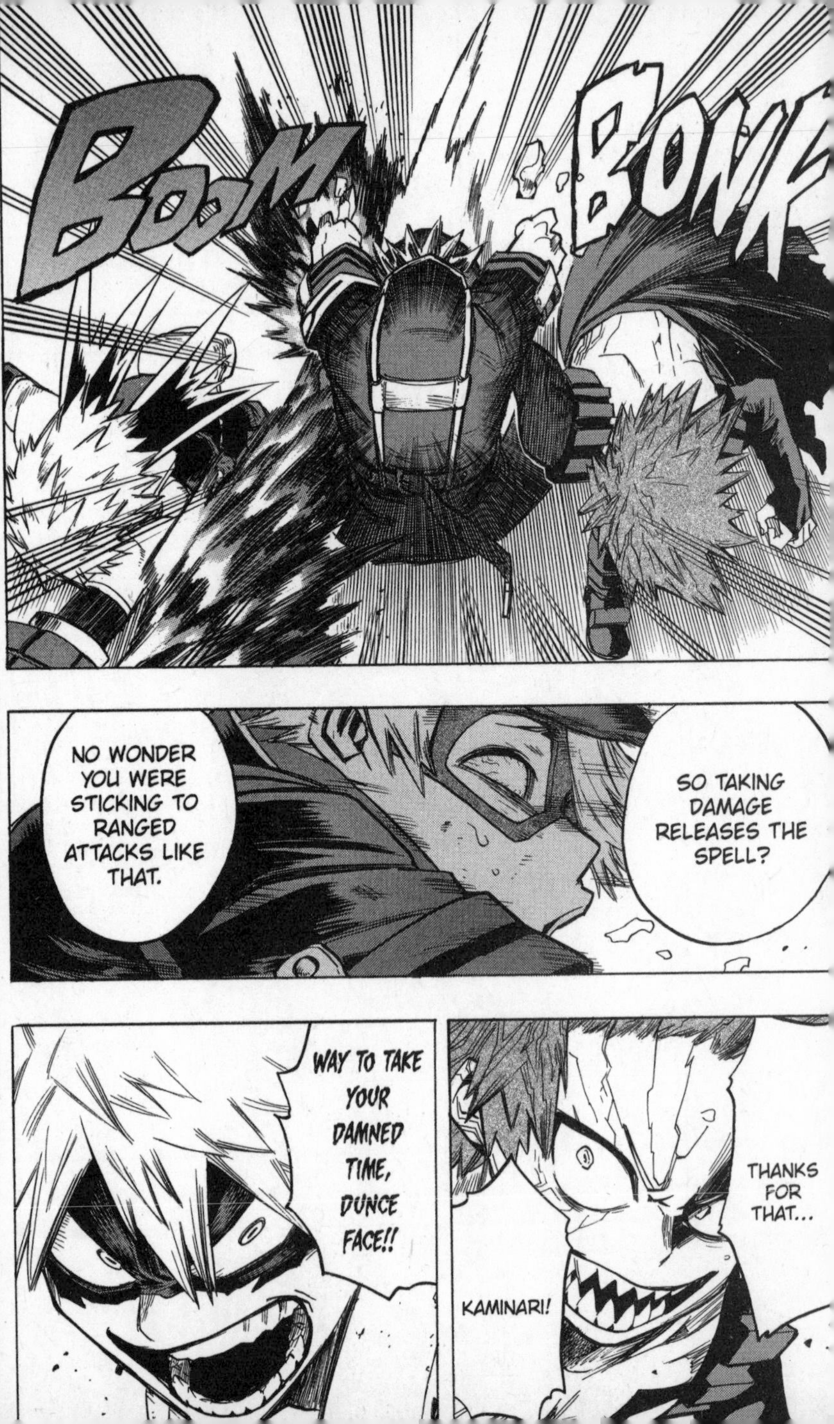

BONK
BOOM
SO TAKING DAMAGE RELEASES THE SPELL?
NO WONDER YOU WERE STICKING TO RANGED ATTACKS LIKE THAT.
THANKS FOR THAT...
KAMINARI!
WAY TO TAKE YOUR DAMNED TIME, DUNCE FACE!!

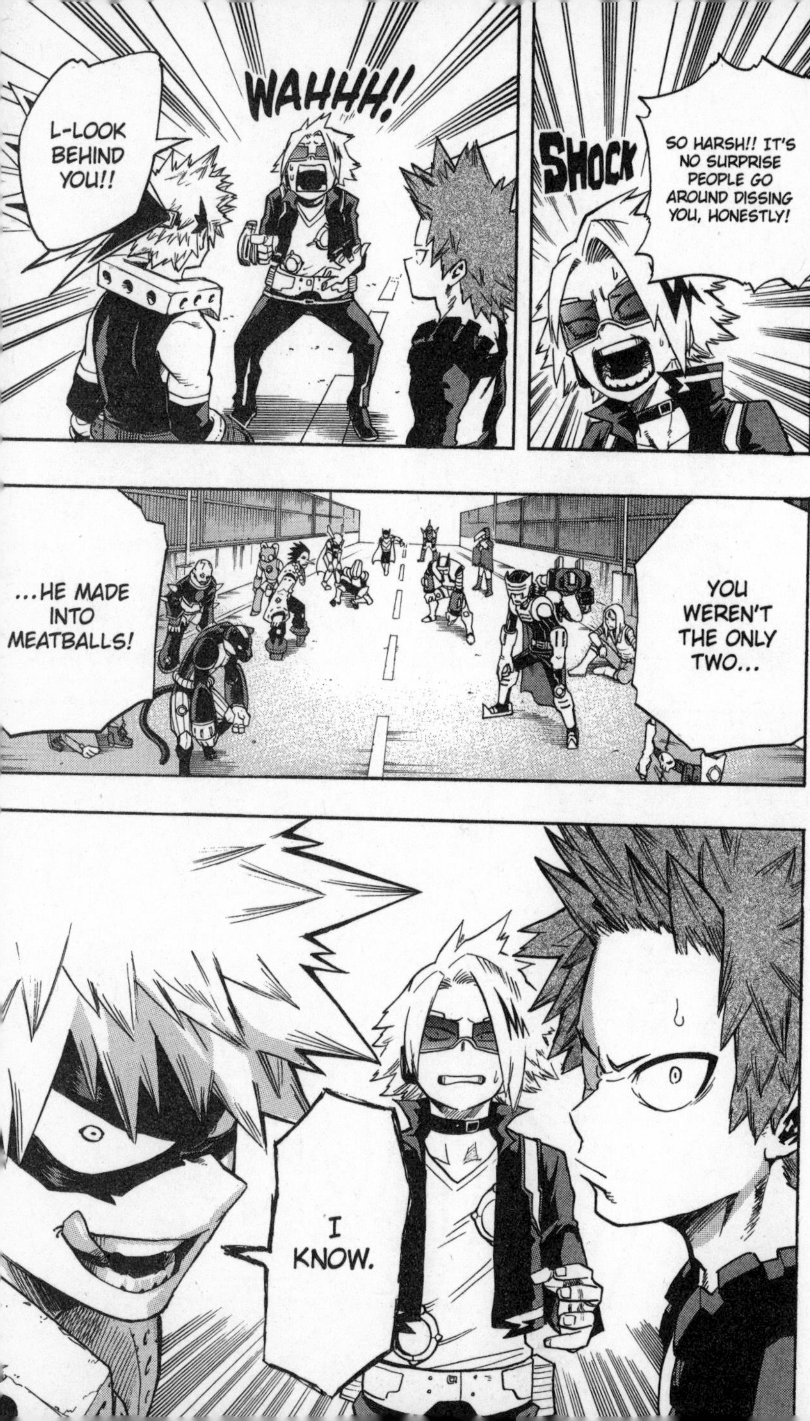
SHOCK
SO HARSH!! IT'S NO SURPRISE PEOPLE GO AROUND DISSING YOU, HONESTLY!
WAHHH!
L-LOOK BEHIND YOU!!
YOU WEREN'T THE ONLY TWO...
...HE MADE INTO MEATBALLS!
I KNOW.

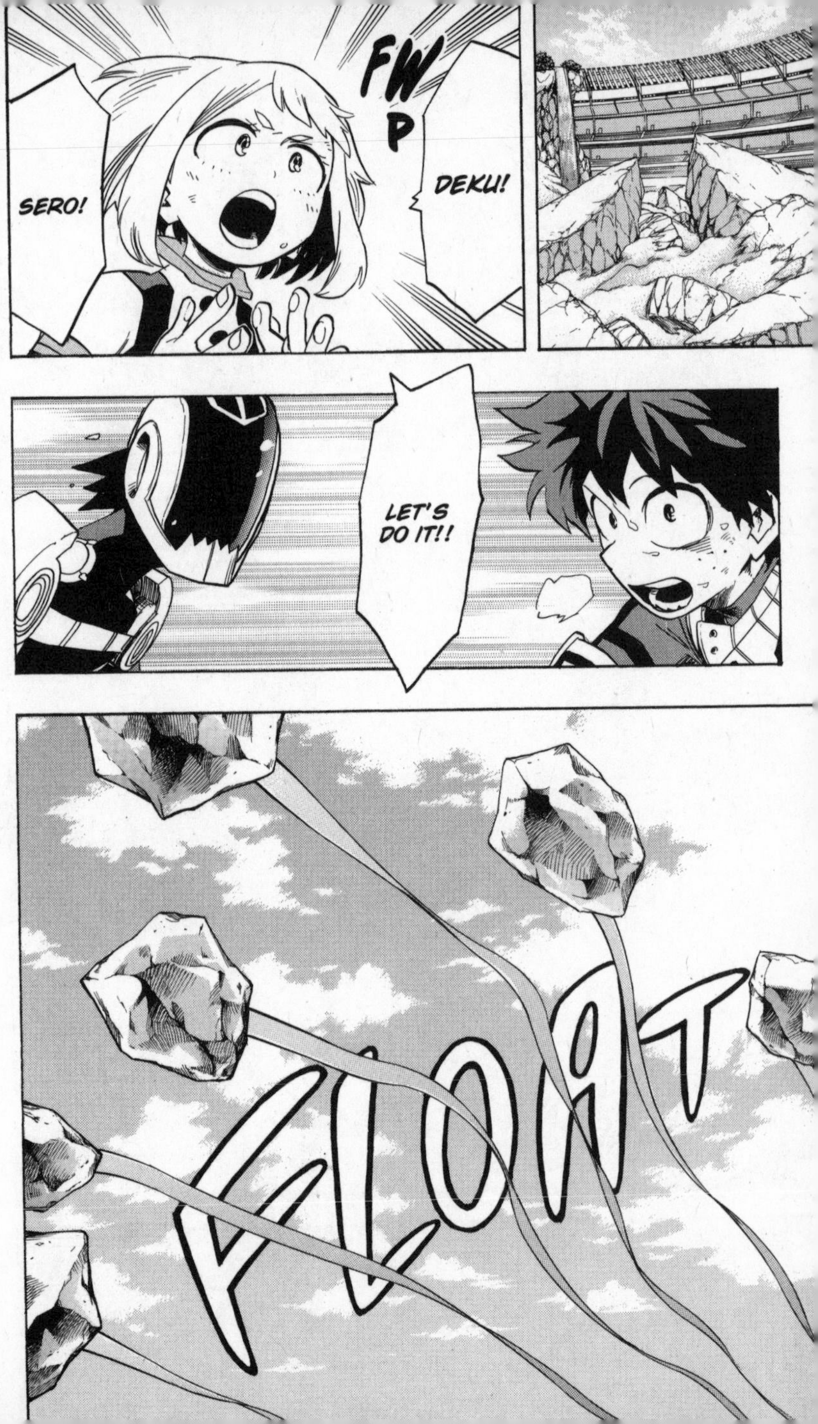
FWP
DEKU!
SERO!
LET'S DO IT!!
FLOAT

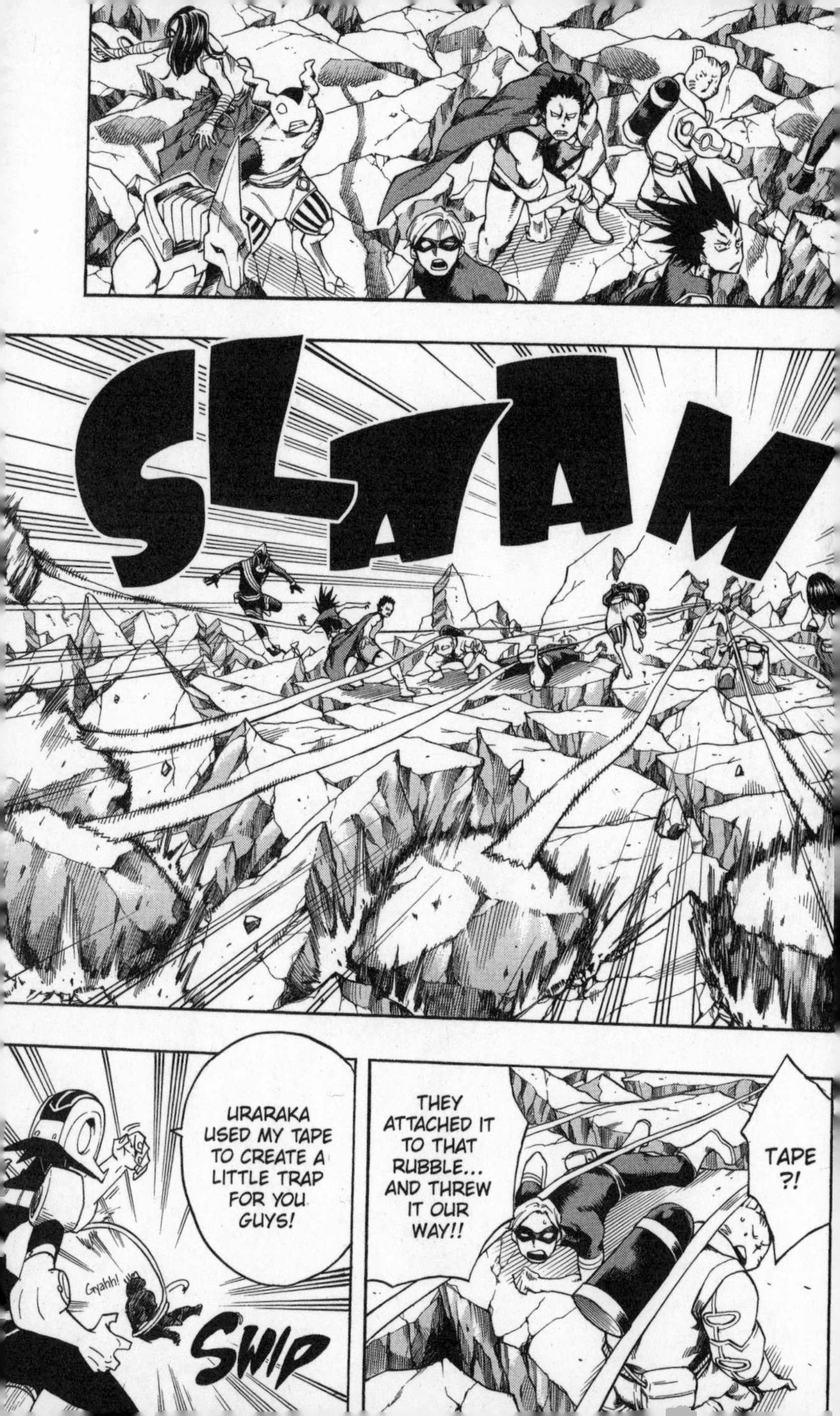
SLAM
TAPE ?!
THEY ATTACHED IT TO THAT RUBBLE... AND THREW IT OUR WAY!!
URARAKA USED MY TAPE TO CREATE A LITTLE TRAP FOR YOU GUYS!
Gyahh!
SWIP

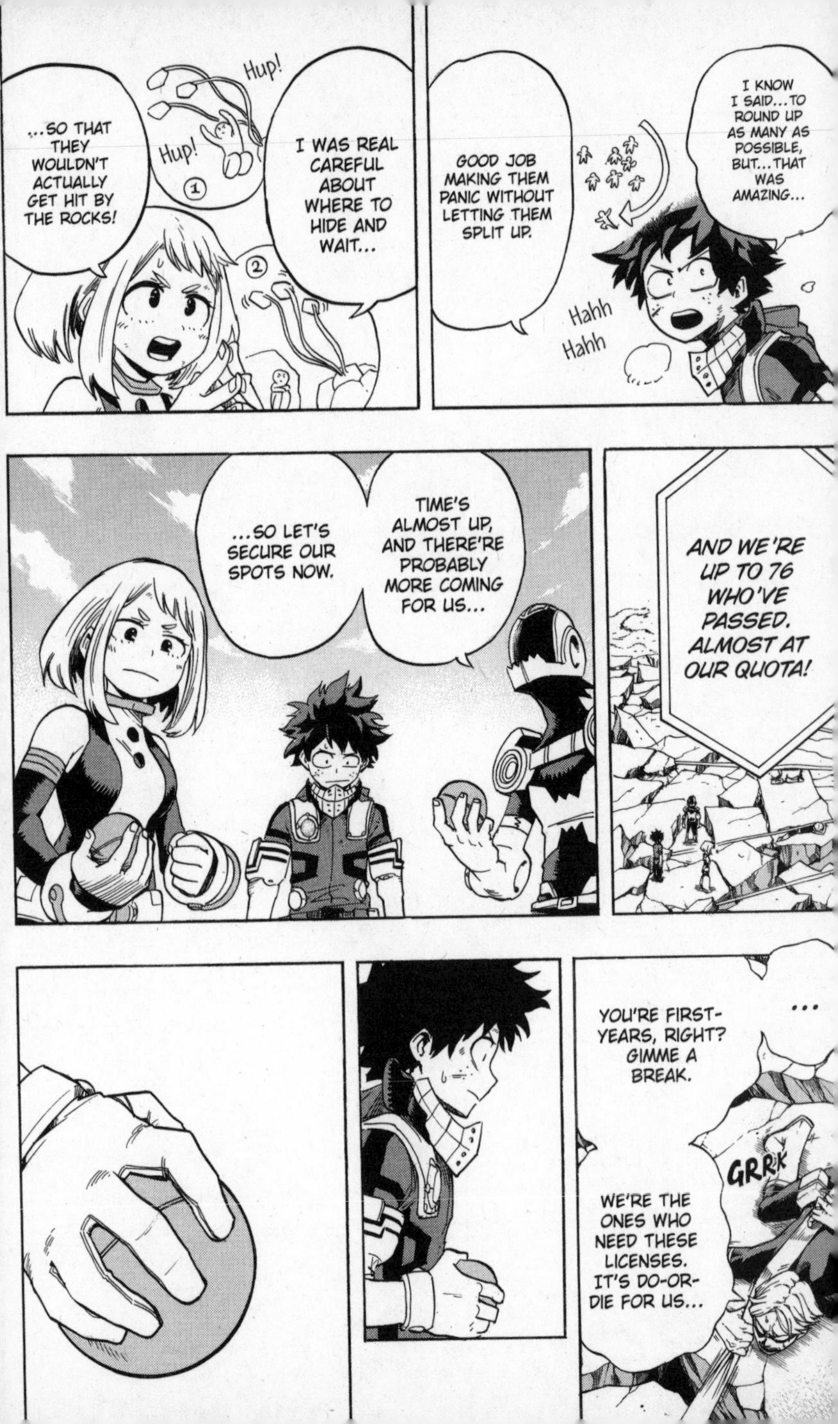
I KNOW I SAID...TO ROUND UP AS MANY AS POSSIBLE, BUT...THAT WAS AMAZING...
GOOD JOB MAKING THEM PANIC WITHOUT LETTING THEM SPLIT UP.
Hahh
Hahh
I WAS REAL CAREFUL ABOUT WHERE TO HIDE AND WAIT...
Hup!
Hup!
1
2
...SO THAT THEY WOULDN'T ACTUALLY GET HIT BY THE ROCKS!
AND WE'RE UP TO 76 WHO'VE PASSED. ALMOST AT OUR QUOTA!
TIME'S ALMOST UP, AND THERE'RE PROBABLY MORE COMING FOR US...
...SO LET'S SECURE OUR SPOTS NOW.
...
YOU'RE FIRST-YEARS, RIGHT? GIMME A BREAK.
GRRK
WE'RE THE ONES WHO NEED THESE LICENSES. IT'S DO-OR-DIE FOR US...

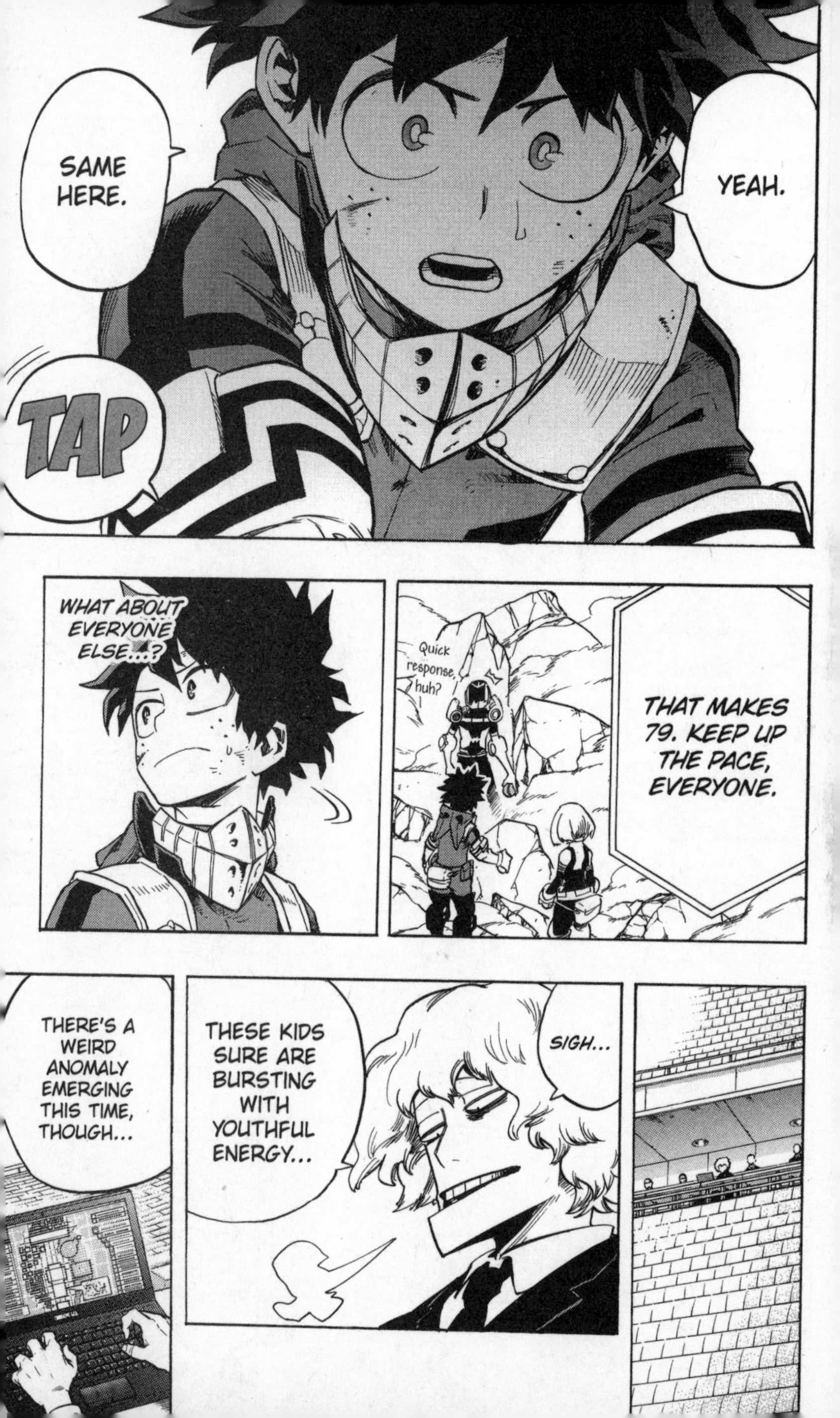
YEAH.
SAME HERE.
TAP
THAT MAKES 79. KEEP UP THE PACE, EVERYONE.
Quick response, huh?
WHAT ABOUT EVERYONE ELSE...?
SIGH...
THESE KIDS SURE ARE BURSTING WITH YOUTHFUL ENERGY...
THERE'S A WEIRD ANOMALY EMERGING THIS TIME, THOUGH...

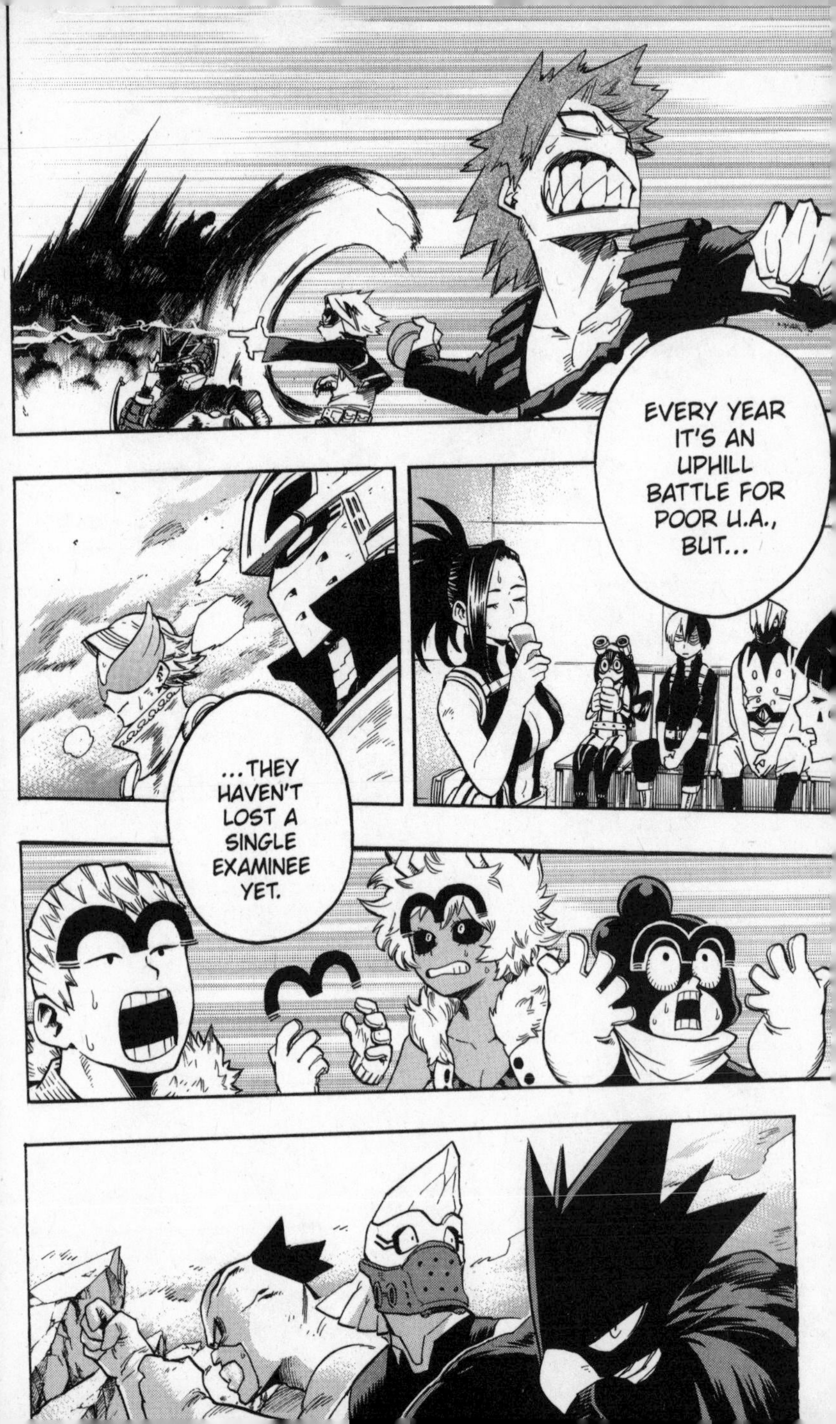
EVERY YEAR IT'S AN UPHILL BATTLE FOR POOR U.A., BUT...
...THEY HAVEN'T LOST A SINGLE EXAMINEE YET.

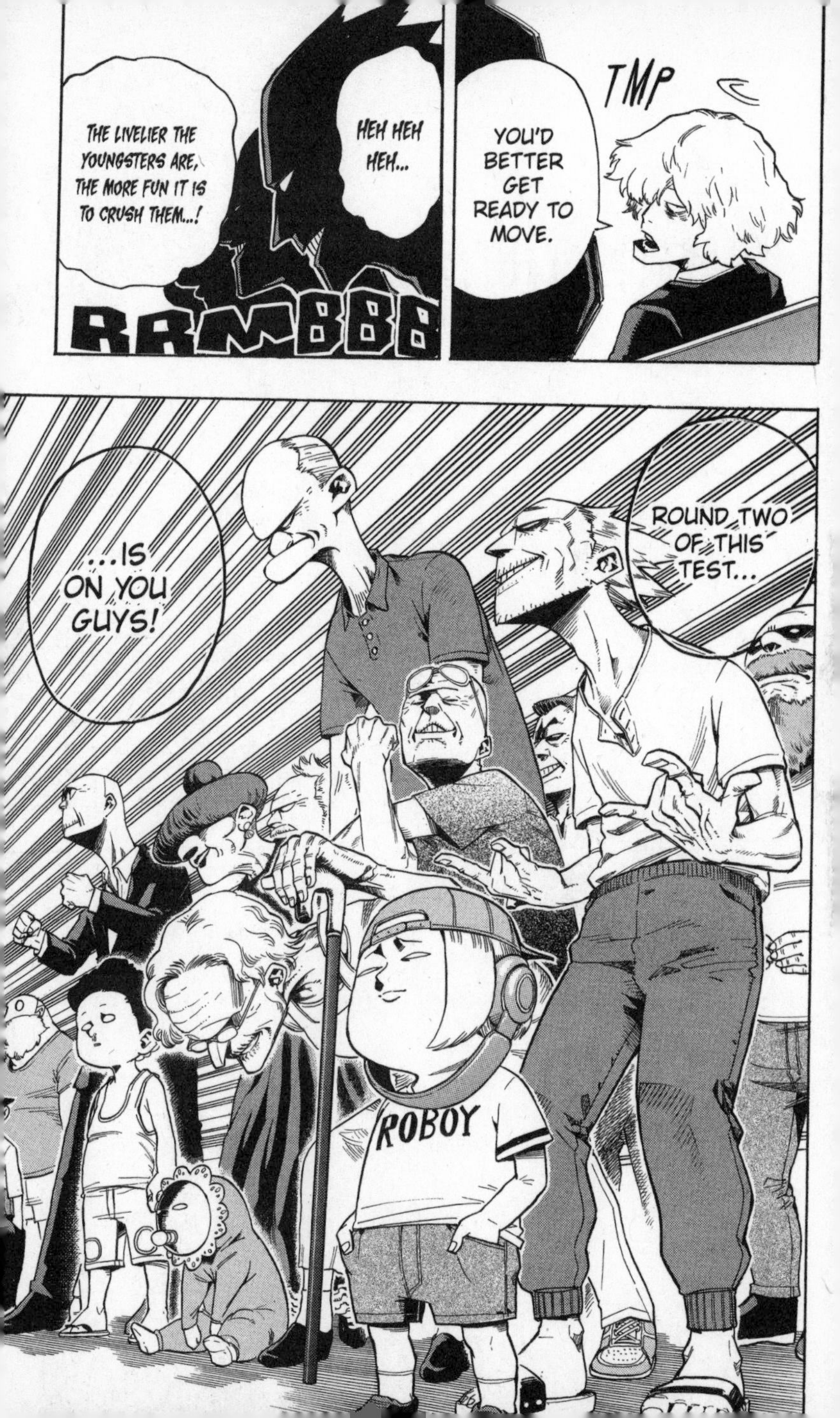
TMP
YOU'D BETTER GET READY TO MOVE.
HEH HEH HEH...
THE LIVELIER THE YOUNGSTERS ARE, THE MORE FUN IT IS TO CRUSH THEM...!
RRMBBB
ROUND TWO OF THIS TEST...
...IS ON YOU GUYS!
ROBOY

STREET CLOTHES

Birthday: 3/9
Height: 171 cm
Favorite Thing: Sleeping

THE SUPPLEMENT
A career man who works a
little too hard. Do your best!!
If you can!!

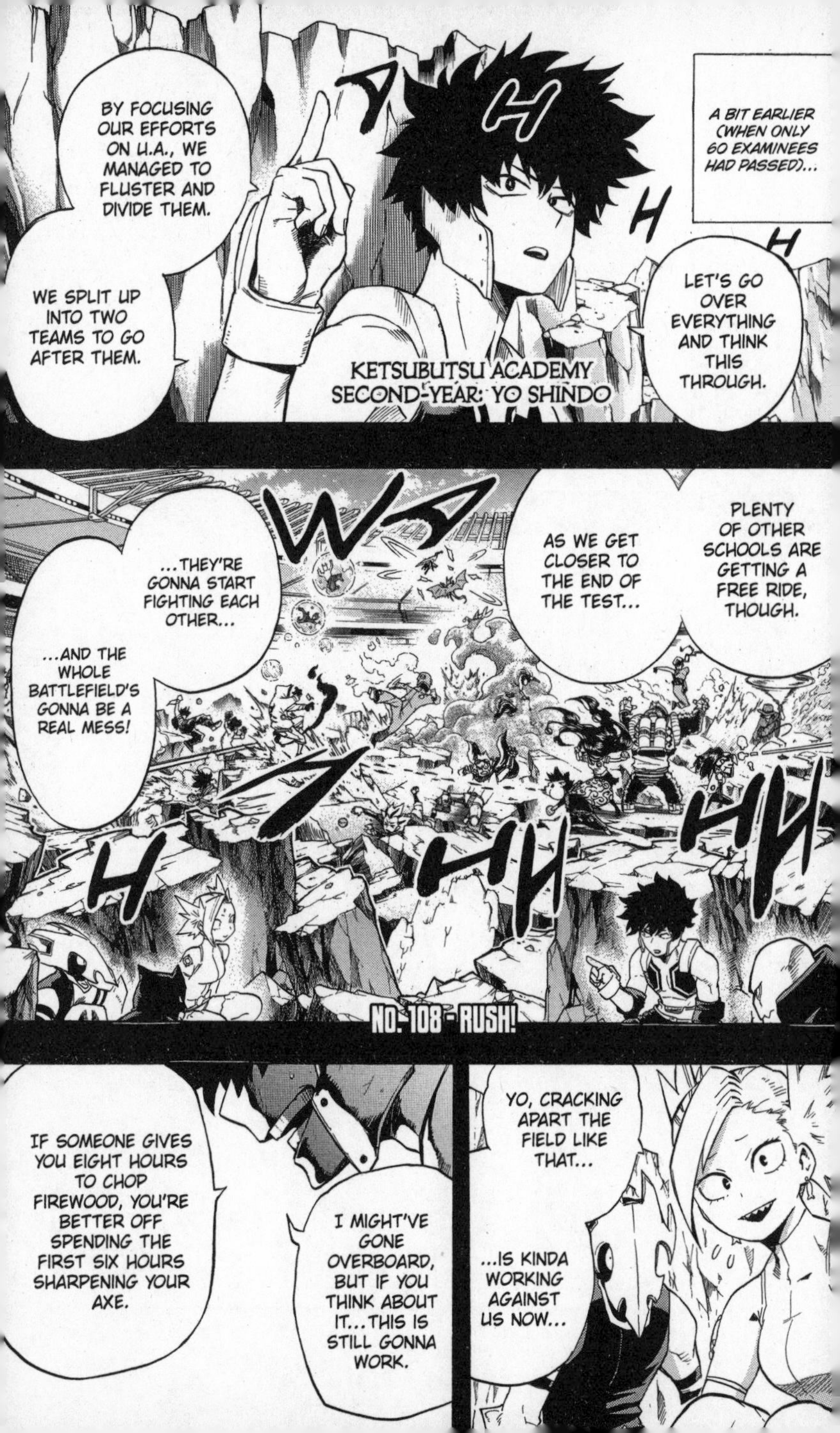
A BIT EARLIER (WHEN ONLY 60 EXAMINEES HAD PASSED)...
LET'S GO OVER EVERYTHING AND THINK THIS THROUGH.
AHHH
BY FOCUSING OUR EFFORTS ON U.A., WE MANAGED TO FLUSTER AND DIVIDE THEM.
WE SPLIT UP INTO TWO TEAMS TO GO AFTER THEM.
KETSUBUTSU ACADEMY SECOND-YEAR: YO SHINDO
PLENTY OF OTHER SCHOOLS ARE GETTING A FREE RIDE, THOUGH.
AS WE GET CLOSER TO THE END OF THE TEST...
...THEY'RE GONNA START FIGHTING EACH OTHER...
...AND THE WHOLE BATTLEFIELD'S GONNA BE A REAL MESS!
NO. 108 - RUSH!
YO, CRACKING APART THE FIELD LIKE THAT...
...IS KINDA WORKING AGAINST US NOW...
I MIGHT'VE GONE OVERBOARD, BUT IF YOU THINK ABOUT IT... THIS IS STILL GONNA WORK.
IF SOMEONE GIVES YOU EIGHT HOURS TO CHOP FIREWOOD, YOU'RE BETTER OFF SPENDING THE FIRST SIX HOURS SHARPENING YOUR AXE.

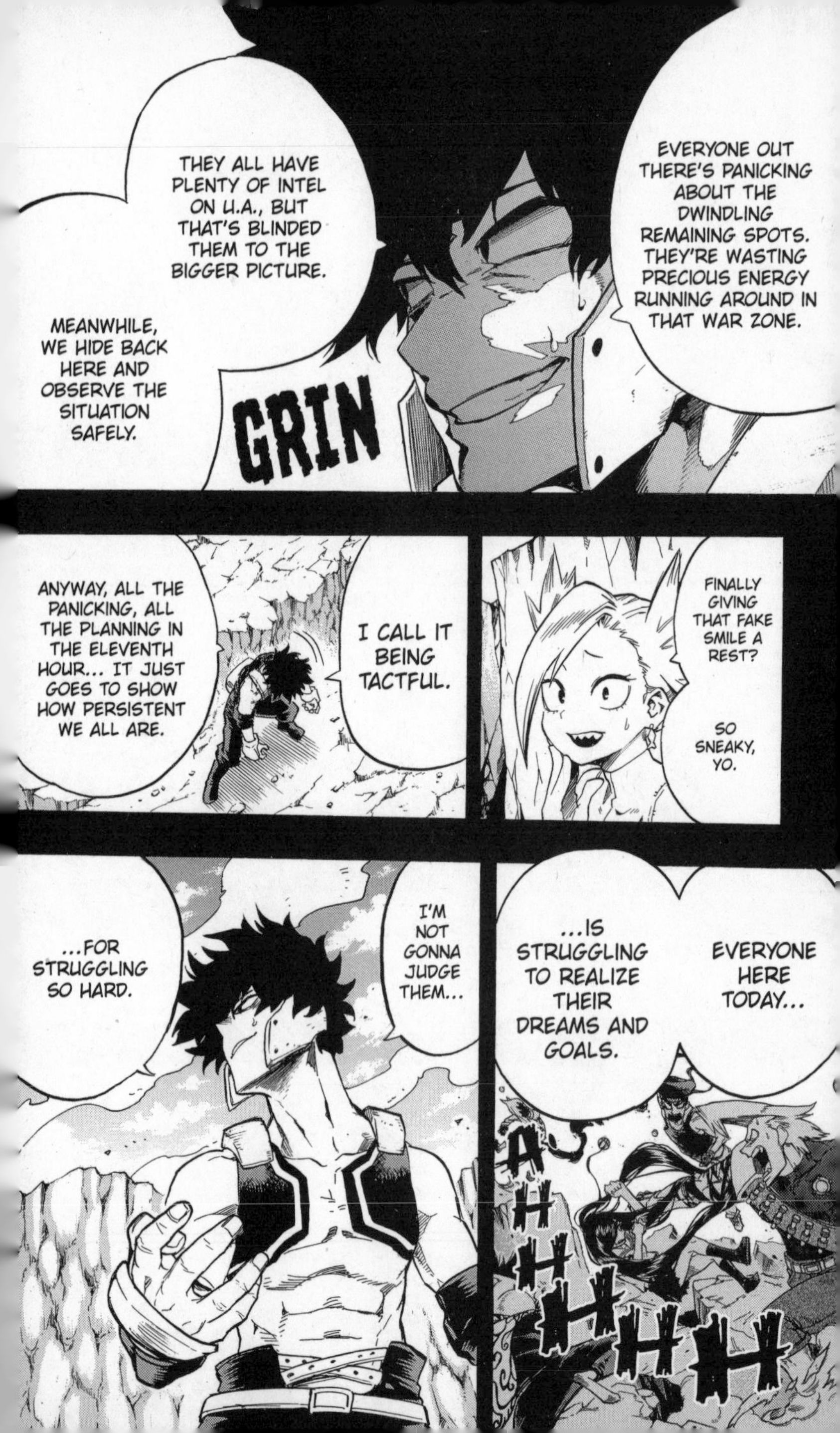
EVERYONE OUT THERE'S PANICKING ABOUT THE DWINDLING REMAINING SPOTS. THEY'RE WASTING PRECIOUS ENERGY RUNNING AROUND IN THAT WAR ZONE.
THEY ALL HAVE PLENTY OF INTEL ON U.A., BUT THAT'S BLINDED THEM TO THE BIGGER PICTURE.
MEANWHILE, WE HIDE BACK HERE AND OBSERVE THE SITUATION SAFELY.
GRIN
FINALLY GIVING THAT FAKE SMILE A REST?
SO SNEAKY, YO.
I CALL IT BEING TACTFUL.
ANYWAY, ALL THE PANICKING, ALL THE PLANNING IN THE ELEVENTH HOUR... IT JUST GOES TO SHOW HOW PERSISTENT WE ALL ARE.
EVERYONE HERE TODAY...
...IS STRUGGLING TO REALIZE THEIR DREAMS AND GOALS.
AHHHHHHH
I'M NOT GONNA JUDGE THEM...
...FOR STRUGGLING SO HARD.

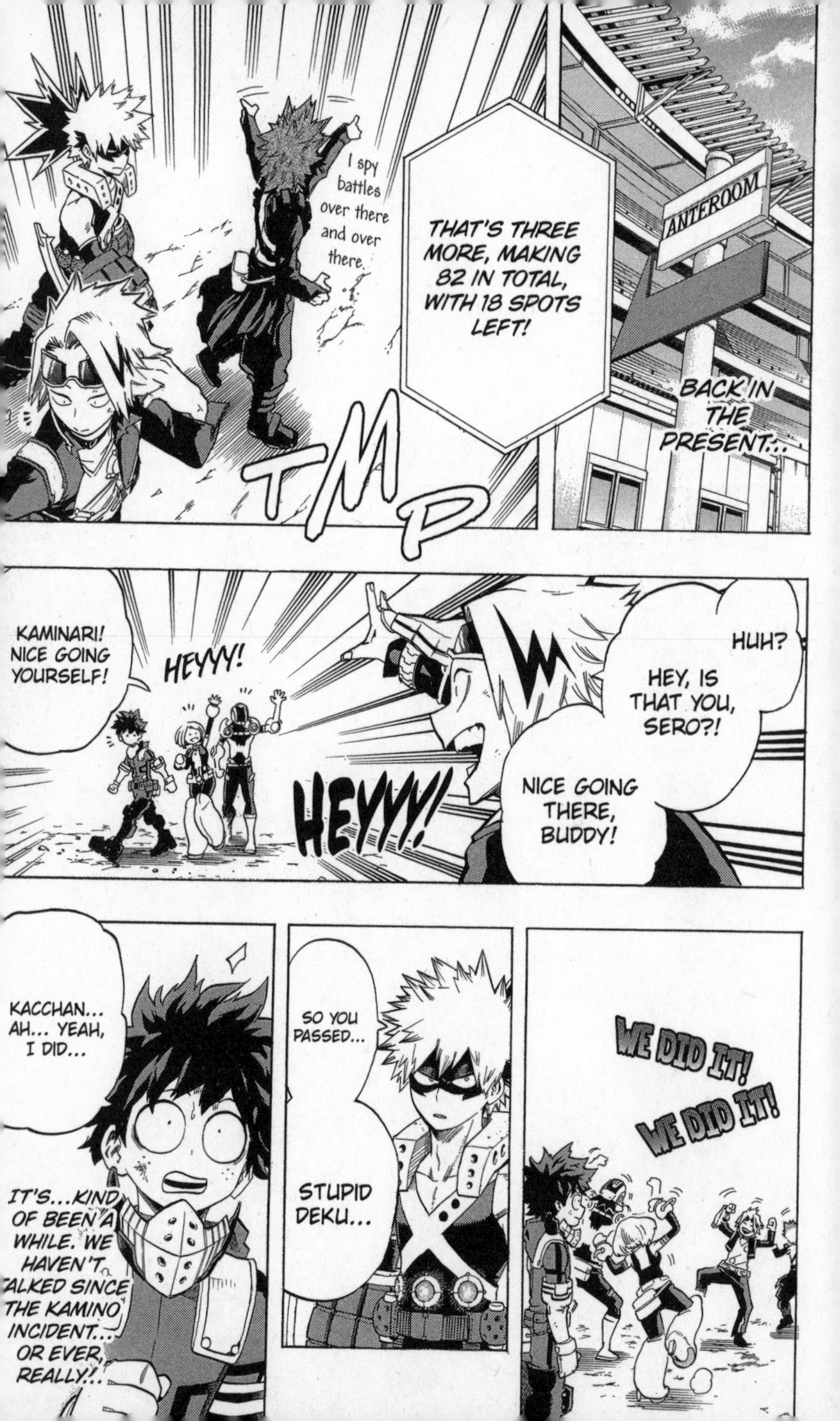
ANTEROOM
BACK IN THE PRESENT...
THAT'S THREE MORE, MAKING 82 IN TOTAL, WITH 18 SPOTS LEFT!
I spy battles over there and over there.
TMP
HUH?
HEY, IS THAT YOU, SERO?!
NICE GOING THERE, BUDDY!
HEYYY!
HEYYY!
KAMINARI! NICE GOING YOURSELF!
WE DID IT!
WE DID IT!
SO YOU PASSED...
STUPID DEKU...
KACCHAN... AH... YEAH, I DID...
IT'S...KIND OF BEEN A WHILE. WE HAVEN'T TALKED SINCE THE KAMINO INCIDENT... OR EVER, REALLY...

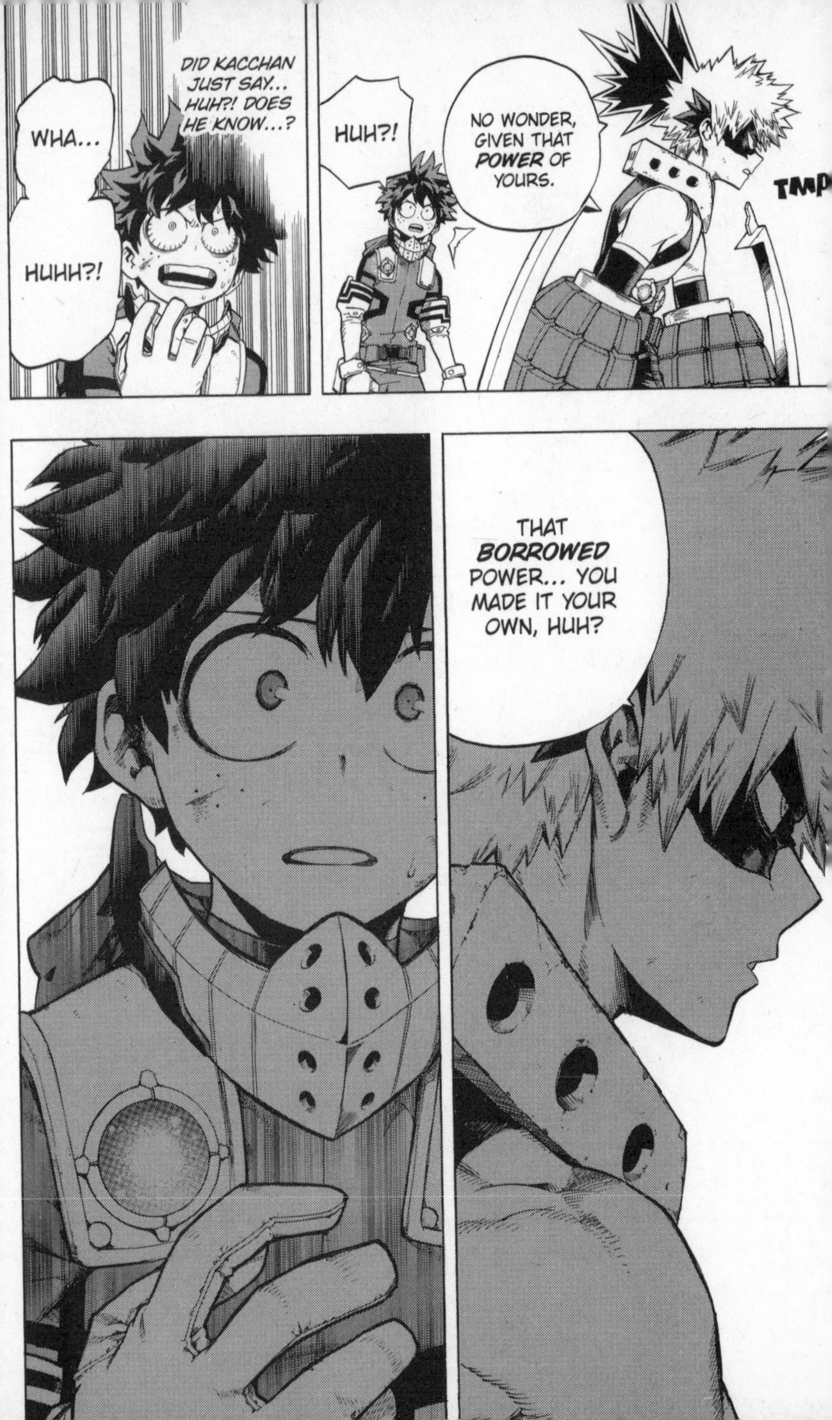
NO WONDER, GIVEN THAT **POWER** OF YOURS.
TMP
HUH?!
DID KACCHAN JUST SAY... HUH?! DOES HE KNOW...?
WHA...
HUHH?!
THAT **BORROWED** POWER... YOU MADE IT YOUR OWN, HUH?

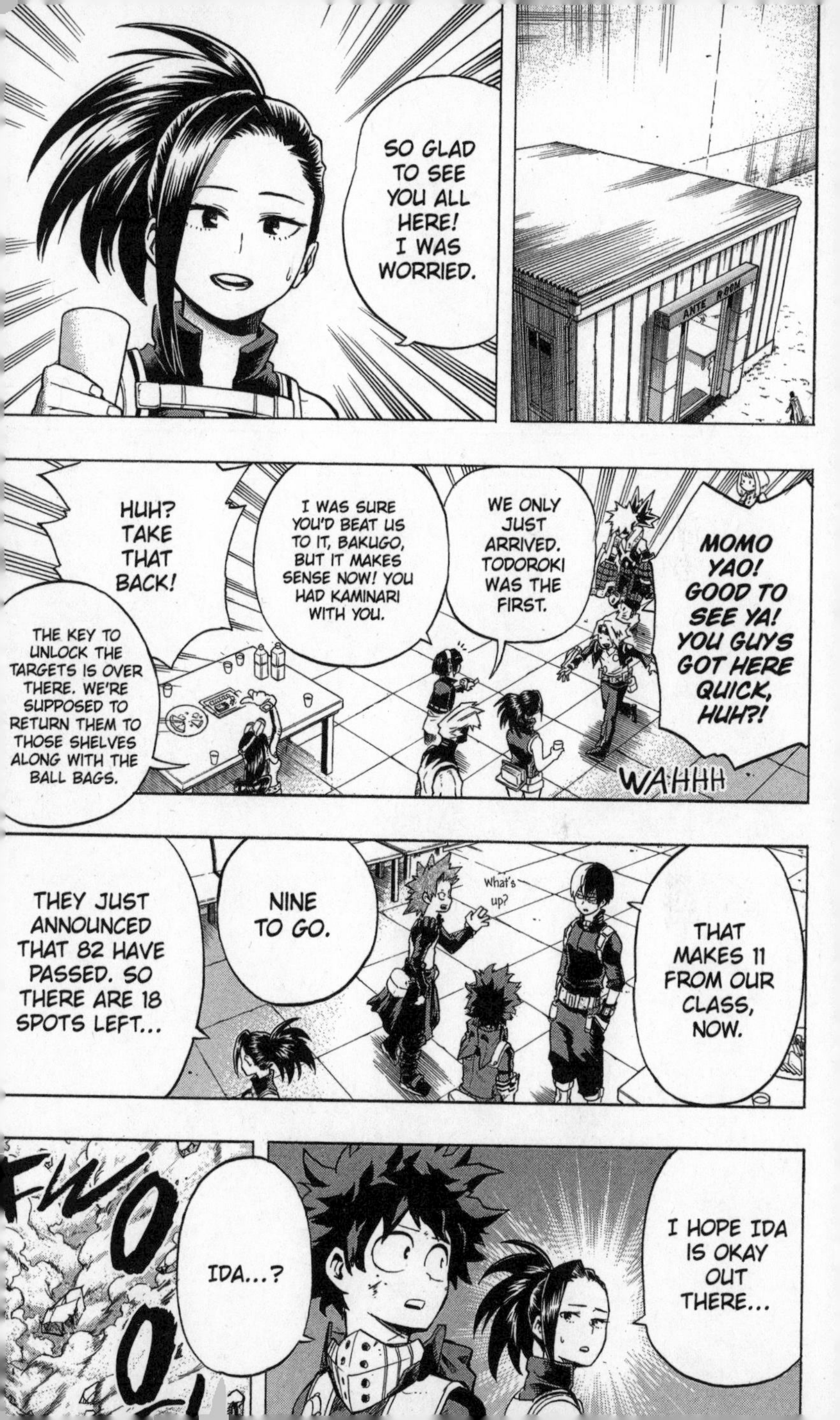
ANTE ROOM
SO GLAD TO SEE YOU ALL HERE! I WAS WORRIED.
MOMO YAO! GOOD TO SEE YA! YOU GUYS GOT HERE QUICK, HUH?!
WAHHH
WE ONLY JUST ARRIVED. TODOROKI WAS THE FIRST.
I WAS SURE YOU'D BEAT US TO IT, BAKUGO, BUT IT MAKES SENSE NOW! YOU HAD KAMINARI WITH YOU.
HUH? TAKE THAT BACK!
THE KEY TO UNLOCK THE TARGETS IS OVER THERE. WE'RE SUPPOSED TO RETURN THEM TO THOSE SHELVES ALONG WITH THE BALL BAGS.
THAT MAKES 11 FROM OUR CLASS, NOW.
What's up?
NINE TO GO.
THEY JUST ANNOUNCED THAT 82 HAVE PASSED. SO THERE ARE 18 SPOTS LEFT...
I HOPE IDA IS OKAY OUT THERE...
IDA...?
FWOO

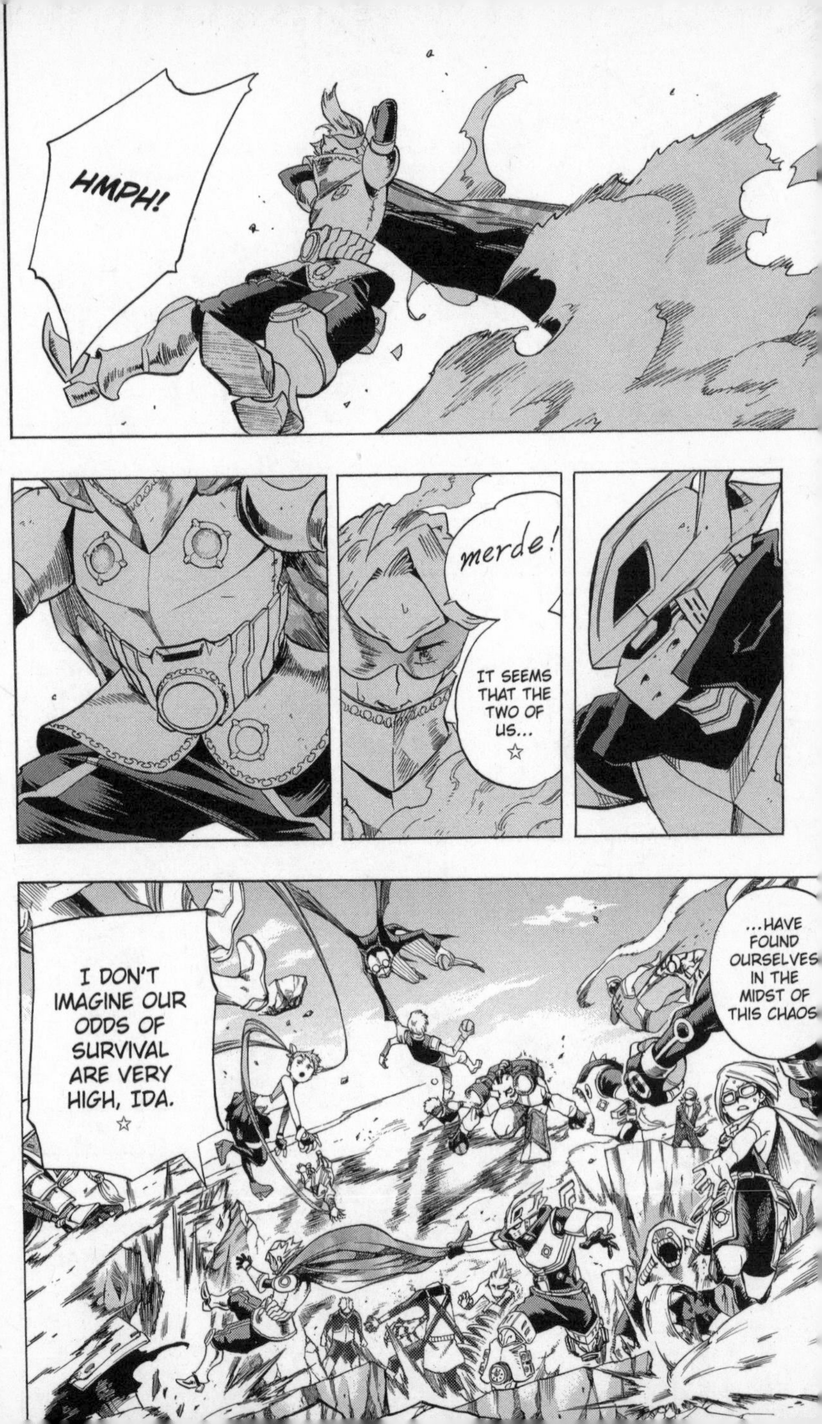
HMPH!
merde!
IT SEEMS THAT THE TWO OF US... ☆
...HAVE FOUND OURSELVES IN THE MIDST OF THIS CHAOS
I DON'T IMAGINE OUR ODDS OF SURVIVAL ARE VERY HIGH, IDA. ☆

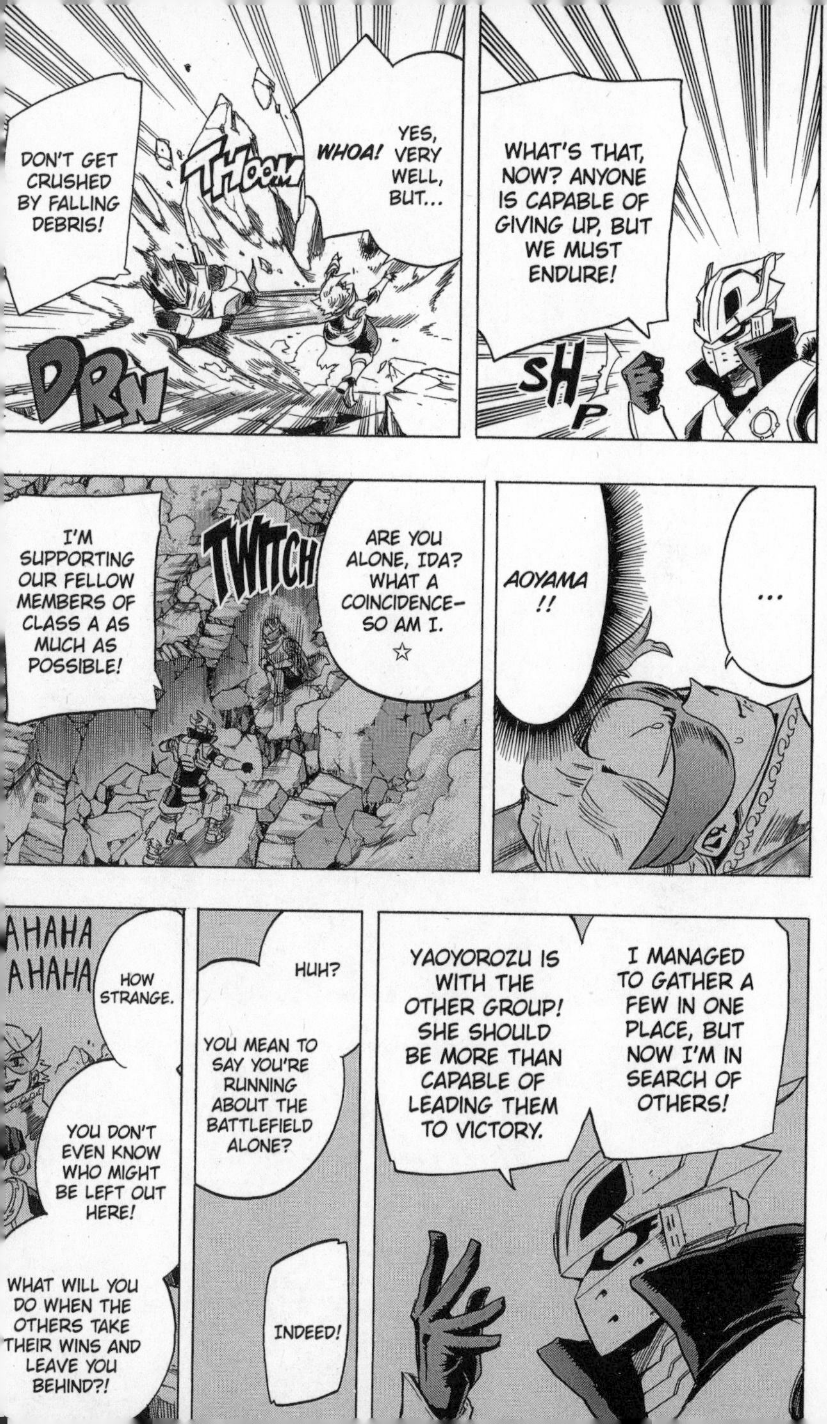
WHAT'S THAT, NOW? ANYONE IS CAPABLE OF GIVING UP, BUT WE MUST ENDURE!
SHP
YES, VERY WELL, BUT...
WHOA!
THOOM
DON'T GET CRUSHED BY FALLING DEBRIS!
DRN
...
AOYAMA!!
ARE YOU ALONE, IDA? WHAT A COINCIDENCE—SO AM I. ☆
TWITCH
I'M SUPPORTING OUR FELLOW MEMBERS OF CLASS A AS MUCH AS POSSIBLE!
I MANAGED TO GATHER A FEW IN ONE PLACE, BUT NOW I'M IN SEARCH OF OTHERS!
YAOYOROZU IS WITH THE OTHER GROUP! SHE SHOULD BE MORE THAN CAPABLE OF LEADING THEM TO VICTORY.
HUH?
YOU MEAN TO SAY YOU'RE RUNNING ABOUT THE BATTLEFIELD ALONE?
INDEED!
AHAHA AHAHA
HOW STRANGE.
YOU DON'T EVEN KNOW WHO MIGHT BE LEFT OUT HERE!
WHAT WILL YOU DO WHEN THE OTHERS TAKE THEIR WINS AND LEAVE YOU BEHIND?!

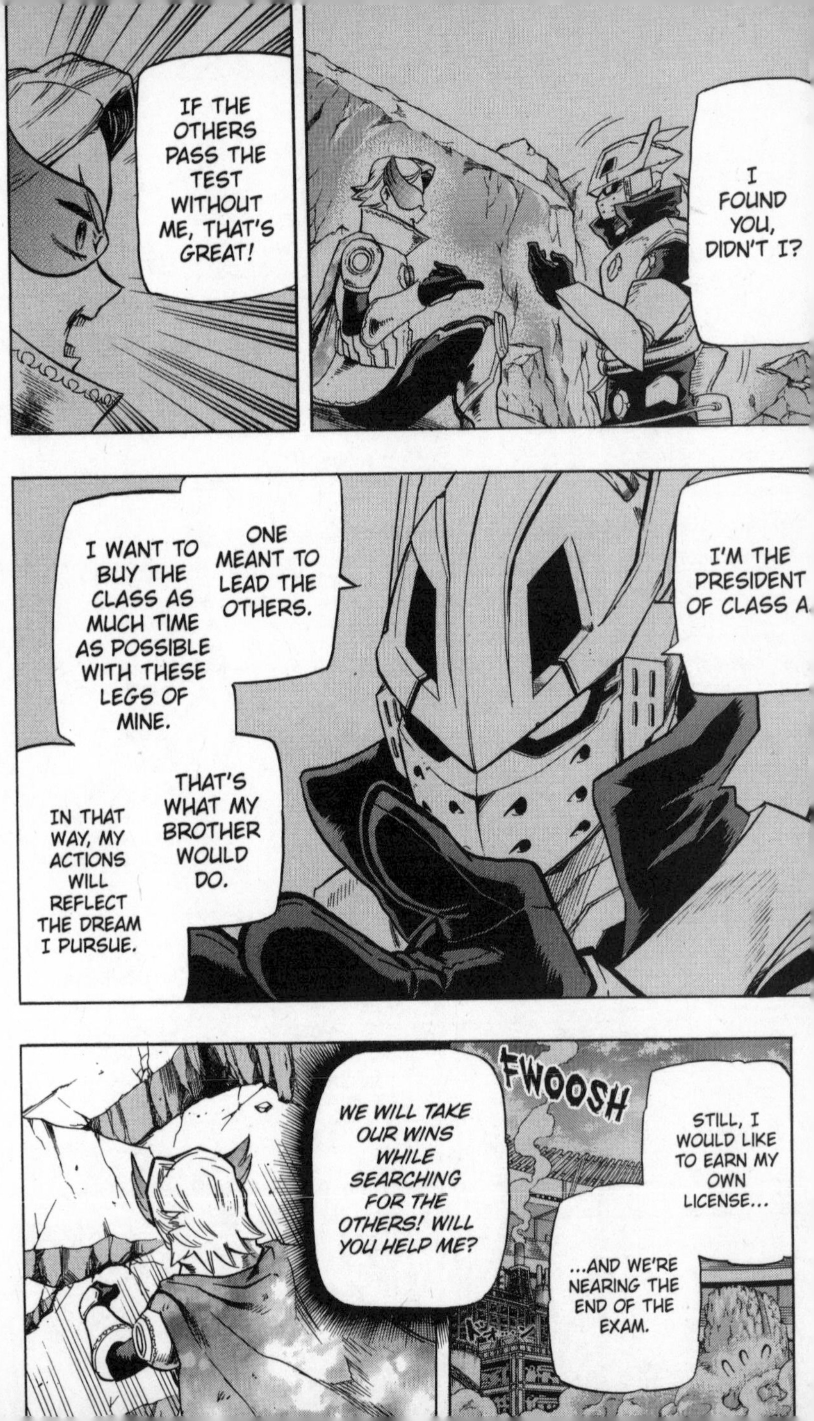

I FOUND YOU, DIDN'T I?
IF THE OTHERS PASS THE TEST WITHOUT ME, THAT'S GREAT!
I'M THE PRESIDENT OF CLASS A.
ONE MEANT TO LEAD THE OTHERS.
I WANT TO BUY THE CLASS AS MUCH TIME AS POSSIBLE WITH THESE LEGS OF MINE.
THAT'S WHAT MY BROTHER WOULD DO.
IN THAT WAY, MY ACTIONS WILL REFLECT THE DREAM I PURSUE.
FWOOSH
STILL, I WOULD LIKE TO EARN MY OWN LICENSE...
...AND WE'RE NEARING THE END OF THE EXAM.
WE WILL TAKE OUR WINS WHILE SEARCHING FOR THE OTHERS! WILL YOU HELP ME?

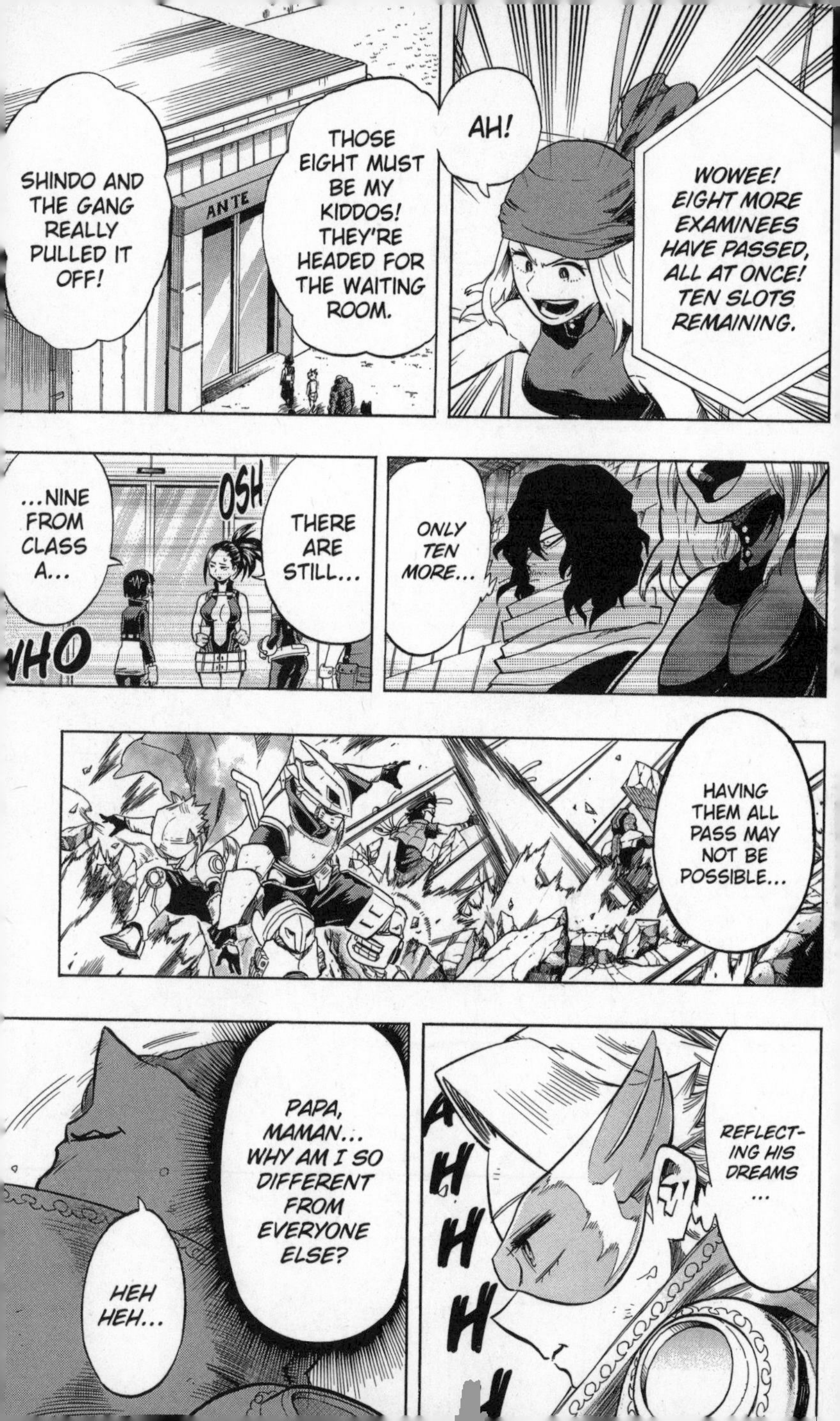
WOWEE! EIGHT MORE EXAMINEES HAVE PASSED, ALL AT ONCE! TEN SLOTS REMAINING.
AH!
THOSE EIGHT MUST BE MY KIDDOS! THEY'RE HEADED FOR THE WAITING ROOM.
SHINDO AND THE GANG REALLY PULLED IT OFF!
ANTE
ONLY TEN MORE...
THERE ARE STILL...
OSH
...NINE FROM CLASS A...
WHO
HAVING THEM ALL PASS MAY NOT BE POSSIBLE...
REFLECT-ING HIS DREAMS ...
AHHHHH
PAPA, MAMAN... WHY AM I SO DIFFERENT FROM EVERYONE ELSE?
HEH HEH...

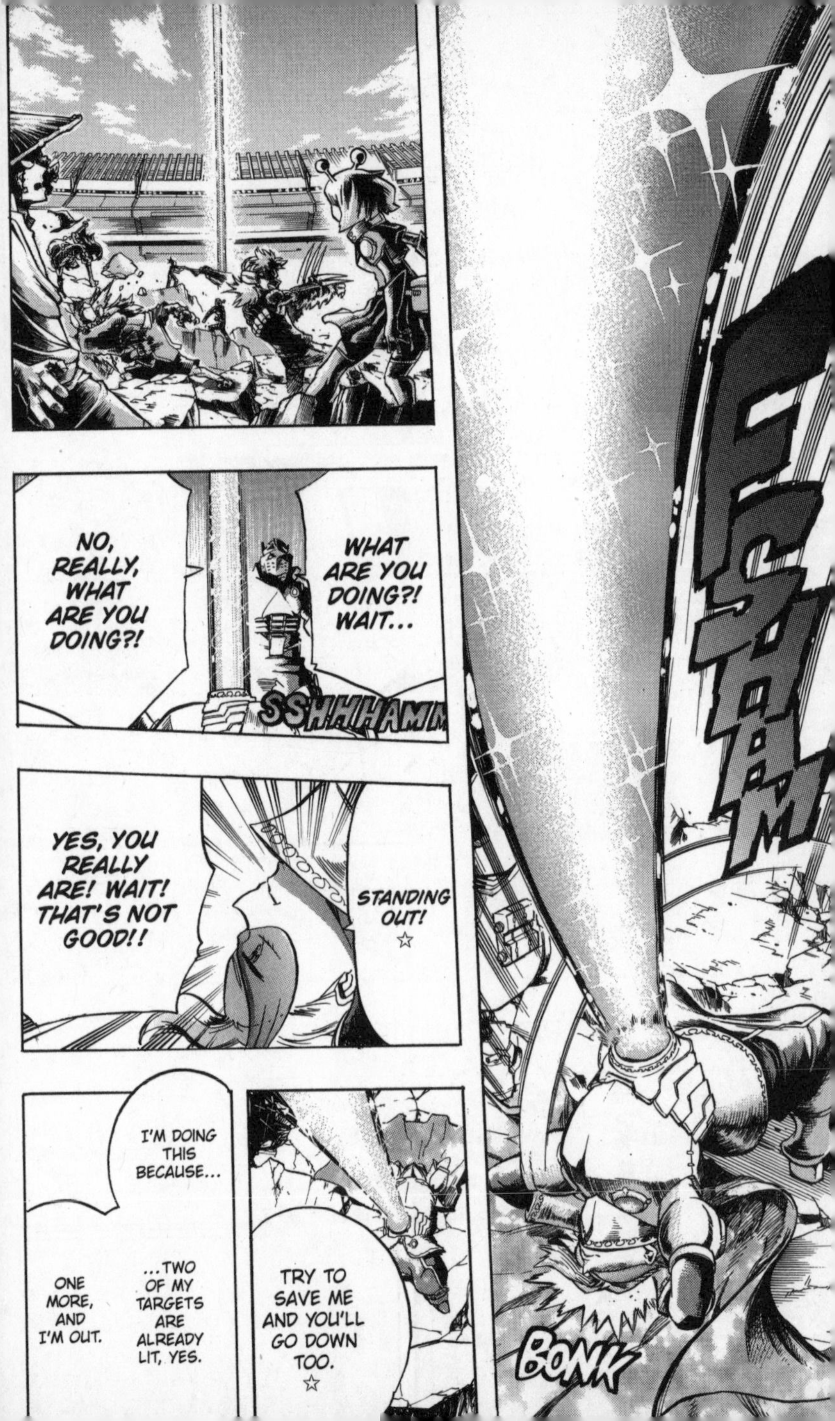
BONK
WHAT ARE YOU DOING?! WAIT...
NO, REALLY, WHAT ARE YOU DOING?!
SSHHHAMM
STANDING OUT! ☆
YES, YOU REALLY ARE! WAIT! THAT'S NOT GOOD!!
TRY TO SAVE ME AND YOU'LL GO DOWN TOO. ☆
I'M DOING THIS BECAUSE...
...TWO OF MY TARGETS ARE ALREADY LIT, YES.
ONE MORE, AND I'M OUT.

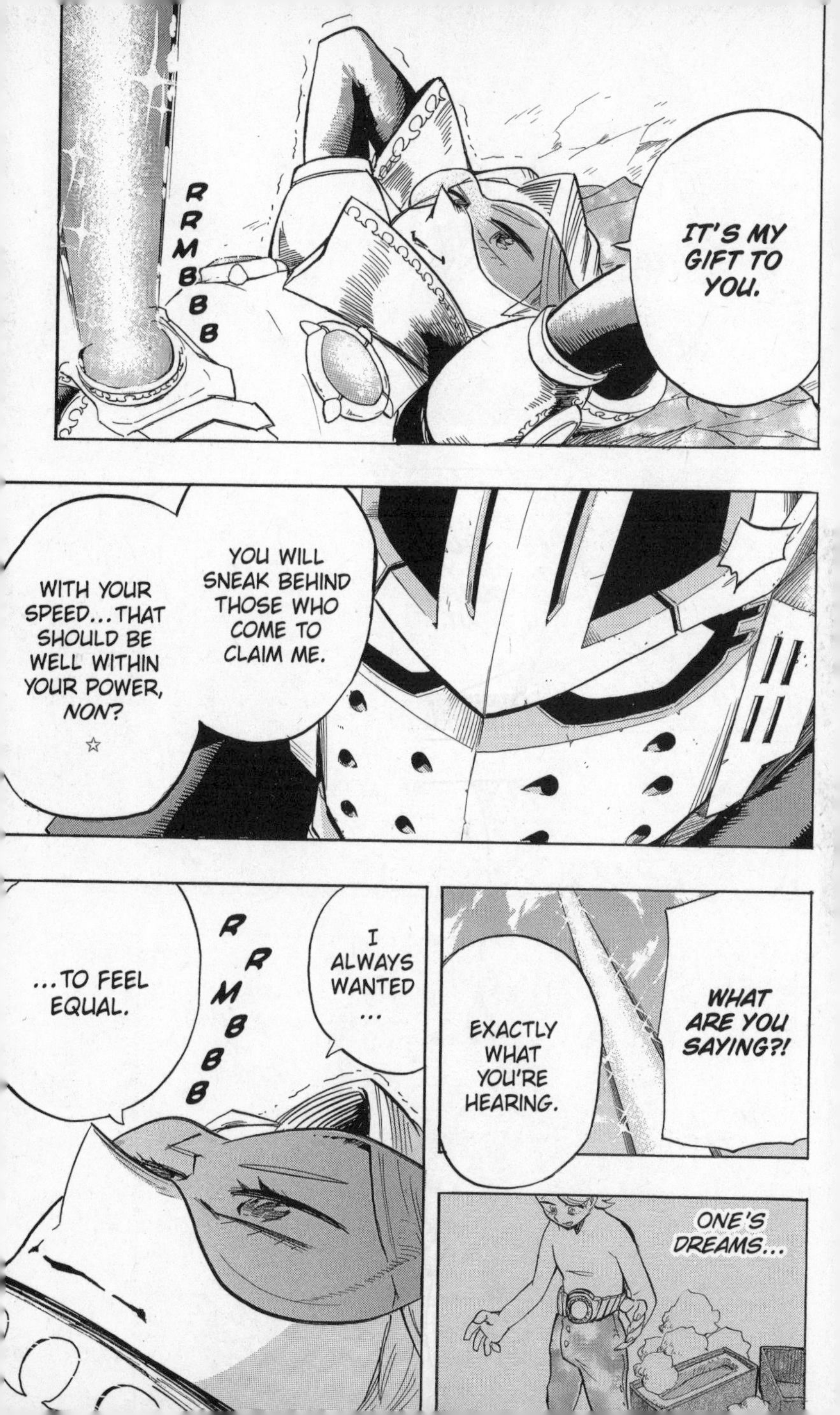
IT'S MY GIFT TO YOU.
RRMBBB
YOU WILL SNEAK BEHIND THOSE WHO COME TO CLAIM ME.
WITH YOUR SPEED...THAT SHOULD BE WELL WITHIN YOUR POWER, *NON?* ☆
WHAT ARE YOU SAYING?!
EXACTLY WHAT YOU'RE HEARING.
ONE'S DREAMS...
I ALWAYS WANTED...
RRMBBB
...TO FEEL EQUAL.

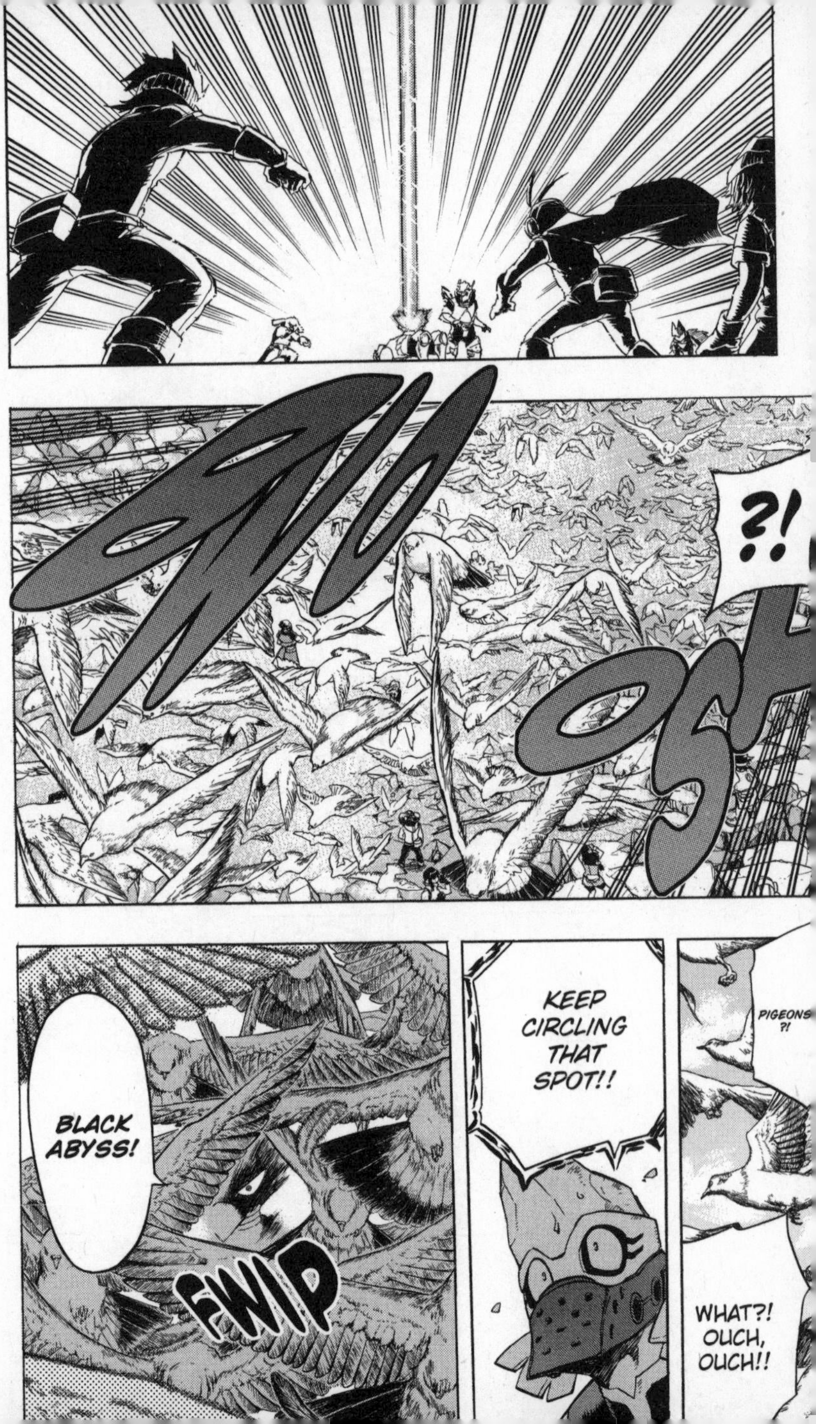
?!
PIGEONS ?!
WHAT?! OUCH, OUCH!!
KEEP CIRCLING THAT SPOT!!
BLACK ABYSS!
FWIP

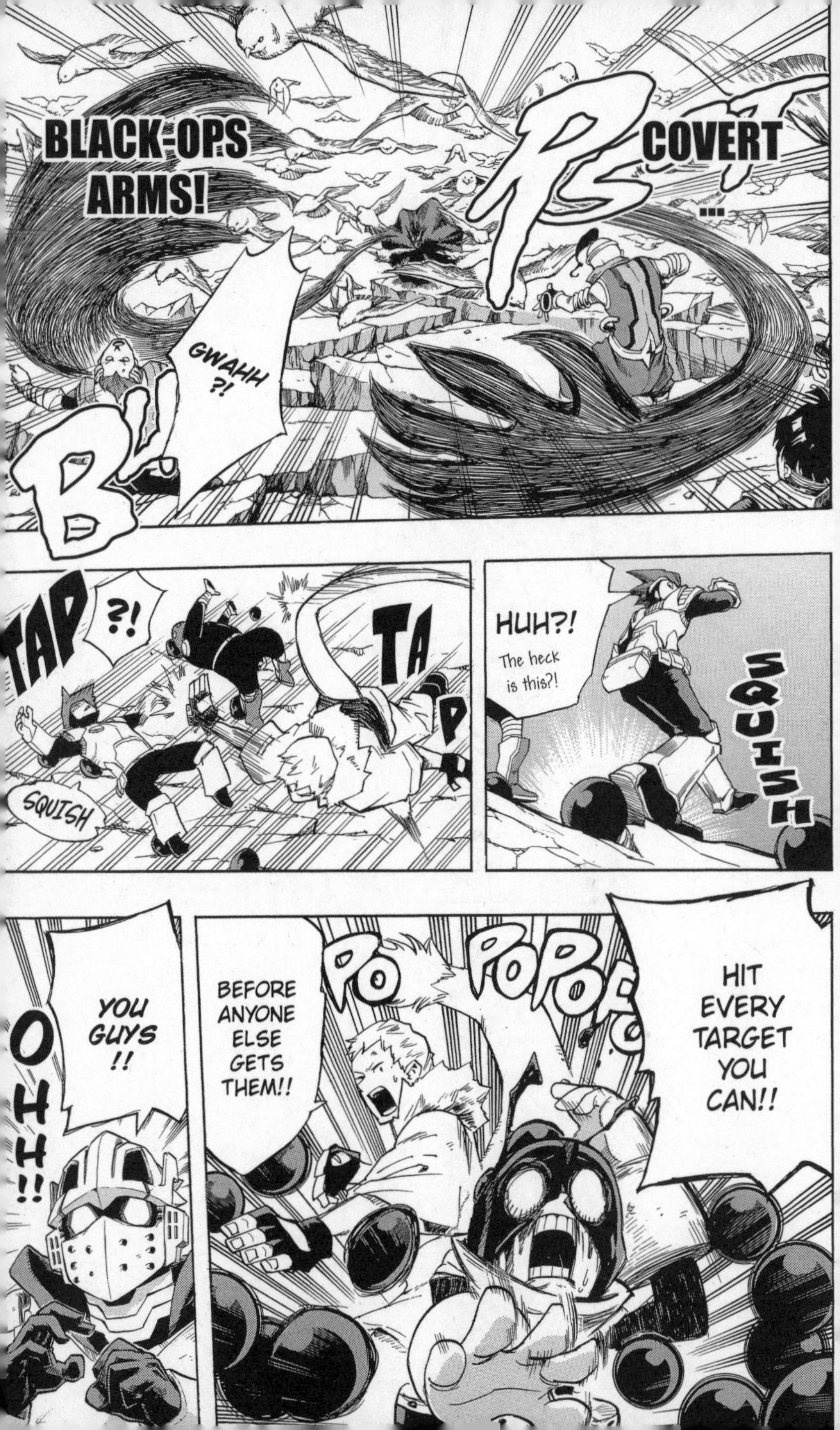
COVERT ...
BLACK-OPS ARMS!
GWAHH ?!
B
HUH?!
The heck is this?!
SQUISH
TA
TAP
?!
TAP
SQUISH
HIT EVERY TARGET YOU CAN!!
POPOPO
PO
BEFORE ANYONE ELSE GETS THEM!!
YOU GUYS !!
OHHH!!

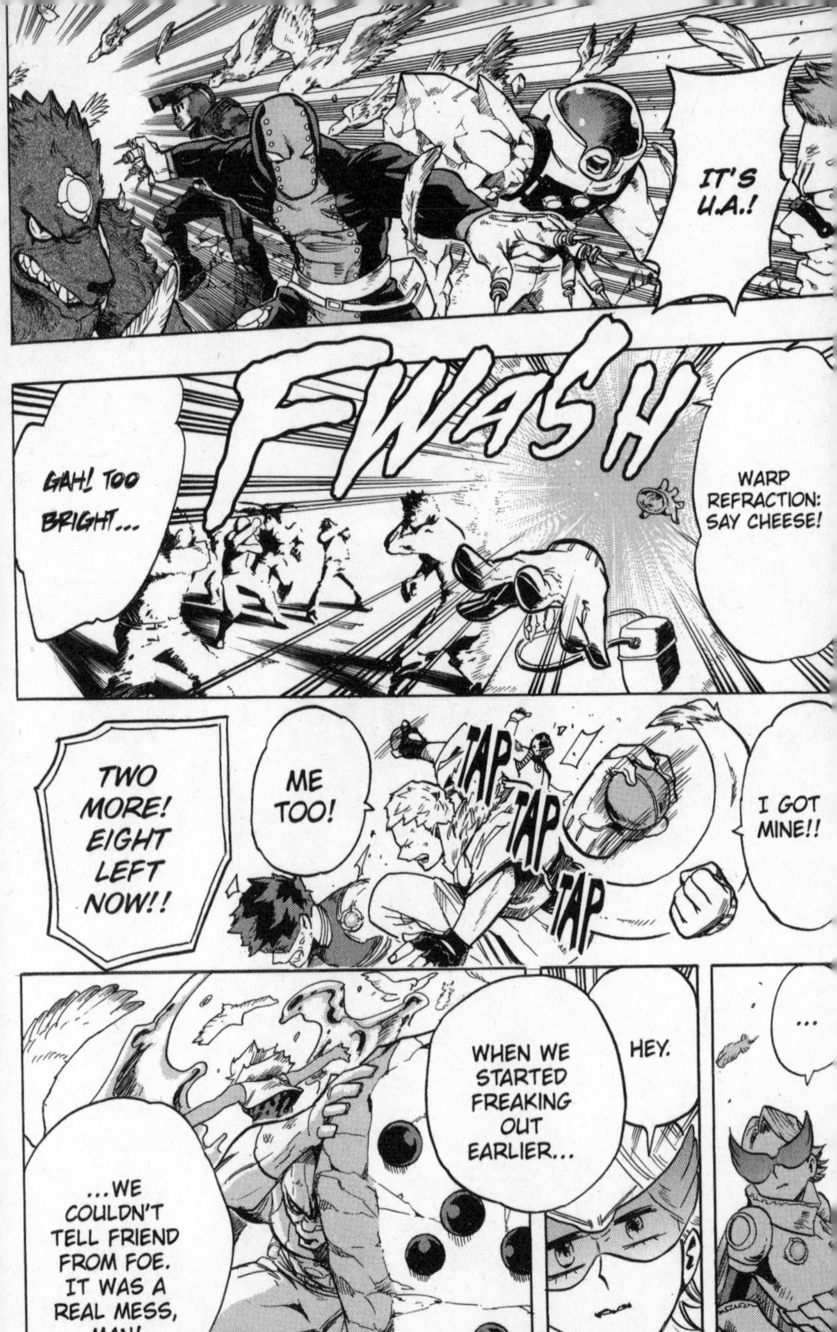
IT'S U.A.!
WARP REFRACTION: SAY CHEESE!
FWASH
GAH! TOO BRIGHT...
I GOT MINE!!
TAP TAP TAP
ME TOO!
TWO MORE! EIGHT LEFT NOW!!
...
HEY.
WHEN WE STARTED FREAKING OUT EARLIER...
...WE COULDN'T TELL FRIEND FROM FOE. IT WAS A REAL MESS, MAN!

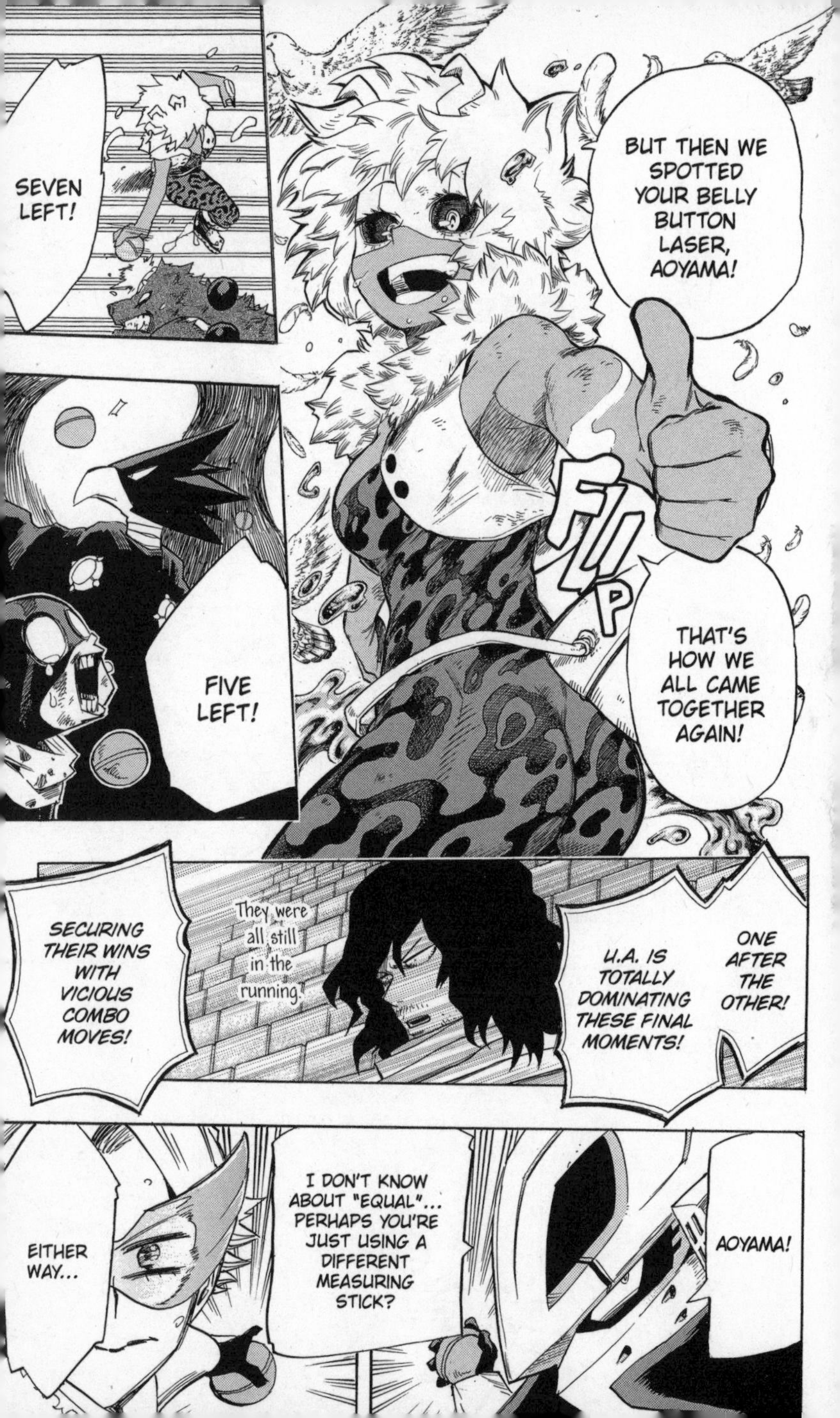
BUT THEN WE SPOTTED YOUR BELLY BUTTON LASER, AOYAMA!
FLIP
THAT'S HOW WE ALL CAME TOGETHER AGAIN!
SEVEN LEFT!
FIVE LEFT!
ONE AFTER THE OTHER!
U.A. IS TOTALLY DOMINATING THESE FINAL MOMENTS!
They were all still in the running.
SECURING THEIR WINS WITH VICIOUS COMBO MOVES!
AOYAMA!
I DON'T KNOW ABOUT "EQUAL"... PERHAPS YOU'RE JUST USING A DIFFERENT MEASURING STICK?
EITHER WAY...

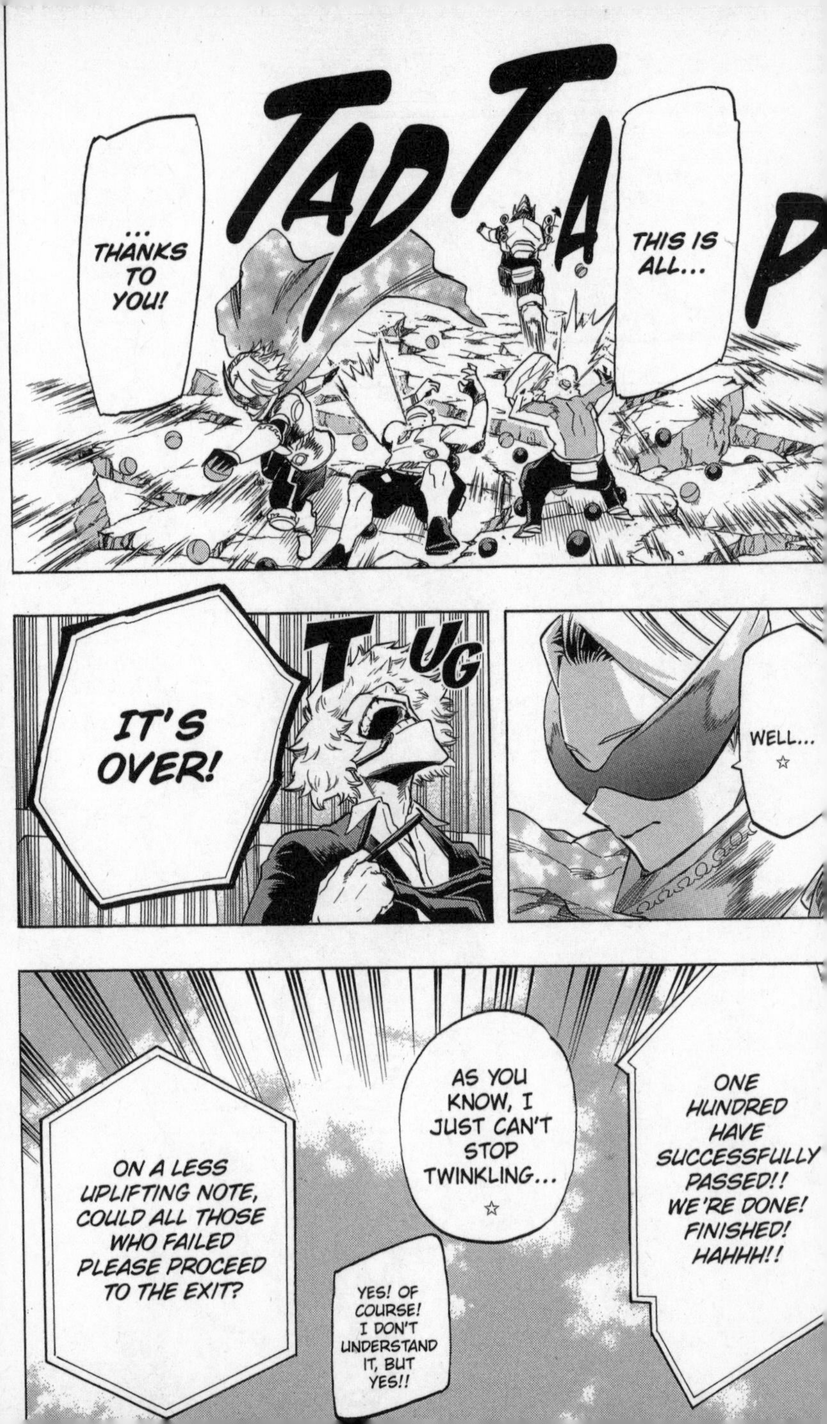
TAPTAP
THIS IS ALL...
... THANKS TO YOU!
WELL... ☆
TUG
IT'S OVER!
ONE HUNDRED HAVE SUCCESSFULLY PASSED!! WE'RE DONE! FINISHED! HAHHH!!
AS YOU KNOW, I JUST CAN'T STOP TWINKLING... ☆
ON A LESS UPLIFTING NOTE, COULD ALL THOSE WHO FAILED PLEASE PROCEED TO THE EXIT?
YES! OF COURSE! I DON'T UNDERSTAND IT, BUT YES!!

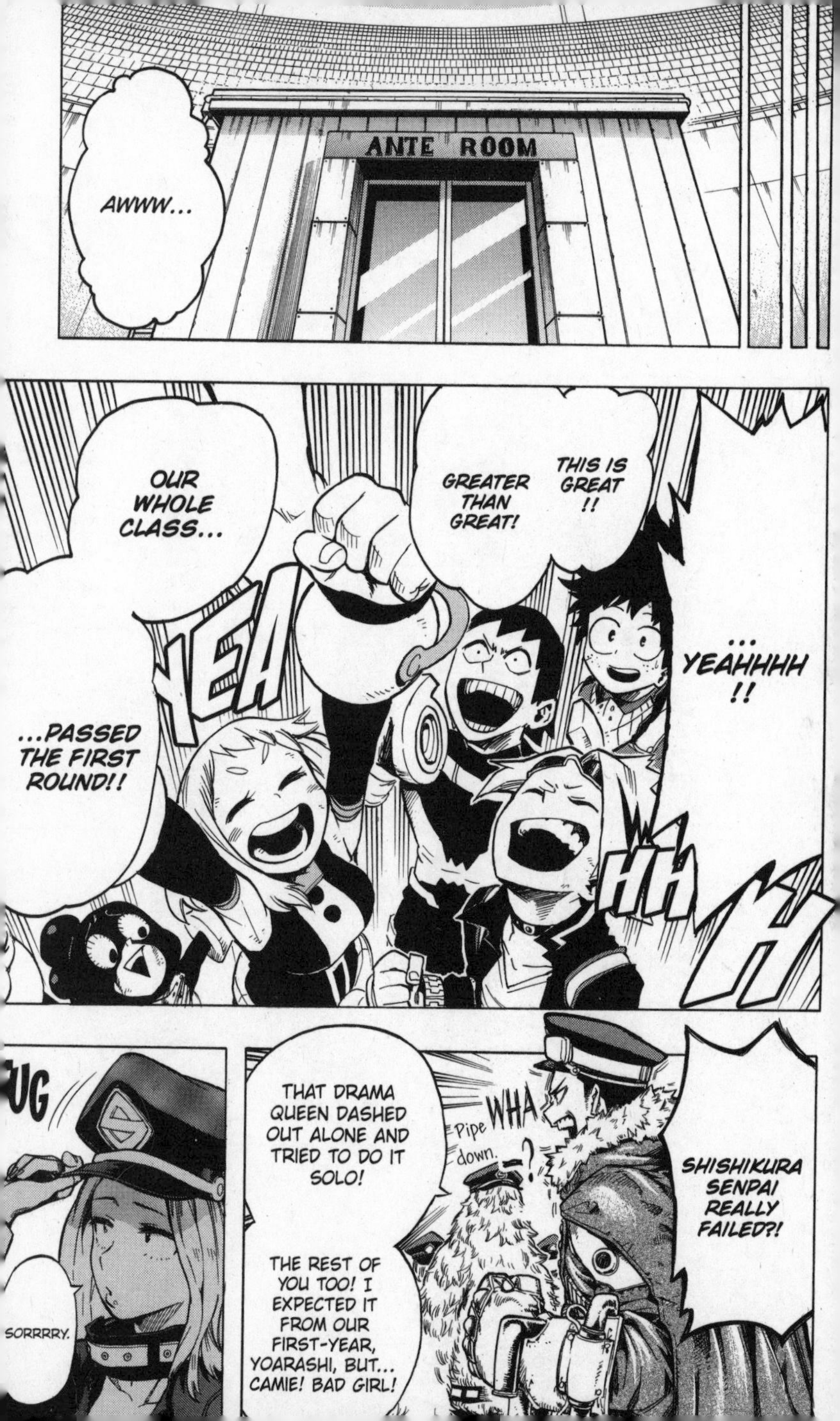
ANTE ROOM
AWWW...
...YEAHHHH!!
THIS IS GREAT!!
GREATER THAN GREAT!
OUR WHOLE CLASS...
YEA
HH
H
...PASSED THE FIRST ROUND!!
SHISHIKURA SENPAI REALLY FAILED?!
WHA
-?
Pipe down.
THAT DRAMA QUEEN DASHED OUT ALONE AND TRIED TO DO IT SOLO!
THE REST OF YOU TOO! I EXPECTED IT FROM OUR FIRST-YEAR, YOARASHI, BUT... CAMIE! BAD GIRL!
UG
SORRRRY.

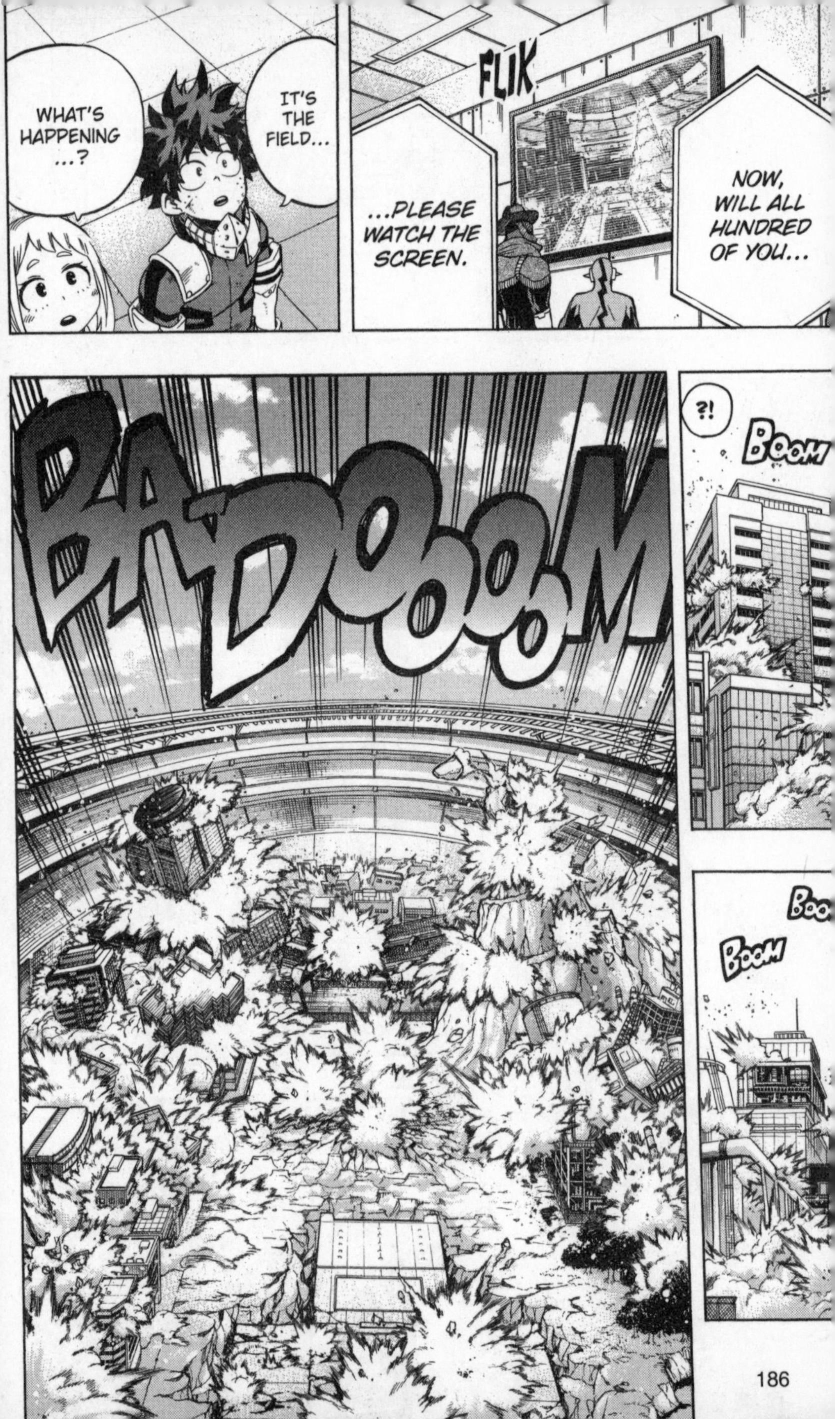

NOW, WILL ALL HUNDRED OF YOU...
FLIK
...PLEASE WATCH THE SCREEN.
IT'S THE FIELD...
WHAT'S HAPPENING ...?
?!
BOOM
BOO
BOOM
BADOOOOM

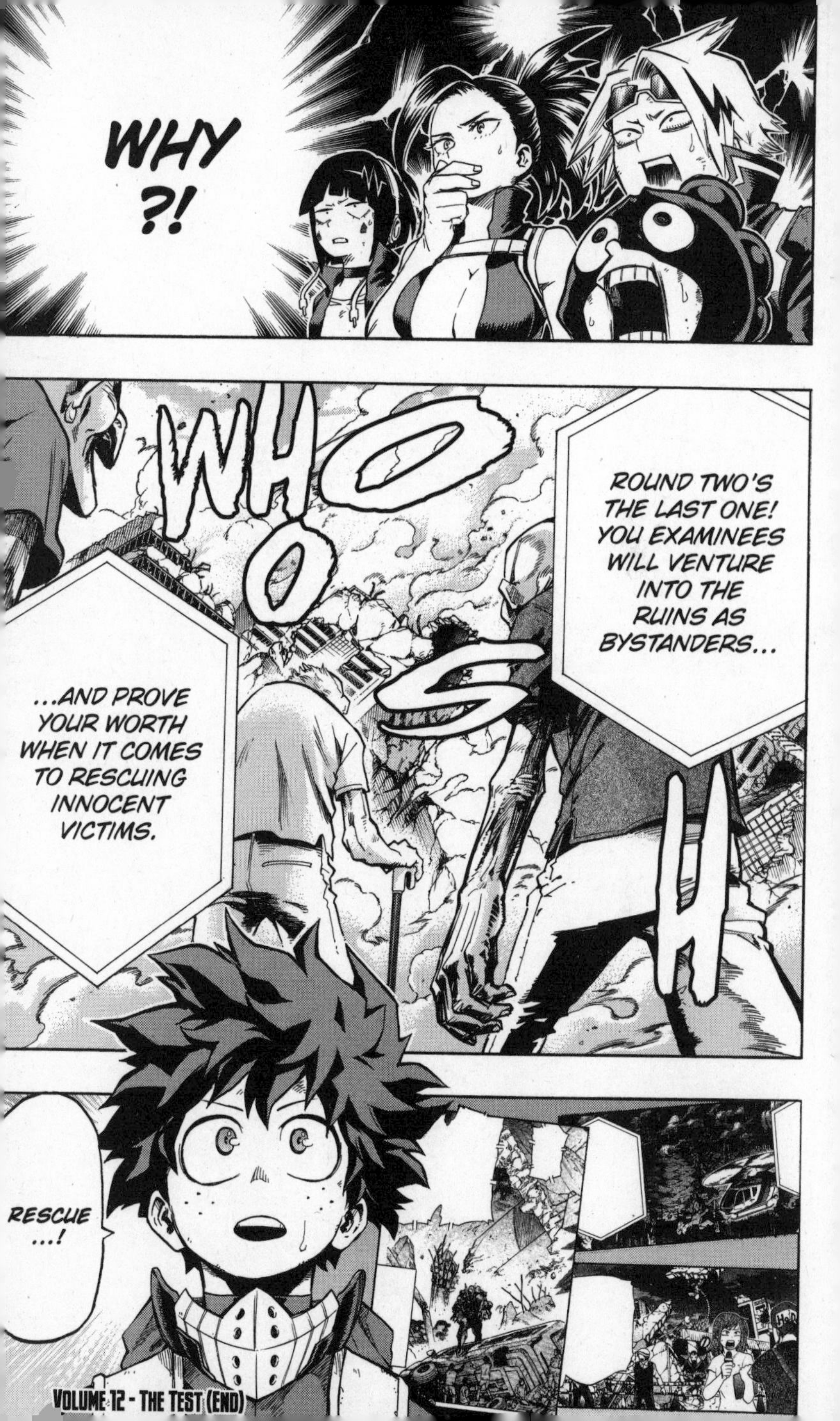

WHY ?!
WHOOSH
ROUND TWO'S THE LAST ONE! YOU EXAMINEES WILL VENTURE INTO THE RUINS AS BYSTANDERS...
...AND PROVE YOUR WORTH WHEN IT COMES TO RESCUING INNOCENT VICTIMS.
RESCUE ...!
VOLUME 12 - THE TEST (END)

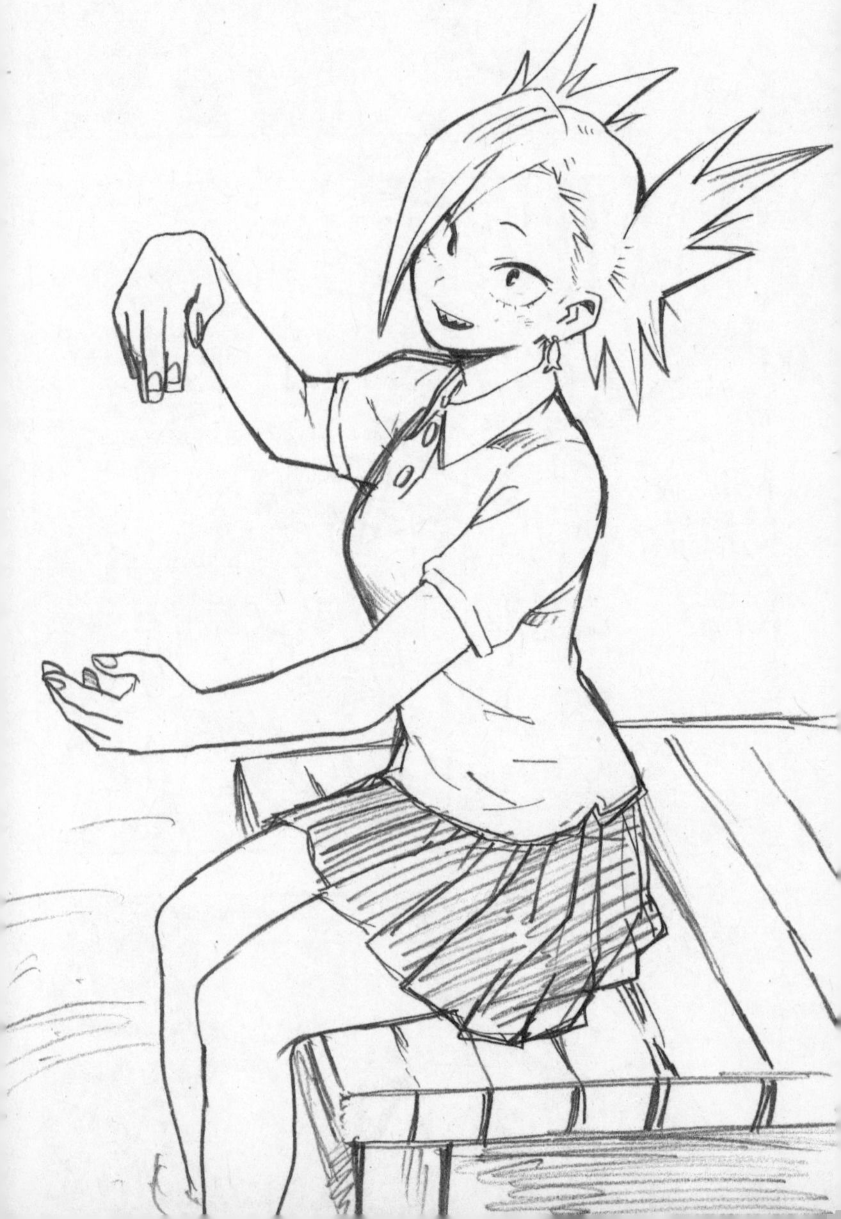

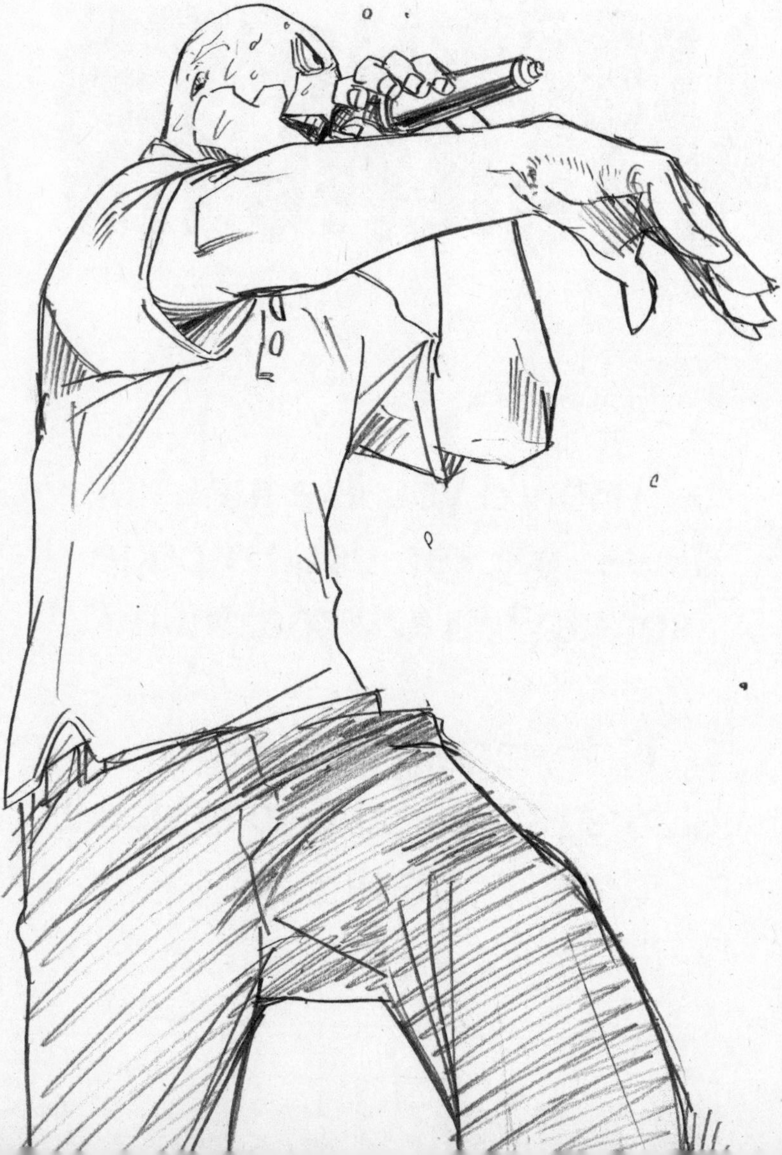

AFTERWORD

How'd you like that power-packed double-page spread? Crazy cool, huh.

I'll try again in the next volume, so be sure to check it out!!!